Microsoft® OUTLOOK® 2010

COMPLETE

Gary B. Shelly

Jill E. Romanoski

Steven M. Freund

Raymond E. Enger

COURSE TECHNOLOGY
CENGAGE Learning™

SHELLY CASHMAN SERIES®

Australia • Brazil • Japan • Korea • Mexico • Singapore • Spain • United Kingdom • United States

COURSE TECHNOLOGY
CENGAGE Learning™

Microsoft® Outlook® 2010: Complete
Gary B. Shelly, Jill E. Romanoski,
Steven M. Freund, Raymond E. Enger

Vice President, Publisher: Nicole Pinard

Executive Editor: Kathleen McMahon

Senior Product Manager: Mali Jones

Associate Product Manager: Aimee Poirier

Editorial Assistant: Lauren Brody

Director of Marketing: Cheryl Costantini

Marketing Manager: Tristen Kendall

Marketing Coordinator: Stacey Leasca

Print Buyer: Julio Esperas

Director of Production: Patty Stephan

Content Project Manager: Matthew Hutchinson

Development Editor: Lisa Ruffolo

Copyeditor: Foxxe Editorial

Proofreader: Chris Clark

Indexer: Rich Carlson

QA Manuscript Reviewers: Chris Scriver,
  Susan Pedicini

Art Director: Marissa Falco

Cover Designer: Lisa Kuhn, Curio Press, LLC

Cover Photo: Tom Kates Photography

Text Design: Joel Sadagursky

Compositor: PreMediaGlobal

For product information and technology assistance, contact us at
Cengage Learning Customer & Sales Support, 1-800-354-9706

For permission to use material from this text or product,
submit all requests online at **cengage.com/permissions**
Further permissions questions can be emailed to
permissionrequest@cengage.com

Library of Congress Control Number: 2010933770

ISBN-13: 978-0-538-47530-3

ISBN-10: 0-538-47530-7

Course Technology
20 Channel Center Street
Boston, MA 02210
USA

Cengage Learning is a leading provider of customized learning solutions with office locations around the globe, including Singapore, the United Kingdom, Australia, Mexico, Brazil, and Japan. Locate your local office at:
international.cengage.com/region

Cengage Learning products are represented in Canada by Nelson Education, Ltd.

Visit our Web site **www.cengage.com/ct/shellycashman** to share and gain ideas on our textbooks!

To learn more about Course Technology,
visit **www.cengage.com/coursetechnology**

Purchase any of our products at your local college bookstore or at our preferred online store at **www.cengagebrain.com**

We dedicate this book to the memory of James S. Quasney (1940 – 2009), who for 18 years co-authored numerous books with Tom Cashman and Gary Shelly and provided extraordinary leadership to the Shelly Cashman Series editorial team. As series editor, Jim skillfully coordinated, organized, and managed the many aspects of our editorial development processes and provided unending direction, guidance, inspiration, support, and advice to the Shelly Cashman Series authors and support team members. He was a trusted, dependable, loyal, and well-respected leader, mentor, and friend. We are forever grateful to Jim for his faithful devotion to our team and eternal contributions to our series.

The Shelly Cashman Series Team

Printed in the United States of America
2 3 4 5 6 7 12 11

Microsoft® OUTLOOK® 2010
COMPLETE

Contents

Microsoft **Outlook 2010**

CHAPTER ONE
Managing E-Mail Messages with Outlook

CHAPTER TWO
Managing Calendars

Appendices

Preface

The Shelly Cashman Series® offers the finest textbooks in computer education. We are proud that since Mircosoft Office 4.3, our series of Microsoft Office textbooks have been the most widely used books in education. With each new edition of our Office books, we make significant improvements based on the software and comments made by instructors and students. For this Microsoft Outlook 2010 text, the Shelly Cashman Series development team carefully reviewed our pedagogy and analyzed its effectiveness in teaching today's Office student. Students today read less, but need to retain more. They need not only to be able to perform skills, but to retain those skills and know how to apply them to different settings. Today's students need to be continually engaged and challenged to retain what they're learning.

With this Microsoft Outlook 2010 text, we continue our commitment to focusing on the user and how they learn best.

Objectives of This Textbook

Microsoft Outlook 2010: Complete is intended for a six- to nine-week period in a course that teaches Outlook 2010 in conjunction with another application or computer concepts. No experience with a computer is assumed, and no mathematics beyond the high school freshman level is required. The objectives of this book are:

- To offer an in-depth presentation of Microsoft Outlook 2010

- To expose students to practical examples of the computer as a useful tool

- To acquaint students with the proper procedures to create e-mail and calendars suitable for coursework, professional purposes, and personal use

- To help students discover the underlying functionality of Outlook 2010 so they can become more productive

- To develop an exercise-oriented approach that allows learning by doing

New to This Edition

Microsoft Outlook 2010: Complete offers a number of new features and approaches, which improve student understanding, retention, transference, and skill in using Outlook 2010. The following enhancements will enrich the learning experience:

- Office 2010 and Windows 7: Essential Concepts and Skills chapter presents basic Office 2010 and Windows 7 skills.

- Streamlined first chapter allows the ability to cover more advanced skills earlier.

- Chapter topic redistribution offers concise chapters that ensure complete skill coverage.

- New pedagogical elements enrich material creating an accessible and user-friendly approach.

  - Break Points, a new boxed element, identify logical stopping points and give students instructions regarding what they should do before taking a break.

  - Within step instructions, Tab | Group Identifiers, such as (Home tab | Bold button), help students more easily locate elements in the groups and on the tabs on the Ribbon.

  - Modified step-by-step instructions tell the student what to do and provide the generic reason why they are completing a specific task, which helps students easily transfer given skills to different settings.

The Shelly Cashman Approach

A Proven Pedagogy with an Emphasis on Project Planning

Each chapter presents a practical problem to be solved, within a project planning framework. The project orientation is strengthened by the use of Plan Ahead boxes, which encourage critical thinking about how to proceed at various points in the project. Step-by-step instructions with supporting screens guide students through the steps. Instructional steps are supported by the Q&A, Experimental Step, and BTW features.

A Visually Engaging Book that Maintains Student Interest

The step-by-step tasks, with supporting figures, provide a rich visual experience for the student. Call-outs on the screens that present both explanatory and navigational information provide students with information they need when they need to know it.

Supporting Reference Materials (Appendices, Quick Reference)

The appendices provide additional information about the Application at hand and include such topics as project planning guidelines and certification. With the Quick Reference, students can quickly look up information about a single task, such as keyboard shortcuts, and find page references of where in the book the task is illustrated.

Integration of the World Wide Web

The World Wide Web is integrated into the Outlook 2010 learning experience by (1) BTW annotations; (2) BTW, Q&A, and Quick Reference Summary Web pages; and (3) the Learn It Online section for each chapter.

End-of-Chapter Student Activities

Extensive end-of-chapter activities provide a variety of reinforcement opportunities for students where they can apply and expand their skills.

Instructor Resources

The Instructor Resources include both teaching and testing aids and can be accessed via CD-ROM or at login.cengage.com.

Instructor's Manual Includes lecture notes summarizing the chapter sections, figures and boxed elements found in every chapter, teacher tips, classroom activities, lab activities, and quick quizzes in Microsoft Word files.

Syllabus Easily customizable sample syllabi that cover policies, assignments, exams, and other course information.

Figure Files Illustrations for every figure in the textbook in electronic form.

PowerPoint Presentations A multimedia lecture presentation system that provides slides for each chapter. Presentations are based on chapter objectives.

Solutions To Exercises Includes solutions for all end-of-chapter and chapter reinforcement exercises.

Test Bank & Test Engine Test Banks include 112 questions for every chapter, featuring objective-based and critical thinking question types, and including page number references and figure references, when appropriate. Also included is the test engine, ExamView, the ultimate tool for your objective-based testing needs.

Data Files For Students Includes all the files that are required by students to complete the exercises.

Additional Activities For Students Consists of Chapter Reinforcement Exercises, which are true/false, multiple-choice, and short answer questions that help students gain confidence in the material learned.

> **Book Resources**
> 🔒 Additional Faculty Files
> 🔒 Blackboard Testbank
> 🔒 Data Files
> 🔒 Instructor's Manual
> 🔒 Lecture Success System
> 🔒 PowerPoint Presentations
> 🔒 Solutions to Exercises
> 🔒 Syllabus
> 🔒 Test Bank and Test Engine
> 🔒 WebCT Testbank
> Chapter Reinforcement Exercises
> Student Downloads

SAM: Skills Assessment Manager

SAM 2010 is designed to help bring students from the classroom to the real world. It allows students to train on and test important computer skills in an active, hands-on environment.

SAM's easy-to-use system includes powerful interactive exams, training, and projects on the most commonly used Microsoft Office applications. SAM simulates the Microsoft Office 2010 application environment, allowing students to demonstrate their knowledge and think through the skills by performing real-world tasks such as bolding word text or setting up slide transitions. Add in live-in-the-application projects, and students are on their way to truly learning and applying skills to business-centric documents.

Designed to be used with the Shelly Cashman Series, SAM includes handy page references so that students can print helpful study guides that match the Shelly Cashman textbooks used in class. For instructors, SAM also includes robust scheduling and reporting features.

Content for Online Learning

Course Technology has partnered with the leading distance learning solution providers and class-management platforms today. To access this material, instructors will visit our password-protected instructor resources available at login.cengage.com. Instructor resources include the following: additional case projects, sample syllabi, PowerPoint presentations per chapter, and more. For additional information or for an instructor user name and password, please contact your sales representative. For students to access this material, they must have purchased a WebTutor PIN-code specific to this title and your campus platform. The resources for students may include (based on instructor preferences), but are not limited to: topic review, review questions, and practice tests.

CourseNotes

Course Technology's CourseNotes are six-panel quick reference cards that reinforce the most important and widely used features of a software application in a visual and user-friendly format. CourseNotes serve as a great reference tool during and after the student completes the course. CourseNotes are available for software applications such as Microsoft Office 2010, Word 2010, Excel 2010, Access 2010, PowerPoint 2010, and Windows 7. Topic-based CourseNotes are available for Best Practices in Social Networking, Hot Topics in Technology, and Web 2.0. Visit www.cengagebrain.com coursenotes to learn more!

A Guided Tour

Add excitement and interactivity to your classroom with "*A Guided Tour*" product line. Play one of the brief mini-movies to spice up your lecture and spark classroom discussion. Or, assign a movie for homework and ask students to complete the correlated assignment that accompanies each topic. "*A Guided Tour*" product line takes the prep work out of providing your students with information about new technologies and applications and helps keep students engaged with content relevant to their lives; all in under an hour!

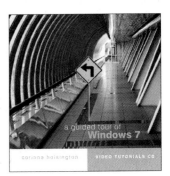

About Our Covers

The Shelly Cashman Series is continually updating our approach and content to reflect the way today's students learn and experience new technology. This focus on student success is reflected on our covers, which feature real students from the University of Rhode Island using the Shelly Cashman Series in their courses, and reflect the varied ages and backgrounds of the students learning with our books. When you use the Shelly Cashman Series, you can be assured that you are learning computer skills using the most effective courseware available.

Textbook Walk-Through

The Shelly Cashman Series Pedagogy: Project-Based — Step-by-Step — Variety of Assessments

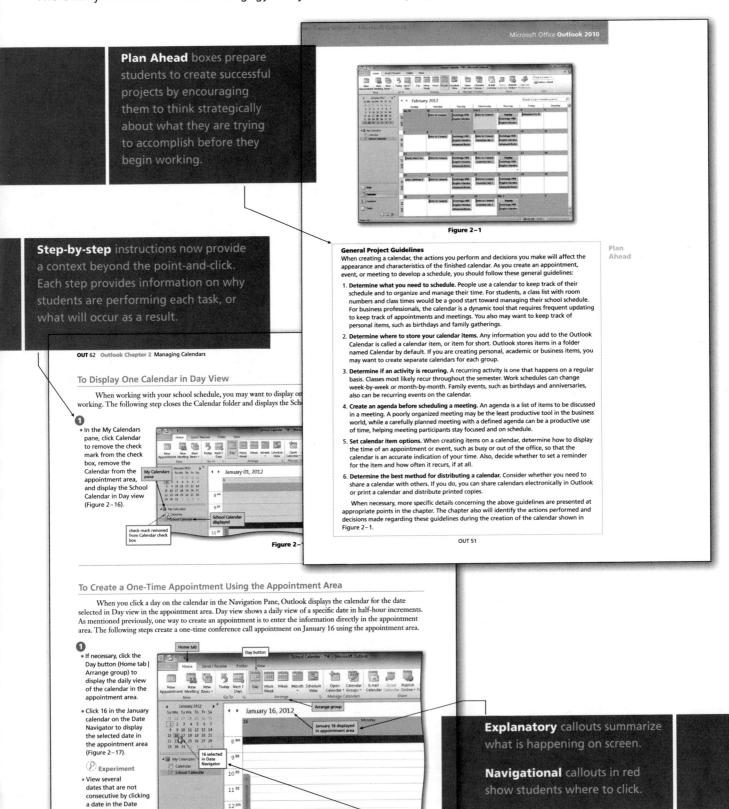

Plan Ahead boxes prepare students to create successful projects by encouraging them to think strategically about what they are trying to accomplish before they begin working.

Step-by-step instructions now provide a context beyond the point-and-click. Each step provides information on why students are performing each task, or what will occur as a result.

Figure 2–1

General Project Guidelines

When creating a calendar, the actions you perform and decisions you make will affect the appearance and characteristics of the finished calendar. As you create an appointment, event, or meeting to develop a schedule, you should follow these general guidelines:

1. **Determine what you need to schedule.** People use a calendar to keep track of their schedule and to organize and manage their time. For students, a class list with room numbers and class times would be a good start toward managing their school schedule. For business professionals, the calendar is a dynamic tool that requires frequent updating to keep track of appointments and meetings. You also may want to keep track of personal items, such as birthdays and family gatherings.

2. **Determine where to store your calendar items.** Any information you add to the Outlook Calendar is called a calendar item, or item for short. Outlook stores items in a folder named Calendar by default. If you are creating personal, academic or business items, you may want to create separate calendars for each group.

3. **Determine if an activity is recurring.** A recurring activity is one that happens on a regular basis. Classes most likely recur throughout the semester. Work schedules can change week-by-week or month-by-month. Family events, such as birthdays and anniversaries, also can be recurring events on the calendar.

4. **Create an agenda before scheduling a meeting.** An agenda is a list of items to be discussed in a meeting. A poorly organized meeting may be the least productive tool in the business world, while a carefully planned meeting with a defined agenda can be a productive use of time, helping meeting participants stay focused and on schedule.

5. **Set calendar item options.** When creating items on a calendar, determine how to display the time of an appointment or event, such as busy or out of the office, so that the calendar is an accurate indication of your time. Also, decide whether to set a reminder for the item and how often it recurs, if at all.

6. **Determine the best method for distributing a calendar.** Consider whether you need to share a calendar with others. If you do, you can share calendars electronically in Outlook or print a calendar and distribute printed copies.

When necessary, more specific details concerning the above guidelines are presented at appropriate points in the chapter. The chapter also will identify the actions performed and decisions made regarding these guidelines during the creation of the calendar shown in Figure 2–1.

Plan Ahead

OUT 51

To Display One Calendar in Day View

When working with your school schedule, you may want to display on working. The following step closes the Calendar folder and displays the Sch

1
- In the My Calendars pane, click Calendar to remove the check mark from the check box, remove the Calendar from the appointment area, and display the School Calendar in Day view (Figure 2–16).

My Calendars pane

School Calendar displayed

check mark removed from Calendar check box

Figure 2–1

To Create a One-Time Appointment Using the Appointment Area

When you click a day on the calendar in the Navigation Pane, Outlook displays the calendar for the date selected in Day view in the appointment area. Day view shows a daily view of a specific date in half-hour increments. As mentioned previously, one way to create an appointment is to enter the information directly in the appointment area. The following steps create a one-time conference call appointment on January 16 using the appointment area.

1
- If necessary, click the Day button (Home tab | Arrange group) to display the daily view of the calendar in the appointment area.

- Click 16 in the January calendar on the Date Navigator to display the selected date in the appointment area (Figure 2–17).

Experiment
- View several dates that are not consecutive by clicking a date in the Date Navigator, holding down the CTRL key, and then clicking additional days.

Home tab

Day button

January 16, 2012

Arrange group

January 16 displayed in appointment area

16 selected in Date Navigator

Figure 2–17

Explanatory callouts summarize what is happening on screen.

Navigational callouts in red show students where to click.

To Display the Calendar in Month View

Month view resembles a standard monthly calendar page and displays a schedule for an entire month. Appointments are listed in each date in the calendar. The following step displays the calendar in Month view.

1

- Click the Month button (Home tab | Arrange group) to display one full month in the appointment area (Figure 2–13).

Experiment

- By default, Month view displays dates from the beginning to the end of a calendar month. To select several weeks across two calendar months, click the Date Navigator and then drag to select the weeks you want to view.

Q&A

What if I accidentally click the Month button arrow instead of the Month button?

Click the Month button arrow again to remove the list of options displayed when you clicked the Month button arrow.

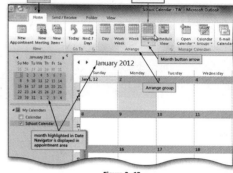

Figure 2–13

Other Ways

1. Press CTRL+ALT+4

To Display the Calendar in Schedule View

Schedule View, new to Outlook 2010, displays multiple calendars at the same time in a horizontal layout of ... isplay the default Calendar and the School Calendar in Schedule View so ...

Figure 2–14

Outlook Chapter 2

2

- Click the Delete button (Calendar Tools Appointment Series tab | Actions group) to display the Delete menu (Figure 2–49).

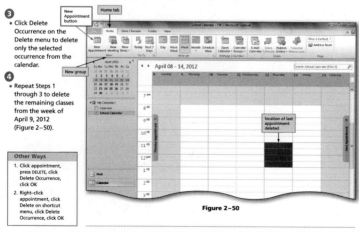

Figure 2–49

3

- Click Delete Occurrence on the Delete menu to delete only the selected occurrence from the calendar.

4

- Repeat Steps 1 through 3 to delete the remaining classes from the week of April 9, 2012 (Figure 2–50).

Other Ways

1. Click appointment, press DELETE, click Delete Occurrence, click OK
2. Right-click appointment, click Delete on shortcut menu, click Delete Occurrence, click OK

Figure 2–50

Break Point: If you wish to take a break, this is a good place to do so. To resume at a later time, start Outlook and continue following the steps from this location forward.

Textbook Walk-Through

Chapter Summary

Chapter Summary A concluding paragraph, followed by a listing of the tasks completed within a chapter together with the pages on which the step-by-step, screen-by-screen explanations appear.

In this chapter, you have learned how to use Outlook to create a personal schedule by entering appointments, creating recurring appointments, moving appointments to new dates, and scheduling events. You also learned how to invite attendees to a meeting, accept a meeting request, and propose and change the time of a meeting. To review your schedule, you learned to view and print your calendar in different views and print styles. Finally, you learned how to export your personal folder to an external storage device. The following list includes all the new Outlook skills you have learned in this chapter.

1. Create a Personal Folder (OUT 54)
2. Display a Personal Calendar (OUT 56)
3. Remove the Default Calendar from the Appointment Area (OUT 56)
4. Go to a Specific Date (OUT 57)
5. Display the Calendar in Work Week View (OUT 58)
6. Display the Calendar in Week View (OUT 59)
7. Display the Calendar in Month View (OUT 60)
8. Display the Calendar in Schedule View (OUT 60)
9. Create a One-Time Appointment Using the Appointment Area (OUT 62)
10. Create a One-Time Appointment Using the Appointment Window (OUT 64)
11. Change the Status of an Appointment (OUT 67)
12. Set a Reminder for an Appointment (OUT 68)
13. Save the Appointment (OUT 69)
14. Create a Recurring Appointment Using the Appointment Window (OUT 71)
15. Set Recurrence Options for an Recurring Appointment (OUT 72)
16. Set a Reminder and Show As Options for an Appointment (OUT 74)
17. Enter an Appointment Date and Time Using Natural Language Phrases (OUT 77)

19. Move an Appointment to a Different Date (OUT 80)
20. Move an Appointment to a Different Month (OUT 81)
21. Delete a Single Occurrence of a Recurring Appointment (OUT 82)
22. Create a One-Time Event in the Appointment Window (OUT 84)
23. Move a One-Time Event to a New Date and Change the Event Status (OUT 86)
24. Delete a One-Time Event (OUT 87)
25. Create a Recurring Event Using the Appointment Window (OUT 88)
26. Move a Recurring Event to a Different Day (OUT 90)
27. Delete a Recurring Event (OUT 92)
28. View the School Calendar in Overlay Mode (OUT 92)
29. Create and Send a Meeting (OUT 93)
30. Change the Time of a Meeting and Send an Update (OUT 95)
31. Reply to a Meeting Request (OUT 96)
32. Cancel a Meeting (OUT 98)
33. Print the Calendar in Weekly Calendar Style (OUT 100)
34. Change the Current View to List View (OUT 102)
35. Export a Subfolder to a USB Flash Drive (OUT 104)
36. Delete a Personal Subfolder (OUT 108)

...me on the...

...profile, your instructor may have assigned an autogradable ...so, log into the SAM 2010 Web site at www.cengage.com/sam2010 ...and start files.

Learn It Online

Test your knowledge of chapter content and key terms.

Instructions: To complete the Learn It Online exercises, start your browser, click the Address bar, and then enter the Web address **scsite.com/out2010/learn**. When the Outlook 2010 Learn It Online page is displayed, click the link for the exercise you want to complete and then read the instructions.

Chapter Reinforcement TF, MC, and SA
A series of true/false, multiple choice, and short answer questions that test your knowledge of the chapter content.

Flash Cards
An interactive learning environment where you identify chapter key terms associated with displayed definitions.

Practice Test
A series of multiple choice questions that test your knowledge of chapter content and key terms.

Who Wants To Be a Computer Genius?
An interactive game that challenges your knowledge of chapter content in the style of a television quiz show.

Wheel of Terms
An interactive game that challenges your knowledge of chapter key terms in the style of the television show *Wheel of Fortune*.

Crossword Puzzle Challenge
A crossword puzzle that challenges your knowledge of key terms presented in the chapter.

Learn It Online Every chapter features a Learn It Online section that is comprised of six exercises. These exercises include True/False, Multiple Choice, Short Answer, Flash Cards, Practice Test, and Learning Games.

Apply Your Knowledge

Reinforce the skills and apply the concepts you learned in this chapter.

Editing a Calendar
Instructions: Start Outlook. Edit the calendar provided in the file called Apply Your Knowledge 2-1 Calendar, located on the Data Files for Students. See the inside back cover of this book for instructions for downloading the Data Files for Students, or see your instructor for information about accessing the files required in this book.

The Apply Your Knowledge 2-1 Calendar is a personal calendar with appointments for personal activities, class schedules, and events. Many of the scheduled items have changed and you now need to revise these scheduled items.

Perform the following tasks:
1. Create a folder called Apply your Knowledge and import the Apply Your Knowledge 2-1 Calendar folder into the newly created folder.
2. Display only the Apply Your Knowledge 2-1 Calendar in the Outlook Calendar window. Use Week view to display the calendar.
3. Change Kelly's Birthday Party from February 17 to February 19. The party is at the same time.
4. Reschedule the work on February 9 to February 12. The work starts at 12:00 PM and continues until 4:00 PM.
5. Reschedule the two-hour Chemistry Study Lab on Wednesday evenings from 5:00 PM – 7:00 PM to 6:00 PM – 8:00 PM in CHM 225.
6. Change Intramural Basketball from Mondays and Wednesdays to Tuesdays and Thursdays at the same time.

Apply Your Knowledge This exercise usually requires students to open and manipulate a file from the Data Files that parallels the activities learned in the chapter. To obtain a copy of the Data Files for Students, follow the instructions on the inside back cover of this text.

Continued >

Extend Your Knowledge

Extend the skills you learned in this chapter and experiment with new skills. You may need to use Help to complete the assignment.

Managing E-Mail Messages
Instructions: Start Outlook. Open the Extend 1-1.pst mailbox file from the Data Files for Students. See the inside back cover of this book for instructions on downloading the Data Files for Students, or contact your instructor for information about accessing the required files.

You will create three folders, rename the folders, and then move messages into the appropriate folders. You also will apply a follow-up flag for the messages in one of the folders. Use Outlook Help to learn about how to add a flag to a message for follow-up and how to create an Outlook Data File (.pst).

1. Create three new subfolders in the Inbox folder. Name one folder New folder 1, another folder New folder 2, and the third folder New folder 3. Make sure that only mail items are contained in the new folders.

2. In the Navigation Pane, rename the newly created folders. Rename New folder 1 to USB Problems. Rename New folder 2 to Monitor Problems. Rename New folder 3 to Printer Problems. (*Hint:* To rename the folders, right-click the folder you want to rename in the Navigation Pane to open a shortcut menu. Select Rename Folder on the shortcut menu. Type the new name of the folder, and then press the ENTER key).

3. Based on the message headers and content of the e-mail messages in the Extend 1-1 mailbox, move each message to one of the folders you created. Figure 1–52 shows the mailbox with the messages moved to the new folders.

4. In the Monitor Problems folder, assign a flag for follow-up for next week to all messages.

5. Export the Inbox mailbox to an Outlook data file (.pst) on a USB flash drive using the file name, Extend.pst, and then submit it in the format specified by your instructor.

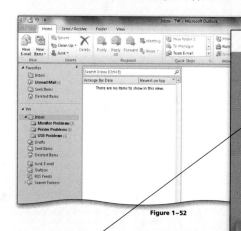

Figure 1–52

Make It Right

Analyze a calendar and correct all errors and/or improve the design.

Correcting Appointment Times
Instructions: Start Outlook. Import the Make It Right 2-1 Calendar folder in the Data Files for Students folder into Outlook.

Note: To complete this assignment, you may be required to use the Data Files for Students. See the inside back cover of this book for instructions on downloading the Data Files for Students, or contact your instructor for information about accessing the required files.

While reviewing your Outlook calendar, you realize that you created several appointments incorrectly. You will identify and open the incorrect appointments, edit them so that they reflect the correct information, and then save all changes.

Perform the following tasks:

1. Display only the Make It Right 2–1 Calendar in the Outlook Calendar window.

2. While adding a dentist appointment to the Calendar, you inadvertently recorded the appointment time as 2:00 AM instead of 2:00 PM. Edit the appointment on April 2, 2012, and change the Start time to 2:00 PM. The appointment still will last one hour.

3. The Yoga class scheduled for April 19, 2012, should be a recurring appointment on your calendar. Change the appointment to reflect the Yoga class meeting every Thursday through the end of June from 7:00 PM until 9:00 PM.

4. Your monthly homeowner's association board meeting has modified their meeting schedule to meet on the second Thursday of each month instead of on the thirteenth of each month. Update the calendar to reflect this change.

5. An appointment during the week of April 16, 2012, has been added to your calendar two times with the same start time and end time. Remove one of these appointments from the calendar.

6. Print the calendar using the Monthly style for the month of April, 2012 (Figure 2–96).

Figure 2–96

Extend Your Knowledge projects at the end of each chapter allow students to extend and expand on the skills learned within the chapter. Students use critical thinking to experiment with new skills to complete each project.

Make It Right projects call on students to analyze a file, discover errors in it, and fix them using the skills they learned in the chapter.

Textbook Walk-Through

In the Lab

Lab 3: Creating a Schedule

Problem: Start Outlook. Create a new Calendar folder using your name as the name of the new folder. You are to create a schedule of classes and other appointments using the information in Table 2–10. This calendar is for the spring semester that begins Monday, January 30, 2012, and ends Friday, May 11, 2012. The calendar you create is shown in Figure 2–98.

March 2012

Figure 2–98

> **In the Lab** Three all new in-depth assignments per chapter require students to utilize the chapter concepts and techniques to solve problems on a computer.

Table 2–10 Appointment Information

Subject	Location	Start Date	Time	Show As
Doctor Appointment	Drs. office	2/3/2012	2:00 PM – 3:00 PM	Out of Off
Work		1/31/2012	7:00 AM – 3:30 PM	Out of Off
Volunteer for New Student Orientation	Student Union	1/21/2012	8:30 AM – 12:00 PM	Out of Off
Chemistry	Science 300	1/30/2012	8:00 AM – 9:30 AM	Busy
Technical Report Writing	HRB 201	1/30/2012	11:30 AM – 1:00 PM	Busy
Marketing	HRB 300	1/31/2012	7:00 PM – 8:30 PM	Busy

Perform the following tasks:

1. Create a one-time appointment for the first item in Table 2–10. Enter Doctor's Appointment, as the appointment subject. Enter the location in Table 2–10. Show the time as Out of Office in your calendar and se

In the Lab *continued*

2. Create a recurring appointment for the Work item in Table 2–10. Enter the subject, start date, and time as shown. Show the time as Out of Office in your calendar and set a one-hour reminder. Set the appointment to recur weekly on Tuesdays, Thursdays, and Saturdays with no end date.

3. Create a one-time appointment for the Volunteer for New Student Orientation item in Table 2–10. Enter the subject, start date, and time as shown. Show the time as Out of Office in your calendar and set a 15-minute reminder.

4. Create a recurring appointment for the Chemistry item in Table 2–10. Enter the subject, start date, and time as shown. Show the time as busy and set a 15-minute reminder. Set the appointment to recur weekly on Mondays and Wednesdays for 30 occurrences.

5. Create a recurring appointment for the Technical Report Writing item in Table 2–10. Enter the subject, start date, and time as shown. Show the time as busy and set a 10-minute reminder. Set the appointment to recur weekly on Mondays and Wednesdays for 30 occurrences.

6. Create a recurring appointment for the Marketing item in Table 2–10. Enter the subject, start date, and time as shown. Show the time as busy and set a 30-minute reminder. Set the appointment to recur weekly on Tuesdays and Thursdays for 30 occurrences.

7. Print the February 2012 calendar in Month view, and then submit it in the format specified by your instructor.

Cases and Places

Apply your creative thinking and problem solving skills to design and implement a solution.

Note: To complete these assignments, you may be required to use the Data Files for Students. See the inside back cover of this book for instructions on downloading the Data Files for Students, or contact your instructor for information about accessing the required files.

1: Create a Personal Schedule

Academic

Create a personal schedule for the next month using the information provided in Table 2–11. Include your appointments for work, classes, and study time. You also can include any extracurricular activities in which you participate. Use recurring appointments when possible. Schedule all-day activities as events. Print the calendar in Monthly Style and submit it in the format specified by your instructor.

> **Cases & Places** exercises call on students to create open-ended projects that reflect academic, personal, and business settings.

Table 2–11 Academic Calendar Items

Description	Location	Date	Time	Show As	Reminder	Recurrence
Financial Planning Workshop	Columbia Inn	March 11, 2012	1:00 PM – 4:00 PM	Busy	30 minutes	None
Spring Fling	Quad	March 3, 2012	12:00 PM – 2:00 PM	Out of Office	10 minutes	None
Department Meeting		Every Monday	2:00 PM – 3:00 PM	Busy	5 minutes	Weekly, end after 12 occurrences
Petition to Graduate		March 15, 2012	All Day Event	Free	1 day	None
Parents Anniversary		October 20, 2012	All Day Event	Free	1 day	Yearly
NJCAA D3 Women's Lacrosse Nationals		March 6, 2012 – March 8, 2012	All Day Event	Tentative	None	None
SGA Meeting		March 21, 2012	11:30 PM – 12:30 PM	Out of Office	30 minutes	None
Work Schedule		2/28/2012	2:00 PM – 5:30 PM	Out of Office	15 minutes	Tuesdays and Thursdays

Office 2010 and Windows 7: Essential Concepts and Skills

Objectives

You will have mastered the material in this chapter when you can:

- Perform basic mouse operations
- Start Windows and log on to the computer
- Identify the objects on the Windows 7 desktop
- Identify the programs in and versions of Microsoft Office
- Start a program
- Identify the components of the Microsoft Office Ribbon

- Create folders
- Save files
- Change screen resolution
- Perform basic tasks in Microsoft Office programs
- Manage files
- Use Microsoft Office Help and Windows Help

Office 2010 and Windows 7: Essential Concepts and Skills

Office 2010 and Windows 7

This introductory chapter covers features and functions common to Office 2010 programs, as well as the basics of Windows 7.

Overview

As you read this chapter, you will learn how to perform basic tasks in Windows and Office programs by performing these general activities:

- Start programs using Windows.
- Use features common across Office programs.
- Organize files and folders.
- Change screen resolution.
- Quit Office programs.

Introduction to the Windows 7 Operating System

Windows 7 is the newest version of Microsoft Windows, which is the most popular and widely used operating system. An **operating system** is a computer program (set of computer instructions) that coordinates all the activities of computer hardware such as memory, storage devices, and printers, and provides the capability for you to communicate with the computer.

The Windows 7 operating system simplifies the process of working with documents and programs by organizing the manner in which you interact with the computer. Windows 7 is used to run **application software**, which consists of programs designed to make users more productive and/or assist them with personal tasks, such as word processing.

Windows 7 has two interface variations, Windows 7 Basic and Windows 7 Aero. Computers with up to 1 GB of RAM display the Windows 7 Basic interface (Figure 1a). Computers with more than 1 GB of RAM also can display the Windows Aero interface (Figure 1b), which provides an enhanced visual appearance. The Windows 7 Professional, Windows 7 Enterprise, Windows 7 Home Premium, and Windows 7 Ultimate editions have the capability to use Windows Aero.

Using a Mouse

Windows users work with a mouse that has at least two buttons. For a right-handed user, the left button usually is the primary mouse button, and the right mouse button is the secondary mouse button. Left-handed people, however, can reverse the function of these buttons.

(a) Windows 7 Basic interface

(b) Windows 7 Aero interface

Figure 1

Table 1 explains how to perform a variety of mouse operations. Some programs also use keys in combination with the mouse to perform certain actions. For example, when you hold down the CTRL key while rolling the mouse wheel, text on the screen becomes larger or smaller based on the direction you roll the wheel. The function of the mouse buttons and the wheel varies depending on the program.

Table 1 Mouse Operations		
Operation	**Mouse Action**	**Example***
Point	Move the mouse until the pointer on the desktop is positioned on the item of choice.	Position the pointer on the screen.
Click	Press and release the primary mouse button, which usually is the left mouse button.	Select or deselect items on the screen or start a program or program feature.
Right-click	Press and release the secondary mouse button, which usually is the right mouse button.	Display a shortcut menu.
Double-click	Quickly press and release the left mouse button twice without moving the mouse.	Start a program or program feature.
Triple-click	Quickly press and release the left mouse button three times without moving the mouse.	Select a paragraph.
Drag	Point to an item, hold down the left mouse button, move the item to the desired location on the screen, and then release the left mouse button.	Move an object from one location to another or draw pictures.
Right-drag	Point to an item, hold down the right mouse button, move the item to the desired location on the screen, and then release the right mouse button.	Display a shortcut menu after moving an object from one location to another.
Rotate wheel	Roll the wheel forward or backward.	Scroll vertically (up and down).
Free-spin wheel	Whirl the wheel forward or backward so that it spins freely on its own.	Scroll through many pages in seconds.
Press wheel	Press the wheel button while moving the mouse.	Scroll continuously.
Tilt wheel	Press the wheel toward the right or left.	Scroll horizontally (left and right).
Press thumb button	Press the button on the side of the mouse with your thumb.	Move forward or backward through Web pages and/or control media, games, etc.

*Note: the examples presented in this column are discussed as they are demonstrated in this chapter.

Scrolling

A **scroll bar** is a horizontal or vertical bar that appears when the contents of an area may not be visible completely on the screen (Figure 2). A scroll bar contains **scroll arrows** and a **scroll box** that enable you to view areas that currently cannot be seen. Clicking the up and down scroll arrows moves the screen content up or down one line. You also can click above or below the scroll box to move up or down a section, or drag the scroll box up or down to move up or down to move to a specific location.

Shortcut Keys

In many cases, you can use the keyboard instead of the mouse to accomplish a task. To perform tasks using the keyboard, you press one or more keyboard keys, sometimes identified as

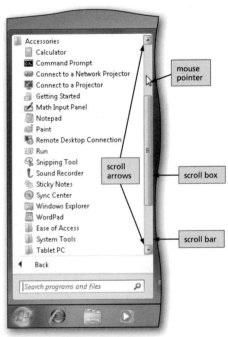

Figure 2

a **shortcut key** or **keyboard shortcut**. Some shortcut keys consist of a single key, such as the F1 key. For example, to obtain help about Windows 7, you can press the F1 key. Other shortcut keys consist of multiple keys, in which case a plus sign separates the key names, such as CTRL+ESC. This notation means to press and hold down the first key listed, press one or more additional keys, and then release all keys. For example, to display the Start menu, press CTRL+ESC, that is, hold down the CTRL key, press the ESC key, and then release both keys.

Starting Windows 7

It is not unusual for multiple people to use the same computer in a work, educational, recreational, or home setting. Windows 7 enables each user to establish a **user account**, which identifies to Windows 7 the resources, such as programs and storage locations, a user can access when working with a computer.

Each user account has a user name and may have a password and an icon, as well. A **user name** is a unique combination of letters or numbers that identifies a specific user to Windows 7. A **password** is a private combination of letters, numbers, and special characters associated with the user name that allows access to a user's account resources. A **user icon** is a picture associated with a user name.

When you turn on a computer, an introductory screen consisting of the Windows logo and copyright messages is displayed. The Windows logo is animated and glows as the Windows 7 operating system is loaded. After the Windows logo appears, depending on your computer's settings, you may or may not be required to log on to the computer. **Logging on** to a computer opens your user account and makes the computer available for use. If you are required to log on to the computer, the **Welcome screen** is displayed, which shows the user names of users on the computer (Figure 3). Clicking the user name or picture begins the process of logging on to the computer.

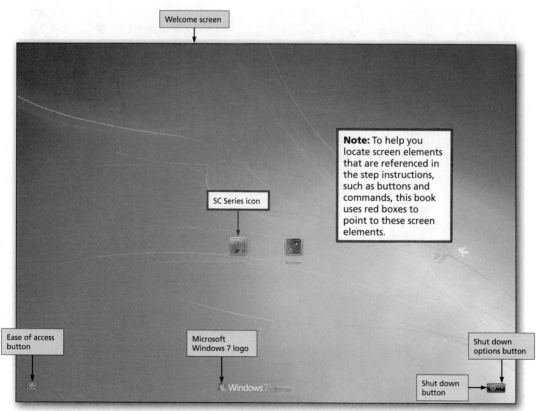

Figure 3

At the bottom of the Welcome screen is the 'Ease of access' button, Windows 7 logo, a Shut down button, and a 'Shut down options' button. The following list identifies the functions of the buttons and commands that typically appear on the Welcome screen:

- Clicking the 'Ease of access' button displays the Ease of Access Center, which provides tools to optimize your computer to accommodate the needs of the mobility, hearing, and vision impaired users.
- Clicking the Shut down button shuts down Windows 7 and the computer.
- Clicking the 'Shut down options' button, located to the right of the Shut down button, provides access to a menu containing commands that perform actions such as restarting the computer, putting the computer in a low-powered state, and shutting down the computer. The commands available on your computer may differ.
  - The **Restart command** closes open programs, shuts down Windows 7, and then restarts Windows 7 and displays the Welcome screen.
  - The **Sleep command** waits for Windows 7 to save your work and then turns off the computer fans and hard disk. To wake the computer from the Sleep state, press the power button or lift a notebook computer's cover, and log on to the computer.
  - The **Shut down command** shuts down and turns off the computer.

To Log On to the Computer

After starting Windows 7, you might need to log on to the computer. The following steps log on to the computer based on a typical installation. You may need to ask your instructor how to log on to your computer. This set of steps uses SC Series as the user name. The list of user names on your computer will be different.

- Click the user icon (SC Series, in this case) on the Welcome screen (shown in Figure 3 on the previous page); depending on settings, this either will display a password text box (Figure 4) or will log on to the computer and display the Windows 7 desktop.

Q&A Why do I not see a user icon?

Your computer may require you to type a user name instead of clicking an icon.

Q&A What is a text box?

A text box is a rectangular box in which you type text.

Q&A Why does my screen not show a password text box?

Your account does not require a password.

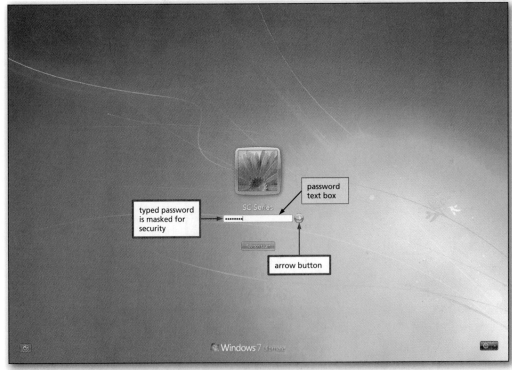

Figure 4

2

- If Windows 7 displays a password text box, type your password in the text box and then click the arrow button to log on to the computer and display the Windows 7 desktop (Figure 5).

Q&A

Why does my desktop look different from the one in Figure 5?

The Windows 7 desktop is customizable, and your school or employer may have modified the desktop to meet its needs. Also, your screen resolution, which affects the size of the elements on the screen, may differ from the screen resolution used in this book. Later in this chapter, you learn how to change screen resolution.

Figure 5

The Windows 7 Desktop

The Windows 7 desktop (Figure 5) and the objects on the desktop emulate a work area in an office. Think of the Windows desktop as an electronic version of the top of your desk. You can perform tasks such as placing objects on the desktop, moving the objects around the desktop, and removing items from the desktop.

When you start a program in Windows 7, it appears on the desktop. Some icons also may be displayed on the desktop. For instance, the icon for the **Recycle Bin**, the location of files that have been deleted, appears on the desktop by default. A **file** is a named unit of storage. Files can contain text, images, audio, and video. You can customize your desktop so that icons representing programs and files you use often appear on your desktop.

Introduction to Microsoft Office 2010

Microsoft Office 2010 is the newest version of Microsoft Office, offering features that provide users with better functionality and easier ways to work with the various files they create. These features include enhanced design tools, such as improved picture formatting tools and new themes, shared notebooks for working in groups, mobile versions of Office programs, broadcast presentation for the Web, and a digital notebook for managing and sharing multimedia information.

Microsoft Office 2010 Programs

Microsoft Office 2010 includes a wide variety of programs such as Word, PowerPoint, Excel, Access, Outlook, Publisher, OneNote, InfoPath, SharePoint Workspace, Communicator, and Web Apps:

- **Microsoft Word 2010**, or Word, is a full-featured word processing program that allows you to create professional-looking documents and revise them easily.
- **Microsoft PowerPoint 2010**, or PowerPoint, is a complete presentation program that allows you to produce professional-looking presentations.
- **Microsoft Excel 2010**, or Excel, is a powerful spreadsheet program that allows you to organize data, complete calculations, make decisions, graph data, develop professional-looking reports, publish organized data to the Web, and access real-time data from Web sites.
- **Microsoft Access 2010**, or Access, is a database management system that allows you to create a database; add, change, and delete data in the database; ask questions concerning the data in the database; and create forms and reports using the data in the database.
- **Microsoft Outlook 2010**, or Outlook, is a communications and scheduling program that allows you to manage e-mail accounts, calendars, contacts, and access to other Internet content.
- **Microsoft Publisher 2010**, or Publisher, is a desktop publishing program that helps you create professional-quality publications and marketing materials that can be shared easily.
- **Microsoft OneNote 2010**, or OneNote, is a note taking program that allows you to store and share information in notebooks with other people.
- **Microsoft InfoPath 2010**, or InfoPath, is a form development program that helps you create forms for use on the Web and gather data from these forms.
- **Microsoft SharePoint Workspace 2010**, or SharePoint, is collaboration software that allows you to access and revise files stored on your computer from other locations.
- **Microsoft Communicator** is communications software that allows you to use different modes of communications such as instant messaging, video conferencing, and sharing files and programs.
- **Microsoft Web Apps** is a Web application that allows you to edit and share files on the Web using the familiar Office interface.

Microsoft Office 2010 Suites

A **suite** is a collection of individual programs available together as a unit. Microsoft offers a variety of Office suites. Table 2 lists the Office 2010 suites and their components.

Programs in a suite, such as Microsoft Office, typically use a similar interface and share features. In addition, Microsoft Office programs use **common dialog boxes** for performing actions such as opening and saving files. Once you are comfortable working with these elements and this interface and performing tasks in one program, the similarity can help you apply the knowledge and skills you have learned to another Office program(s). For example, the process for saving a file in Word is the same in PowerPoint, Excel, and the other Office programs. While briefly showing how to use several Office programs, this chapter illustrates some of the common functions across the programs and also identifies the characteristics unique to these programs.

Table 2 Microsoft Office 2010 Suites

	Microsoft Office Professional Plus 2010	Microsoft Office Professional 2010	Microsoft Office Home and Business 2010	Microsoft Office Standard 2010	Microsoft Office Home and Student 2010
Microsoft Word 2010	✓	✓	✓	✓	✓
Microsoft PowerPoint 2010	✓	✓	✓	✓	✓
Microsoft Excel 2010	✓	✓	✓	✓	✓
Microsoft Access 2010	✓	✓	✗	✗	✗
Microsoft Outlook 2010	✓	✓	✓	✓	✗
Microsoft Publisher 2010	✓	✓	✗	✓	✗
Microsoft OneNote 2010	✓	✓	✓	✓	✓
Microsoft InfoPath 2010	✓	✗	✗	✗	✗
Microsoft SharePoint Workspace 2010	✓	✗	✗	✗	✗
Microsoft Communicator	✓	✗	✗	✗	✗

Starting and Using a Program

To use a program, you must instruct the operating system to start the program. Windows 7 provides many different ways to start a program, one of which is presented in this section (other ways to start a program are presented throughout this chapter). After starting a program, you can use it to perform a variety of tasks. The following pages use Word to discuss some elements of the Office interface and to perform tasks that are common to other Office programs.

Word

Word is a full-featured word processing program that allows you to create many types of personal and business documents, including flyers, letters, memos, resumes, reports, fax cover sheets, mailing labels, and newsletters. Word also provides tools that enable you to create Web pages and save these Web pages directly on a Web server. Word has many features designed to simplify the production of documents and add visual appeal. Using Word, you easily can change the shape, size, and color of text. You also can include borders, shading, tables, images, pictures, charts, and Web addresses in documents.

To Start a Program Using the Start Menu

Across the bottom of the Windows 7 desktop is the taskbar. The taskbar contains the **Start button**, which you use to access programs, files, folders, and settings on a computer. A **folder** is a named location on a storage medium that usually contains related documents. The taskbar also displays a button for each program currently running on a computer.

Clicking the Start button displays the Start menu. The **Start menu** allows you to access programs, folders, and files on the computer and contains commands that allow you to start programs, store and search for documents, customize the computer, and obtain help about thousands of topics. A **menu** is a list of related items, including folders, programs, and commands. Each **command** on a menu performs a specific action, such as saving a file or obtaining help.

The following steps, which assume Windows 7 is running, use the Start menu to start an Office program based on a typical installation. You may need to ask your instructor how to start Office programs for your computer. Although the steps illustrate starting the Word program, the steps to start any Office program, such as Outlook, are similar.

1

- Click the Start button on the Windows 7 taskbar to display the Start menu (Figure 6).

Q&A Why does my Start menu look different?

It may look different depending on your computer's configuration. The Start menu may be customized for several reasons, such as usage requirements or security restrictions.

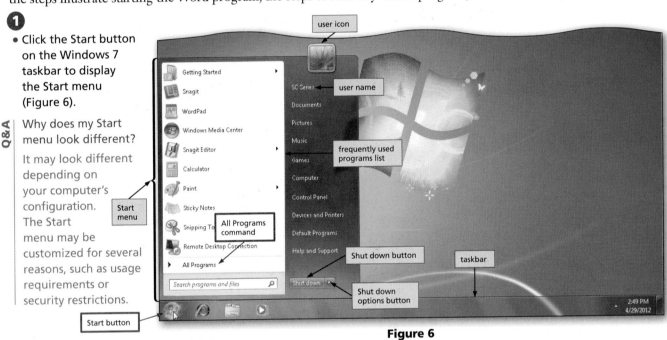

Figure 6

2

- Click All Programs at the bottom of the left pane on the Start menu to display the All Programs list (Figure 7).

Q&A What is a pane?

A **pane** is an area of a window that displays related content. For example, the left pane on the Start menu contains a list of frequently used programs, as well as the All Programs command.

Q&A Why might my All Programs list look different?

Most likely, the programs installed on your computer will differ from those shown in Figure 7. Your All Programs list will show the programs that are installed on your computer.

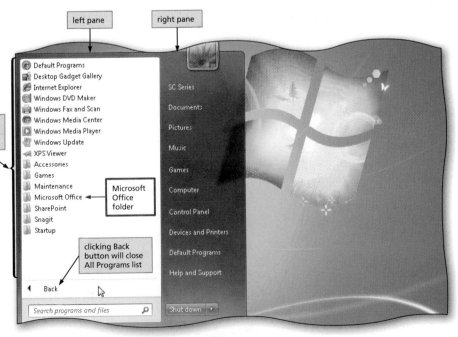

Figure 7

3

- If the program you wish to start is located in a folder, click or scroll to and then click the folder (Microsoft Office, in this case) in the All Programs list to display a list of the folder's contents (Figure 8).

Q&A

Why is the Microsoft Office folder on my computer?

During installation of Microsoft Office 2010, the Microsoft Office folder was added to the All Programs list.

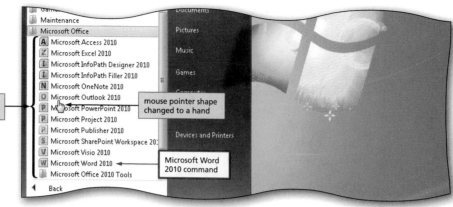

Figure 8

4

- Click, or scroll to and then click, the program name (Microsoft Word 2010, in this case) in the list to start the selected program (Figure 9).

Q&A

What happens when you start a program?

Many programs initially display a blank document in a program window, as shown in the Word window in Figure 9; others provide a means for you to create a blank document. A **window** is a rectangular area that displays data and information. The top of a window has a **title bar**, which is a horizontal space that contains the window's name.

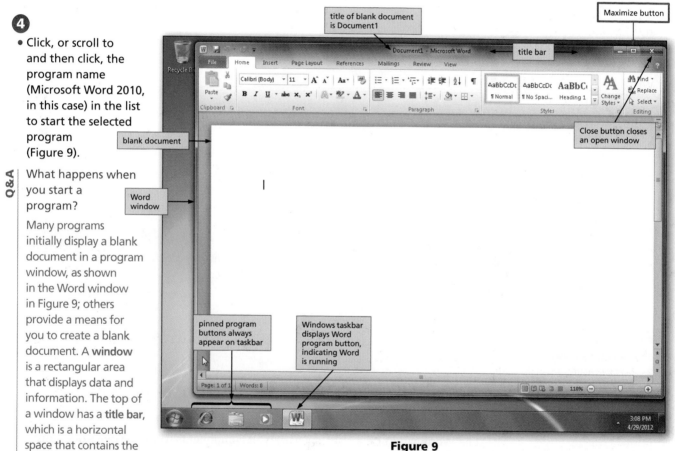

Figure 9

Q&A

Why is my program window a different size?

The Word window shown in Figure 9 is not maximized. Your Word window already may be maximized. The next steps maximize a window.

Other Ways
1. Double-click program icon on desktop, if one is present   3. Display Start menu, type program name in search box, click program name
2. Click program name in left pane of Start menu, if present   4. Double-click file created using program you want to start

To Maximize a Window

Sometimes content is not visible completely in a window. One method of displaying the entire contents of a window is to **maximize** it, or enlarge the window so that it fills the entire screen. The following step maximizes the Word window; however, any Office program's window, including Outlook's window, can be maximized using this step.

- If the program window is not maximized already, click the Maximize button (shown in Figure 9 on the previous page) next to the Close button on the window's title bar (the Word window title bar, in this case) to maximize the window (Figure 10).

Q&A What happened to the Maximize button?

It changed to a Restore Down button, which you can use to return a window to its size and location before you maximized it.

Q&A How do I know whether a window is maximized?

A window is maximized if it fills the entire display area and the Restore Down button is displayed on the title bar.

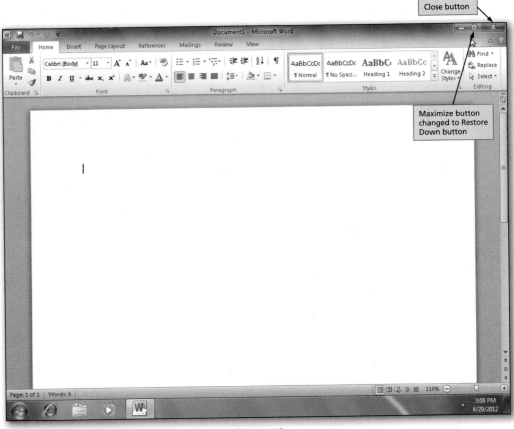

Figure 10

Other Ways

1. Double-click title bar
2. Drag title bar to top of screen

BTW

Scrolling in Outlook
Scrolling often is required in Outlook when you are reading a long e-mail message, perusing the message list, or viewing appointments and events on your calendar.

The Word Document Window, Ribbon, and Elements Common to Office Programs

The Word window consists of a variety of components to make your work more efficient and documents more professional. These include the document window, Ribbon, Mini toolbar, shortcut menus, and Quick Access Toolbar. Most of these components are common to other Microsoft Office 2010 programs; others are unique to Word.

You view a portion of a document on the screen through a **document window** (Figure 11). The default (preset) view is **Print Layout view**, which shows the document on a mock sheet of paper in the document window.

Scroll Bars You use a scroll bar to display different portions of a document in the document window. At the right edge of the document window is a vertical scroll bar. If a document is too wide to fit in the document window, a horizontal scroll bar also appears at the bottom of the document window. On a scroll bar, the position of the scroll box reflects the location of the portion of the document that is displayed in the document window.

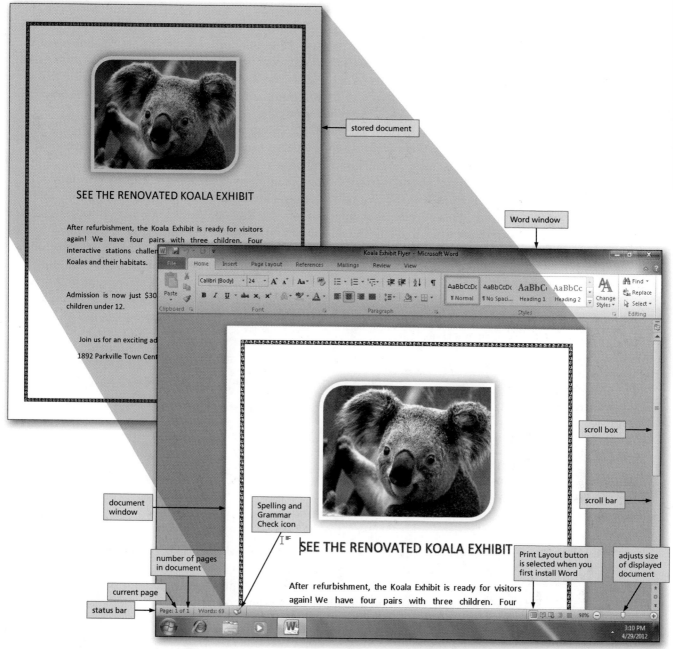

Figure 11

Status Bar The **status bar**, located at the bottom of the document window above the Windows 7 taskbar, presents information about the document, the progress of current tasks, and the status of certain commands and keys; it also provides controls for viewing the document. As you type text or perform certain tasks, various indicators and buttons may appear on the status bar.

The left side of the status bar in Figure 11 shows the current page followed by the total number of pages in the document, the number of words in the document, and an icon to check spelling and grammar. The right side of the status bar includes buttons and controls you can use to change the view of a document and adjust the size of the displayed document.

BTW

Outlook Status Bar
The Outlook status bar contains information such as how many e-mail messages are in the current folder, the number of unread messages, and whether the folder is up to date. You also can change the view or zoom level using the status bar.

Ribbon The Ribbon, located near the top of the window below the title bar, is the control center in Word and other Office programs (Figure 12). The Ribbon provides easy, central access to the tasks you perform while creating a document. The Ribbon consists of tabs, groups, and commands. Each **tab** contains a collection of groups, and each **group** contains related functions. When you start an Office program, such as Word, it initially displays several main tabs, also called default tabs. All Office programs have a **Home tab**, which contains the more frequently used commands.

In addition to the main tabs, Office programs display **tool tabs**, also called contextual tabs (Figure 13), when you perform certain tasks or work with objects such as pictures or tables. If you insert a picture in a Word document, for example, the Picture Tools tab and its related subordinate Format tab appear, collectively referred to as the Picture Tools Format tab. When you are finished working with the picture, the Picture Tools Format tab disappears from the Ribbon. Word and other Office programs determine when tool tabs should appear and disappear based on tasks you perform. Some tool tabs, such as the Table Tools tab, have more than one related subordinate tab.

Items on the Ribbon include buttons, boxes (text boxes, check boxes, etc.), and galleries (Figure 12). A **gallery** is a set of choices, often graphical, arranged in a grid or in a list. You can scroll through choices in an in-Ribbon gallery by clicking the gallery's scroll arrows. Or, you can click a gallery's More button to view more gallery options on the screen at a time.

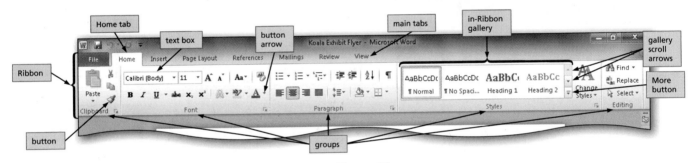

Figure 12

Some buttons and boxes have arrows that, when clicked, also display a gallery; others always cause a gallery to be displayed when clicked. Most galleries support **live preview**, which is a feature that allows you to point to a gallery choice and see its effect in the document — without actually selecting the choice (Figure 13).

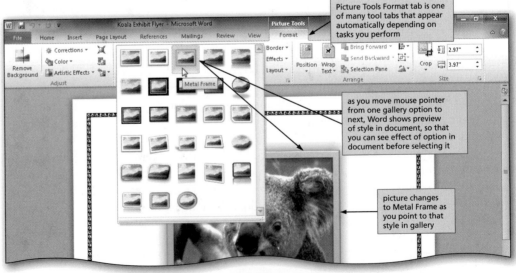

Figure 13

Some commands on the Ribbon display an image to help you remember their function. When you point to a command on the Ribbon, all or part of the command glows in shades of yellow and orange, and an Enhanced ScreenTip appears on the screen. An **Enhanced ScreenTip** is an on-screen note that provides the name of the command, available keyboard shortcut(s), a description of the command, and sometimes instructions for how to obtain help about the command (Figure 14). Enhanced ScreenTips are more detailed than a typical ScreenTip, which usually displays only the name of the command.

Some groups on the Ribbon have a small arrow in the lower-right corner, called a **Dialog Box Launcher**, that when clicked, displays a dialog box or a task pane with additional options for the group (Figure 15). When presented with a dialog box, you make selections and must close the dialog box before returning to the document. A **task pane**, in contrast to a dialog box, is a window that can remain open and visible while you work in the document.

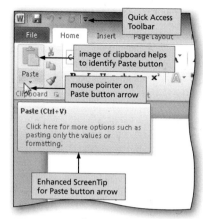

Figure 14

Mini Toolbar   The **Mini toolbar**, which appears automatically based on tasks you perform, contains commands related to changing the appearance of text. All commands on the Mini toolbar also exist on the Ribbon. The purpose of the Mini toolbar is to minimize mouse movement.

When the Mini toolbar appears, it initially is transparent (Figure 16a). If you do not use the transparent Mini toolbar, it disappears from the screen. To use the Mini toolbar, move the mouse pointer into the toolbar, which causes the Mini toolbar to change from a transparent to bright

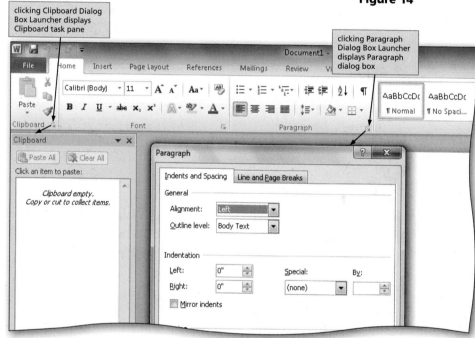

Figure 15

appearance (Figure 16b). If you right-click an item in the document window, Word displays both the Mini toolbar and a shortcut menu, which is discussed in a later section in this chapter.

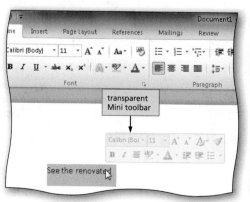

(a) transparent Mini toolbar

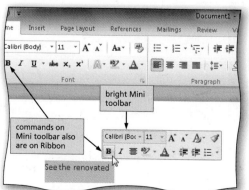

(b) bright Mini toolbar

Figure 16

BTW

Outlook Quick Access Toolbar
The buttons on the Quick Access Toolbar vary slightly from those in most other Office programs. For instance, when you are viewing the message list, the default buttons on the Quick Access Toolbar include the Send/Receive All Folders button and the Undo button. These buttons will change depending on the task you are performing currently in Outlook.

Quick Access Toolbar   The **Quick Access Toolbar**, located initially (by default) above the Ribbon at the left edge of the title bar, provides convenient, one-click access to frequently used commands (Figure 14 on the previous page). The commands on the Quick Access Toolbar always are available, regardless of the task you are performing. The Quick Access Toolbar is discussed in more depth later in the chapter.

KeyTips   If you prefer using the keyboard instead of the mouse, you can press the ALT key on the keyboard to display **KeyTips**, or keyboard code icons, for certain commands (Figure 17). To select a command using the keyboard, press the letter or number displayed in the KeyTip, which may cause additional KeyTips related to the selected command to appear. To remove KeyTips from the screen, press the ALT key or the ESC key until all KeyTips disappear, or click the mouse anywhere in the program window.

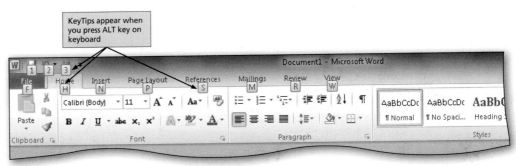

Figure 17

To Display a Different Tab on the Ribbon

When you start Word, the Ribbon displays eight main tabs: File, Home, Insert, Page Layout, References, Mailings, Review, and View. The tab currently displayed is called the **active tab**.

The following step displays the Insert tab, that is, makes it the active tab.

1

- Click Insert on the Ribbon to display the Insert tab (Figure 18).

🔎 **Experiment**

- Click the other tabs on the Ribbon to view their contents. When you are finished, click the Insert tab to redisplay the Insert tab.

Q&A

If I am working in a different Office program, such as Outlook, how do I display a different tab on the Ribbon?

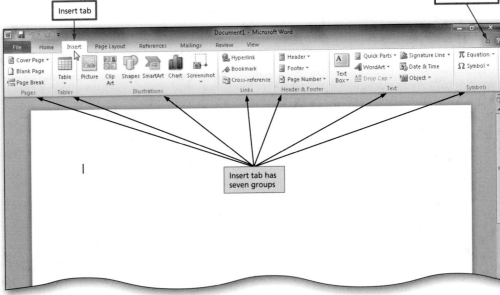

Figure 18

Follow this same procedure; that is, click the desired tab on the Ribbon.

To Minimize, Display, and Restore the Ribbon

To display more of a document or other item, such as an e-mail message, in the window of an Office program, some users prefer to minimize the Ribbon, which hides the groups on the Ribbon and displays only the main tabs. Each time you start an Office program, the Ribbon appears the same way it did the last time you used that Office program. The chapters in this book, however, begin with the Ribbon appearing as it did at the initial installation of the software.

The following steps minimize, display, and restore the Ribbon in an Office program.

- Click the Minimize the Ribbon button on the Ribbon (shown in Figure 18) to minimize the Ribbon (Figure 19).

Q&A What happened to the groups on the Ribbon?

When you minimize the Ribbon, the groups disappear so that the Ribbon does not take up as much space on the screen.

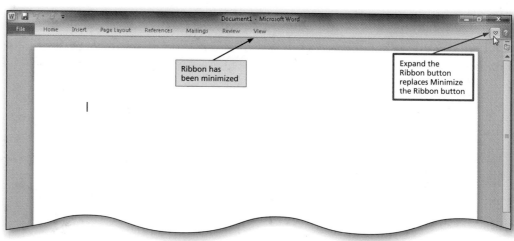

Figure 19

Q&A What happened to the Minimize the Ribbon button?

The Expand the Ribbon button replaces the Minimize the Ribbon button when the Ribbon is minimized.

- Click Home on the Ribbon to display the Home tab (Figure 20).

Q&A Why would I click the Home tab?

If you want to use a command on a minimized Ribbon, click the main tab to display the groups for that tab. After you select a command on the Ribbon, the groups will be hidden once again. If you decide not to use a command on the Ribbon, you can hide the groups by clicking the same main tab or clicking in the program window.

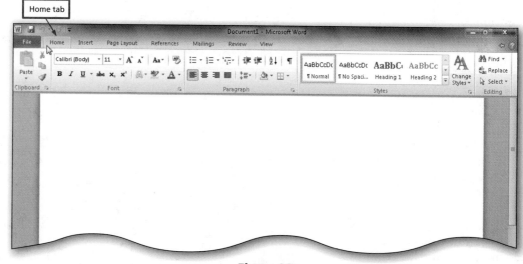

Figure 20

- Click Home on the Ribbon to hide the groups again (shown in Figure 19).

- Click the Expand the Ribbon button on the Ribbon (shown in Figure 19) to restore the Ribbon.

Other Ways

1. Double-click Home on the Ribbon
2. Press CTRL+F1

To Display and Use a Shortcut Menu

When you right-click certain areas of the Word and other program windows, a shortcut menu will appear. A **shortcut menu** is a list of frequently used commands that relate to the right-clicked object. When you right-click a scroll bar, for example, a shortcut menu appears with commands related to the scroll bar. When you right-click the Quick Access Toolbar, a shortcut menu appears with commands related to the Quick Access Toolbar. You can use shortcut menus to access common commands quickly. The following steps use a shortcut menu to move the Quick Access Toolbar, which by default is located on the title bar.

- Right-click the Quick Access Toolbar to display a shortcut menu that presents a list of commands related to the Quick Access Toolbar (Figure 21).

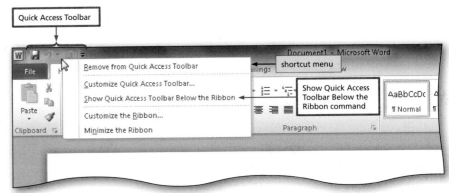

Figure 21

- Click Show Quick Access Toolbar Below the Ribbon on the shortcut menu to display the Quick Access Toolbar below the Ribbon (Figure 22).

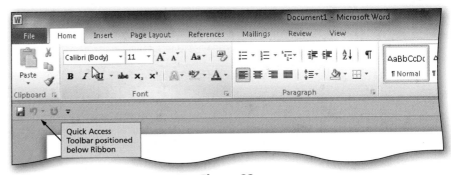

Figure 22

- Right-click the Quick Access Toolbar to display a shortcut menu (Figure 23).

- Click Show Quick Access Toolbar Above the Ribbon on the shortcut menu to return the Quick Access Toolbar to its original position (shown in Figure 21).

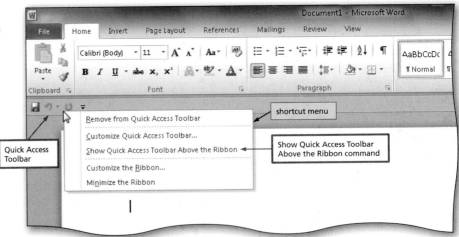

Figure 23

To Customize the Quick Access Toolbar

The Quick Access Toolbar provides easy access to some of the more frequently used commands in Office programs. You can customize the Quick Access Toolbar by changing its location in the window, as shown in the previous steps, and by adding more buttons to reflect commands you would like to access easily. The following steps add the Quick Print button to the Quick Access Toolbar.

- Click the Customize Quick Access Toolbar button to display the Customize Quick Access Toolbar menu (Figure 24).

Q&A Which commands are listed on the Customize Quick Access Toolbar menu?

It lists commands that commonly are added to the Quick Access Toolbar.

Q&A What do the check marks next to some commands signify?

Check marks appear next to commands that already are on the Quick Access Toolbar. When you add a button to the Quick Access Toolbar, a check mark will be displayed next to its command name.

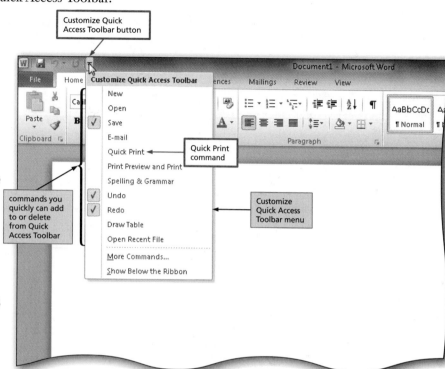

Figure 24

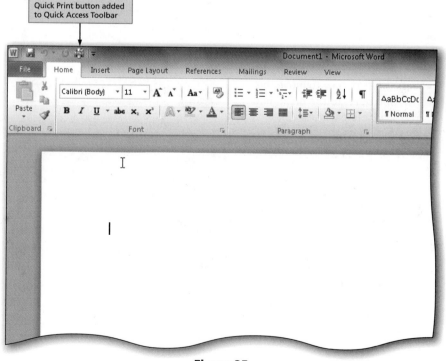

- Click Quick Print on the Customize Quick Access Toolbar menu to add the Quick Print button to the Quick Access Toolbar (Figure 25).

Q&A How would I remove a button from the Quick Access Toolbar?

You would right-click the button you wish to remove and then click Remove from Quick Access Toolbar on the shortcut menu.

Q&A Why does the Quick Print command not appear in Outlook?

Depending on the window you currently are viewing in Outlook, the Quick Print command might not appear. The Quick Access Toolbar contains only commands representing the tasks that can be performed in the current window.

Figure 25

To Enter Text in a Document

The first step in creating a document is to enter its text by typing on the keyboard. By default, Word positions text at the left margin as you type. To begin creating a flyer, for example, you type the headline in the document window. The following steps type this first line of text, a headline, in a document.

1

- Type **SEE THE RENOVATED KOALA EXHIBIT** as the text (Figure 26).

Q&A What is the blinking vertical bar to the right of the text?

The insertion point. It indicates where text, graphics, and other items will be inserted in the document. As you type, the insertion point moves to the right, and when you reach the end of a line, it moves downward to the beginning of the next line.

Q&A What if I make an error while typing?

You can press the BACKSPACE key until you have deleted the text in error and then retype the text correctly.

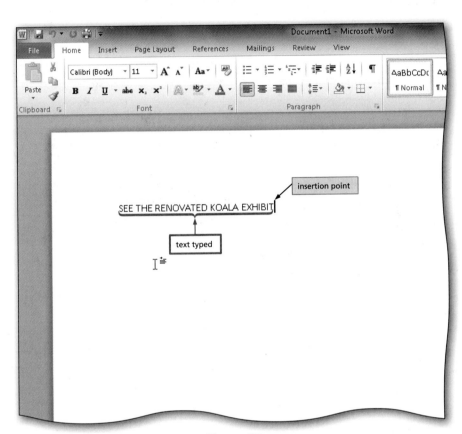

Figure 26

2

- Press the ENTER key to move the insertion point to the beginning of the next line (Figure 27).

Q&A Why did blank space appear between the entered text and the insertion point?

Each time you press the ENTER key, Word creates a new paragraph and inserts blank space between the two paragraphs.

Q&A Can I enter text in an e-mail message in a similar fashion?

Yes. Entering text in an e-mail message is very similar to entering text in a document.

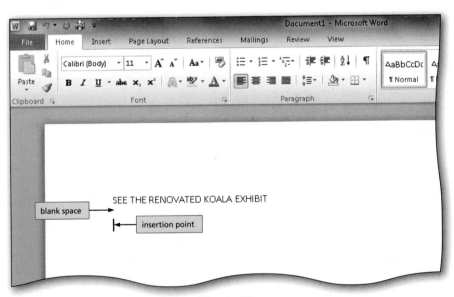

Figure 27

Saving and Organizing Files

While you are creating a document, the computer stores it in memory. When you save a document, the computer places it on a storage medium such as a hard disk, USB flash drive, or optical disc. A saved document is referred to as a file. A **file name** is the name assigned to a file when it is saved. It is important to save a document frequently for the following reasons:

- The document in memory might be lost if the computer is turned off or you lose electrical power while a program is running.
- If you run out of time before completing a project, you may finish it at a future time without starting over.

When saving files, you should organize them so that you easily can find them later. Windows 7 provides tools to help you organize files.

Organizing Files and Folders

A file contains data. This data can range from a research paper to an accounting spreadsheet to an electronic math quiz. You should organize and store these files in folders to avoid misplacing a file and to help you find a file quickly.

If you are a freshman taking an introductory computer class (CIS 101, for example), you may want to design a series of folders for the different subjects covered in the class. To accomplish this, you can arrange the folders in a hierarchy for the class, as shown in Figure 28.

BTW

File Type
Depending on your Windows 7 settings, the file type may be displayed immediately to the right of the file name after you save the file. The file type .docx is a Word 2010 document and the file type .msg is an Outlook e-mail message.

BTW

Saving Files in Outlook
Users typically do not save files in Outlook as often as they might in another Office program such as Word, PowerPoint, or Excel. However, Outlook provides features to save items such as individual e-mail messages, calendar items, contacts, and e-mail attachments.

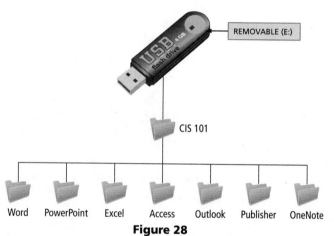

Figure 28

The hierarchy contains three levels. The first level contains the storage device, in this case a USB flash drive. Windows 7 identifies the storage device with a letter, and, in some cases, a name. In Figure 28, the USB flash drive is identified as REMOVABLE (E:). The second level contains the class folder (CIS 101, in this case), and the third level contains seven folders, one each for a different Office program that will be covered in the class (Word, PowerPoint, Excel, Access, Outlook, Publisher, and OneNote).

When the hierarchy in Figure 28 is created, the USB flash drive is said to contain the CIS 101 folder, and the CIS 101 folder is said to contain the separate Office folders (i.e., Word, PowerPoint, Excel, etc.). In addition, this hierarchy easily can be expanded to include folders from other classes taken during additional semesters.

The vertical and horizontal lines in Figure 28 form a pathway that allows you to navigate to a drive or folder on a computer or network. A **path** consists of a drive letter (preceded by a drive name when necessary) and colon, to identify the storage device, and one or more folder names. Each drive or folder in the hierarchy has a corresponding path.

Table 3 shows examples of paths and their corresponding drives and folders.

Table 3 Paths and Corresponding Drives and Folders	
Path	**Drive and Folder**
Computer ▶ REMOVABLE (E:)	Drive E (REMOVABLE (E:))
Computer ▶ REMOVABLE (E:) ▶ CIS 101	CIS 101 folder on drive E
Computer ▶ REMOVABLE (E:) ▶ CIS 101 ▶ Word	Word folder in CIS 101 folder on drive E

The following pages illustrate the steps to organize the folders for this class and save a file in one of those folders:

1. Create the folder identifying your class.
2. Create the Word folder in the folder identifying your class.
3. Create the remaining folders in the folder identifying your class (one each for PowerPoint, Excel, Access, Outlook, Publisher, and OneNote).
4. Save a file in the Word folder.
5. Verify the location of the saved file.

To Create a Folder

When you create a folder, such as the CIS 101 folder shown in Figure 28 on the previous page, you must name the folder. A folder name should describe the folder and its contents. A folder name can contain spaces and any uppercase or lowercase characters, except a backslash (\), slash (/), colon (:), asterisk (*), question mark (?), quotation marks ("), less than symbol (<), greater than symbol (>), or vertical bar (|). Folder names cannot be CON, AUX, COM1, COM2, COM3, COM4, LPT1, LPT2, LPT3, PRN, or NUL. The same rules for naming folders also apply to naming files.

To store files and folders on a USB flash drive, you must connect the USB flash drive to an available USB port on a computer. The following steps create your class folder (CIS 101, in this case) on a USB flash drive.

1

- Connect the USB flash drive to an available USB port on the computer to open the AutoPlay window (Figure 29).

Q&A Why does the AutoPlay window not open?

Some computers are not configured to open an AutoPlay window. Instead, they might display the contents of the USB flash drive automatically, or you might need to access contents of the USB flash drive using the Computer window. To use the Computer window to display the USB flash drive's contents, click the Start button, click Computer on the Start menu, and then click the icon representing the USB flash drive.

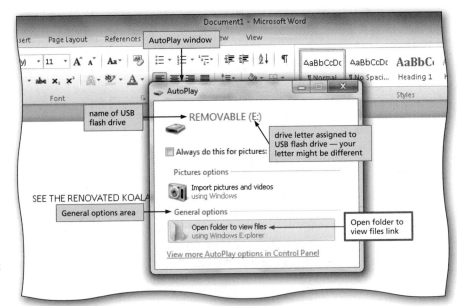

Figure 29

Q&A Why does the AutoPlay window look different from the one in Figure 29?

The AutoPlay window that opens on your computer might display different options. The type of USB flash drive, its contents, and the next available drive letter on your computer all will determine which options are displayed in the AutoPlay window.

2

- Click the 'Open folder to view files' link in the AutoPlay window to open the USB flash drive window (Figure 30).

Q&A

Why does Figure 30 show REMOVABLE (E:) for the USB flash drive?

REMOVABLE is the name of the USB flash drive used to illustrate these steps. The (E:) refers to the drive letter assigned by Windows 7 to the USB flash drive. The name and drive letter of your USB flash drive probably will be different.

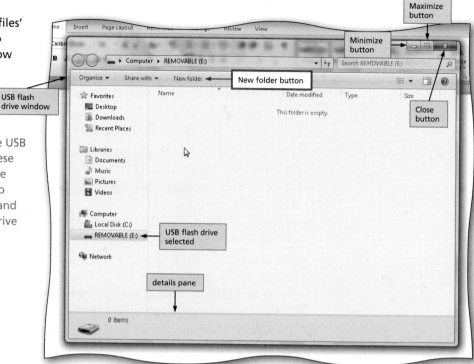

Figure 30

3

- Click the New folder button on the toolbar to display a new folder icon with the name, New folder, selected in a text box.

- Type CIS 101 (or your class code) in the text box to name the folder.

- Press the ENTER key to create a folder identifying your class on the selected drive (Figure 31). If the CIS 101 folder does not appear in the navigation pane, double-click REMOVABLE (E:) in the navigation pane to display the folder just added.

Q&A

What happens when I press the ENTER key?

The class folder (CIS 101, in this case) is displayed in the File list, which contains the folder name, date modified, type, and size.

Q&A

Why is the folder icon displayed differently on my computer?

Windows might be configured to display contents differently on your computer.

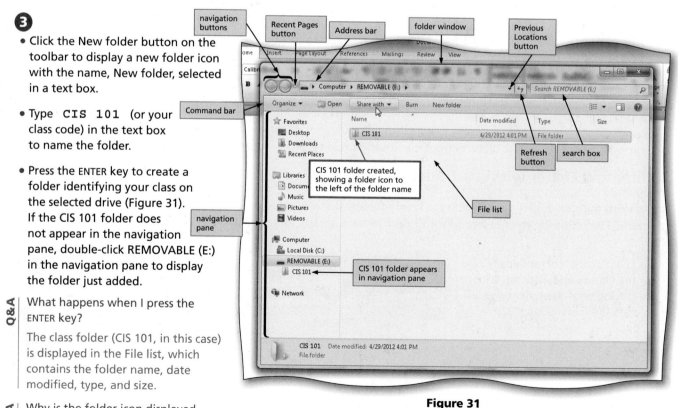

Figure 31

Folder Windows

The USB flash drive window (shown in Figure 31 on the previous page) is called a folder window. Recall that a folder is a specific named location on a storage medium that contains related files. Most users rely on **folder windows** for finding, viewing, and managing information on their computer. Folder windows have common design elements, including the following (Figure 31).

- The **Address bar** provides quick navigation options. The arrows on the Address bar allow you to visit different locations on the computer.
- The buttons to the left of the Address bar allow you to navigate the contents of the left pane and view recent pages. Other buttons allow you to specify the size of the window.
- The **Previous Locations button** saves the locations you have visited and displays the locations when clicked.
- The **Refresh button** on the right side of the Address bar refreshes the contents of the right pane of the folder window.
- The **search box** to the right of the Address bar contains the dimmed word, Search. You can type a term in the search box for a list of files, folders, shortcuts, and elements containing that term within the location you are searching. A **shortcut** is an icon on the desktop that provides a user with immediate access to a program or file.
- The **Command bar** contains five buttons used to accomplish various tasks on the computer related to organizing and managing the contents of the open window.
- The **navigation pane** on the left contains the Favorites area, Libraries area, Computer area, and Network area.
- The **Favorites area** contains links to your favorite locations. By default, this list contains only links to your Desktop, Downloads, and Recent Places.
- The **Libraries area** shows links to files and folders that have been included in a library.

A **library** helps you manage multiple folders and files stored in various locations on a computer. It does not store the files and folders; rather, it displays links to them so that you can access them quickly. For example, you can save pictures from a digital camera in any folder on any storage location on a computer. Normally, this would make organizing the different folders difficult; however, if you add the folders to a library, you can access all the pictures from one location regardless of where they are stored.

To Create a Folder within a Folder

With the class folder created, you can create folders that will store the files you create using each Office program. The following steps create a Word folder in the CIS 101 folder (or the folder identifying your class).

1
- Double-click the icon or folder name for the CIS 101 folder (or the folder identifying your class) in the File list to open the folder (Figure 32).

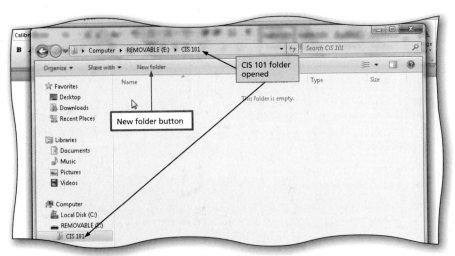

Figure 32

2

- Click the New folder button on the toolbar to display a new folder icon and text box for the folder.

- Type **Word** in the text box to name the folder.

- Press the ENTER key to create the folder (Figure 33).

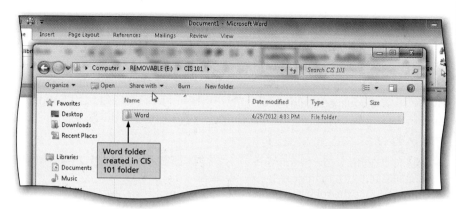

Figure 33

To Create the Remaining Folders

The following steps create the remaining folders in the folder identifying your class (in this case, CIS 101).

1 Click the New folder button on the toolbar to display a new folder icon and text box.

2 Type **PowerPoint** in the text box and then press the ENTER key to create and name the folder.

3 Repeat Steps 1 and 2 to create each of the remaining folders, using the names Excel, Access, Outlook, Publisher, and OneNote as the folder names (Figure 34).

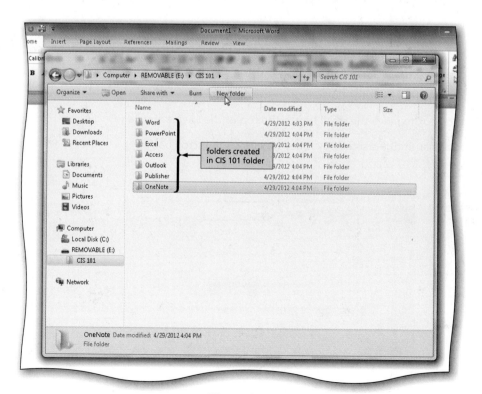

Figure 34

To Expand a Folder, Scroll through Folder Contents, and Collapse a Folder

Folder windows display the hierarchy of items and the contents of drives and folders in the right pane. You might want to expand a drive in the navigation pane to view its contents, scroll through its contents, and collapse it when you are finished viewing its contents. When a folder is expanded, it lists all the folders it contains. By contrast, a collapsed folder does not list the folders it contains. The following steps expand, scroll through, and then collapse the folder identifying your class (CIS 101, in this case).

- Double-click the folder identifying your class (CIS 101, in this case), which expands the folder to display its contents and displays a black arrow to the left of the folder icon (Figure 35).

Q&A Why are the subject folders indented below the CIS 101 folder in the navigation pane?

It shows that the folders are contained within the CIS 101 folder.

Q&A Why did a scroll bar appear in the navigation pane?

When all contents cannot fit in a window or pane, a scroll bar appears. As described earlier, you can view areas currently not visible by (1) clicking the scroll arrows, (2) clicking above or below the scroll bar, and (3) dragging the scroll box.

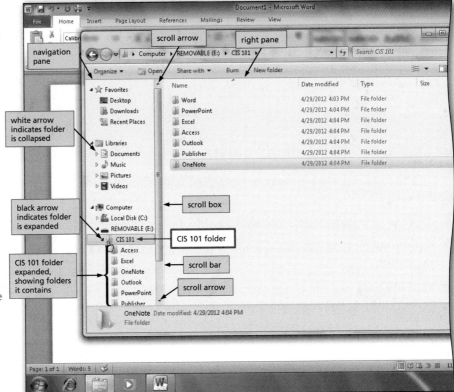

Figure 35

Experiment

- Click the down scroll arrow on the vertical scroll bar to display additional folders at the bottom of the navigation pane.

- Click the scroll bar above the scroll box to move the scroll box to the top of the navigation pane.

- Drag the scroll box down the scroll bar until the scroll box is halfway down the scroll bar.

2

- Double-click the folder identifying your class (CIS 101, in this case) to collapse the folder (Figure 36).

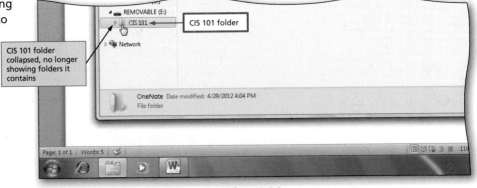

Figure 36

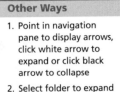

Other Ways

1. Point in navigation pane to display arrows, click white arrow to expand or click black arrow to collapse

2. Select folder to expand or collapse using arrow keys, press RIGHT ARROW to expand; press LEFT ARROW to collapse.

To Switch from One Program to Another

The next step is to save the Word file containing the headline you typed earlier. Word, however, currently is not the active window. You can use the program button on the taskbar and live preview to switch to Word and then save the document in the Word document window.

If Windows Aero is active on your computer, Windows displays a live preview window whenever you move your mouse on a button or click a button on the taskbar. If Aero is not supported or enabled on your computer, you will see a window title instead of a live preview. The steps below use the Word program; however, the steps are the same for any active Office program currently displayed as a program button on the taskbar.

The following steps switch to the Word window.

- Point to the Word program button on the taskbar to see a live preview of the open document(s) or the window title(s) of the open document(s), depending on your computer's configuration (Figure 37).

- Click the program button or the live preview to make the program associated with the program button the active window (shown in Figure 27 on page OFF 20).

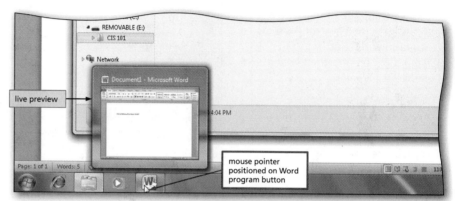

Figure 37

Q&A

What if multiple windows are open in a program?

If Aero is enabled on your computer, click the desired live preview. If Aero is not supported or not enabled, click the window title.

To Save a File in a Folder

Now that you have created the folders for storing files, you can save the Word document. The following steps save a file on a USB flash drive in the Word folder contained in your class folder (CIS 101, in this case) using the file name, Koala Exhibit.

- With a USB flash drive connected to one of the computer's USB ports, click the Save button on the Quick Access Toolbar to display the Save As dialog box (Figure 38).

Q&A

Why does a file name already appear in the File name text box?

Word automatically suggests a file name the first time you save a document. The file name normally consists of the first few words contained in the document. Because the suggested file name is selected, you do not need to delete it; as soon as you begin typing, the new file name replaces the selected text. In Outlook, the default file name might be the subject of an e-mail message you are saving.

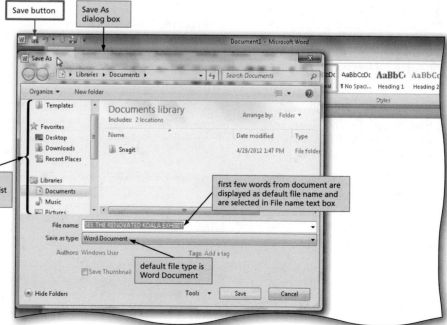

Figure 38

2

- Type **Koala Exhibit** in the File name text box (Save As dialog box) to change the file name. Do not press the ENTER key after typing the file name because you do not want to close the dialog box at this time (Figure 39).

Q&A

What characters can I use in a file name?

The only invalid characters are the backslash (\), slash (/), colon (:), asterisk (*), question mark (?), quotation mark ("), less than symbol (<), greater than symbol (>), and vertical bar (|).

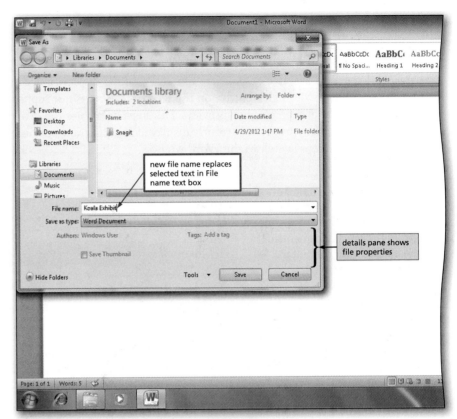

Figure 39

3

- Navigate to the desired save location (in this case, the Word folder in the CIS 101 folder [or your class folder] on the USB flash drive) by performing the tasks in Steps 3a, 3b, and 3c.

- If the navigation pane is not displayed in the dialog box, click the Browse Folders button to expand the dialog box.

- If Computer is not displayed in the navigation pane, drag the navigation pane scroll bar until Computer appears.

- If Computer is not expanded in the navigation pane, double-click Computer to display a list of available storage devices in the navigation pane.

- If necessary, scroll through the dialog box until your USB flash drive appears in the list of available storage devices in the navigation pane (Figure 40).

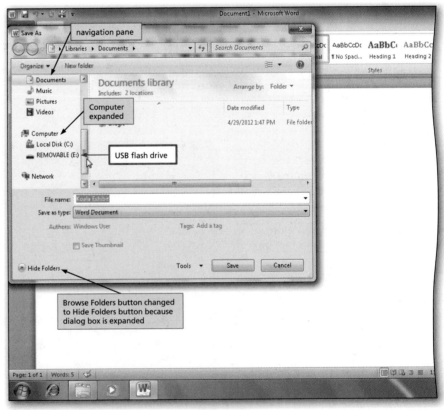

Figure 40

- If your USB flash drive is not expanded, double-click the USB flash drive in the list of available storage devices in the navigation pane to select that drive as the new save location and display its contents in the right pane.

- If your class folder (CIS 101, in this case) is not expanded, double-click the CIS 101 folder to select the folder and display its contents in the right pane.

Q&A

What if I do not want to save in a folder?

Although storing files in folders is an effective technique for organizing files, some users prefer not to store files in folders. If you prefer not to save this file in a folder, skip all instructions in Step 3c and proceed to Step 4.

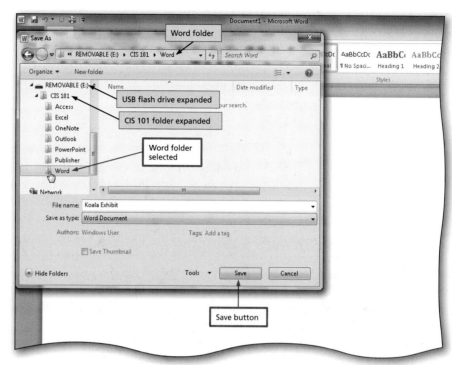

Figure 41

- Click the Word folder to select the folder and display its contents in the right pane (Figure 41).

- Click the Save button (Save As dialog box) to save the document in the selected folder on the selected drive with the entered file name (Figure 42).

Q&A

How do I know that the file is saved?

While an Office program is saving a file, it briefly displays a message on the status bar indicating the amount of the file saved. In addition, the USB flash drive may have a light that flashes during the save process.

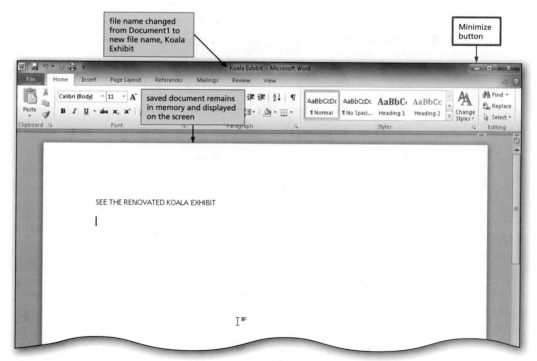

Figure 42

Other Ways
1. Click File on Ribbon, click Save, type file name, navigate to desired save location, click Save button
2. Press CTRL+S or press SHIFT+F12, type file name, navigate to desired save location, click Save button

Navigating in Dialog Boxes

Navigating is the process of finding a location on a storage device. While saving the Koala Exhibit file, for example, Steps 3a – 3c in the previous set of steps navigated to the Word folder located in the CIS 101 folder. When performing certain functions in Windows programs, such as saving a file, opening a file, or inserting a picture in an existing document, you most likely will have to navigate to the location where you want to save the file or to the folder containing the file you want to open or insert. Most dialog boxes in Windows programs requiring navigation follow a similar procedure; that is, the way you navigate to a folder in one dialog box, such as the Save As dialog box, is similar to how you might navigate in another dialog box, such as the Open dialog box. If you chose to navigate to a specific location in a dialog box, you would follow the instructions in Steps 3a – 3c on pages OFF 28 and OFF 29.

To Minimize and Restore a Window

Before continuing, you can verify that the Word file was saved properly. To do this, you will minimize the Word window and then open the USB flash drive window so that you can verify the file is stored on the USB flash drive. A **minimized window** is an open window hidden from view but that can be displayed quickly by clicking the window's program button on the taskbar.

In the following example, Word is used to illustrate minimizing and restoring windows; however, you would follow the same steps regardless of the Office program you are using.

The following steps minimize the Word window, verify that the file is saved, and then restore the minimized window.

1

- Click the Minimize button on the program's title bar (shown in Figure 42 on the previous page) to minimize the window (Figure 43).

Q&A

Is the minimized window still available?

The minimized window, Word in this case, remains available but no longer is the active window. It is minimized as a program button on the taskbar.

- If necessary, click the Windows Explorer program button on the taskbar to open the USB flash drive window.

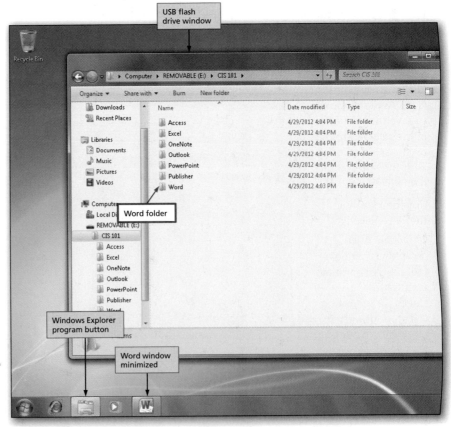

Figure 43

• Double-click the Word folder to select the folder and display its contents (Figure 44).

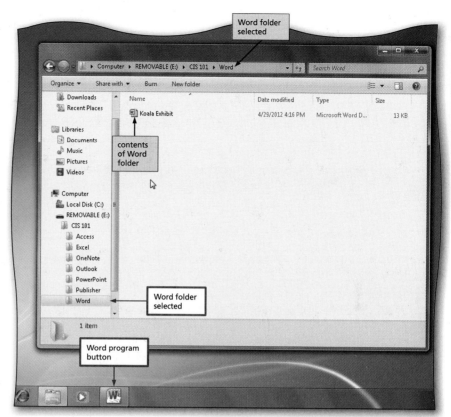

Figure 44

Q&A

Why does the Windows Explorer button on the taskbar change?

The button changes to reflect the status of the folder window (in this case, the USB flash drive window). A selected button indicates that the folder window is active on the screen. When the button is not selected, the window is open but not active.

3

• After viewing the contents of the selected folder, click the Word program button on the taskbar to restore the minimized window (as shown in Figure 42 on page OFF 29).

Other Ways
1. Right-click title bar, click Minimize on shortcut menu, click taskbar button in taskbar button area
2. Press WINDOWS+M, press WINDOWS+SHIFT+M

Screen Resolution

Screen resolution indicates the number of pixels (dots) that the computer uses to display the letters, numbers, graphics, and background you see on the screen. When you increase the screen resolution, Windows displays more information on the screen, but the information decreases in size. The reverse also is true: as you decrease the screen resolution, Windows displays less information on the screen, but the information increases in size.

Screen resolution usually is stated as the product of two numbers, such as 1024×768 (pronounced "ten twenty-four by seven sixty-eight"). A 1024×768 screen resolution results in a display of 1,024 distinct pixels on each of 768 lines, or about

786,432 pixels. Changing the screen resolution affects how the Ribbon appears in Office programs. Figure 45 shows the Word Ribbon at screen resolutions of 1024 × 768 and 1280 × 800. All of the same commands are available regardless of screen resolution. Word, however, makes changes to the groups and the buttons within the groups to accommodate the various screen resolutions. The result is that certain commands may need to be accessed differently depending on the resolution chosen. A command that is visible on the Ribbon and available by clicking a button at one resolution may not be visible and may need to be accessed using its Dialog Box Launcher at a different resolution.

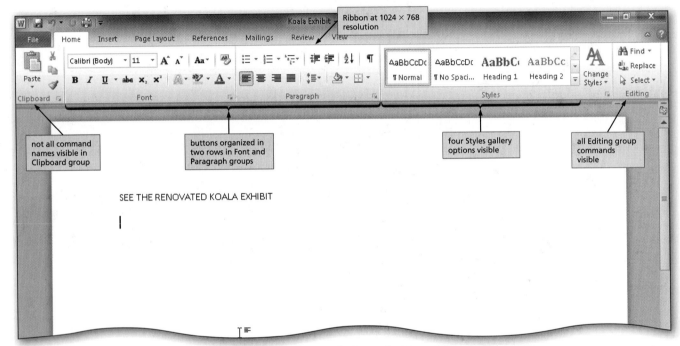

(a) Ribbon at resolution of 1024 x 768

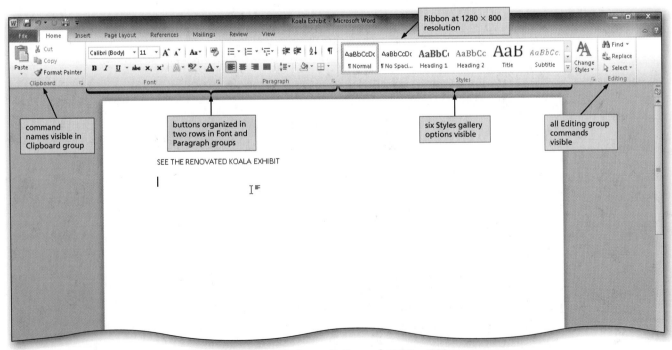

(b) Ribbon at resolution of 1280 x 800

Figure 45

Comparing the two Ribbons in Figure 45, notice the changes in content and layout of the groups and galleries. In some cases, the content of a group is the same in each resolution, but the layout of the group differs. For example, the same gallery and buttons appear in the Styles groups in the two resolutions, but the layouts differ. In other cases, the content and layout are the same across the resolution, but the level of detail differs with the resolution. In the Clipboard group, when the resolution increases to 1280×800, the names of all the buttons in the group appear in addition to the buttons themselves. At the lower resolution, only the buttons appear.

To Change the Screen Resolution

If you are using a computer to step through the chapters in this book and you want your screen to match the figures, you may need to change your screen's resolution. The figures in this book use a screen resolution of 1024×768. The following steps change the screen resolution to 1024×768. Your computer already may be set to 1024×768 or some other resolution. Keep in mind that many computer labs prevent users from changing the screen resolution; in that case, read the following steps for illustration purposes.

- Click the Show desktop button on the taskbar to display the Windows 7 desktop.

- Right-click an empty area on the Windows 7 desktop to display a shortcut menu that displays a list of commands related to the desktop (Figure 46).

Q&A

Why does my shortcut menu display different commands?

Depending on your computer's hardware and configuration, different commands might appear on the shortcut menu.

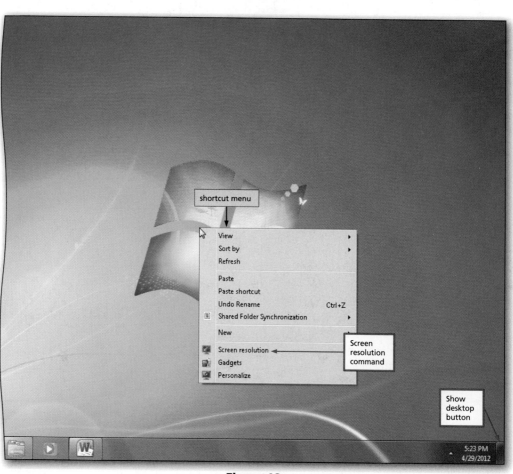

Figure 46

2

- Click Screen resolution on the shortcut menu to open the Screen Resolution window (Figure 47).

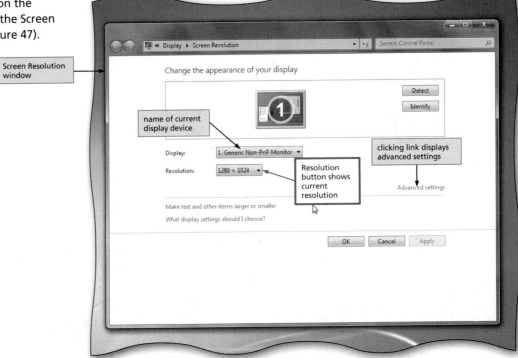

Figure 47

3

- Click the Resolution button in the Screen Resolution window to display the resolution slider.

Q&A

What is a slider?

A **slider** is an object that allows users to choose from multiple predetermined options. In most cases, these options represent some type of numeric value. In most cases, one end of the slider (usually the left or bottom) represents the lowest of available values, and the opposite end (usually the right or top) represents the highest available value.

4

- If necessary, drag the resolution slider until the desired screen resolution (in this case, 1024 × 768) is selected (Figure 48).

Q&A

What if my computer does not support the 1024 × 768 resolution?

Some computers do not support the 1024 × 768 resolution. In this case, select a resolution that is close to the 1024 × 768 resolution.

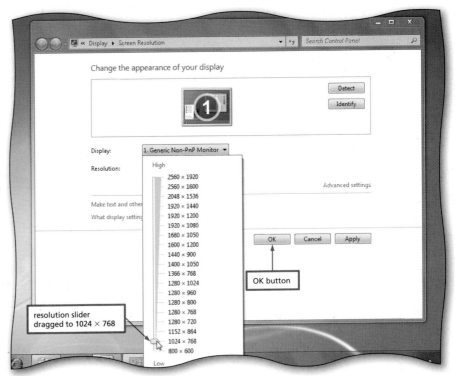

Figure 48

- Click an empty area of the Screen Resolution window to close the resolution slider.

- Click the OK button to change the screen resolution and display the Display Settings dialog box (Figure 49).

- Click the Keep changes button (Display Settings dialog box) to accept the new screen resolution.

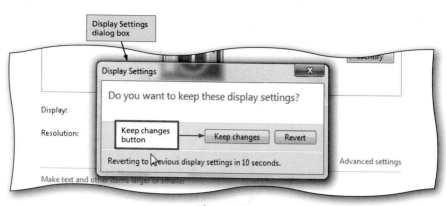

Figure 49

Q&A Why does a message display stating that the image quality can be improved?

Some computer monitors are designed to display contents better at a certain screen resolution, sometimes referred to as an optimal resolution.

To Quit an Office Program with One Document Open

When you quit some Office programs, such as Word, if you have made changes to a file since the last time the file was saved, the Office program displays a dialog box asking if you want to save the changes you made to the file before it closes the program window. The dialog box contains three buttons with these resulting actions: the Save button saves the changes and then quits the Office program, the Don't Save button quits the Office program without saving changes, and the Cancel button closes the dialog box and redisplays the file without saving the changes.

If no changes have been made to an open document since the last time the file was saved, the Office program will close the window without displaying a dialog box.

The following steps quit an Office program. In the following example, Word is used to illustrate quitting an Office program; however, you would follow the same steps regardless of the Office program you were using.

- If necessary, click the Word program button on the taskbar to display the Word window on the desktop.

- Point to the Close button on the right side of the program's title bar, Word in this case (Figure 50).

Figure 50

2

- Click the Close button to close the document and quit Word.

Q&A What if I have multiple windows open in Outlook?

Clicking the Close button in the Microsoft Outlook window closes all other Outlook windows that currently are open.

Q&A What is the Backstage view?

The **Backstage view** contains a set of commands that enable you to manage documents and data about the documents. The Backstage view is discussed in more depth later in this chapter.

3

- If a Microsoft Word dialog box appears, click the Save button to save any changes made to the document since the last save.

Other Ways

1. Right-click the Office program button on Windows 7 taskbar, click Close window or 'Close all windows' on shortcut menu

2. Press ALT + F4

Break Point: If you wish to take a break, this is a good place to do so. To resume at a later time, continue to follow the steps from this location forward.

Additional Microsoft Office Programs

The previous section used Word to illustrate common features of Office and some basic elements unique to Word. The following sections present elements unique to PowerPoint, Excel, and Access, as well as illustrate additional common features of Office.

In the following pages, you will learn how to do the following:

1. Start an Office program (PowerPoint) using the search box.
2. Create two small documents in the same Office program (PowerPoint).
3. Close one of the documents.
4. Reopen the document just closed.
5. Create a document in a different Office program (Excel).
6. Save the document with a new file name.
7. Create a file in a different Office program (Access).
8. Close the file and then open the file.

PowerPoint

PowerPoint is a complete presentation program that allows you to produce professional-looking presentations (Figure 51). A PowerPoint **presentation** also is called a **slide show**. PowerPoint contains several features to simplify creating a slide show. To make presentations more impressive, you can add diagrams, tables, pictures, video, sound, and animation effects. Additional PowerPoint features include the following:

- **Word processing** — Create bulleted lists, combine words and images, find and replace text, and use multiple fonts and font sizes.
- **Outlining** — Develop a presentation using an outline format. You also can import outlines from Microsoft Word or other word processing programs, including single-level and multilevel lists.
- **Charting** — Create and insert charts into presentations and then add effects and chart elements.
- **Drawing** — Create and modify diagrams using shapes such as arcs, arrows, cubes, rectangles, stars, and triangles. Then, customize and add effects to the diagrams, and arrange these objects by sizing, scaling, and rotating them.
- **Inserting multimedia** — Insert artwork and multimedia effects into a slide show. The Microsoft Clip Organizer, included with Office programs, contains hundreds of media files, including pictures, sounds, and movies.
- **Saving to the Web** — Save presentations or parts of a presentation so that they can be viewed in a Web browser. You can publish your slide show to the Internet or to an intranet.
- **E-mailing** — Send an entire slide show as an attachment to an e-mail message.
- **Collaborating** — Share a presentation with friends and coworkers. Ask them to review the slides and then insert comments that offer suggestions to enhance the presentation.
- **Preparing delivery** — Rehearse integrating PowerPoint slides into your speech by setting timings, using presentation tools, showing only selected slides in a presentation, and packaging the presentation for an optical disc.

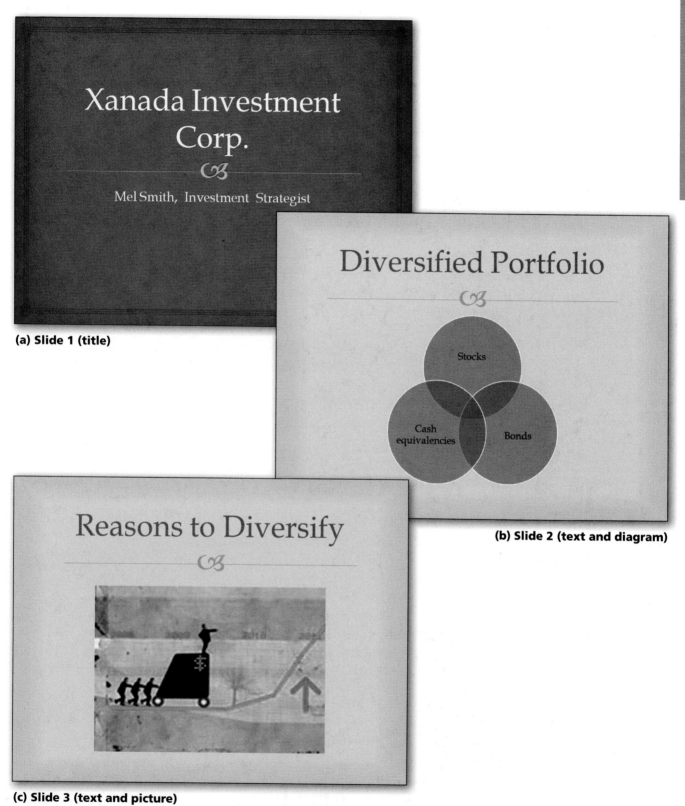

(a) Slide 1 (title)

(b) Slide 2 (text and diagram)

(c) Slide 3 (text and picture)

Figure 51

To Start a Program Using the Search Box

The steps on the next page, which assume Windows 7 is running, use the search box to start the PowerPoint Office program based on a typical installation; however, you would follow similar steps to start any Office program. You may need to ask your instructor how to start programs for your computer.

1

• Click the Start button on the Windows 7 taskbar to display the Start menu.

2

• Type **Microsoft PowerPoint** as the search text in the 'Search programs and files' text box and watch the search results appear on the Start menu (Figure 52).

Q&A

Do I need to type the complete program name or correct capitalization?

No, just enough of it for the program name to appear on the Start menu. For example, if you want to start Outlook, you may be able to type Outlook or outlook, instead of Microsoft Outlook.

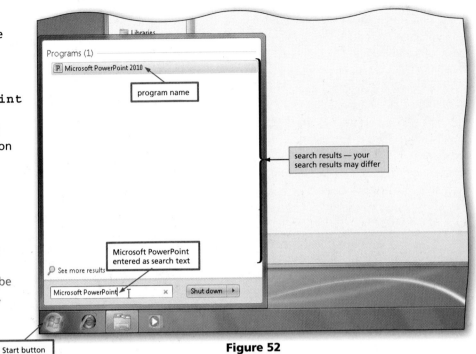

Figure 52

3

• Click the program name, Microsoft PowerPoint 2010 in this case, in the search results on the Start menu to start PowerPoint and display a new blank presentation in the PowerPoint window.

• If the program window is not maximized, click the Maximize button on its title bar to maximize the window (Figure 53).

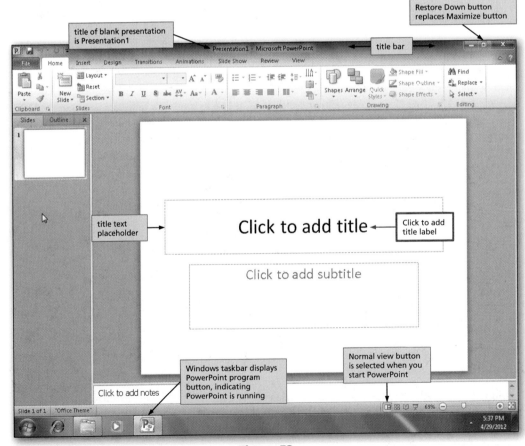

Figure 53

The PowerPoint Window and Ribbon

The PowerPoint window consists of a variety of components to make your work more efficient and documents more professional: the window, Ribbon, Mini toolbar, shortcut menus, and Quick Access Toolbar. Many of these components are common to other Office programs and have been discussed earlier in this chapter. Other components, discussed in the following paragraphs and later in subsequent chapters, are unique to PowerPoint.

The basic unit of a PowerPoint presentation is a **slide**. A slide may contain text and objects, such as graphics, tables, charts, and drawings. **Layouts** are used to position this content on the slide. When you create a new presentation, the default **Title Slide** layout appears (Figure 54). The purpose of this layout is to introduce the presentation to the audience. PowerPoint includes eight other built-in standard layouts.

The default slide layouts are set up in **landscape orientation**, where the slide width is greater than its height. In landscape orientation, the slide size is preset to 10 inches wide and 7.5 inches high when printed on a standard sheet of paper measuring 11 inches wide and 8.5 inches high.

BTW

Portrait Orientation
If your slide content is dominantly vertical, such as a skyscraper or a person, consider changing the slide layout to a portrait orientation. To change the orientation to portrait, click the Slide Orientation button (Design tab | Page Setup group) and then click Portrait. You can use both landscape and portrait orientation in the same slide show.

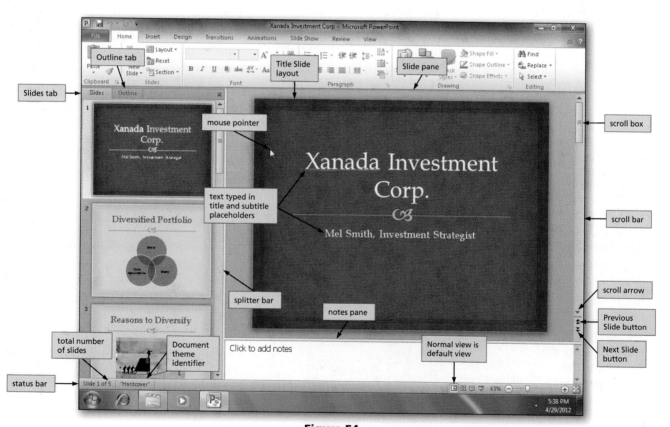

Figure 54

Placeholders   **Placeholders** are boxes with dotted or hatch-marked borders that are displayed when you create a new slide. All layouts except the Blank slide layout contain placeholders. Depending on the particular slide layout selected, title and subtitle placeholders are displayed for the slide title and subtitle; a content text placeholder is displayed for text, art, or a table, chart, picture, graphic, or movie. The title slide in Figure 53 has two text placeholders for the main heading, or title, of a new slide and the subtitle.

Ribbon   The Ribbon in PowerPoint is similar to the one in Word and the other Microsoft Office programs. When you start PowerPoint, the Ribbon displays nine main tabs: File, Home, Insert, Design, Transitions, Animations, Slide Show, Review, and View.

To Enter Content in a Title Slide

With the exception of a blank slide and a slide with a picture and caption, PowerPoint assumes every new slide has a title. Many of PowerPoint's layouts have both a title text placeholder and at least one content placeholder. To make creating a presentation easier, any text you type after a new slide appears becomes title text in the title text placeholder. As you begin typing text in the title text placeholder, the title text also is displayed in the Slide 1 thumbnail in the Slides tab. The presentation title for this presentation is Xanada Investments. The following steps enter a presentation title on the title slide.

1
- Click the label 'Click to add title' located inside the title text placeholder (shown in Figure 53 on page OFF 38) to select the placeholder (Figure 55).

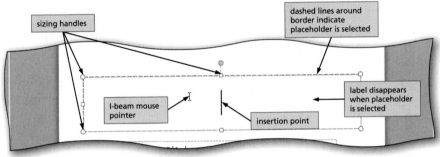

Figure 55

2
- Type **Xanada Investments** in the title text placeholder. Do not press the ENTER key because you do not want to create a new line of text (Figure 56).

Q&A

What are the white squares and circles that appear around the title text placeholder as I type the presentation title?

The white squares and circles are sizing handles, which you can drag to change the size of the title text placeholder. Sizing handles also can be found around other placeholders and objects within a presentation.

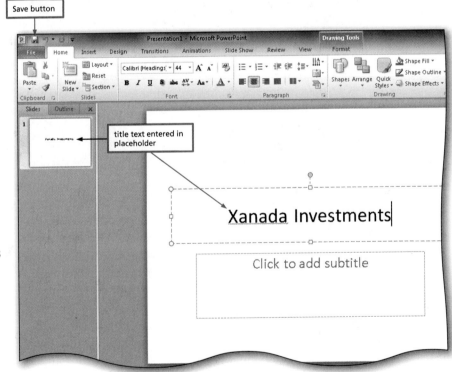

Figure 56

To Save a File in a Folder

The following steps save the presentation in the PowerPoint folder in the class folder (CIS 101, in this case) on a USB flash drive using the file name, Xanada Investments.

1 With a USB flash drive connected to one of the computer's USB ports, click the Save button on the Quick Access Toolbar to display the Save As dialog box.

2 If necessary, type `Xanada Investments` in the File name text box to change the file name. Do not press the ENTER key after typing the file name because you do not want to close the dialog box at this time.

3 Navigate to the desired save location (in this case, the PowerPoint folder in the CIS 101 folder [or your class folder] on the USB flash drive). For specific instructions, perform the tasks in Steps 3a through 3g.

3a If a navigation pane is not displayed in the Save As dialog box, click the Browse Folders button to expand the dialog box.

3b If Computer is not displayed in the navigation pane, drag the navigation pane scroll bar (Save As dialog box) until Computer appears.

3c If Computer is not expanded in the navigation pane, double-click Computer to display a list of available storage devices in the navigation pane.

3d If necessary, scroll through the Save As dialog box until your USB flash drive appears in the list of available storage devices in the navigation pane.

3e If your USB flash drive is not expanded, double-click the USB flash drive in the list of available storage devices in the navigation pane to select that drive as the new save location and display its contents in the right pane.

3f If your class folder (CIS 101, in this case) is not expanded, double-click the CIS 101 folder to select the folder and display its contents.

3g Click the PowerPoint folder to select it as the new save location and display its contents in the right pane.

4 Click the Save button (Save As dialog box) to save the presentation in the selected folder on the selected drive with the entered file name.

To Create a New Office Document from the Backstage View

As discussed earlier, the Backstage view contains a set of commands that enable you to manage documents and data about the documents. From the Backstage view in PowerPoint, for example, you can create, open, print, and save presentations. You also can share documents, manage versions, set permissions, and modify document properties. In other Office 2010 programs, the Backstage view may contain features specific to those programs. The steps on the following pages create a file, a blank presentation in this case, from the Backstage view.

1

● Click File on the Ribbon to open the Backstage view (Figure 57).

Q&A What is the purpose of the File tab?

The **File** tab is used to display the Backstage view for each Office program, including Outlook.

Q&A What commands does the Backstage view contain in Microsoft Outlook?

The Backstage view in Microsoft Outlook allows you to save files such as e-mail messages, retrieve and modify e-mail account settings, open files, print items in Outlook, obtain help, change Outlook options, and exit Outlook.

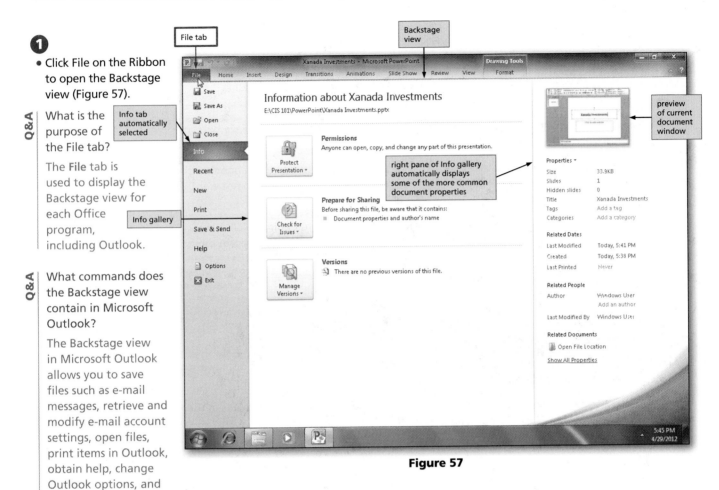

Figure 57

2

● Click the New tab in the Backstage view to display the New gallery (Figure 58).

Q&A Can I create documents through the Backstage view in other Office programs?

Yes. If the Office program has a New tab in the Backstage view, the New gallery displays various options for creating a new file. Outlook, however, does not have a New tab in the Backstage view.

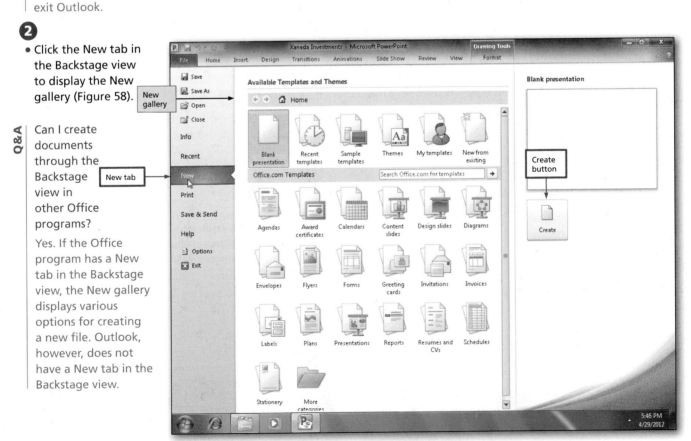

Figure 58

• Click the Create button in the New gallery to create a new presentation (Figure 59).

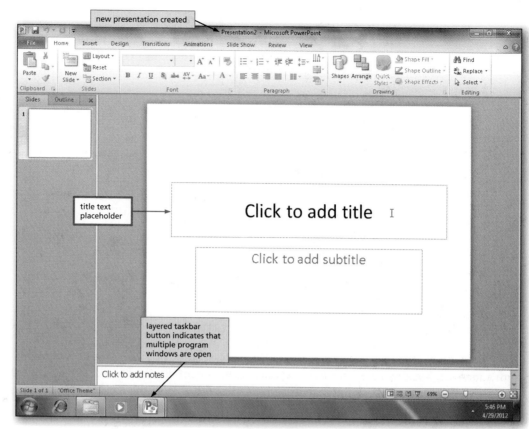

Figure 59

Other Ways

1. Press CTRL+N

To Enter Content in a Title Slide of a Second PowerPoint Presentation

The presentation title for this presentation is Koala Exhibit Gala. The following steps enter a presentation title on the title slide.

1 Click the title text placeholder (shown in Figure 59) to select it.

2 Type **Koala Exhibit Gala** in the title text placeholder. Do not press the ENTER key (Figure 60).

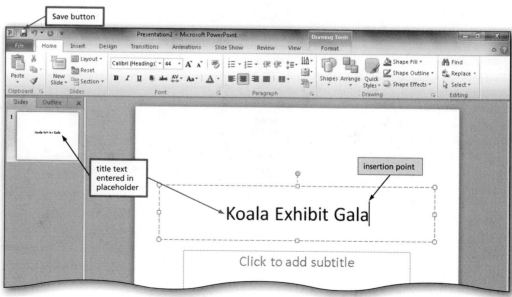

Figure 60

To Save a File in a Folder

The following steps save the second presentation in the PowerPoint folder in the class folder (CIS 101, in this case) on a USB flash drive using the file name, Koala Exhibit Gala.

1 With a USB flash drive connected to one of the computer's USB ports, click the Save button on the Quick Access Toolbar to display the Save As dialog box.

2 If necessary, type **Koala Exhibit Gala** in the File name text box to change the file name. Do not press the ENTER key after typing the file name because you do not want to close the dialog box at this time.

3 If necessary, navigate to the desired save location (in this case, the PowerPoint folder in the CIS 101 folder [or your class folder] on the USB flash drive).

4 Click the Save button (Save As dialog box) to save the presentation in the selected folder on the selected drive with the entered file name.

To Close an Office File Using the Backstage View

Sometimes, you may want to close an Office file, such as a PowerPoint presentation, entirely and start over with a new file. You also may want to close a file when you are finished working with it so that you can begin a new file. The following steps close the current active Office file, that is, the Koala Exhibit Gala presentation, without quitting the active program (PowerPoint in this case).

1
- Click File on the Ribbon to open the Backstage view (Figure 61).

2
- Click Close in the Backstage view to close the open file (Koala Exhibit Gala, in this case) without quitting the active program.

Q&A What if the Office program displays a dialog box about saving?

Click the Save button if you want to save the changes, click the Don't Save button if you want to ignore the changes since the last time you saved, and click the Cancel button if you do not want to close the document.

Q&A Can I use the Backstage view to close an e-mail message without quitting Outlook?

Yes.

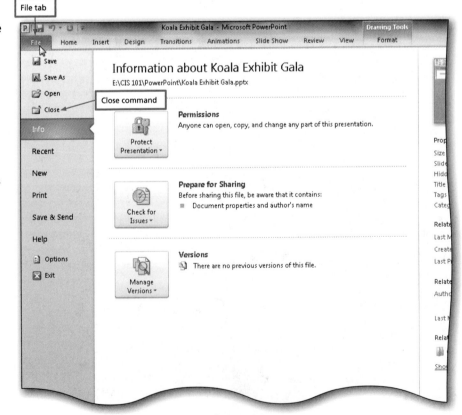

Figure 61

To Open a Recent Office File Using the Backstage View

You sometimes need to open a file that you recently modified. You may have more changes to make such as adding more content or correcting errors. The Backstage view allows you to access recent files easily. The following steps reopen the Koala Exhibit Gala file just closed.

1

- Click File on the Ribbon to open the Backstage view.

- Click the Recent tab in the Backstage view to display the Recent gallery (Figure 62).

2

- Click the desired file name in the Recent gallery, Koala Exhibit Gala in this case, to open the file (shown in Figure 60 on page OFF 43).

Q&A

Can I use the Backstage view to open a recent file in other Office programs, such as Word and Excel?

Yes, programs containing the Recent tab in the Backstage view allow you to open recent files.

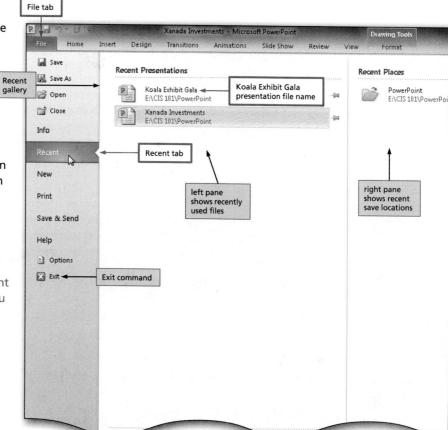

Figure 62

Other Ways

1. Click Start button, point to program name, click file name on submenu

2. Click File on Ribbon, click Open in Backstage view, navigate to file (Open dialog box), click Open button

To Quit an Office Program

You are finished using PowerPoint. Thus, you should quit this Office program. The following steps quit PowerPoint.

1 If you have one Office document open, click the Close button on the right side of the title bar to close the document and quit the Office program; or if you have multiple Office documents open, click File on the Ribbon to open the Backstage view and then click Exit in the Backstage view to close all open documents and quit the Office program.

2 If a dialog box appears, click the Save button to save any changes made to the document since the last save.

Excel

Excel is a powerful spreadsheet program that allows users to organize data, complete calculations, make decisions, graph data, develop professional-looking reports (Figure 63), publish organized data to the Web, and access real-time data from Web sites. The four major parts of Excel are:

- **Workbooks and Worksheets** - A **workbook** is like a notebook. Inside the workbook are sheets, each of which is called a **worksheet**. In other words, a workbook is a collection of worksheets. Worksheets allow users to enter, calculate, manipulate, and analyze data such as numbers and text. The terms worksheet and spreadsheet are interchangeable.

- **Charts** - Excel can draw a variety of charts.

- **Tables** - Tables organize and store data within worksheets. For example, once a user enters data into a worksheet, an Excel table can sort the data, search for specific data, and select data that satisfies defined criteria.

- **Web Support -** Web support allows users to save Excel worksheets or parts of a worksheet in HTML format, so that a user can view and manipulate the worksheet using a browser. Excel Web support also provides access to real-time data, such as stock quotes, using Web queries.

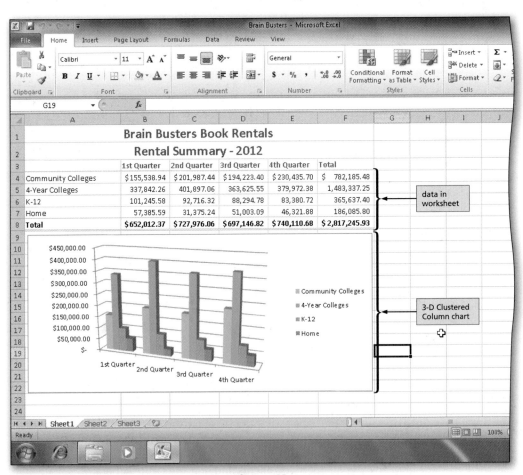

Figure 63

To Create a New Blank Office Document from Windows Explorer

Windows Explorer provides a means to create a blank Office document without ever starting an Office program. The following steps use Windows Explorer to create a blank Excel document.

1

- If necessary, click the Windows Explorer program button on the taskbar to make the folder window the active window in Windows Explorer.

- Double-click your class folder (CIS 101, in this case) in the navigation pane to display the contents of the selected folder.

- Double-click the Excel folder to display its contents in the right pane.

- With the Excel folder selected, right-click an open area in the right pane to display a shortcut menu.

- Point to New on the shortcut menu to display the New submenu (Figure 64).

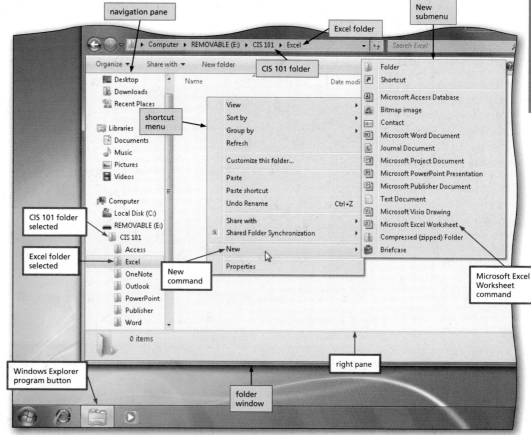

Figure 64

2

- Click Microsoft Excel Worksheet on the New submenu to display an icon and text box for a new file in the current folder window (Figure 65).

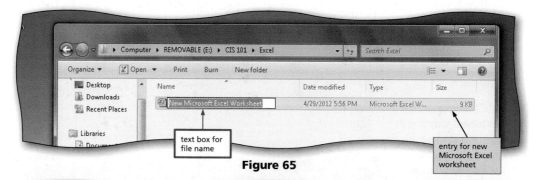

Figure 65

3

- Type **Brain Busters** in the text box and then press the ENTER key to assign a name to the new file in the current folder (Figure 66).

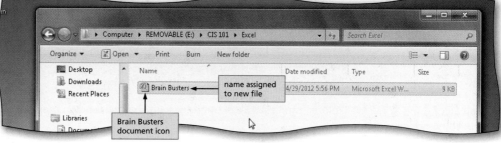

Figure 66

To Start a Program from Windows Explorer and Open a File

Previously, you learned how to start an Office program using the Start menu and the search box. Another way start an Office program is to open an existing file from Windows Explorer, which causes the program in which the file was created to start and then open the selected file. The following steps, which assume Windows 7 is running, use Windows Explorer to start the Excel Office program based on a typical installation. You may need to ask your instructor how to start Office programs for your computer.

 1

- If necessary, display the file to open in the folder window in Windows Explorer (shown in Figure 66 on the previous page).

- Right-click the file icon or file name (Brain Busters, in this case) to display a shortcut menu (Figure 67).

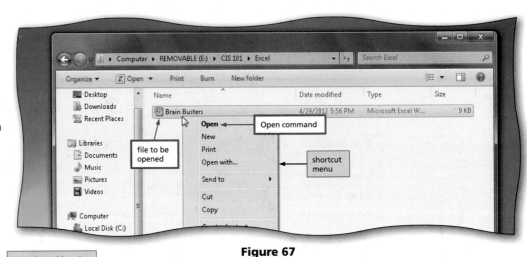

Figure 67

2

- Click Open on the shortcut menu to open the selected file in the program used to create the file, Microsoft Excel in this case (Figure 68).

- If the program window is not maximized, click the Maximize button on the title bar to maximize the window.

- For Excel users, if the worksheet window in Excel is not maximized, click the worksheet window Maximize button to maximize the worksheet window within Excel.

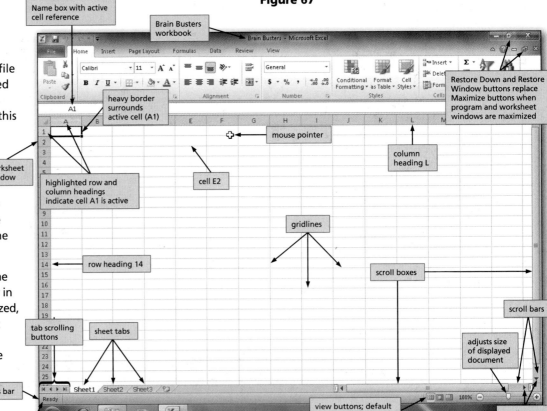

Figure 68

Q&A

Instead of using Windows Explorer, can I start Excel using the same method shown previously for Word and PowerPoint?

Yes, you can use any method of starting an Office program to start Excel.

Unique Features of Excel

The Excel window consists of a variety of components to make your work more efficient and worksheets more professional. These include the document window, Ribbon, Mini toolbar and shortcut menus, Quick Access Toolbar, and the Backstage view. Some of these components are common to other Microsoft Office 2010 programs; others are unique to Excel.

Excel opens a new workbook with three worksheets. If necessary, you can add additional worksheets as long as your computer has enough memory to accommodate them.

Each worksheet has a sheet name that appears on a **sheet tab** at the bottom of the workbook. For example, Sheet1 is the name of the active worksheet displayed in the Brain Busters workbook. If you click the sheet tab labeled Sheet2, Excel displays the Sheet2 worksheet.

The Worksheet   The worksheet is organized into a rectangular grid containing vertical columns and horizontal rows. A column letter above the grid, also called the **column heading**, identifies each column. A row number on the left side of the grid, also called the **row heading**, identifies each row. With the screen resolution set to 1024×768 and the Excel window maximized, Excel displays 15 columns (A through O) and 25 rows (1 through 25) of the worksheet on the screen, as shown in Figure 68.

The intersection of each column and row is a cell. A **cell** is the basic unit of a worksheet into which you enter data. Each worksheet in a workbook has 16,384 columns and 1,048,576 rows for a total of 17,179,869,180 cells. Only a small fraction of the active worksheet appears on the screen at one time.

A cell is referred to by its unique address, or **cell reference**, which is the coordinates of the intersection of a column and a row. To identify a cell, specify the column letter first, followed by the row number. For example, cell reference E2 refers to the cell located at the intersection of column E and row 2 (Figure 68).

One cell on the worksheet, designated the **active cell**, is the one into which you can enter data. The active cell in Figure 68 is A1. The active cell is identified in three ways. First, a heavy border surrounds the cell; second, the active cell reference shows immediately above column A in the Name box; and third, the column heading A and row heading 1 are highlighted so it is easy to see which cell is active (Figure 68).

The horizontal and vertical lines on the worksheet itself are called **gridlines**. Gridlines make it easier to see and identify each cell in the worksheet. If desired, you can turn the gridlines off so that they do not show on the worksheet, but it is recommended that you leave them on for now.

The mouse pointer in Figure 68 has the shape of a block plus sign. The mouse pointer appears as a block plus sign whenever it is located in a cell on the worksheet. Another common shape of the mouse pointer is the block arrow. The mouse pointer turns into the block arrow when you move it outside the worksheet or when you drag cell contents between rows or columns. The other mouse pointer shapes are described when they appear on the screen.

Ribbon   When you start Excel, the Ribbon displays eight main tabs: File, Home, Insert, Page Layout, Formulas, Data, Review, and View. The Formulas and Data tabs are specific to Excel. The Formulas tab allows you to work with Excel formulas, and the Data tab allows you to work with data processing features such as importing and sorting data.

BTW

The Worksheet Size and Window
The 16,384 columns and 1,048,576 rows in Excel make for a huge worksheet that – if you could imagine – takes up the entire side of a building to display in its entirety. Your computer screen, by comparison, is a small window that allows you to view only a minute area of the worksheet at one time. While you cannot see the entire worksheet, you can move the window over the worksheet to view any part of it.

BTW

Customizing the Ribbon
In addition to customizing the Quick Access Toolbar, you can add items to and remove items from the Ribbon. To customize the Ribbon, click File on the Ribbon to open the Backstage view, click Options in the Backstage view, and then click Customize Ribbon in the left pane of the Options dialog box. More information about customizing the Ribbon is presented in a later chapter.

Formula Bar The formula bar appears below the Ribbon (Figure 69). As you type, Excel displays the entry in the **formula bar**. You can make the formula bar larger by dragging the sizing handle at the bottom of the formula bar or clicking the expand button to the right of the formula bar. Excel also displays the active cell reference in the **Name box** on the left side of the formula bar.

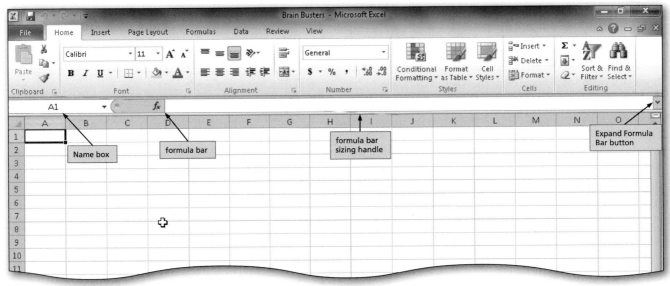

Figure 69

To Enter a Worksheet Title

To enter data into a cell, you first must select it. The easiest way to select a cell (make it active) is to use the mouse to move the block plus sign mouse pointer to the cell and then click. An alternative method is to use the arrow keys that are located just to the right of the typewriter keys on the keyboard. An arrow key selects the cell adjacent to the active cell in the direction of the arrow on the key.

In Excel, any set of characters containing a letter, hyphen (as in a telephone number), or space is considered text. **Text** is used to place titles, such as worksheet titles, column titles, and row titles, on the worksheet. The following steps enter the worksheet title in cell A1.

• If it is not already the active cell, click cell A1 to make it the active cell (Figure 70).

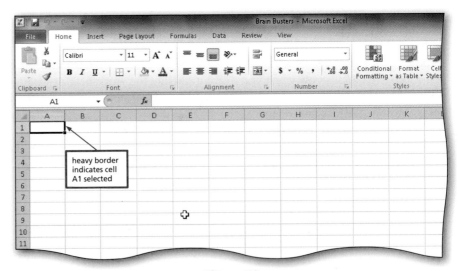

Figure 70

• Type **Brain Buster Book Rentals** in cell A1 (Figure 71).

Q&A

Why did the appearance of the formula bar change?

Excel displays the title in the formula bar and in cell A1. When you begin typing a cell entry, Excel displays two additional boxes in the formula bar: the Cancel box and the Enter box. Clicking the Enter box completes an entry. Clicking the Cancel box cancels an entry.

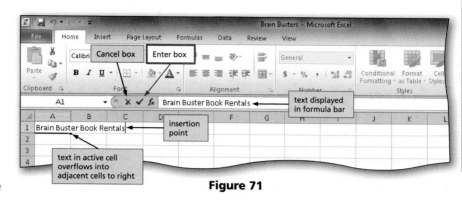

Figure 71

❸

• Click the Enter box to complete the entry and enter the worksheet title in cell A1 (Figure 72).

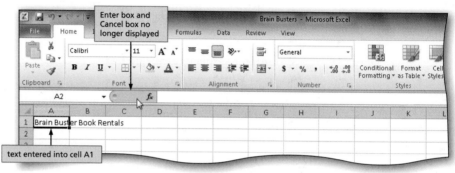

Figure 72

Other Ways		
1. To complete entry, click any cell other than active cell	2. To complete entry, press ENTER, HOME, PAGE UP, PAGE DOWN, END,	UP, DOWN, LEFT ARROW, or RIGHT ARROW

To Save an Existing Office Document with the Same File Name

Saving frequently cannot be overemphasized. You have made modifications to the file (spreadsheet) since you created it. Thus, you should save again. Similarly, you should continue saving files frequently so that you do not lose your changes since the time you last saved the file. You can use the same file name, such as Brain Busters, to save the changes made to the document. The following step saves a file again.

❶

• Click the Save button on the Quick Access Toolbar to overwrite the previously saved file (Brain Busters, in this case) on the USB flash drive (Figure 73).

Q&A

Why did the Save As dialog box not appear?

Office programs, including Excel, overwrite the document using the setting specified the first time you saved the document.

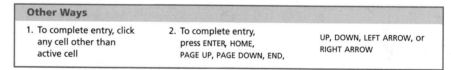

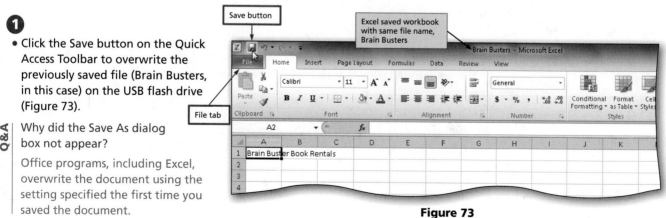

Figure 73

Other Ways
1. Press CTRL+S or press SHIFT+F12

To Use Save As to Change the Name of a File

You might want to save a file with a different name and even to a different location. For example, you might start a homework assignment with a data file and then save it with a final file name for submitting to your instructor, saving it to a location designated by your instructor. The following steps save a file with a different file name.

1 With your USB flash drive connected to one of the computer's USB ports, click File on the Ribbon to open the Backstage view.

2 Click Save As in the Backstage view to display the Save As dialog box.

3 Type `Brain Busters Rental Summary` in the File name text box (Save As dialog box) to change the file name. Do not press the ENTER key after typing the file name because you do not want to close the dialog box at this time.

4 Navigate to the desired save location (the Excel folder in the CIS 101 folder [or your class folder] on the USB flash drive, in this case). For specific instructions, perform the tasks in steps 4a through 4g.

4a If a navigation pane is not displayed in the Save As dialog box, click the Browse Folders button to expand the dialog box.

4b If Computer is not displayed in the navigation pane, drag the navigation pane scroll bar (Save As dialog box) until Computer appears.

4c If Computer is not expanded in the navigation pane, double-click Computer to display a list of available storage devices in the navigation pane.

4d If necessary, scroll through the Save As dialog box until your USB flash drive appears in the list of available storage devices in the navigation pane.

4e If your USB flash drive is not expanded, double-click the USB flash drive in the list of available storage devices in the navigation pane to select that drive as the new save location and display its contents in the right pane.

4f If your class folder (CIS 101, in this case) is not expanded, double-click the CIS 101 folder to select the folder and display its contents.

4g Double-click the Excel folder to select it and display its contents in the right pane.

5 Click the Save button (Save As dialog box) to save the file in the selected folder on the selected drive with the new file name.

To Quit an Office Program

You are finished using Excel. The following steps quit Excel.

1 If you have one Office document open, click the Close button on the right side of the title bar to close the document and quit the Office program; or if you have multiple Office documents open, click File on the Ribbon to open the Backstage view and then click Exit in the Backstage view to close all open documents and quit the Office program.

2 If a dialog box appears, click the Save button to save any changes made to the file since the last save.

Access

The term **database** describes a collection of data organized in a manner that allows access, retrieval, and use of that data. **Microsoft Access 2010**, usually referred to as simply **Access,** is a database management system. A **database management system** is software that allows you to use a computer to create a database; add, change, and delete data in the database; create queries that allow you to ask questions concerning the data in the database; and create forms and reports using the data in the database.

To Start a Program

The following steps, which assume Windows 7 is running, start the Access program based on a typical installation. You may need to ask your instructor how to start programs for your computer.

1 Click the Start button on the Windows 7 taskbar to display the Start menu.

2 Type the name of the program, `Microsoft Access` in this case, as the search text in the 'Search programs and files' text box and watch the search results appear on the Start menu.

3 Click the name of the program, Microsoft Access 2010 in this case, in the search results on the Start menu to start Access.

4 If the program window is not maximized, click the Maximize button on its title bar to maximize the window (Figure 74).

Q&A Do I have to start Access using these steps?

No. You can use any previously discussed method of starting an Office program to start Access.

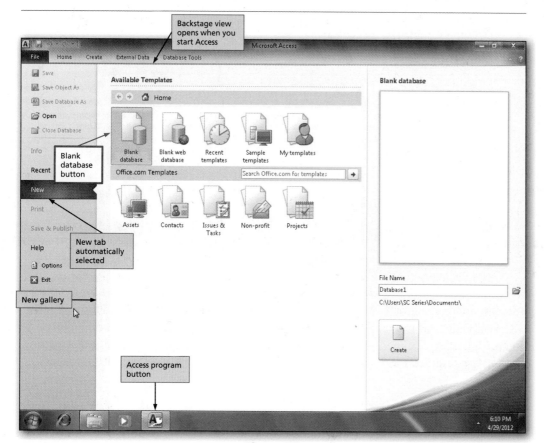

Figure 74

Unique Elements in Access

You work on objects such as tables, forms, and reports in the **Access work area**. In Figure 74, the Access window contains no open objects. Figure 75 shows a work area with multiple objects open. **Object tabs** for the open objects appear at the top of the work area. You select an open object by clicking its tab. In the figure, the Suppliers Split Form is the selected object. To the left of the work area is the Navigation Pane, which contains a list of all the objects in the database. You use this pane to open an object. You also can customize the way objects are displayed in the Navigation Pane.

Because the Navigation Pane can take up space in the window, you may not have as much open space for working as you would with Word or Excel. You can use the Shutter Bar Open/Close button to minimize the Navigation Pane when you are not using it, which allows more space to work with tables, forms, reports, and other database elements.

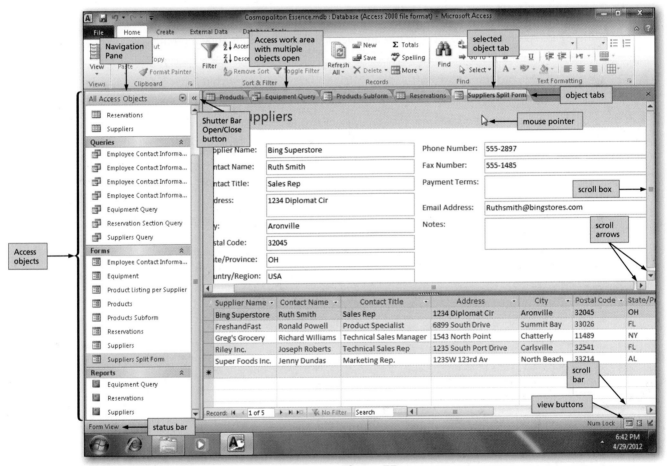

Figure 75

Ribbon When you start Access, the Ribbon displays five main tabs: File, Home, Create, External Data, and Database Tools. Access has unique groupings such as Sort & Filter and Records that are designed specifically for working with databases. Many of the formatting options are reserved for the tool tabs that appear when you are working with forms and reports.

To Create an Access Database

Unlike the other Office programs, Access saves a database when you first create it. When working in Access, you will add data to an Access database. As you add data to a database, Access automatically saves your changes rather than waiting until you manually save the database or quit Access. Recall that in Word and Excel, you entered the data first and then saved it.

Because Access automatically saves the database as you add and change data, you do not have to always click the Save button. In fact, the Save button in Access is used for saving the objects (including tables, queries, forms, reports, and other database objects) a database contains. You can use either the Blank Database option or a template to create a new database. If you already know the organization of your database, you would use the Blank Database option. If not, you can use a template. Templates can guide you by suggesting some commonly used database organizations.

The following steps use the Blank Database option to create a database named Charmed Excursions in the Access folder in the class folder (CIS 101, in this case) on a USB flash drive.

- If necessary, click the Blank database button in the New gallery (shown in Figure 74 on page OFF 53) in the Backstage view to select the template type.

- Click the File Name text box to select the default database name.

- Type **Charmed Excursions** in the File Name text box to enter the new file name. Do not press the ENTER key after typing the file name because you do not want to create the database at this time (Figure 76).

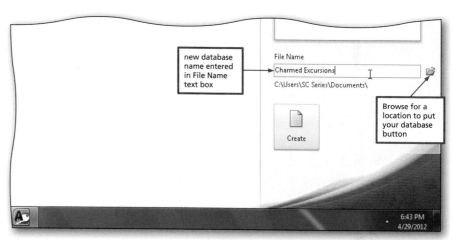

Figure 76

Q&A   Why is the Backstage view automatically open when you start Access?

Unlike other Office programs, you first must save a database before adding any data. For this reason, the Backstage view opens automatically when you start Access.

- Click the 'Browse for a location to put your database' button to display the File New Database dialog box.

- Navigate to the location for the database, that is, the USB flash drive, then to the folder identifying your class (CIS 101, in this case), and then to the Access folder (Figure 77). For detailed steps about navigating, see Steps 3a – 3c on pages OFF 28 and OFF 29.

Q&A   Why does the 'Save as type' box say Microsoft Access 2007 Databases?

Microsoft Access database formats change with some new versions of Microsoft Access. The most recent format is the Microsoft Access 2007 Databases format, which was released with Access 2007.

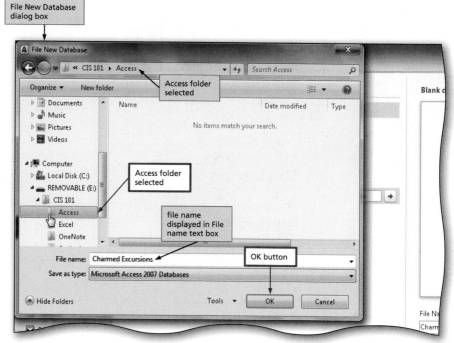

Figure 77

3

• Click the OK button (File New Database dialog box) to select the Access folder as the location for the database and close the dialog box (Figure 78).

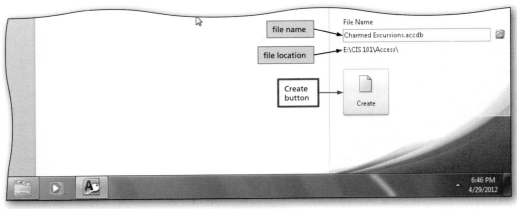

Figure 78

4

• Click the Create button in the Backstage view to create the database on the selected drive in the selected folder with the file name, Charmed Excursions. If necessary, click the Enable Content button (Figure 79).

How do I know that the Charmed Excursions database is created?

The name of the database appears on the title bar.

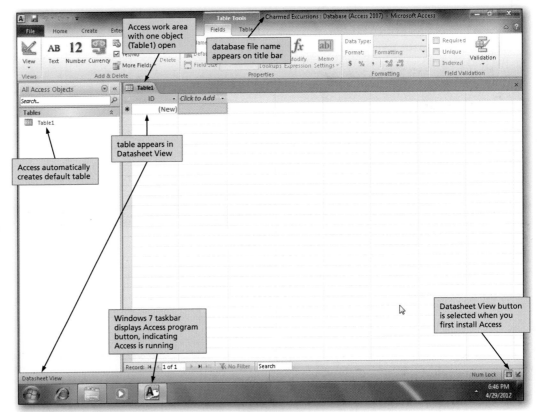

Figure 79

To Close an Office File

Assume you need to close the Access database and return to it later. The following step closes an Office file.

1 Click File on the Ribbon to open the Backstage view and then click Close Database in the Backstage view to close the open file (Charmed Excursions, in this case) without quitting the active program.

Why is Access still on the screen?

When you close a database, the program remains open.

To Open an Existing Office File

Assume you wish to continue working on an existing file, that is, a file you previously saved. Earlier in this chapter, you learned how to open a recently used file through the Backstage view. The following steps open a database, specifically the Charmed Excursions database, from the USB flash drive.

- With your USB flash drive connected to one of the computer's USB ports, if necessary, click File on the Ribbon to open the Backstage view.

- Click Open in the Backstage view to display the Open dialog box (Figure 80).

- Navigate to the location of the file to be opened (in this case, the USB flash drive, then to the CIS 101 folder [or your class folder], and then to the Access folder). For detailed steps about navigating, see Steps 3a – 3c on pages OFF 28 and OFF 29.

Q&A

What if I did not save my file in a folder?

If you did not save your file in a folder, the file you wish to open should be displayed in the Open dialog box before navigating to any folders.

Figure 80

- Click the file to be opened, Charmed Excursions in this case, to select the file (Figure 81).

- Click the Open button (Open dialog box) to open the selected file and display the opened file in the current program window (shown in Figure 79).

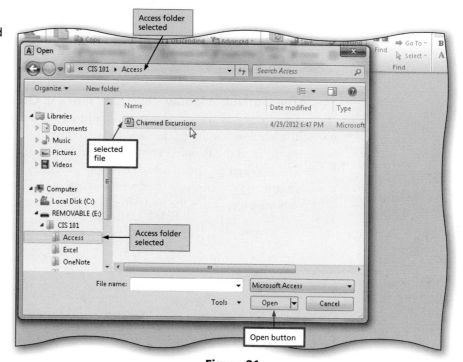

Figure 81

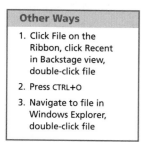

Other Ways

1. Click File on the Ribbon, click Recent in Backstage view, double-click file
2. Press CTRL+O
3. Navigate to file in Windows Explorer, double-click file

To Quit an Office Program

You are finished using Access. The following step quits Access.

1 Click the Close button on the right side of the title bar to close the file and quit the Office program.

Other Office Programs

In addition to the Office programs discussed thus far, three other programs are useful when collaborating and communicating with others: Outlook, Publisher, and OneNote.

Outlook

Outlook is a powerful communications and scheduling program that helps you communicate with others, keep track of contacts, and organize your calendar. Personal information manager (PIM) programs such as Outlook provide a way for individuals and workgroups to organize, find, view, and share information easily. Outlook allows you to send and receive electronic mail (e-mail) and permits you to engage in real-time messaging with family, friends, or coworkers using instant messaging. Outlook also provides a means to organize contacts. Users can track e-mail messages, meetings, and notes related to a particular contact. Outlook's Calendar, Contacts, Tasks, and Notes components aid in this organization. Contact information readily is available from the Outlook Calendar, Mail, Contacts, and Task components by accessing the Find a Contact feature.

Electronic mail (e-mail) is the transmission of messages and files over a computer network. E-mail has become an important means of exchanging information and files between business associates, classmates and instructors, friends, and family. Businesses find that using e-mail to send documents electronically saves both time and money. Parents with students away at college or relatives who live across the country find that communicating by e-mail is an inexpensive and easy way to stay in touch with their family members. Exchanging e-mail messages is one of the more widely used features of the Internet.

The Outlook Window Figure 82 shows an Outlook window, which is divided into six panes: the Favorites folder pane, Mail folder pane, and Navigation Pane on the left side of the window, the Inbox message pane to the left of center, the Reading Pane to the right of center, and the People Pane just below the Reading Pane.

When an e-mail message is open in Outlook, it is displayed in a Message window (Figure 83). When you open a message, the Message window Ribbon displays the Message tab, which contains the more frequently used commands.

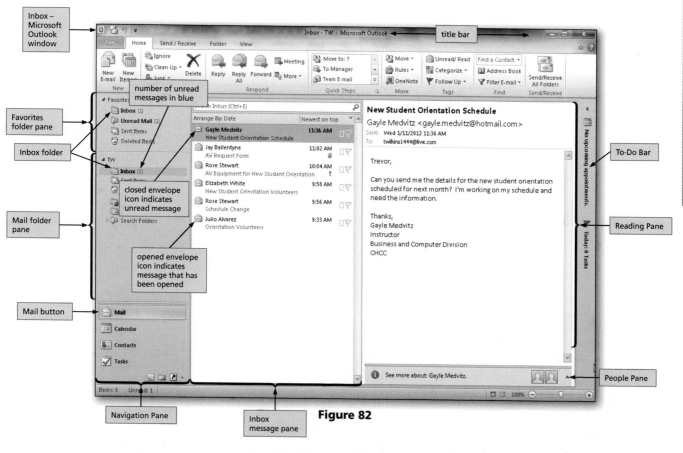

Figure 82

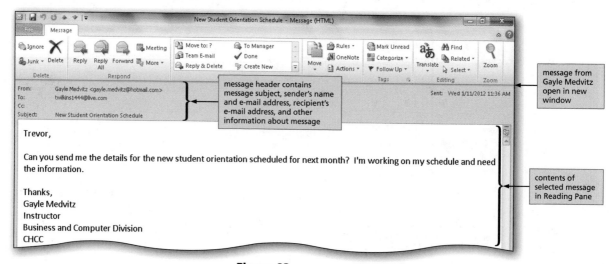

Figure 83

Publisher

Publisher is a powerful desktop publishing (DTP) program that assists you in designing and producing professional-quality documents that combine text, graphics, illustrations, and photos. DTP software provides additional tools beyond those typically found in word processing programs, including design templates, graphic manipulation tools, color schemes or libraries, advanced layout and printing tools, and Web components. For large jobs, businesses use DTP software to design publications that are camera ready, which means the files are suitable for outside commercial printing. In addition, DTP software can be used to create Web pages and interactive Web forms.

Publisher is used by people who regularly produce high-quality color publications, such as newsletters, brochures, flyers, logos, signs, catalogs, cards, and business forms. Saving publications as Web pages or complete Web sites is a powerful component of Publisher. All publications can be saved in a format that easily is viewed and manipulated using a browser.

Publisher has many features designed to simplify production and make publications visually appealing. Using Publisher, you easily can change the shape, size, and color of text and graphics. You can include many kinds of graphical objects, including mastheads, borders, tables, images, pictures, charts, and Web objects in publications, as well as integrate spreadsheets and databases.

BTW

Starting Publisher
When you first start Publisher, the New templates gallery usually is displayed in the Backstage view. If it is not displayed, click File on the Ribbon, click Options in the Backstage view, click General (Options dialog box), and then click Show the New template gallery when starting Publisher to select the check box in the General panel.

The Publisher Window   On the right side of the Backstage view, Publisher displays the New template gallery, which includes a list of publication types. **Publication types** are typical publications used by desktop publishers. The more popular types are displayed in the center of the window. Each publication type is a link to display various templates and blank publications from which you may choose.

Once you select a publication type, the window changes to allow you to select a specific template (Figure 84). Some templates are installed with Publisher, and others are available online. Clicking a publication type causes template previews to be displayed in the center of the window. The templates are organized by purpose (for example, Sales) and then alphabetically by design type. On the right, Publisher will display a larger preview of the selected template, along with some customization options if the template is installed or a download option if the template is online. In Figure 84, the installed Arrows template is selected so that the customize options appear.

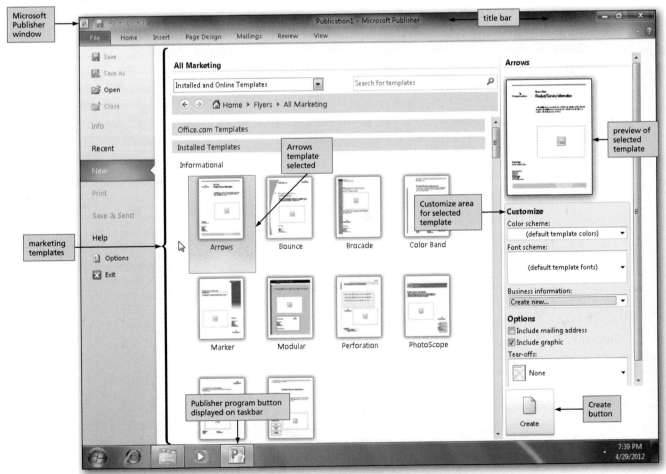

Figure 84

When you click the Create button, Publisher creates the document and sets it up for you to edit. Figure 85 shows the Arrows document that Publisher creates when default options are selected.

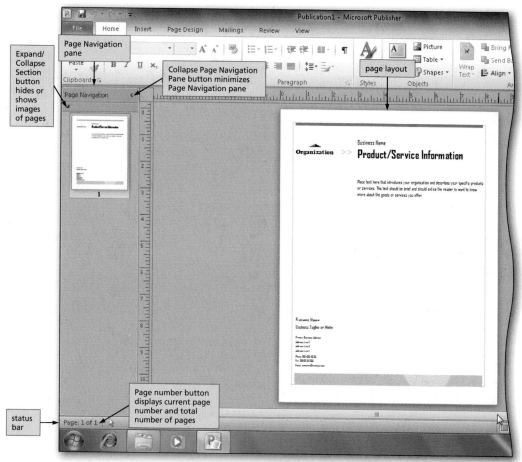

Figure 85

OneNote

OneNote is a note taking program that assists you in entering, saving, organizing, searching, and using notes. It enables you to create pages, which are organized in sections, just as in a physical notebook. In OneNote, you can type notes anywhere on a page and then easily move the notes around on the page. You can create lists and outlines, use handwriting to enter notes, and create drawings. If you use a Tablet PC to add handwritten notes to a document, OneNote can convert the handwriting to text. It also can perform searches on the handwritten entries. Pictures and data from other programs easily are incorporated in your notes.

In addition to typing and handwriting, you can take audio notes. For example, you could record conversations during a meeting or lecture. As you record, you can take additional notes. When you play back the audio notes, you can synchronize the additional notes you took; that is, OneNote will show you during playback the exact points at which you added the notes. A variety of note flags, which are symbols that call your attention to notes on a page, enable you to flag notes as being important. You then can use the Note Flags summary to view the flagged notes, which can be sorted in a variety of ways.

OneNote includes tools to assist you with organizing a notebook and navigating its contents. It also includes a search facility, making it easy to find the specific notes in which you are interested. For short notes that you always want to have available readily, you can use Side Notes, which are used much like the sticky notes that you might use in a physical notebook.

OneNote Window   All activity in OneNote takes place in the **notebook** (Figure 86). Like a physical notebook, the OneNote notebook consists of notes that are placed on **pages**. The pages are grouped into **sections**, which can be further grouped into **folders**. (No folders are shown in the notebook in the figure.) You can use the Search All Notebooks box to search for specific text in your notes.

You can add pages to the notebook using the New Page button in the Page Tabs pane. If Page Tabs are displayed, then you can switch to a page by clicking its tab. Figure 86 shows the Top Uses page being displayed for the General notebook.

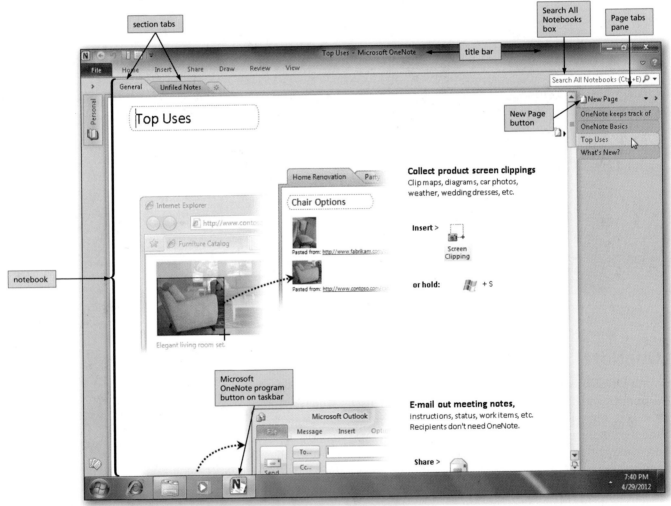

Figure 86

Break Point: If you wish to take a break, this is a good place to do so. To resume at a later time, continue to follow the steps from this location forward.

Moving, Renaming, and Deleting Files

Earlier in this chapter, you learned how to organize files in folders, which is part of a process known as **file management**. The following sections cover additional file management topics including renaming, moving, and deleting files.

To Rename a File

In some circumstances, you may want to change the name of, or rename, a file or a folder. For example, you may want to distinguish a file in one folder or drive from a copy of a similar file, or you may decide to rename a file to better identify its contents. The Word folder shown in Figure 87 contains the Word document, Koala Exhibit. The following steps change the name of the Koala Exhibit file in the Word folder to Koala Exhibit Flyer.

1

- If necessary, click the Windows Explorer program button on the taskbar to display the folder window in Windows Explorer.

- Navigate to the location of the file to be renamed (in this case, the Word folder in the CIS 101 [or your class folder] folder on the USB flash drive) to display the file(s) it contains in the right pane.

- Right-click the Koala Exhibit icon or file name in the right pane to select the Koala Exhibit file and display a shortcut menu that presents a list of commands related to files (Figure 87).

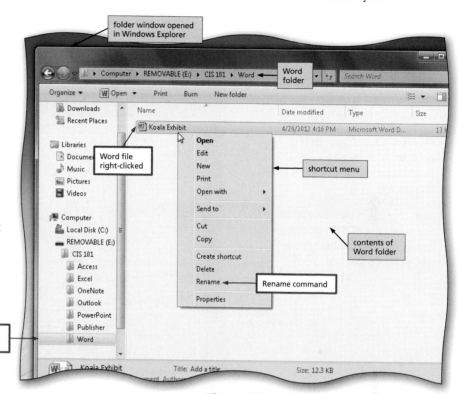

Figure 87

2

- Click Rename on the shortcut menu to place the current file name in a text box.

- Type **Koala Exhibit Flyer** in the text box and then press the ENTER key (Figure 88).

 Q&A
Are any risks involved in renaming files that are located on a hard disk?

If you inadvertently rename a file that is associated with certain programs, the programs may not be able to find the file and, therefore, may not execute properly. Always use caution when renaming files.

Q&A
Can I rename a file when it is open?

No, a file must be closed to change the file name.

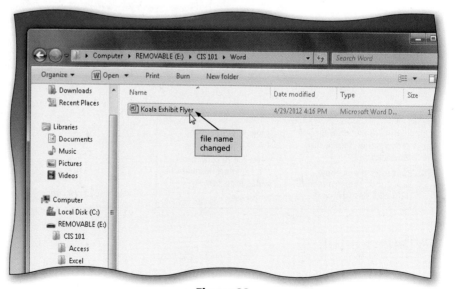

Figure 88

Other Ways

1. Select file, press F2, type new file name, press ENTER

To Move a File

At some time, you may want to move a file from one folder, called the source folder, to another, called the destination. When you move a file, it no longer appears in the original folder. If the destination and the source folders are on the same disk drive, you can move a file by dragging it. If the folders are on different disk drives, then you will need to right-drag the file. The following step moves the Brain Busters Rental Summary file from the Excel folder to the OneNote folder.

- In Windows Explorer, navigate to the location of the file to be moved (in this case, the Excel folder in the CIS 101 folder [or your class folder] on the USB flash drive).

- Click the Excel folder in the navigation pane to display the files it contains in the right pane (Figure 89).

- Drag the Brain Busters Rental Summary file in the right pane to the OneNote folder in the navigation pane.

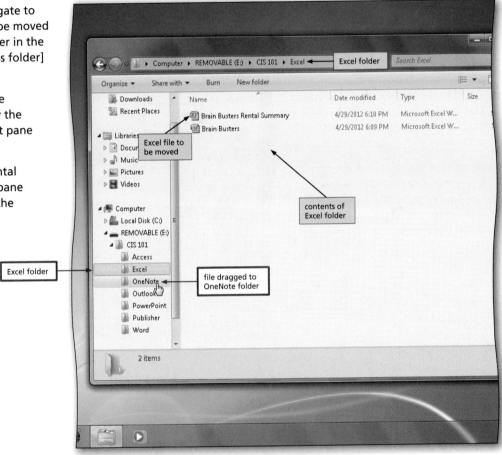

Figure 89

Other Ways
1. Right-click file, drag file to destination folder, click Move here
2. Right-click file to copy, click Cut on shortcut menu, right-click destination
folder, click Paste on shortcut menu
3. Select file to copy, press CTRL+X, select destination folder, press CTRL+V

To Delete a File

A final task you may want to perform is to delete a file. Exercise extreme caution when deleting a file or files. When you delete a file from a hard disk, the deleted file is stored in the Recycle Bin where you can recover it until you empty the Recycle Bin. If you delete a file from removable media, such as a USB flash drive, the file is deleted permanently. The next steps delete the Koala Exhibit Gala file from the PowerPoint folder.

1

- In Windows Explorer, navigate to the location of the file to be deleted (in this case, the PowerPoint folder in the CIS 101 folder [or your class folder] on the USB flash drive).

- Click the PowerPoint folder in the navigation pane to display the files it contains in the right pane.

- Right-click the Koala Exhibit Gala icon or file name in the right pane to select the file and display a shortcut menu (Figure 90).

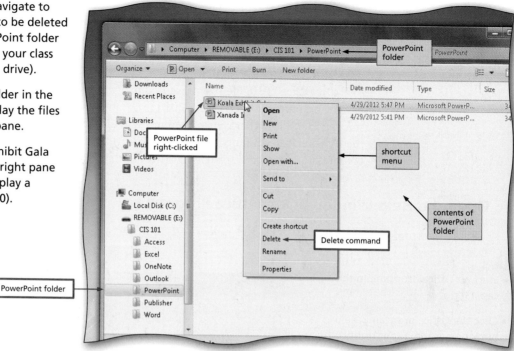

Figure 90

2

- Click Delete on the shortcut menu to display the Delete File dialog box (Figure 91).

- Click the Yes button (Delete File dialog box) to delete the selected file.

Q&A Can I use this same technique to delete a folder?

Yes. Right-click the folder and then click Delete on the shortcut menu. When you delete a folder, all of the files and folders contained in the folder you are deleting, together with any files and folders on lower hierarchical levels, are deleted as well.

Q&A When might I delete Outlook files?

If you are storing e-mail messages, calendar items, or other Outlook files for an extended period of time, you might want to delete older files you are sure you no longer need.

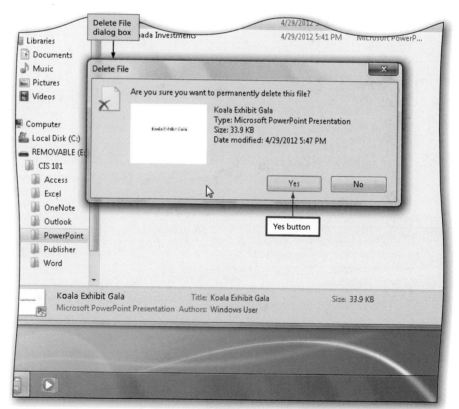

Figure 91

Other Ways
1. Select icon, press DELETE

Microsoft Office and Windows Help

At any time while you are using one of the Microsoft Office 2010 programs, you can use Office Help to display information about all topics associated with the program. To illustrate the use of Office Help, this section uses Outlook. Help in other Office 2010 programs operates in a similar fashion.

In Office 2010, Help is presented in a window that has Web-browser-style navigation buttons. Each Office 2010 program has its own Help home page, which is the starting Help page that is displayed in the Help window. If your computer is connected to the Internet, the contents of the Help page reflect both the local help files installed on the computer and material from Microsoft's Web site.

To Open the Help Window in an Office Program

The following step opens the Word Help window.

1

- Start an Office program, in this case Outlook.

- Click the Office program's Help button near the upper-right corner of the program window (the Microsoft Outlook Help button, in this case) to open the program's Help window (Figure 92).

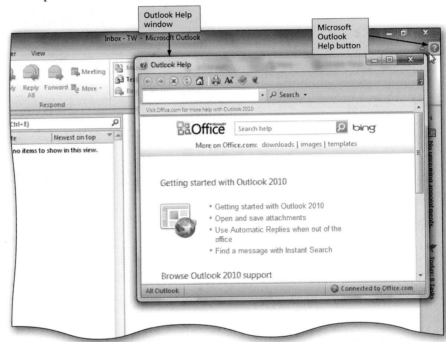

Figure 92

Other Ways

1. Press F1

Moving and Resizing Windows

Up to this point, this chapter has used minimized and maximized windows. At times, however, it is useful, or even necessary, to have more than one window open and visible on the screen at the same time. You can resize and move these open windows so that you can view different areas of and elements in the window. In the case of the Help window, for example, it could be covering an e-mail message in the Outlook window that you need to see.

To Move a Window by Dragging

You can move any open window that is not maximized to another location on the desktop by dragging the title bar of the window. The following step drags the Outlook Help window to the top left of the desktop.

- Drag the window title bar (the Outlook Help window title bar, in this case) so that the window moves near the top left of the desktop, as shown in Figure 93.

Q&A What should I do if the Outlook Help window is maximized when it is moved to the top of the desktop?

Click the Restore Down button and then move the window again as shown in Figure 93.

Figure 93

Other Ways

1. Right-click title bar, click Move on shortcut menu, drag window

To Resize a Window by Dragging

Sometimes, information is not visible completely in a window. A method used to change the size of the window is to drag the window borders. The following step changes the size of the Outlook Help window by dragging its borders.

- Point to the lower-right corner of the window (the Outlook Help window, in this case) until the mouse pointer changes to a two-headed arrow.

- Drag the bottom border downward to display more of the active window (Figure 94).

Q&A Can I drag other borders on the window to enlarge or shrink the window?

Yes, you can drag the left, right, and top borders and any window corner to resize a window.

Q&A Will Windows 7 remember the new size of the window after I close it?

Yes. When you reopen the window, Windows 7 will display it at the same size it was when you closed it.

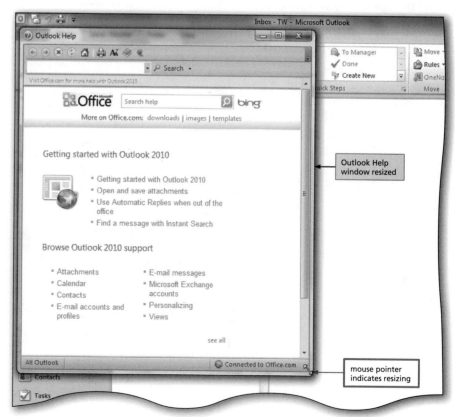

Figure 94

Using Office Help

Once an Office program's Help window is open, several methods exist for navigating Help. You can search for help by using any of the three following methods from the Help window:

1. Enter search text in the 'Type words to search for' text box.
2. Click the links in the Help window.
3. Use the Table of Contents.

To Obtain Help Using the 'Type words to search for' Text Box

Assume for the following example that you want to know more about the Backstage view. The following steps use the 'Type words to search for' text box to obtain useful information about the Backstage view by entering the word, Backstage, as search text.

1

- Type **Backstage** in the 'Type words to search for' text box at the top of the Outlook Help window to enter the search text.

- Click the Search button arrow to display the Search menu (Figure 95).

- If it is not selected already, click All Outlook on the Search menu, so that Help performs the most complete search of the current program (Outlook, in this case). If All Outlook already is selected, click the Search button arrow again to close the Search menu.

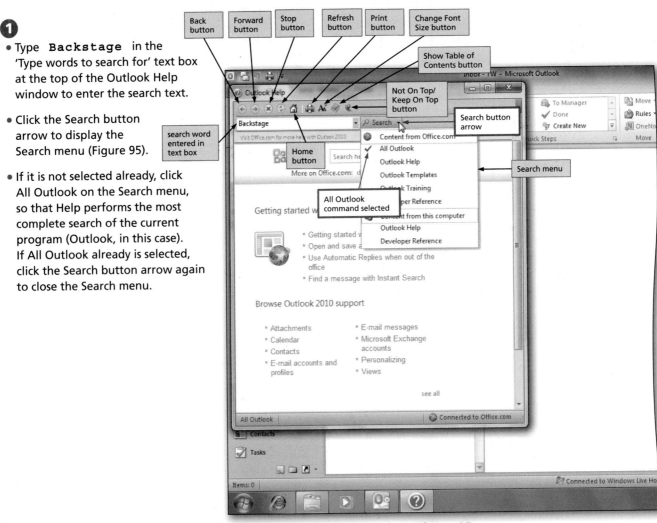

Figure 95

Q&A

Why select All Outlook on the Search menu?

Selecting All Outlook on the Search menu ensures that Outlook Help will search all possible sources for information about your search term. It will produce the most complete search results.

2

- Click the Search button to display the search results (Figure 96).

Q&A Why do my search results differ?

If you do not have an Internet connection, your results will reflect only the content of the Help files on your computer. When searching for help online, results also can change as material is added, deleted, and updated on the online Help Web pages maintained by Microsoft.

Q&A Why were my search results not very helpful?

When initiating a search, be sure to check the spelling of the search text; also, keep your search specific, with fewer than seven words, to return the most accurate results.

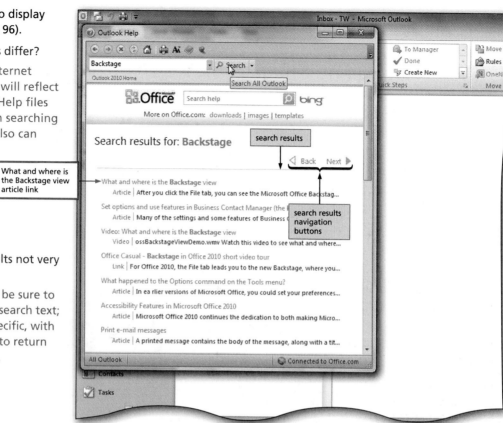

Figure 96

3

- Click the What and where is the Backstage view link to open the Help document associated with the selected topic (Figure 97).

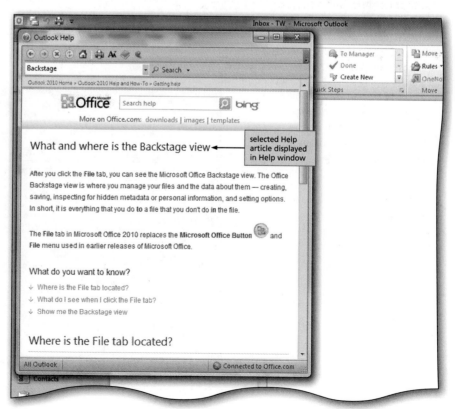

Figure 97

4
- Click the Home button on the toolbar to clear the search results and redisplay the Help home page (Figure 98).

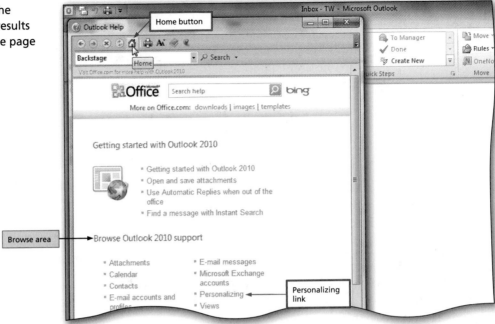

Figure 98

To Obtain Help Using the Help Links

If your topic of interest is listed in the Browse area of the Help window, you can click the link to begin browsing the Help categories instead of entering search text. You browse Help just as you would browse a Web site. If you know which category contains your Help information, you may wish to use these links. The following step finds the Personalizing Outlook information using the category links from the Outlook Help home page.

1
- Click the Personalizing link on the Help home page (shown in Figure 98) to display the Personalizing Outlook page (Figure 99).

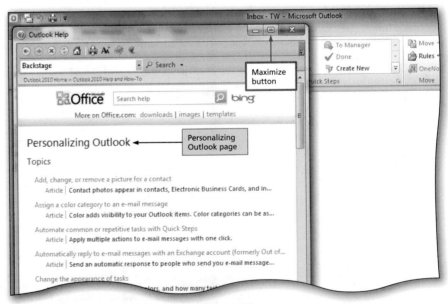

Figure 99

To Obtain Help Using the Help Table of Contents

A third way to find Help in Office programs is through the Help Table of Contents. You can browse through the Table of Contents to display information about a particular topic or to familiarize yourself with an Office program. The following steps access the Help information about automatic replies by browsing through the Table of Contents.

1

- Click the Home button on the toolbar to display the Help home page.

- Click the Show Table of Contents button on the toolbar to display the Table of Contents pane on the left side of the Help window. If necessary, click the Maximize button on the Help title bar to maximize the window (Figure 100).

Q&A

Why does the appearance of the Show Table of Contents button change?

When the Table of Contents is displayed in the Help window, the Hide Table of Contents button replaces the Show Table of Contents button.

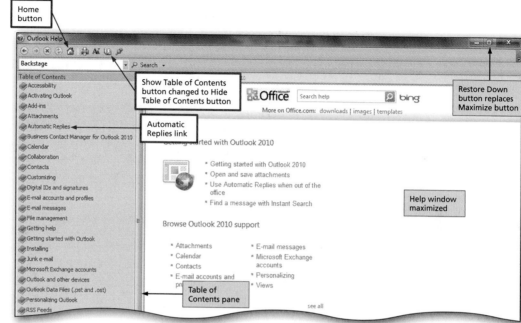

Figure 100

2

- Click the Automatic Replies link in the Table of Contents pane to view a list of Help subtopics.

- Click the 'Automatically reply to e-mail messages' link in the Table of Contents pane to view the selected Help document in the right pane (Figure 101).

- After reviewing the page, click the Close button to quit Help.

- Click the Office program's Close button (Outlook, in this case) to quit the Office program.

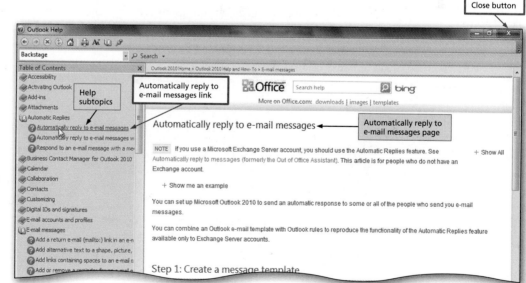

Figure 101

Q&A

How do I remove the Table of Contents pane when I am finished with it?

The Show Table of Contents button acts as a toggle. When the Table of Contents pane is visible, the button changes to Hide Table of Contents. Clicking it hides the Table of Contents pane and changes the button to Show Table of Contents.

Obtaining Help while Working in an Office Program

Help in the Office programs provides you with the ability to obtain help directly, without the need to open the Help window and initiate a search. For example, you may be unsure about how a particular command works, or you may be presented with a dialog box that you are not sure how to use.

Figure 102 shows one option for obtaining help while working in Outlook. If you want to learn more about a command, point to the command button and wait for the Enhanced ScreenTip to appear. If the Help icon appears in the Enhanced ScreenTip, press the F1 key while pointing to the command to open the Help window associated with that command.

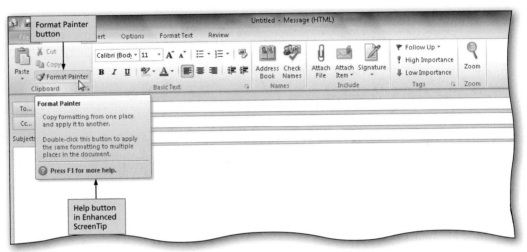

Figure 102

Figure 103 shows a dialog box that contains a Help button. Pressing the F1 key while the dialog box is displayed opens a Help window. The Help window contains help about that dialog box, if available. If no help file is available for that particular dialog box, then the main Help window opens.

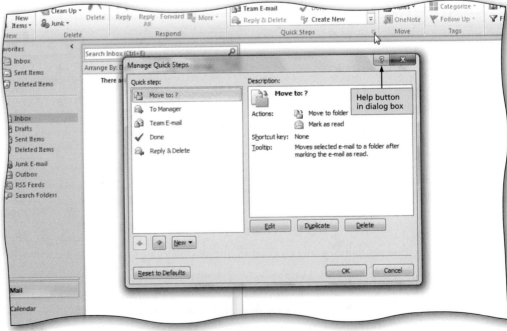

Figure 103

Using Windows Help and Support

One of the more powerful Windows 7 features is Windows Help and Support. **Windows Help and Support** is available when using Windows 7 or when using any Microsoft program running under Windows 7. This feature is designed to assist you in using Windows 7 or the various programs. Table 4 describes the content found in the Help and Support Center. The same methods used for searching Microsoft Office Help can be used in Windows Help and Support. The difference is that Windows Help and Support displays help for Windows 7, instead of for Microsoft Office.

Table 4 Windows Help and Support Center Content Areas	
Area	**Function**
Find an answer quickly	This area contains instructions about how to do a quick search using the search box.
Not sure where to start?	This area displays three topics to help guide a user: How to get started with your computer, Learn about Windows Basics, and Browse Help topics. Clicking one of the options navigates to corresponding Help and Support pages.
More on the Windows Website	This area contains links to online content from the Windows Web site. Clicking the links navigates to the corresponding Web pages on the Web site.

To Start Windows Help and Support

The following steps start Windows Help and Support and display the Windows Help and Support window, containing links to more information about Windows 7.

1

- Click the Start button on the taskbar to display the Start menu (Figure 104).

Q&A

Why are the programs that are displayed on the Start menu different?

Windows adds the programs you have used recently to the left pane on the Start menu. You have started several programs while performing the steps in this chapter, so those programs now are displayed on the Start menu.

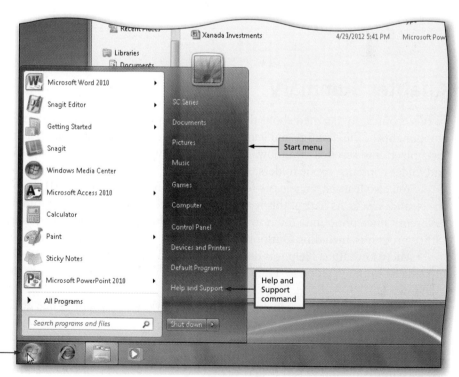

Figure 104

2

- Click Help and Support on the Start menu to open the Windows Help and Support window (Figure 105).

- After reviewing the Windows Help and Support window, click the Close button to quit Windows Help and Support.

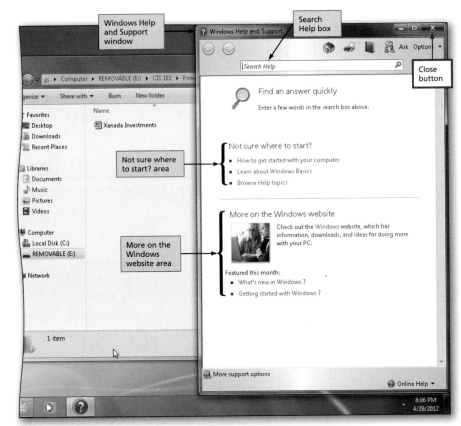

Figure 105

Other Ways

1. Press CTRL+ESC, press RIGHT ARROW, press UP ARROW, press ENTER
2. Press WINDOWS+F1

Chapter Summary

In this chapter, you learned about the Windows 7 interface. You started Windows 7, were introduced to the components of the desktop, and learned several mouse operations. You opened, closed, moved, resized, minimized, maximized, and scrolled a window. You used folder windows to expand and collapse drives and folders, display drive and folder contents, create folders, and rename and then delete a file.

You also learned some basic features of some Microsoft Office 2010 programs, including Word, PowerPoint, Excel, and Access. As part of this learning process, you discovered the common elements that exist among these different Office programs. You now can save basic document, presentation, spreadsheet, and database files. Additional Office programs, including Outlook, Publisher, and OneNote also were discussed.

Microsoft Office Help was demonstrated, and you learned how to use the Office Help window. You were introduced to the Windows 7 Help and Support Center and learned how to use it to obtain more information about Windows 7.

The items listed below include all of the new Windows 7 and Office 2010 skills you have learned in this chapter.

1. Log On to the Computer (OFF 6)
2. Start a Program Using the Start Menu (OFF 10)
3. Maximize a Window (OFF 12)
4. Display a Different Tab on the Ribbon (OFF 16)
5. Minimize, Display, and Restore the Ribbon (OFF 17)
6. Display and Use a Shortcut Menu (OFF 18)
7. Customize the Quick Access Toolbar (OFF 19)
8. Enter Text in a Document (OFF 20)
9. Create a Folder (OFF 22)
10. Create a Folder within a Folder (OFF 24)
11. Expand a Folder, Scroll through Folder Contents, and Collapse a Folder (OFF 26)
12. Switch from One Program to Another (OFF 27)
13. Save a File in a Folder (OFF 27)
14. Minimize and Restore a Window (OFF 30)
15. Change the Screen Resolution (OFF 33)

16. Quit an Office Program with One Document Open (OFF 35)
17. Start a Program Using the Search Box (OFF 37)
18. Enter Content in a Title Slide (OFF 40)
19. Create a New Office Document from the Backstage View (OFF 41)
20. Close an Office File Using the Backstage View (OFF 44)
21. Open a Recent Office File Using the Backstage View (OFF 45)
22. Create a New Blank Office Document from Windows Explorer (OFF 47)
23. Start a Program from Windows Explorer and Open a File (OFF 48)
24. Enter a Worksheet Title (OFF 50)
25. Save an Existing Document with the Same File Name (OFF 51)

26. Create an Access Database (OFF 55)
27. Open an Existing Office File (OFF 57)
28. Rename a File (OFF 63)
29. Move a File (OFF 64)
30. Delete a File (OFF 64)
31. Open the Help Window in an Office Program (OFF 66)
32. Move a Window by Dragging (OFF 66)
33. Resize a Window by Dragging (OFF 67)
34. Obtain Help Using the 'Type words to search for' Text Box (OFF 68)
35. Obtain Help Using the Help Links (OFF 70)
36. Obtain Help Using the Help Table of Contents (OFF 71)
37. Start Windows Help and Support (OFF 73)

 If you have a SAM 2010 user profile, your instructor may have assigned an autogradable version of this assignment. If so, log into the SAM 2010 Web site at www.cengage.com/sam2010 to download the instruction and start files.

Learn It Online

Test your knowledge of chapter content and key terms.

Instructions: To complete the Learn It Online exercises, start your browser, click the Address bar, and then enter the Web address **scsite.com/out2010/learn**. When the Office 2010 Learn It Online page is displayed, click the link for the exercise you want to complete and then read the instructions.

Chapter Reinforcement TF, MC, and SA
A series of true/false, multiple choice, and short answer questions that test your knowledge of the chapter content.

Flash Cards
An interactive learning environment where you identify chapter key terms associated with displayed definitions.

Practice Test
A series of multiple choice questions that test your knowledge of chapter content and key terms.

Who Wants To Be a Computer Genius?
An interactive game that challenges your knowledge of chapter content in the style of a television quiz show.

Wheel of Terms
An interactive game that challenges your knowledge of chapter key terms in the style of the television show *Wheel of Fortune*.

Crossword Puzzle Challenge
A crossword puzzle that challenges your knowledge of key terms presented in the chapter.

Apply Your Knowledge

Reinforce the skills and apply the concepts you learned in this chapter.

Creating a Folder and a Document

Instructions: You will create a Word folder and then create a Word document and save it in the folder.

Perform the following tasks:

1. Connect a USB flash drive to an available USB port and then open the USB flash drive window.

2. Click the New folder button on the toolbar to display a new folder icon and text box for the folder name.

3. Type **Word** in the text box to name the folder. Press the ENTER key to create the folder on the USB flash drive.

4. Start Word.

5. Enter the text shown in Figure 106.

6. Click the Save button on the Quick Access Toolbar. Navigate to the Word folder on the USB flash drive and then save the document using the file name, Apply 1 Class List.

7. If your Quick Access Toolbar does not show the Quick Print button, add the Quick Print button to the Quick Access Toolbar. Print the document using the Quick Print button on the Quick Access Toolbar. When you are finished printing, remove the Quick Print button from the Quick Access Toolbar.

8. Submit the printout to your instructor.

9. Quit Word.

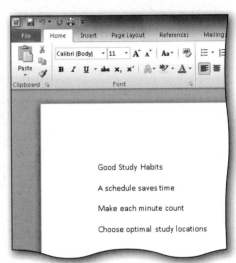

Good Study Habits

A schedule saves time

Make each minute count

Choose optimal study locations

Figure 106

Extend Your Knowledge

Extend the skills you learned in this chapter and experiment with new skills. You will use Help to complete the assignment.

Using Help

Instructions: Use Office Help to perform the following tasks.

Perform the following tasks:

1. Start Word.

2. Click the Microsoft Word Help button to open the Word Help window (Figure 107).

3. Search Word Help to answer the following questions.

   a. What are the steps to add a new group to the Ribbon?

   b. What are Quick Parts?

4. With the Word program still running, start PowerPoint.

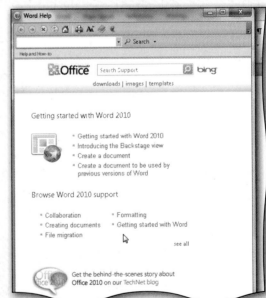

Figure 107

5. Click the Microsoft PowerPoint Help button on the title bar to open the PowerPoint Help window.

6. Search PowerPoint Help to answer the following questions.

    a. What is a slide master?

    b. How do you copy slides from another presentation into the existing presentation?

7. Quit PowerPoint.

8. Start Excel.

9. Click the Microsoft Excel Help button to open the Excel Help window.

10. Search Excel Help to answer the following questions.

    a. What are three different functions available in Excel?

    b. What are sparklines?

11. Quit Excel.

12. Start Access.

13. Click the Microsoft Access Help button to open the Access Help window.

14. Search Access Help to answer the following questions.

    a. What is SQL?

    b. What is a data macro?

15. Quit Access.

16. Type the answers from your searches in the Word document. Save the document with a new file name and then submit it in the format specified by your instructor.

17. Quit Word.

Make It Right

Analyze a file structure and correct all errors and/or improve the design.

Organizing Vacation Photos

Note: To complete this assignment, you will be required to use the Data Files for Students. See the inside back cover of this book for instructions on downloading the Data Files for Students, or contact your instructor for information about accessing the required files.

Instructions: Traditionally, you have stored photos from past vacations together in one folder. The photos are becoming difficult to manage, and you now want to store them in appropriate folders. You will create the folder structure shown in Figure 108. You then will move the photos to the folders so that they will be organized properly.

1. Connect a USB flash drive to an available USB port to open the USB flash drive window.

2. Using the techniques presented in the chapter, create the hierarchical folder structure shown in Figure 108.

3. Using the techniques presented in the chapter, move the vacation photos to their appropriate folders.

4. Submit your work in the format specified by your instructor.

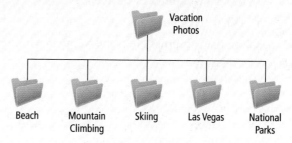

Figure 108

STUDENT ASSIGNMENTS

In the Lab

Use the guidelines, concepts, and skills presented in this chapter to increase your knowledge of Windows 7 and Office 2010. Labs are listed in order of increasing difficulty.

Lab 1: Using Windows Help and Support

Problem: You have a few questions about using Windows 7 and would like to answer these questions using Windows Help and Support.

Instructions: Use Windows Help and Support to perform the following tasks:

1. Display the Start menu and then click Help and Support to start Windows Help and Support.

2. Use the Help and Support Content page to answer the following questions.

   a. How do you reduce computer screen flicker?

   b. Which dialog box do you use to change the appearance of the mouse pointer?

   c. How do you minimize all windows?

   d. What is a VPN?

3. Use the Search Help text box in Windows Help and Support to answer the following questions.

   a. How can you minimize all open windows on the desktop?

   b. How do you start a program using the Run command?

   c. What are the steps to add a toolbar to the taskbar?

   d. What wizard do you use to remove unwanted desktop icons?

4. The tools to solve a problem while using Windows 7 are called **troubleshooters**. Use Windows Help and Support to find the list of troubleshooters (Figure 109), and answer the following questions.

   a. What problems does the HomeGroup troubleshooter allow you to resolve?

   b. List five Windows 7 troubleshooters that are not listed in Figure 109.

5. Use Windows Help and Support to obtain information about software licensing and product activation, and answer the following questions.

   a. What is genuine Windows?

   b. What is activation?

   c. What steps are required to activate Windows?

   d. What steps are required to read the Microsoft Software License Terms?

   e. Can you legally make a second copy of Windows 7 for use at home, work, or on a mobile computer or device?

   f. What is registration?

6. Close the Windows Help and Support window.

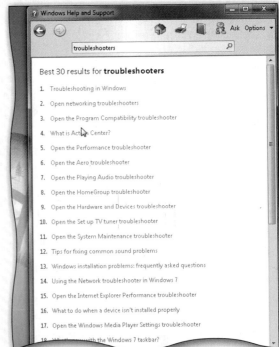

Figure 109

In the Lab

Lab 2: Creating Folders for a Pet Supply Store

Problem: Your friend works for Pete's Pet Supplies. He would like to organize his files in relation to the types of pets available in the store. He has five main categories: dogs, cats, fish, birds, and exotic. You are to create a folder structure similar to Figure 110.

Instructions: Perform the following tasks:

1. Connect a USB flash drive to an available USB port and then open the USB flash drive window.

2. Create the main folder for Pete's Pet Supplies.

3. Navigate to the Pete's Pet Supplies folder.

4. Within the Pete's Pet Supplies folder, create a folder for each of the following: Dogs, Cats, Fish, Birds, and Exotic.

5. Within the Exotic folder, create two additional folders, one for Primates and the second for Reptiles.

6. Submit the assignment in the format specified by your instructor.

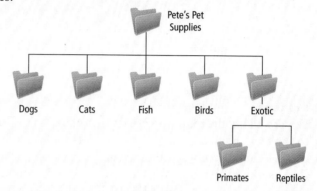

Figure 110

In the Lab

Lab 3: Creating Office Documents

Problem: You are taking a class that requires you to create a Word, PowerPoint, Excel, and Access file. You will save these files to folders named for four different Office programs (Figure 111).

Instructions: Create the folders shown in Figure 111. Then, using the respective Office program, create a small file to save in each folder (i.e., create a Word document to save in the Word folder, a PowerPoint presentation to save in the PowerPoint folder, and so on).

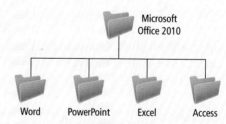

Figure 111

1. Connect a USB flash drive to an available USB port and then open the USB flash drive window.

2. Create the folder structure shown in Figure 111.

3. Navigate to the Word folder.

4. Create a Word document containing the text, My First Word Document, and then save it in the Word folder.

5. Navigate to the PowerPoint folder.

6. Create a PowerPoint presentation containing the title text, My First PowerPoint Presentation, and then save it in the PowerPoint folder.

7. Navigate to the Excel folder.

Continued >

In the Lab *continued*

8. Create an Excel spreadsheet containing the text, My First Excel Spreadsheet, in cell A1 and then save it in the Excel folder.

9. Navigate to the Access folder.

10. Save an Access database named, My First Database, in the Access folder.

11. Close all open Office programs.

12. Submit the assignment in the format specified by your instructor.

Cases and Places

Apply your creative thinking and problem solving skills to design and implement a solution.

1: Creating Beginning Files for Classes

Academic

You are taking the following classes: Introduction to Engineering, Beginning Psychology, Introduction to Biology, and Accounting. Create folders for each of the classes. Use the following folder names: Engineering, Psychology, Biology, and Accounting, when creating the folder structure. In the Engineering folder, use Word to create a Word document with the name of the class and the class meeting location and time (MW 10:30 – 11:45, Room 317). In the Psychology folder, use PowerPoint to create your first lab presentation. It should begin with a title slide containing the text, Behavioral Observations. In the Biology folder, save a database named Research in the Biology folder. In the Accounting folder, create an Excel spreadsheet with the text, Tax Information, in cell A1. Use the concepts and techniques presented in this chapter to create the folders and files.

2: Using Help

Personal

Your parents enjoy working and playing games on their home computers. Your mother uses a notebook computer downstairs, and your father uses a desktop computer upstairs. They expressed interest in sharing files between their computers and sharing a single printer, so you offered to research various home networking options. Start Windows Help and Support, and search Help using the keywords, home networking. Use the link for installing a printer on a home network. Start Word and then type the main steps for installing a printer. Use the link for setting up a HomeGroup and then type the main steps for creating a HomeGroup in the Word document. Use the concepts and techniques presented in this chapter to use Help and create the Word document.

3: Creating Folders

Professional

Your boss at the bookstore where you work part-time has asked for help with organizing her files. After looking through the files, you decided upon a file structure for her to use, including the following folders: books, magazines, tapes, DVDs, and general merchandise. Within the books folder, create folders for hardback and paperback books. Within magazines, create folders for special issues and periodicals. In the tapes folder, create folders for celebrity and major release. In the DVDs folder, create a folder for book to DVD. In the general merchandise folder, create folders for novelties, posters, and games. Use the concepts and techniques presented in this chapter to create the folders.

1 Managing E-Mail Messages with Outlook

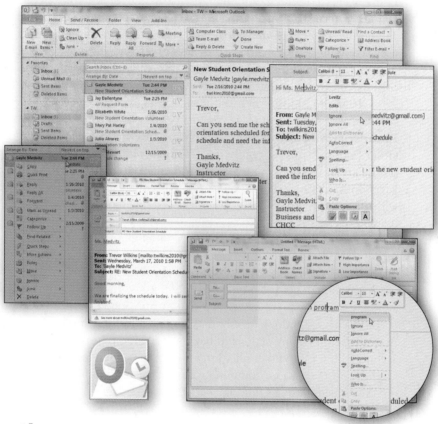

Objectives

You will have mastered the material in this chapter when you can:

- Start and quit Outlook

- Compose, address, and send an e-mail message

- Open, read, print, and close an e-mail message

- Reply to an e-mail message

- Forward an e-mail message

- Delete an e-mail message

- Check spelling as you type an e-mail message

- Save an e-mail message in the Drafts folder

- Retrieve a saved e-mail message

- Attach a file to an outgoing e-mail message

- Copy another person when sending an e-mail message

- Preview and save a file attachment

- Create an e-mail folder

- Move and copy received e-mail messages to a folder

1 | Managing E-Mail Messages with Outlook

Introduction

E-mail (short for **electronic mail**) is the transmission of messages and files over a computer network. Today, e-mail is the primary communication method for both personal and business use. An **e-mail program**, such as Microsoft Outlook 2010, is software in the user's computer that can access the mail servers in a local or remote network. Outlook is used to compose, send, receive, store, print, and delete e-mail messages. Finally, you can organize messages so that you easily can find and respond to them later.

To use Outlook, you must have an e-mail account. An **e-mail account** is an account used to connect to an e-mail service via an Internet service provider. An **Internet service provider (ISP)** delivers Internet access to a geographic location, either regionally or nationally. An e-mail account could be set up by your employer or school, or through a Web application such as Google's Gmail, Yahoo! Mail, or Windows Live Hotmail. Outlook does not create or issue e-mail accounts; it merely provides you with access to them. You may be able to establish e-mail service through your cable or telephone company.

In Outlook, an e-mail account is contained in an e-mail profile. An **e-mail profile** includes the e-mail account(s), data files, and settings that contain information about where a user's e-mail is stored. A **personal folders file (.pst file)** is a data file that stores a user's Outlook items, including e-mail messages, on your computer. A data file is created automatically when you set up an e-mail profile in Outlook, called an Outlook profile. If you are using Outlook on a home computer and starting it for the first time, the Auto Account Setup feature starts and begins to configure e-mail account settings for the e-mail account you want to use. (The process is discussed later in this chapter.) If you are using Outlook on a classroom computer, your instructor will provide the necessary information on how to begin using Outlook.

Project Planning Guidelines

The process of composing an e-mail message that communicates specific information requires some analysis and planning. As a starting point, establish why the e-mail message is needed. Once the purpose is determined, analyze the intended readers of the e-mail message and their unique needs. Then, gather information about the topic and decide what to include in the e-mail message. Details of these guidelines are provided in Appendix A. In addition, each project in this book provides practical applications of these planning considerations.

Project — Composing and Sending E-Mail Messages

The project in this chapter follows the general guidelines for using Outlook to compose, open, and reply to e-mail messages, as shown in Figure 1–1. To communicate with individuals and groups, you typically send or receive some kind of message. Phone calls, faxes, letters, and e-mail are examples of ways to communicate a message. E-mail is a convenient way to send information to multiple people simultaneously, instantly, and inexpensively.

As a student assistant to the director of the Business and Computer Division at Condor Harbor Community College (CHCC), you use Outlook to communicate with faculty, staff, and fellow classmates. This chapter uses the communications features of

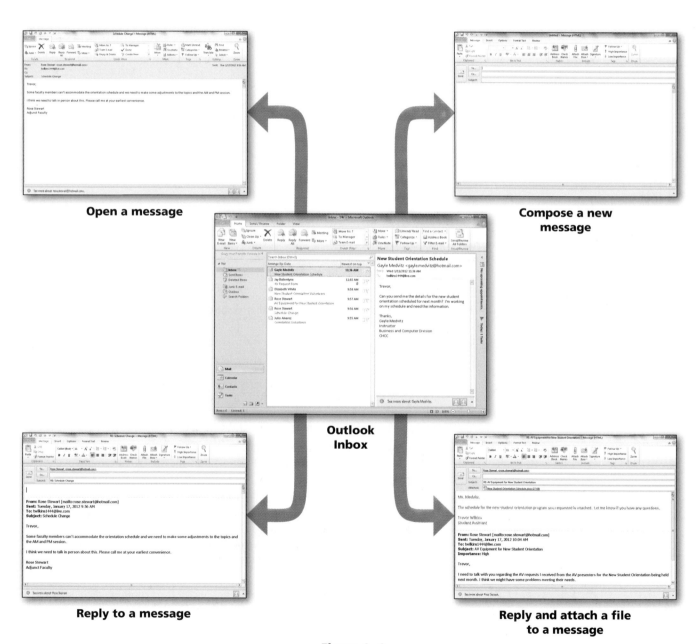

Open a message

Compose a new message

Outlook Inbox

Reply to a message

Reply and attach a file to a message

Figure 1–1

Microsoft Outlook 2010 to compose, send, read, reply to, and forward e-mail messages regarding an upcoming New Student Orientation program. Your responsibilities include collecting information from instructors who are participating in the orientation program, coordinating the resources needed, and scheduling student volunteers to work at the orientation program. Using Outlook, you open e-mail messages from instructors and students regarding these activities. You reply to e-mail messages and include a document containing the schedule that the recipient, or receiver of the e-mail message, can open. To organize messages, you create folders in which to store them.

Overview

As you read this chapter, you will learn how to communicate using e-mail by performing these general tasks:

- Compose and send an e-mail message.
- Open, read, and print an e-mail message.
- Reply to an e-mail message.
- Forward an e-mail message.
- Save an e-mail message.
- Attach a file to an e-mail message.
- Send an e-mail message to multiple recipients.
- Organize e-mail messages in folders.

Plan Ahead

General Project Guidelines

When creating an e-mail message, the actions you perform and decisions you make will affect the appearance and characteristics of the finished message. As you read, respond to, and create e-mail messages, such as those shown in Figure 1–1, you should follow these general guidelines:

1. **Determine the best method for reading e-mail messages you receive.** Although e-mail messages are sent electronically, you can read them on the computer in several ways or print them if you need a paper copy.

2. **Organize the e-mail message.** An e-mail message typically is organized into two areas: the message header and the message area.

3. **Choose the words for the subject line.** The subject line should indicate the main purpose or topic of the e-mail message. Use as few words as possible and never leave the subject line blank because it provides important information for the person receiving the e-mail message.

4. **Choose the words for the message text.** The message text should be clear and concise. Use as few words as possible to make a point. Brief or short message text is more likely to be read than lengthy text.

5. **Ensure that the content of the e-mail message is appropriate for the recipient.** An e-mail message sent to a close friend may be considerably different from one sent to an instructor, coworker, or client. Shortening words or using abbreviations (such as u for you, r for are, and 2 for to) may be appropriate for personal e-mail messages, but should be avoided when sending work-related e-mail messages. These types of abbreviations are too informal for the workplace and often are viewed as unprofessional.

6. **Alert the recipient(s) when sending large file attachments.** An **attachment** is a file, such as a document or picture, which is sent along with an e-mail message. Recipients can open attachments only if they have the appropriate software installed on their computer. Be aware when sending large file attachments that some e-mail services only allow file attachments up to a certain size.

(continued)

(continued)

7. **Be aware of computer viruses and how they spread.** A **virus** is a malicious computer program that can damage files and the operating system. One way that viruses spread is through virus-infected e-mail attachments. You only should open attachments when the e-mail message is from someone you know or when you are expecting the attachment. If you receive an e-mail attachment, you should use an **antivirus program**, which is a program that checks files for viruses, to verify that the attachment is virus free.

When necessary, more specific details concerning the above guidelines are presented at appropriate points in the chapter. The chapter also will identify the actions performed and decisions made regarding these guidelines during the creation of the messages shown in Figure 1–1.

Outlook Account Settings

The first time you start Outlook on a home computer, the Auto Account Setup feature starts automatically to help you provide information that Outlook needs to send and receive e-mail messages. First, you will be prompted to provide your name, which will appear in e-mail messages that you send to other people. You also need to provide an e-mail address. An **e-mail address** identifies a user so that he or she can receive Internet e-mail. Just as you address a letter when using the postal system, you address an e-mail message with the e-mail address of the person receiving the message, or the recipient. Likewise, when someone sends you a message, he or she must have your e-mail address.

An e-mail address is divided into two parts. The first part contains a **user name**, which is a unique combination of characters, such as letters of the alphabet and numbers, which identifies a specific user. The last part is a **domain name**, which is the unique name associated with a specific Internet address and is provided by your ISP or school. In an Internet e-mail address, an @ (pronounced *at*) symbol separates the user name from the domain name. A possible e-mail address for someone named Kiley Barnhill, for example, would be kbarnhill@scsite.com, which would be read as k barnhill at s c site dot com. Figure 1–2 shows the parts of an e-mail address.

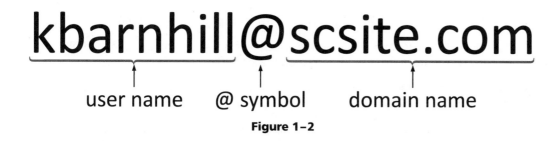

Figure 1–2

After entering an e-mail address, you enter a password for the account. A **password** is a combination of letters, numbers, and symbols that verifies your identity. Typically, the ISP provides a password when you set up your e-mail service. Most people change the password so that they can remember it easily.

Figure 1–3 shows typical entries in the Add New Account dialog box, which is part of the Auto Account Setup feature and can be displayed by clicking File on the Ribbon to open the Backstage view and then clicking the Add Account link in the Backstage view. Notice in Figure 1–3 that the entered password is displayed as asterisks or bullets, which keeps your password private, preventing anyone from learning your password as you type it.

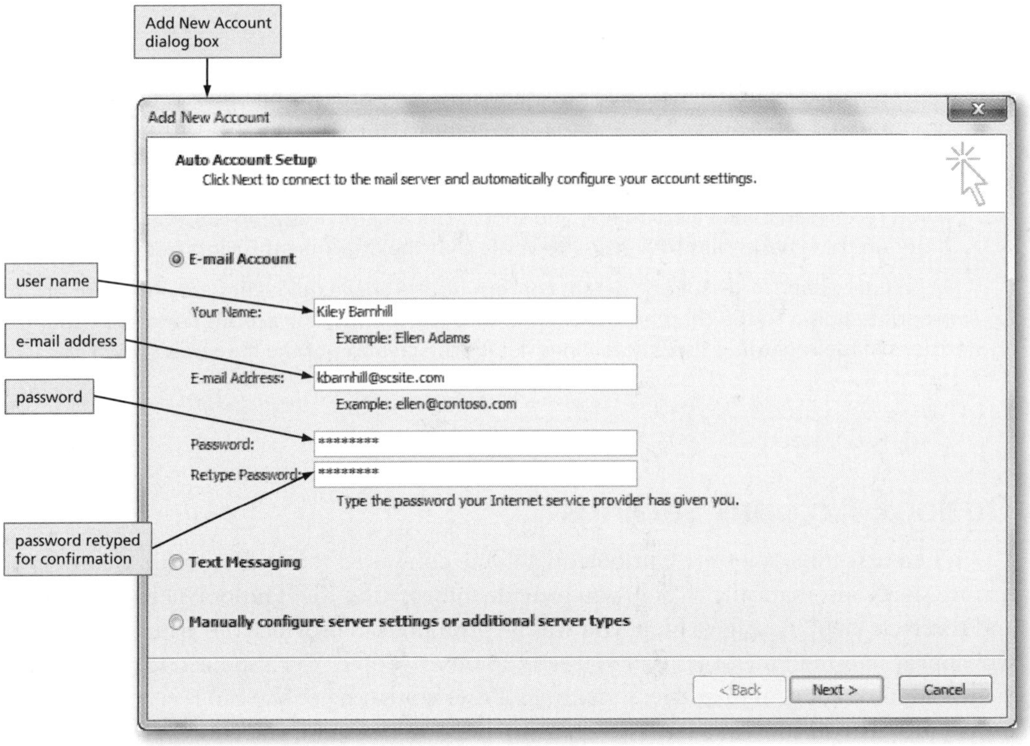

Add New Account
dialog box

user name

e-mail address

password

password retyped
for confirmation

Figure 1–3

To Start Outlook

If you are using a computer to step through the project in this chapter and you want your screens to match the figures in this book, you should change your screen's resolution to 1024 × 768. For information about how to change a computer's resolution, refer to the Office 2010 and Windows 7 chapter at the beginning of this book.

The following steps, which assume Windows 7 is running, start Outlook based on a typical installation. You may need to ask your instructor how to start Outlook for your computer. For a detailed example of the procedure summarized below, refer to the Office 2010 and Windows 7 chapter.

1 Click the Start button on the Windows 7 taskbar to display the Start menu.

2 Type `Microsoft Outlook` as the search text in the 'Search programs and files' text box and watch the search results appear on the Start menu.

3 Click Microsoft Outlook 2010 in the search results on the Start menu to start Outlook and display the Outlook window.

4 If the Outlook window is not maximized, click the Maximize button next to the Close button on its title bar to maximize the window.

5 If the Inbox – Outlook – Microsoft Outlook window is not displayed, click the Mail button in the Navigation Pane to display your mailbox.

Q&A

What does the name in the title bar mean?

The name of your window in the title bar is the name of the profile you set up when starting Outlook for the first time.

Note: If you are stepping through this project on a computer and you want your screens to appear the same as in the figures, then you should ask your instructor for assistance with opening or importing the TW.pst mailbox from the Data Files for Students. See the inside back cover of this book for instructions for downloading the Data Files for Students or see your instructor for information about accessing files for this book.

To Open an Outlook Data File

The e-mail messages you work with in this chapter are stored in a personal folders (.pst) file named TW.pst, which is an Outlook mailbox available on the Data Files for Students. See the inside back cover of this book for instructions on downloading the Data Files for Students, or contact your instructor for information about accessing the required files. The following steps show how to open this personal folders file in Outlook, display the Inbox for the TW file, and then make your TW mailbox match the figures in this chapter. In this example, the TW mailbox is located in the Chapter01 folder in the Outlook folder in the Data Files for Students folder on a USB flash drive.

1

- With your USB flash drive connected to one of the computer's USB ports, click File on the Ribbon to open the Backstage view.

- Click Open in the Backstage view to display the Open commands.

- Click Open Outlook Data File to display the Open Outlook Data File dialog box.

- Navigate to the mailbox location (in this case, the Chapter01 folder in

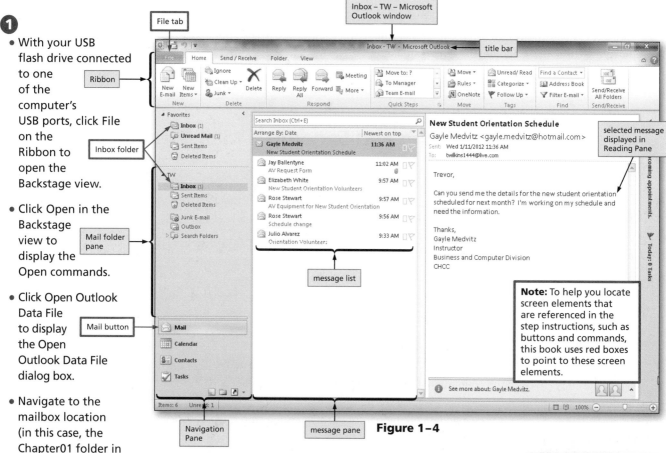

Figure 1–4

the Outlook folder in the Data Files for Students folder on a USB flash drive). For a detailed example of this procedure, refer to Steps 3a – 3c in the To Save a File in a Folder section in the Office 2010 and Windows 7 chapter at the beginning of this book.

- Click TW to select the file, and then click the Open button to open the TW mailbox in your Outlook window.

- Click Inbox below the TW heading in the Navigation Pane to view the TW Inbox (Figure 1–4).

Q&A What is the Navigation Pane?

The **Navigation Pane** is a pane along the left side of the Outlook window that contains shortcuts to your Outlook folders and gives you quick access to them. You use the Navigation Pane to browse all your Outlook folders using one of its views: Mail, Calendar, Contacts, or Tasks. The contents of the Navigation Pane change depending on the folder you are using.

Q&A What is the Inbox?

The **Inbox** is the Outlook folder that contains incoming e-mail messages.

For an introduction to Office 2010 and instruction about how to perform basic tasks in Office 2010 programs, read the Office 2010 and Windows 7 chapter at the beginning of this book, where you can learn how to start a program, use the Ribbon, save a file, open a file, quit a program, use Help, and much more.

2

- Right-click the Arrange By: bar in the Inbox to display the shortcut menu.

- If Date is not selected with a check mark, click Date to select it.

Q&A
My Outlook window includes an option called Date: [Conversations]. Is that the same command as Date?

Yes, the Date command and the Date: [Conversations] commands are the same.

- If Show in Groups is selected with a check mark, click Show in Groups to remove the check mark and deselect this command.

- If Show as Conversations is selected with a check mark, click Show as Conversations to remove the check mark and deselect this command.

BTW

Q&As
For a complete list of the Q&As found in many of the step-by-step sequences in this book, visit the Outlook 2010 Q&A Web page (scsite.com/out2010/qa).

Composing and Sending E-Mail Messages

Composing an e-mail message consists of four basic steps — open a new message window, enter message header information, enter the message text, and add a signature.

Plan Ahead

Organize the e-mail message.
An e-mail message typically is organized into two areas: the message header and the message area.

- The information in the **message header** routes the message to its recipients and identifies the purpose or contents of the message. The message header contains the e-mail address of the recipient(s), the primary person or persons to whom you are sending the message; it also may contain a courtesy copy or carbon copy (cc), which includes one or more additional recipients; and the **subject line**, which states the reason for the message.

- The **message area**, where you type an e-mail message, consists of a greeting line or salutation, the message text, an optional closing, and a signature line(s).

- A **greeting line** or salutation sets the tone of the message and can be formal or informal, depending on the nature of the message. You can use a comma (,) or a colon (:) at the end of the greeting line.

- The **message text** informs the recipient or summarizes or requests information.

- A **closing** signals an end to the message using courtesy words such as *Thank you* or *Regards*. Because the closing is most appropriate for formal e-mail messages, it is optional.

- A **signature line(s)** identifies the sender and may contain additional information, such as a job title and phone number(s). In a signature, the name usually is provided on one line followed by other information listed on separate lines.

BTW

The Outlook Window
The chapters in this book begin with the Outlook window appearing as it did at the initial installation of the software. Your Outlook window may look different depending on your screen resolution and other Outlook settings.

To Compose and Send an E-Mail Message

The first step in this project is to send an e-mail message to Rose Stewart, a faculty member at the college, asking her to send you the morning agenda for the new student orientation program. The following steps compose a new e-mail message to Rose Stewart.

1

- Click the New E-mail button (Home tab | New group) to open the Untitled – Message (HTML) window (Figure 1–5).

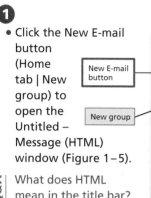

Q&A What does HTML mean in the title bar?

HTML is the format for the new e-mail message. Outlook messages can use two other formats — Rich Text Format (RTF) and Plain Text — all of these are discussed later in this chapter.

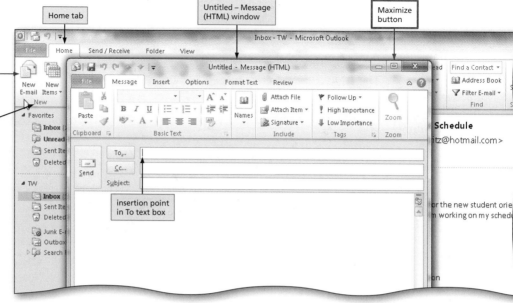

Figure 1–5

2

- If necessary, click the Maximize button in the Untitled – Message (HTML) window to maximize the window.

- With the insertion point in the To text box, type `rose.stewart@hotmail.com` (with no spaces) to enter the e-mail address of the recipient.

- Click the Subject text box to position the insertion point in the Subject text box.

- Type `Draft Agenda` as the subject.

- Press the TAB key to move the insertion point into the message area (Figure 1–6).

Q&A What if I make an error while typing an e-mail message?

Press the BACKSPACE key until you have deleted the error and then retype the text correctly. You also can click the Undo button on the Quick Access Toolbar to undo your most recent action.

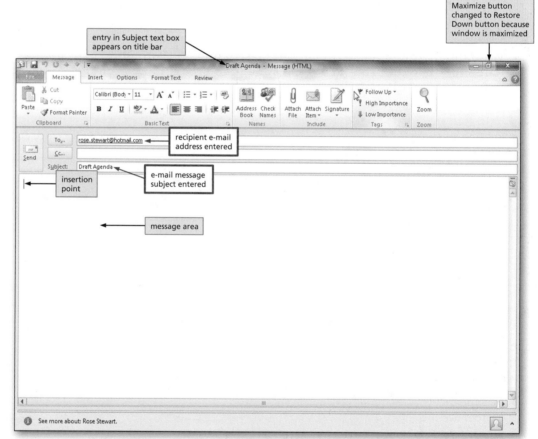

Figure 1–6

BTW | **The Ribbon and Screen Resolution**
Outlook may change how the groups and buttons within the groups appear on the Ribbon, depending on the computer's screen resolution. Thus, your Ribbon may look different from the ones in this book if you are using a screen resolution other than 1024 × 768.

3

- Type **Ms. Stewart,** as the greeting line.

- Press the ENTER key to move the insertion point to the beginning of the next line.

- Press the ENTER key again to insert a blank line between the greeting line and the message text.

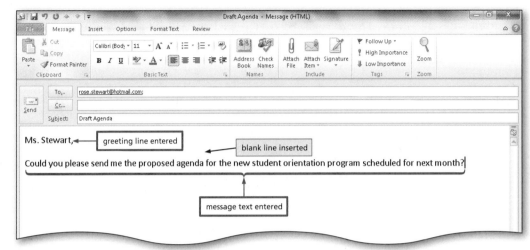

Figure 1–7

Q&A

Why did a blank space appear between the greeting line and the insertion point?

Each time you press the ENTER key, Outlook creates a new paragraph. When you press the ENTER key on a line with no text, Outlook inserts blank space between the two paragraphs.

- Type **Could you please send me the proposed agenda for the new student orientation program scheduled for next month?** to enter the message text (Figure 1–7).

4

- Press the ENTER key two times to insert a blank line below the message text.

- Type **Thanks,** as the closing and then press the ENTER key to move the insertion point to the next line.

- Type **Trevor Wilkins** as signature line 1.

- Press the ENTER key to move the insertion point to the next line and then type **Student Assistant** as signature line 2 (Figure 1–8).

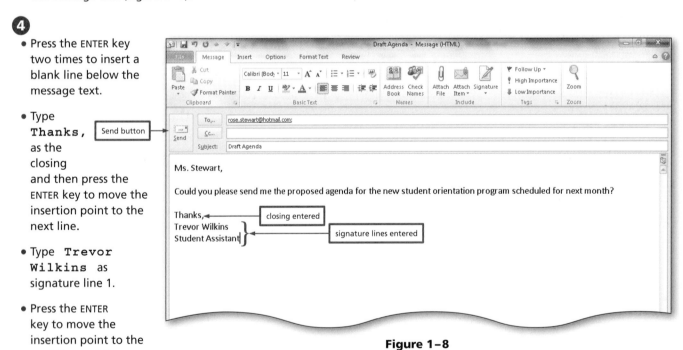

Figure 1–8

Q&A

Do I always need to type my last name in the signature of an e-mail message?

No. If you and your recipient know each other, you can type only your first name as the signature.

Other Ways

1. Click Inbox folder, press CTRL+N

To Send an E-Mail Message

The message to Rose Stewart is created and ready to be sent. The following step sends the completed e-mail message to Rose Stewart.

- Click the Send button in the message header to send the e-mail message and close the message window.

Q&A What happened to the e-mail message?

E-mail messages are sent automatically when you click Send in a new message window.

Other Ways
1. Press ALT+S

How E-Mail Messages Travel from Sender to Receiver

When you send someone an e-mail message, it travels across the Internet to the computer at your ISP that handles outgoing e-mail messages. This computer, called the **outgoing e-mail server,** examines the e-mail address on your message, selects the best route for sending the message across the Internet, and then sends the e-mail message. Many outgoing e-mail servers use **SMTP (Simple Mail Transfer Protocol),** which is a communications protocol, or set of rules for communicating with other computers. An e-mail program such as Outlook contacts the outgoing e-mail server and then transfers the e-mail message(s) in its Outbox to that server. If the e-mail program cannot contact the outgoing e-mail server, the e-mail message(s) remains in the Outbox until the program can connect to the server.

As an e-mail message travels across the Internet, routers direct the e-mail message to a computer at your recipient's ISP that handles incoming e-mail messages. (A **router** is a device that forwards data on a network.) The computer handling incoming e-mail messages, called the **incoming e-mail server,** stores the e-mail message(s) until your recipient uses an e-mail program such as Outlook to retrieve the e-mail message(s). Some e-mail servers use **POP3,** the latest version of **Post Office Protocol (POP),** a communications protocol for incoming e-mail. Figure 1–9 shows how an e-mail message may travel from a sender to a receiver.

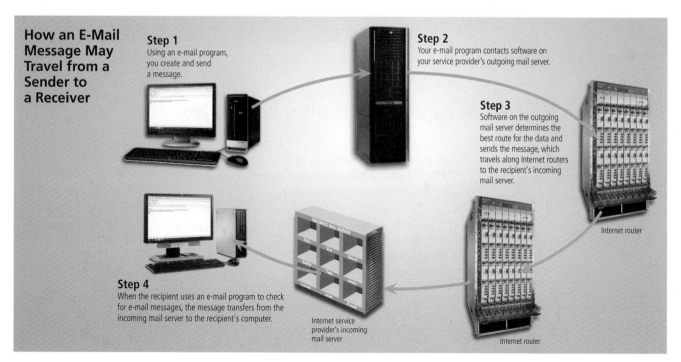

Figure 1–9

In most cases, the user provides Outlook information about the outgoing and incoming e-mail servers when using the Auto Account Setup feature to set up an e-mail account. You can verify these Internet e-mail settings in the Change Account dialog box, which is displayed by clicking File on the Ribbon to open the Backstage view, clicking the Account Settings button in the Backstage view, clicking Account Settings to display the Account Settings dialog box, selecting your e-mail address, and then clicking the Change button on the toolbar. Figure 1–10 shows the Change Account dialog box for Kiley Barnhill. Notice that this account uses a POP3 incoming mail server and an SMTP outgoing mail server with the same domain name as in the e-mail address. Use the Test Account Settings button to test these Internet e-mail settings, if necessary.

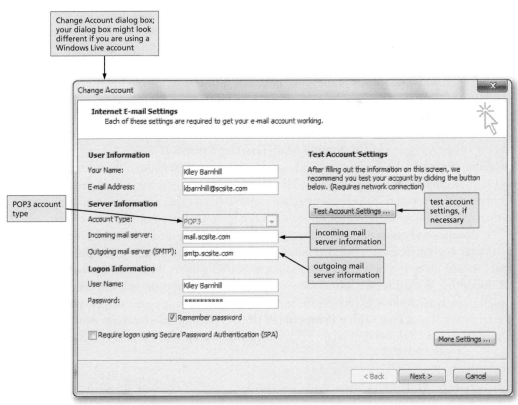

Figure 1–10

BTW

Message Notifications
If Outlook is not the active window on your desktop, it still provides a mail notification alert informing you when you receive a new message. Outlook briefly displays a closed envelope and a semitransparent ScreenTip in the notification area of the taskbar. The ScreenTip includes the sender's name, subject of the message, and the first few words of the message body.

Working with Incoming Messages

When you receive e-mail messages, Outlook directs them to the Inbox and displays them in the **message pane,** which lists the contents of the selected folder, in this case the Inbox (Figure 1–11). The list of messages displayed in the message pane is called the **message list.** A highlighted e-mail message in the message list displays the selected message header, which appears in bold with a **closed envelope icon** to the left of the e-mail message if the e-mail message is unread (unopened). An **open envelope icon** indicates a previously read (opened) message. The blue number next to the Inbox folder shows how many unread messages are stored in the Inbox. The e-mail messages on your computer may be different.

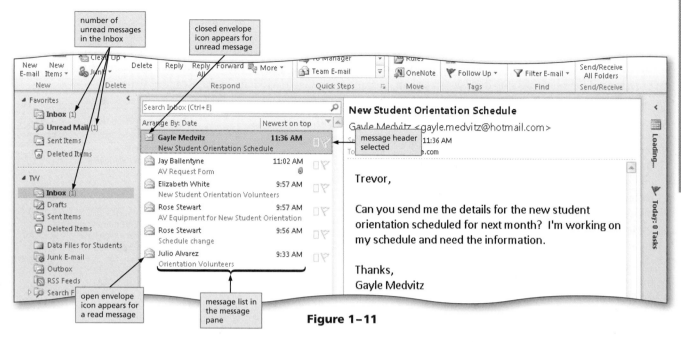

Figure 1–11

You can read incoming messages in three ways: in an open window, in the Reading Pane, or as a hard copy. A **hard copy** (**printout**) is information presented on a physical medium such as paper.

Determine the best method for reading e-mail messages you receive.
Popular methods for reading an e-mail message are to either display it in the Reading Pane or to open it in its own message window. These methods are easy and quick. Reading electronic documents also saves paper and printer supplies. You should be aware of problems, however, that can be caused by reading e-mail messages.

- **Know the sender.** If you receive an e-mail message from someone you do not know, you should not open it because it might trigger a virus. Unsolicited e-mail messages, known as **spam** or **junk e-mail**, are e-mail messages sent from an unknown sender to many e-mail accounts, usually advertising a product or service such as low-cost medication, low-interest loans, or free credit reports. Spam quickly can fill an Inbox with unwanted messages. If a suspicious e-mail message appears to come from someone you know and trust, contact them first to make sure they actually sent the e-mail message.

- **Do not click a hyperlink in an e-mail message from an unknown sender.** A **hyperlink** is a word, phrase, symbol, or picture in an e-mail message or on a Web page that, when clicked, directs you to another document or Web site. One way spammers (senders of spam) verify your e-mail address is by sending messages that request you to click a hyperlink to direct you to a Web site. After spammers know that your e-mail address is valid, they are likely to send you many more e-mail messages.

The next several pages in this chapter read and reply to an e-mail message. The following pages follow these general tasks:

1. Read an e-mail message in the Reading Pane.
2. Open, print, and close an e-mail message.
3. Reply to and forward an e-mail message.
4. Delete an e-mail message.
5. Check the spelling of an e-mail message.
6. Save an e-mail message.
7. Attach a file to an outgoing e-mail message.

BTW

Reading Pane
By default, the Reading Pane is displayed on the right side of the Outlook window. To change its position, click the Reading Pane button (View tab | Layout group), and then click the desired option.

BTW

Junk E-Mail Filters
The Outlook Junk E-mail Filter is turned on by default and evaluates whether an incoming message should be sent to the Junk E-mail folder. By scanning message information such as the content, time the message was sent, and who sent the message, this feature determines whether a message might be spam and diverts it to the Junk E-mail folder. To change junk e-mail settings, click the Junk button (Home tab | Delete group), and then click Junk E-mail Options to display the Junk E-mail Options dialog box. Choose the level of protection you want and click the OK button.

To Read an E-Mail Message in the Reading Pane

You can read an e-mail message without opening it by displaying its contents in the Reading Pane. The **Reading Pane** appears on the right side of the Outlook window by default and displays the contents of a message without opening the message. The following step displays an e-mail message from Gayle Medvitz in the Reading Pane.

1

- If necessary, click the message header from Gayle Medvitz in the Inbox message list to select the e-mail message and display its contents in the Reading Pane (Figure 1–12).

Q&A What happens to the message icon when I select another message?

Outlook automatically marks messages as read after you preview the message in the Reading Pane and select another message to view. A read message is displayed in the message list with an open envelope and is not bold. An unread message is displayed with a closed envelope icon and appears in bold in the message list.

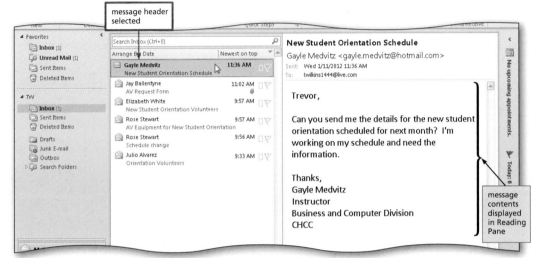

Figure 1–12

To Open an E-Mail Message in a Window

The next step is to open the message in its own window for further evaluation. The following step opens the message from Gayle Medvitz.

1

- Double-click the Gayle Medvitz message in the message list to display the selected e-mail message in its own window (Figure 1–13).

Q&A Does the message header contain additional information about the e-mail message?

Yes. To view the additional information, known as the message properties, make sure the e-mail message is open in its own window, click File on the Ribbon to display the Backstage view, click the Info tab to display the Info gallery, and then click the Properties button.

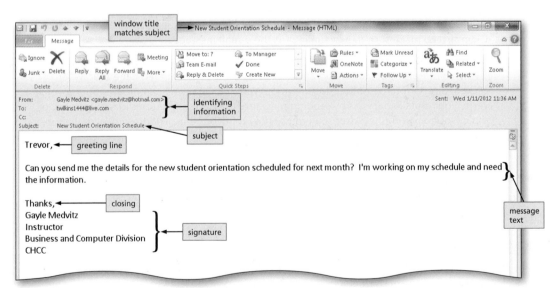

Figure 1–13

Other Ways

1. Select message header, press CTRL+O

To Close an E-Mail Message

You are finished with the e-mail message from Gayle Medvitz, so you can close it. The following steps close the New Student Orientation Schedule – Message (HTML) window.

1

- Point to the Close button on the title bar of the message window to prepare for selecting the button (Figure 1–14).

Figure 1–14

2

- Click the Close button on the title bar of the message window to close the window and display the message icon for Gayle Medvitz as an open envelope (Figure 1–15).

Q&A Can I change the message status from unread to read or from read to unread?

Yes, right-click the message you want to change and select the desired command on the shortcut menu.

Q&A Why did the number next to the Inbox folder change?

When you close a message window, the message header (Gayle Medvitz, in this case) in the message pane no longer appears in bold, the closed envelope icon changes to an open envelope icon to indicate the message has been opened, and the number next to the Inbox folder changes to reflect the number of unread messages.

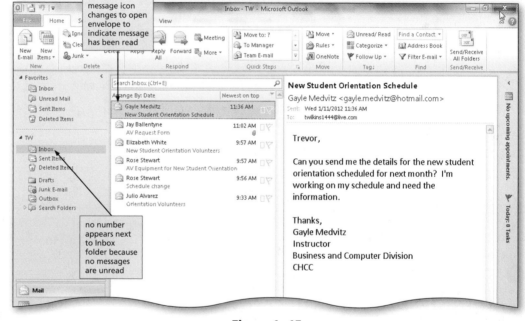

Figure 1–15

Other Ways
1. Click Close (File tab)

To Print an E-Mail Message

Occasionally, you may want to print the contents of an e-mail message. A hard copy of an e-mail message can serve as reference material if your storage medium becomes corrupted and you need to re-create the message or refer to the message when your computer is not readily available. A printed copy of an e-mail message also serves as a **backup**, which is an additional copy of a file or message that you store for safekeeping. You can print the contents of an e-mail message from an open message window or directly from the Inbox window.

You would like to have a hard copy of the message from Gayle Medvitz so that you can keep it with other documents relating to the orientation topic. The following steps print the e-mail message from Gayle Medvitz.

- In the message list, right-click the e-mail message from Gayle Medvitz to display a shortcut menu that presents a list of possible actions (Figure 1–16).

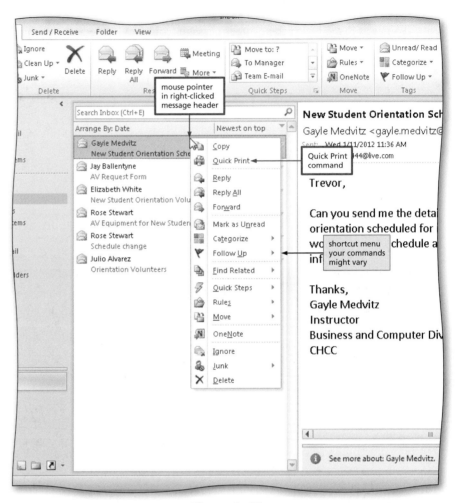

Figure 1–16

- Click Quick Print on the shortcut menu to send the e-mail message to the currently selected printer.

- When the printer stops, retrieve the hard copy (Figure 1–17).

Figure 1–17

Other Ways

1. Press CTRL+P, press ENTER
2. Click File tab, click Print tab (Backstage view), click Print

To Print Multiple Copies of an E-Mail Message

You may need to print multiple copies of an e-mail message if you want to distribute the message to more than one person, or if you want to file one copy for later use and keep a second copy as a backup. If you wanted to print multiple copies of an e-mail message, you would follow these steps.

1. Click File on the Ribbon to open the Backstage view and then click the Print tab in the Backstage view to display the Print gallery.
2. Click the Print Options button in the Print gallery to display the Print dialog box.
3. Change the number in the 'Number of copies' box to the number of desired copies, such as a 2 for 2 copies (Print dialog box).
4. Click the Print button to print the message and close the Print dialog box.

Responding to E-Mail Messages

In this chapter, you respond to e-mail messages by replying to and forwarding them. Thus, the next step is to respond to an e-mail message that has already been received.

Ensure that the content of the e-mail message is appropriate for the recipient. An e-mail message you send to a close friend may be much less formal than one you send to an instructor, coworker, or client. For example, conversational language to a friend, such as "Can't wait to see you!" is not appropriate in professional e-mail messages. All standard grammar rules apply, however, such as punctuation, capitalization, and spelling, no matter the audience.

Plan Ahead

When responding to e-mail messages, you have three options in Outlook: Reply, Reply All, or Forward. Table 1–1 lists the response options and their actions.

Table 1–1 Outlook Response Options	
Response Option	**Action**
Reply	Opens the RE: reply window and sends a reply to the person who sent the message.
Reply All	Opens the RE: reply window and sends a reply to everyone listed in the message header.
Forward	Opens the FW: message window and sends a copy of the selected message to additional people, if you want to share information with others. The original message text is included in the message window.

BTW

Configuring Options for Replies and Forwards
Microsoft Outlook includes multiple options you can configure for replies to e-mail messages and forwarded e-mail messages. To access these options, click the Reply, Reply All, or Forward button to display the appropriate message window, and then click Options on the Ribbon to display the Options tab.

You reply to messages you already have received. You can forward an e-mail message to additional recipients to share information with others. You should receive permission from the sender before forwarding a message, in case the sender intended the original message to remain private. A message that you forward is similar to a new message in that you send the message to someone other than the original sender of the message. A reply sends the message to the person who sent the message.

To Reply to an E-Mail Message

The message from Gayle Medvitz is asking for information and requires a reply. The following steps reply to the e-mail message from Gayle Medvitz.

1

• If necessary, click the Gayle Medvitz message header in the message list to select it and display its contents in the Reading Pane (Figure 1–18).

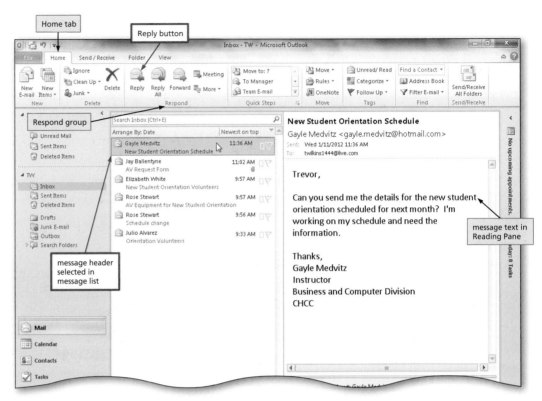

Figure 1–18

2

• Click the Reply button (Home tab | Respond group) to open the RE: New Student Orientation Schedule – Message (HTML) window.

• If the message window is not maximized, click the Maximize button next to the Close button on its title bar to maximize the window (Figure 1–19).

Q&A

Why does RE: appear at the beginning of the subject line and in the title bar?

The RE: indicates this message is a reply to another message. The subject of the original message appears after the RE.

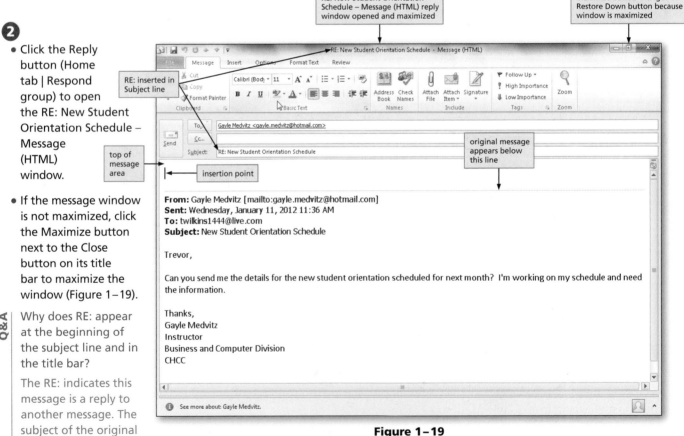

Figure 1–19

3

- If necessary, click the message area below the message header to position the insertion point at the top of the message area.

- Type **Good morning,** as the greeting line.

- Press the ENTER key two times to place a blank line between the greeting line and the message text.

Figure 1–20

- Type **We are finalizing the schedule today. I will send it to you as soon as we are finished.** to enter the message text.

- Press the ENTER key two times to place a blank line between the message text and the signature lines.

- Type **Trevor Wilkins** as signature line 1 and then press the ENTER key to move the insertion point to the next line.

- Type **Student Assistant** as signature line 2 (Figure 1–20).

4

- Click the Send button in the message header to send the e-mail message and display the Inbox window.

Other Ways
1. Right-click message header, click Reply
2. Click message header, press CTRL+R

To Forward an E-Mail Message

Elizabeth White has sent you an e-mail message offering to volunteer for the New Student Orientation program. Because she is not sure you can authorize her volunteer service, she mentions that you can forward her message to the appropriate person. In fact, Julio Alvarez is the person handling the volunteers for the program. The following steps forward Elizabeth White's message to Julio Alvarez.

1

- In the Inbox window, click the Elizabeth White message header in the message list to select the e-mail message (Figure 1–21).

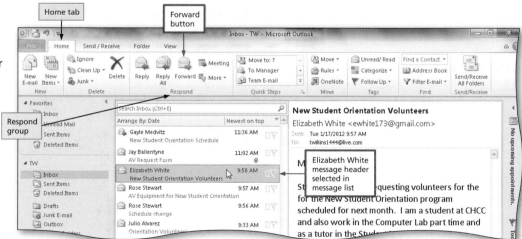

Figure 1–21

• Click the Forward button (Home tab | Respond group) to display the FW: New Student Orientation Volunteers – Message (HTML) window.

• Type **julioa1776@ hotmail.com** (with no spaces) in the To text box as the recipient's e-mail address (unless you are stepping through this task — in that case, enter an actual e-mail address) (Figure 1–22).

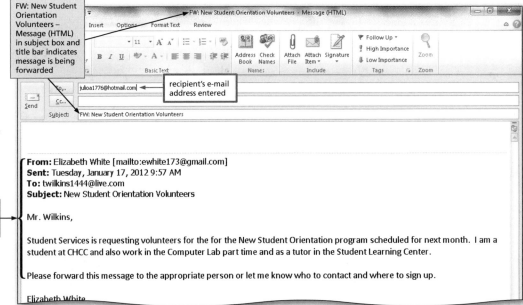

Figure 1–22

Q&A Why does the original message appear in the message area of the window?

By default, Outlook is configured to automatically display the original message below the new message area for all message replies and forwards.

• Click the message area above the original message text and then type **Julio,** as the greeting line.

• Press the ENTER key two times to enter a blank line before the message text.

• Type **I received the message below from Elizabeth White, a new student at CHCC. Because you have been working on the orientation program, could you please handle this request?** to enter the message text.

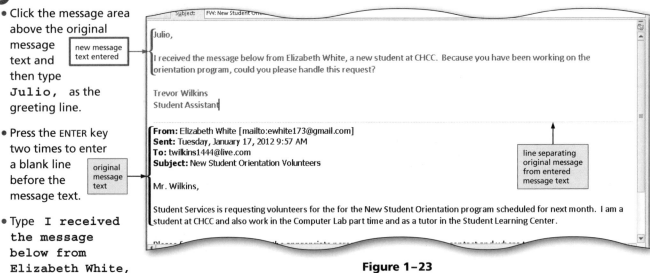

Figure 1–23

• Press the ENTER key two times to place a blank line between the message text and the signature lines.

• Type **Trevor Wilkins** as signature line 1 and then press the ENTER key to move the insertion point to the next line.

• Type **Student Assistant** as signature line 2 (Figure 1–23).

Other Ways

1. Right-click message header, click Forward

2. Click message header, press CTRL+F

Message Formats

As shown in Figure 1–23 on the previous page, Outlook's default (preset) message format is HTML (Hypertext Markup Language), which is a format that allows you to view pictures and text formatted with color and various fonts and font sizes. **Formatting** refers to changing the appearance of text in a document such as the font (typeface), font size, color, and alignment of the text in a document.

Before you send an original e-mail message, reply to an e-mail message, or forward an e-mail message, consider which message format you want to use. A message format determines whether an e-mail message can include pictures or formatted text, such as bold, italic, and colored fonts. Select a message format that is appropriate for your message and your recipient. Outlook offers three message formats: HTML, Plain Text, and Rich Text, summarized in Table 1–2. If you select the HTML format, for example, the e-mail program your recipient uses must be able to display formatted messages or pictures.

Table 1–2 Message Formats	
Message Format	**Description**
HTML	HTML format is the default format for new messages in Outlook. HTML lets you include pictures and basic formatting, such as text formatting, numbering, bullets, and alignment. HTML is the recommended format for Internet mail because the more popular e-mail programs use it.
Plain Text	Plain Text format is recognized by all e-mail programs and is the most likely format to be allowed through a company's virus-filtering program. Plain Text does not support basic formatting, such as bold, italic, colored fonts, or other text formatting. It also does not support pictures displayed directly in the message.
Rich Text	Rich Text Format (RTF) is a Microsoft format that only the latest versions of **Microsoft Exchange** (a Microsoft message system that includes an e-mail program and a mail server) and Outlook recognize. RTF supports more formats than HTML or Plain Text, as well as hyperlinks. A hyperlink can be text, a picture or other object that is displayed in an e-mail message.

Be aware of computer viruses and how they are spread.
Your message may be blocked by the recipient's e-mail server. Some e-mail servers are set up to automatically block messages in the HTML format using antivirus software. If you have concerns about whether the recipient's server is set up to block messages formatted as HTML, use Plain Text as the message format.

BTW

Using Plain Text Formatting to Guard Against E-Mail Viruses
Because HTML-formatted messages can contain viruses, minimize the risk of receiving a virus-infected e-mail message by changing the format of messages you read. You can configure Outlook to format all opened messages in Plain Text. Click File on the Ribbon to open the Backstage view. Click the Trust Center button in the Backstage view, and then click Trust Center Settings to display the Trust Center dialog box. Click the E-mail Security tab (Trust Center dialog box), and in the Read as Plain Text section, click the 'Read all standard mail in plain text' check box.

BTW

Inserting Hyperlinks
To insert a Web address in an e-mail message, click where you want to insert the hyperlink, and then click the Hyperlink button (Insert tab | Links group) to display the Insert Hyperlink dialog box. In the Address text box, type the Web address you want to insert as a hyperlink, and then click the OK button to insert the hyperlink into the message body.

Plan Ahead

To Change the Message Format and Send the Message

The next step in this project is to change the message format of the e-mail message before forwarding it to Julio Alvarez. You want to make sure that your reply is not blocked by an antivirus program, so you will change the message format to Plain Text. The following steps change the message format to Plain Text and then send the message.

1

- In the message window, click Format Text on the Ribbon to display the Format Text tab.

- Click the Plain Text button (Format Text tab | Format group) to select the Plain Text message format, which removes all formatting in the message (Figure 1–24).

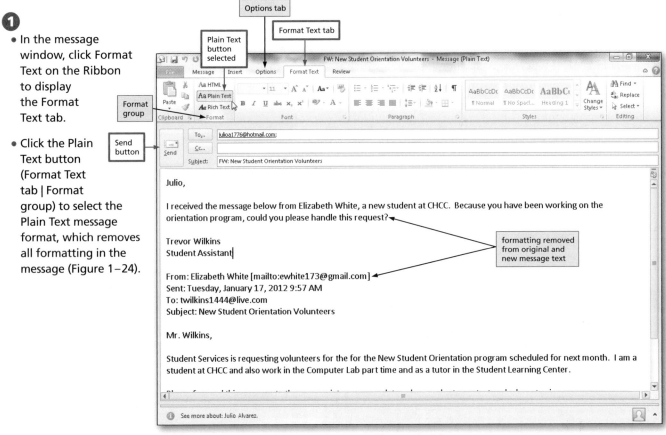

Figure 1–24

Q&A A warning message appeared after I completed Step 1. How should I respond?

Click the Continue button.

Q&A What happened to the line separating the existing message and the new message?

When Plain Text is selected as the message format, all formatting such as text color, font type, and size is removed.

Q&A Can I display additional fields in the message header?

Yes. Outlook allows you to display the From field and the Bcc field. To display these fields, click the Bcc button or the From button (Options tab | Show Fields group) to display the corresponding field(s). To hide a field, click the corresponding button again.

2

- Click the Send button in the message header to send the e-mail message and display the Inbox window.

Q&A Why did the envelope icon for this message change to an open envelope with a forward-pointing blue arrow?

The forward-pointing blue arrow indicates you forwarded the message. The status of the envelope icon represents your last action with the message.

To Delete an E-Mail Message

Now that you have forwarded Elizabeth White's message, you no longer need to keep it in your Inbox and you decide to delete it. When you delete a message from a folder, Outlook removes the message from the folder and moves it to the Deleted Items folder. The following steps delete the e-mail message from Elizabeth White.

1

- If necessary, click the Elizabeth White message header in the message list to select the e-mail message (Figure 1–25).

Q&A Why does the Navigation Pane contain two Deleted Items folders?

By default, Outlook automatically includes the Deleted Items in the Favorites section of the Navigation Pane.

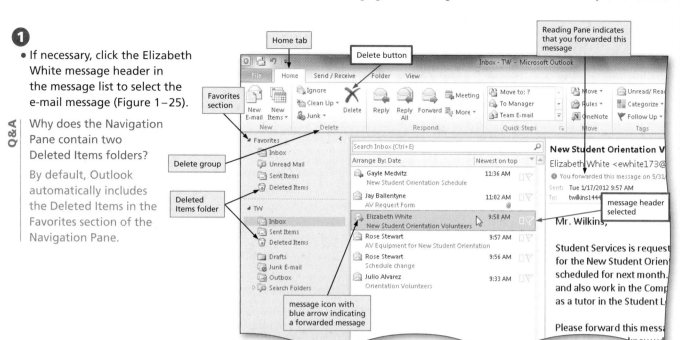

Figure 1–25

2

- Click the Delete button (Home tab | Delete group) to move the e-mail message from the current folder (Inbox, in this case) to the Deleted Items folder.

- If you want to verify the location of the deleted file, click the Deleted Items folder in the Navigation Pane to display the Deleted Items message list in the message pane, which shows all deleted e-mail messages (Figure 1–26).

Q&A Is the e-mail message permanently deleted when I click the Delete button?

No, after Outlook moves the e-mail message to the Deleted Items folder, it stores the deleted e-mail message in that folder until you permanently delete the message. One way to permanently delete a message is to select the Deleted Items folder to view its contents in the message pane and then select the item to be deleted. Click the Delete button (Home tab | Delete group), and then click the Yes button in the Microsoft Office Outlook dialog box to permanently delete the selected item from Outlook.

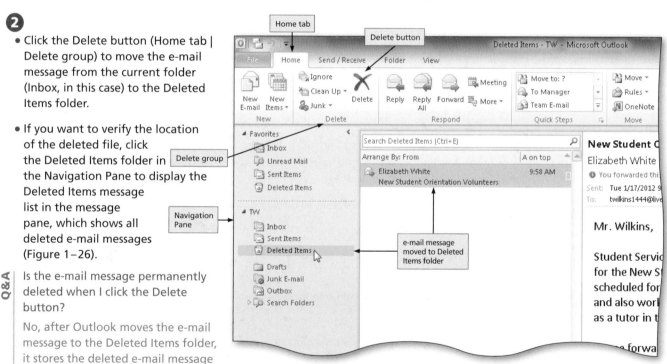

Figure 1–26

Other Ways
1. Drag selected e-mail message to Deleted Items folder   3. Click e-mail message, press CTRL+D
2. Click e-mail message, press DELETE

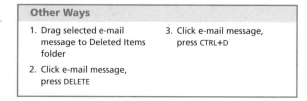

> **Break Point:** If you wish to take a break, this is a good place to do so. You can quit Outlook now (refer to page OUT 38 for instructions). To resume at a later time, start Outlook (refer to page OUT 6 for instructions), and then continue to follow the steps from this location forward.

BTW

Automatic Spelling Correction
As you type an e-mail message, Outlook automatically corrects some misspelled words. For example, if you type recieve, Word automatically corrects the misspelling and displays the word, receive, when you press the spacebar or type a punctuation mark. To see a complete list of automatically corrected words, click File on the Ribbon to open the Backstage view, click Options in the Backstage view, click Mail in the left pane (Outlook Options dialog box), click the Spelling and AutoCorrect button, click the Proofing tab, and then click the AutoCorrect Options button. Scroll through the list near the bottom of the dialog box.

BTW

BTWs
For a complete list of the BTWs found in the margins of this book, visit the Outlook 2010 BTW Web page (scsite.com/out2010/btw).

Spelling and Grammar Check

As you type text in an e-mail message, Outlook checks your typing for possible spelling and grammar errors and flags any potential errors in the message text with a red, green, or blue wavy underline. A red wavy underline means the flagged text is not in Outlook's main dictionary (because it is a proper name or misspelled). A green wavy underline indicates the text may be incorrect grammatically. A blue wavy underline indicates the text may contain a contextual spelling error such as the misuse of homophones (words that are pronounced the same but have different spellings or meanings, such as one and won). Although you can check the entire message for spelling and grammar errors at once, you also can check these flagged errors as they appear on the screen.

A flagged word is not necessarily misspelled. For example, many names, abbreviations, and specialized terms are not in Outlook's main dictionary. In these cases, you instruct Outlook to ignore the flagged word. As you type, Outlook also detects duplicate words while checking for spelling errors. For example, if your e-mail message contains the phrase, to the the store, Outlook places a red wavy underline below the second occurrence of the word, the.

The following pages illustrate how to ignore a correctly typed word and correct an incorrectly typed word in a reply to an e-mail message.

To Reply to an E-Mail Message

You are ready to reply to Gayle Medvitz's e-mail message and send her a copy of the orientation schedule, which now is complete. The following steps begin the reply to the e-mail message.

1 If necessary, click the Inbox folder to display its contents in the message list.

2 Click the Gayle Medvitz message header to select the e-mail message.

3 Click the Reply button (Home tab | Respond group) to send a second reply to Gayle Medvitz.

4 Maximize the message window to provide more room to work.

To Check the Spelling of a Correctly Typed Word

As you start typing the e-mail message, you will notice that Gayle Medvitz's last name has a red wavy line below it even though it is spelled correctly, indicating the word is not in Outlook's main dictionary. The following steps ignore the error and remove the red wavy line.

1

• Type **Ms. Medvitz,** as the greeting line and then press the ENTER key, which causes Outlook to place a red wavy line below the proper name (in this case, Medvitz) (Figure 1–27).

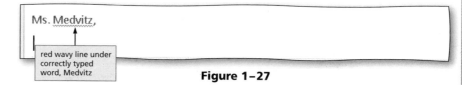

Ms. Medvitz,

red wavy line under correctly typed word, Medvitz

Figure 1–27

Q&A Why does a red wavy line appear below Medvitz even though it is spelled correctly?

Outlook places a red wavy line below any word that is not in the main dictionary when Outlook checks for spelling errors.

Q&A What if Outlook does not flag my spelling and grammar errors with wavy underlines?

To verify that the check spelling and grammar as you type features are enabled, click the File tab on the Ribbon to open the Backstage view and then click Options to display the Outlook Options dialog box. In the Compose messages section, click the Editor Options button to display the Editor Options dialog box. Click Proofing in the left pane (Editor Options dialog box). In the 'When correcting spelling in Outlook' section, ensure the 'Check spelling as you type' check box contains a check mark. Click the OK button two times to close each open dialog box.

2

• Right-click the proper name, Medvitz, to display a shortcut menu that presents a list of suggested spelling corrections for the flagged word, and then point to the Ignore command to prepare for selecting it (Figure 1–28).

Q&A What is the toolbar that appears above the shortcut menu?

The Mini toolbar appears when you right-click text by default and provides quick and easy access formatting options for the selected text.

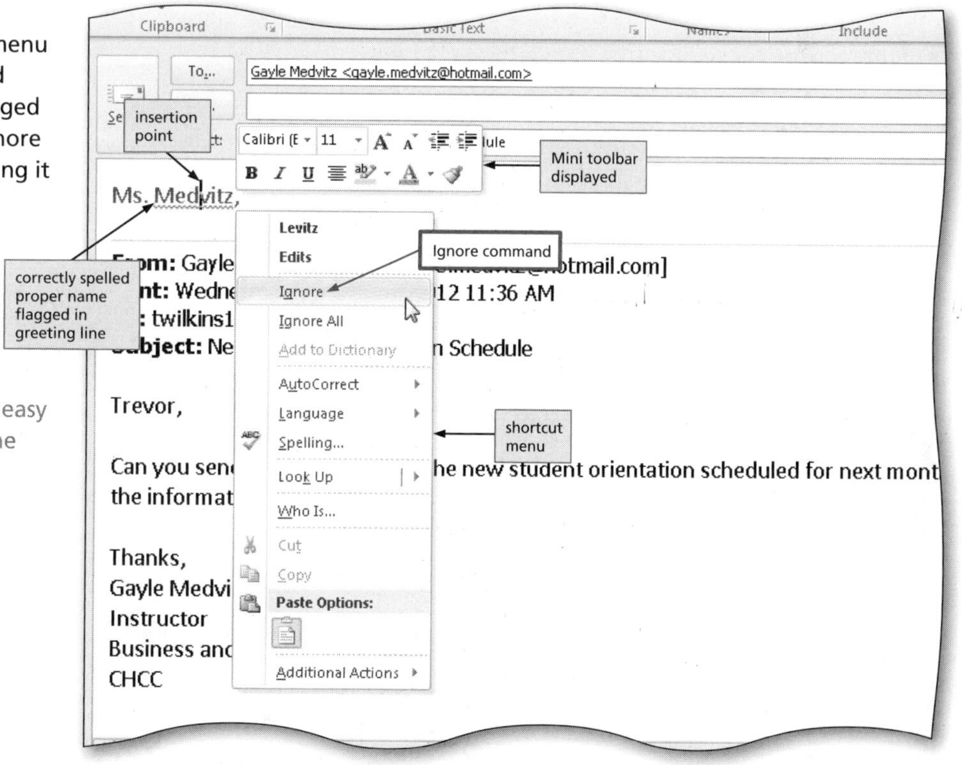

Clipboard | Basic Text | Name> | Include

To... Gayle Medvitz <gayle.medvitz@hotmail.com>

insertion point

Calibri (E ▾ 11 ▾ A˄ A˅ ≔ ≔ lule

Mini toolbar displayed

B *I* U̲ abℓ ▾ A̲ ▾ ✦

Ms. Medvitz,

Levitz

Edits

Ignore command

From: Gayle

nt: Wedne

: twilkins1

Subject: Ne

Ignore

Ignore All

Add to Dictionary

...tmail.com]

12 11:36 AM

n Schedule

correctly spelled proper name flagged in greeting line

Trevor,

AutoCorrect

Language

ABC Spelling...

shortcut menu

Can you sen Look Up he new student orientation scheduled for next mont

the informat

Who Is...

Thanks,

Gayle Medvi

Instructor

Business an

CHCC

Cut

Copy

Paste Options:

Additional Actions

shortcut menu

Figure 1–28

3

• Click Ignore on the shortcut menu to ignore this flagged error, close the shortcut menu, and remove the red wavy line beneath the name (in this case, Medvitz) (Figure 1–29).

Ms. Medvitz,

red wavy line removed

Figure 1–29

To Check the Spelling of Misspelled Text

In the following steps, the word, program, has been misspelled intentionally as profram to illustrate Outlook's check spelling as you type feature. If you are performing the steps in this project, your e-mail message may contain different misspelled words, depending on the accuracy of your typing. The following steps check the spelling of a misspelled word.

 1

- Press the DOWN ARROW key to move the insertion point to the blank paragraph below the greeting line.

- Press the ENTER key, type **The schedule for the new student orientation profram** to begin entering the message text, and then press the SPACEBAR so that a red wavy line appears below the misspelled word.

- Right-click the flagged word (profram, in this case) to display a shortcut menu that presents a list of suggested spelling corrections for the flagged word, and then point to program to prepare for selecting it (Figure 1–30).

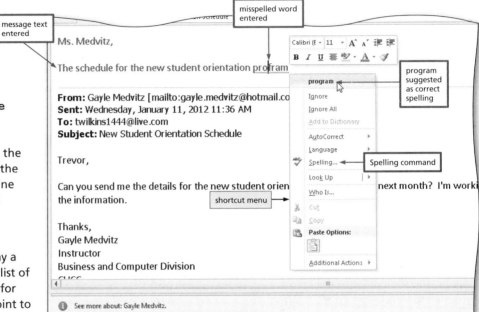

Figure 1–30

Q&A

What should I do if the correction I want to use is not in the list on the shortcut menu?

You can click outside the shortcut menu to close the shortcut menu and then retype the correct word, or you can click Spelling on the shortcut menu to display the Spelling dialog box.

 2

- Click program on the shortcut menu to replace the misspelled word in the e-mail message with a correctly spelled word (Figure 1–31).

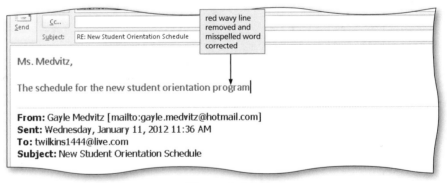

Figure 1–31

Other Ways
1. Click Review tab on Ribbon (message window), click Spelling and Grammar button (Review tab | Proofing group)
2. Press F7

To Enter More Text

In the e-mail message, the text yet to be entered includes the remainder of the message text and the signature lines. The following steps enter the remainder of the message text and signature lines.

1 Type `you requested is attached. Let me know if you have any questions.` to continue entering the message text.

2 Press the ENTER key two times to move the insertion point one blank line below the message text.

3 Type `Trevor Wilkins` as signature line 1.

4 Press the ENTER key and then type `Student Assistant` as signature line 2 (Figure 1–32).

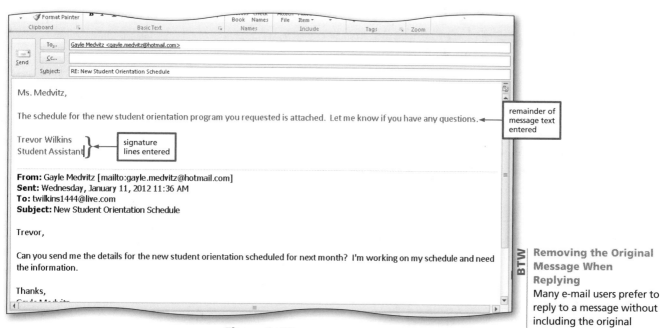

Figure 1–32

Saving and Closing an E-Mail Message

Occasionally, you begin composing a message but cannot complete the process. You may be waiting for information from someone else to include in the message, or you might prefer to complete the message later after you have time to evaluate its content. One option is to save the message, which stores the message in the Drafts folder until you are ready to send it. The Drafts folder is the default location for all saved messages.

BTW

Removing the Original Message When Replying
Many e-mail users prefer to reply to a message without including the original e-mail message along with their response. To remove the original message from *all* e-mail replies, click the File to open the Backstage view, and then click the Mail tab. In the Replies and forwards section, click the 'When replying to a message box' arrow, select the 'Do not include original message' option, and then click OK.

To Save and Close an E-Mail Message without Sending It

The orientation schedule that Gayle Medvitz requested still is being drafted, so you are not ready to send the e-mail message to her. The following steps save the RE: New Student Orientation Schedule – message in the Drafts folder for completion at a later time.

1

- Click the Save button on the Quick Access Toolbar to save the message in the Drafts folder (Figure 1–33).

Q&A How does Outlook know where to store the saved message?

The Drafts folder is the default folder where Outlook automatically stores all saved messages.

Q&A Can I save the message to a location other than the Drafts folder?

To save the message on a USB flash drive, click File on the Ribbon to open the Backstage view and then click Save As in the Backstage view to display the Save As dialog box. Click Computer to display a list of available devices and select a USB flash drive. In the File name text box, type the name of the message and then click the Save button.

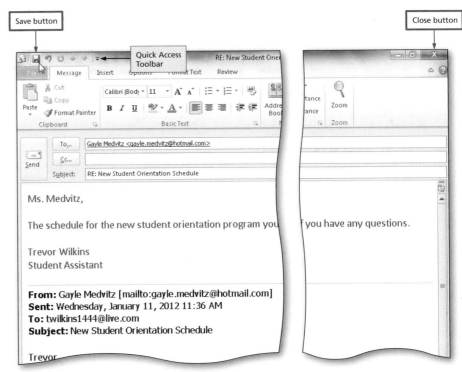

Figure 1–33

2

- Click the Close button on the title bar to close the RE: New Student Orientation Schedule - Message (HTML) window.

Q&A What happens if I click the Close button without saving the message?

If you create a message and then click the Close button, Outlook displays a dialog box asking you if you want to save the changes. If you click Yes, Outlook saves the file to the Drafts folder and closes the message window. If you click No, Outlook discards the e-mail message and closes the message window.

3

- If you want to view the saved message, click the Drafts folder to view any saved messages (Figure 1–34).

Q&A Do I need to view the messages in the Drafts folder?

No, they are stored in the Drafts folder until you need them.

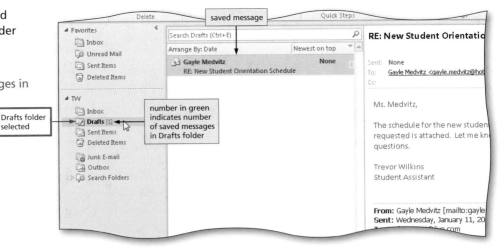

Figure 1–34

Other Ways

1. Click Close button, click Yes to keep saved draft of message
2. Press F12

Opening and Modifying a Saved E-Mail Message

The Word document containing the New Orientation Schedule that Gayle Medvitz requested has been completed. The next step is to modify the saved message to Gayle Medvitz by attaching the Word file. You also want to include Rose Stewart as a courtesy copy recipient. By including her e-mail address as a courtesy copy in the message header, Rose Stewart receives a copy of the message but is not the primary recipient. As such, she neither is required to reply nor is a reply expected from her.

To Open a Saved E-Mail Message

To complete the message to Gayle Medvitz, you first must open it. The following steps open the previously saved New Student Orientation Schedule message, located in the Drafts folder.

1

- If necessary, click the Drafts folder in the Mail folder list to display the message header for the Gayle Medvitz e-mail message in the message list (Figure 1–35).

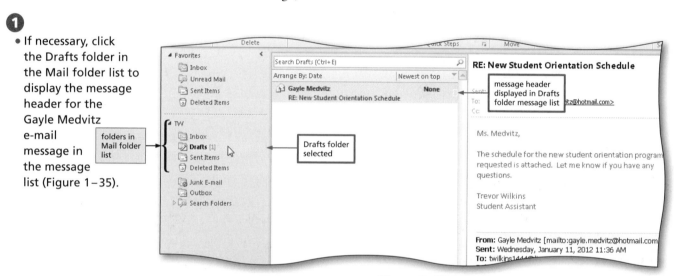

Figure 1–35

2

- Double-click the Gayle Medvitz message header in the Drafts folder to open the e-mail message (Figure 1–36).

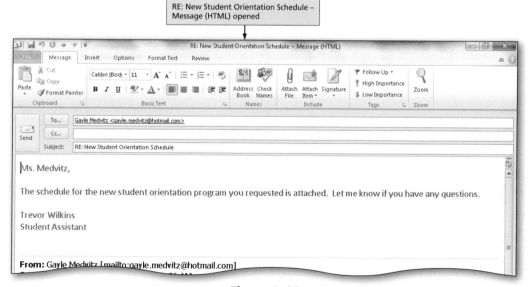

Figure 1–36

Other Ways

1. Right-click message, click Open

2. With message selected, press CTRL+O

To Include a Courtesy Copy Recipient in an E-Mail Message

The following step includes Rose Stewart as a courtesy copy recipient of the message to Gayle Medvitz.

1
- Click the Cc text box to select it and then type `rose.stewart@ hotmail.com` (with no spaces) to include a courtesy copy e-mail address in the message header (Figure 1–37).

Q&A

Why does Rose Stewart's complete e-mail address appear when I start typing the address?

As you type in the Cc text box, Outlook uses a feature called **AutoComplete**, which begins to suggest possible matches based on names you have typed before. Because you have typed Rose Stewart's e-mail address before, AutoComplete suggests the complete address before you finish typing. Press the ENTER key to add the suggested e-mail address to the Cc text box.

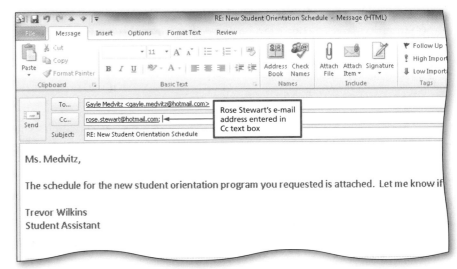

Figure 1–37

To Attach a File to an E-Mail Message

Many of the messages you receive and respond to are likely to contain an attachment, that is, a file such as a document or picture sent along with a message. You typically attach a file to an e-mail message to provide additional information to a recipient.

Before you send the e-mail message, you need to attach a file to the message to Gayle Medvitz to include the schedule she requested. The following steps attach a file to an e-mail message.

1
- Click the Attach File button (Message tab | Include group) to display the Insert File dialog box (Figure 1–38).

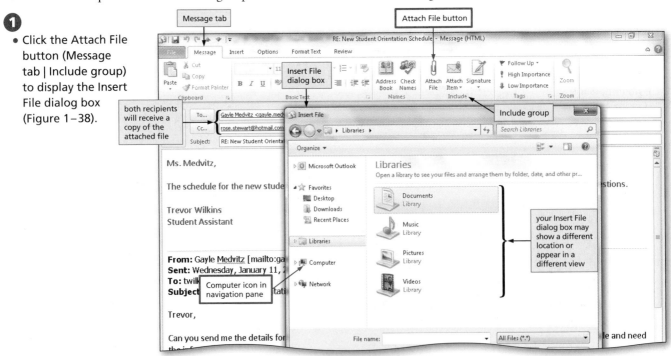

Figure 1–38

2

- If Computer is not displayed in the navigation pane, drag the navigation pane scroll bar (Insert File dialog box) until Computer appears.

- Click Computer in the navigation pane to display a list of available storage devices in the Insert File dialog box.

- If necessary, scroll through the Insert File dialog box until your USB flash drive appears in the list of available storage devices, and then click the USB flash drive to select it (Figure 1–39).

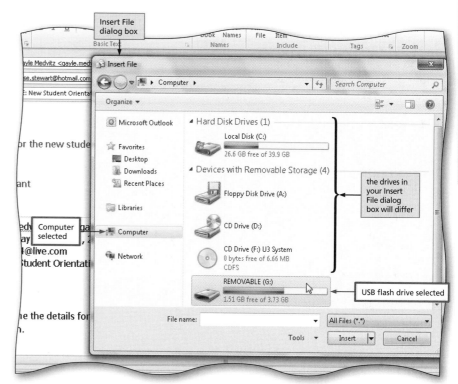

Figure 1–39

3

- Double-click your USB flash drive in the list of available storage devices to display a list of files and folders on the selected USB flash drive.

- If necessary, navigate to the folder containing the data files for this chapter, and then double-click that folder to open it and display the data files for this chapter.

- Click New Student Orientation Schedule to select the file to attach (Figure 1–40).

Why does my screen show .docx after the file name?

Windows does not display file name extensions by default, so your system has been changed to display the file extension with the name of the file. To change this, open a folder window. Press ALT+T to display the Tools menu. Click Folder options to open the Folder Options dialog box and then click the View tab. In the Advanced settings section, click the appropriate check box to hide or unhide the file extensions.

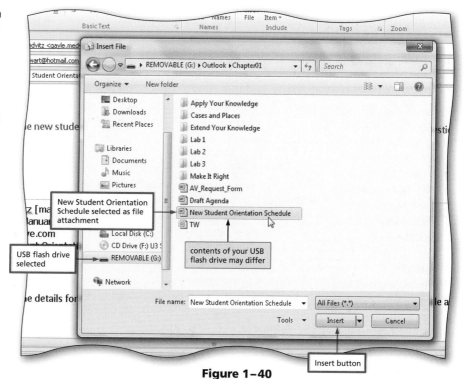

Figure 1–40

- Click the Insert button (Insert File dialog box) to attach the selected file to the e-mail message and close the Insert File dialog box (Figure 1–41).

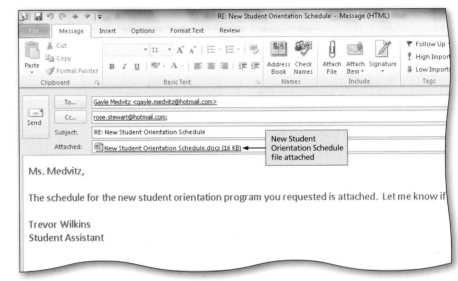

Other Ways

1. Click Insert tab, click Attach File button (Insert or Message tab | Include group)
2. Drag file to message area
3. Right-click file, click Copy, right-click message area, click Paste

Figure 1–41

To Set Message Importance for a Single E-Mail Message and Send the Message

Outlook provides the option to assign an **importance level** to a message, which indicates to the recipient the priority level of an e-mail message. The default importance level for all new messages is normal importance, but you can change the importance level to high or low, depending on the priority level of the e-mail message. A message sent with **high importance** displays a red exclamation point in the message header and indicates to the recipient that the message requires a higher priority than other messages he or she might have received. The **low importance** option displays with a blue arrow and indicates to the recipient a low priority for the message.

Your e-mail message to Gayle Medvitz and Rose Stewart requires their immediate attention so you decide to send the message with high importance. The following steps set the high importance option for a single e-mail message and then send the message.

1

- With the message to Gayle Medvitz and Rose Stewart open, click the High Importance button (Message tab | Tags group) to add a high importance level to the e-mail message (Figure 1–42).

Q&A

How would I set a low importance to an e-mail message?

Click the Low Importance button (Message tab | Tags group).

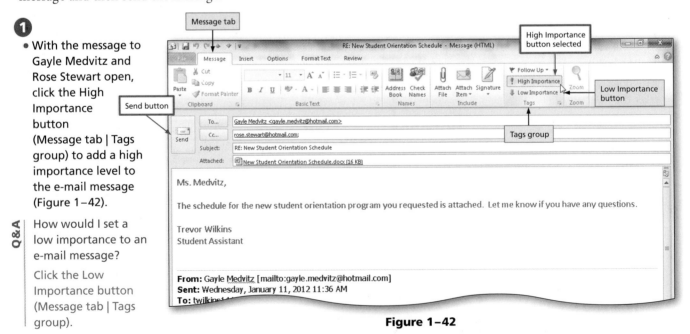

Figure 1–42

2

• Click the Send button in the message header to send the e-mail message.

◄ | **Q&A** | What happens to the e-mail message I just sent?

After Outlook closes the message window, it stores the e-mail message reply in the Outbox folder while it sends the message to the two recipients. You might not see the message in the Outbox because Outlook usually stores it there only briefly. Next, Outlook moves the message to the Sent Items folder. The original message in the message list now shows an open envelope icon with a purple arrow to indicate a reply was sent.

File Attachments

Users typically attach a file to an e-mail message to provide additional information to the recipient. The **Attachment Preview** feature in Outlook allows you to preview an attachment you receive in an e-mail message from either the Reading Pane in an unopened message or the message area of an opened message.

Outlook has built-in previewers for several file types, such as other Office programs, pictures, text, and Web pages. Outlook includes attachment previewers that work with other Microsoft Office programs so that users can preview an attachment without opening it. These attachment previewers are turned on by default. To preview an attached file created in an Office 2010 application, you must have that Office application installed on your computer. For example, to preview an Excel attachment in Outlook, you must have Excel installed. Third-party software vendors may provide previewers that support additional attachment file types.

The previewers in Microsoft Office 2010 are designed to provide additional security against potentially harmful code, allowing you to preview attachments more safely. Turning off the attachment previewers removes that layer of protection. Using Attachment Preview, you quickly can see the contents of the attachment without opening it, thus eliminating the need to save the attachment. If you do not have the program that was used to create the attached file, you cannot open an attachment.

If Outlook does not have a built-in previewer for an attachment's file type, Outlook displays a message explaining why it cannot preview the attachment. It also asks if you want to save the file and open it with the program in which it was created.

You should be aware of the limitations of Attachment Preview. For example, Outlook can preview attachments in the HTML or Plain Text message format, but not attachments formatted in Rich Text. In addition, you should preview or open attachments from trustworthy sources only. Sometimes, malicious code such as scripts, macros, and Active X controls is embedded in an e-mail message. For your protection, Outlook disables this type of active content when it previews a document. The Trust Center allows you to configure the way Outlook handles attachments.

BTW

Printing Attachments
You sometimes may want to print a file attached to an e-mail message you receive. To print an attachment, right-click the attachment to display the shortcut menu, and then click Quick Print.

BTW

Outlook Help
At any time while using Outlook, you can find answers to questions and display information about various topics through Outlook Help. Used properly, this form of assistance can increase your productivity and reduce your frustrations by minimizing the time you spend learning how to use Outlook. For instruction about Outlook Help and exercises that will help you gain confidence in using it, read the Introduction to Windows 7 and Office 2010 chapter at the beginning of this book.

To Preview and Save an Attachment

When you receive a message with an attachment, you can preview an attached file without opening it to see its contents. After Trevor Wilkins receives the e-mail message and attachment from Jay Ballentyne, he previews the contents of the attached file and then saves the attachment in a folder on his computer. The following steps preview and store the attachment from Jay Ballentyne.

1

- If necessary, click Inbox to display the TW Inbox.

- In the message list, click the message header from Jay Ballentyne with the AV Request Form subject line to select the e-mail message and display its contents in the Reading Pane (Figure 1–43).

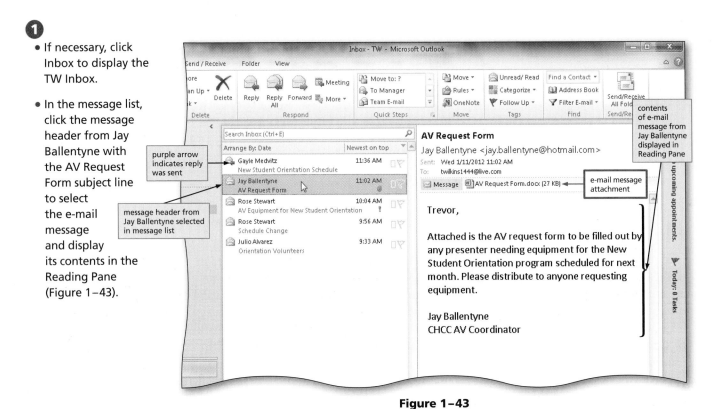

Figure 1–43

2

- In the Reading Pane, click the attachment to preview the document in the Reading Pane and display the Attachment Tools Attachments tab (Figure 1–44).

Q&A What if I do not have a message from Jay Ballentyne in my Inbox?

If you sent the message with the AV Request Form attachment to yourself, that message should appear in your Inbox. Otherwise, you can read but not perform these steps.

Figure 1–44

3

- Click the Save As button (Attachment Tools Attachments tab | Actions group) to display the Save Attachment dialog box.

- If Computer is not displayed in the navigation pane, drag the navigation pane scroll bar (Save Attachment dialog box) until Computer appears.

- Click Computer in the navigation pane to display a list of available storage devices in the Save Attachment dialog box.

- If necessary, scroll through the Save Attachment dialog box until your USB flash drive appears in the list of available storage devices.

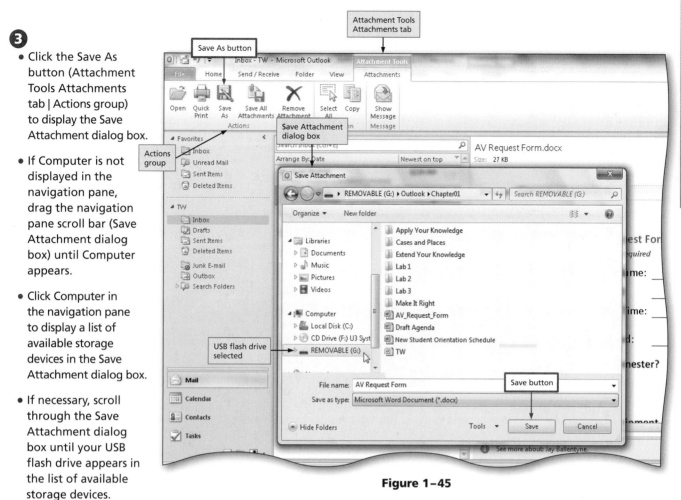

Figure 1–45

- Double-click your USB flash drive to display a list of files and folders on the selected USB flash drive.

- If necessary, navigate to the folder containing the files for this chapter, and then double-click that folder to open it (Figure 1–45).

4

- Click the Save button (Save Attachment dialog box) to save the attached file and close the Save Attachment dialog box.

Q&A After I save the attachment, is there a way to keep the e-mail message but not the attachment?

Yes, click the attachment in the Reading Pane and then click the Remove Attachment button (Attachment Tools Attachments tab | Actions group) to remove the attachment from the e-mail message.

Other Ways

1. Right-click attachment, click Save As

Using Outlook Folders to Organize the Inbox

Keeping track of incoming messages and other Outlook items can be a challenge, especially if you receive many e-mail messages. Outlook provides a basic set of **folders**, which are containers that store Outlook items of a specific type, such as messages, appointments, or contacts. For example, the Inbox is a mail folder created to store e-mail messages. One way to organize your Outlook items is to create folders. The process for creating folders in Outlook is similar to that for creating folders in Windows.

To Create a New Folder in the Inbox Folder

You anticipate receiving several messages throughout the semester from faculty and classmates and want to create a folder in the Inbox folder, known as a subfolder, to store these e-mail messages. The following steps create a subfolder called Volunteers in Trevor Wilkins' Inbox folder.

1

- If it is not already selected, click the Inbox folder to select it.

- Click the Folder tab on the Ribbon to display the Folder tab commands.

- Click the New Folder button (Folder tab | New group) to display the Create New Folder dialog box (Figure 1–46).

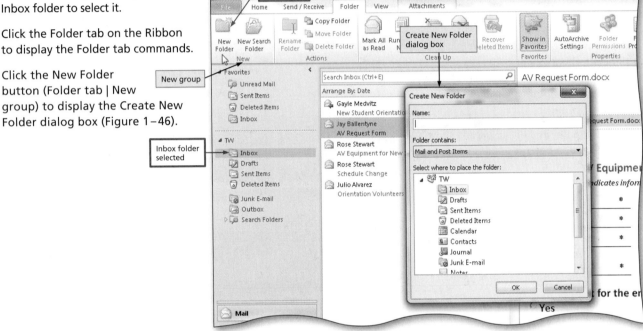

Figure 1–46

2

- Type **Volunteers** as the subfolder name in the Name text box.

- If Mail and Post Items is not already selected, click the Folder contains button arrow and then click Mail and Post Items to place only e-mail messages in the new folder.

- If necessary, click Inbox in the 'Select where to place the folder' list to place the new folder in the selected folder (in this case, Inbox) (Figure 1–47).

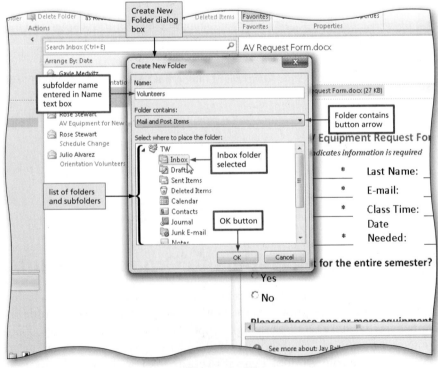

Figure 1–47

3

- Click the OK button to create the Volunteers folder and close the Create New Folder dialog box (Figure 1–48).

Q&A Why is the Volunteers folder indented below the Inbox folder?

A folder within a folder is called a subfolder. When you create a subfolder, Outlook indents the folder in the list to indicate that it is a subfolder of a main folder.

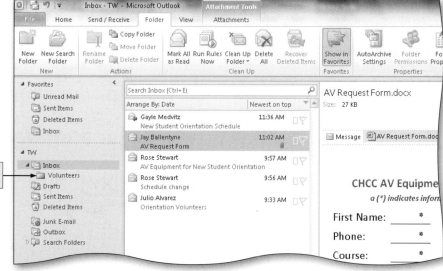

Figure 1–48

Other Ways

1. Right-click folder in Folder pane, click New Folder

To Move an E-Mail Message to a Folder

With the folder for e-mail messages regarding volunteers created, the next step is to move messages about volunteers to that folder. Specifically, you will move the message from Julio Alvarez from the Inbox folder to the Volunteers folder. In this case, the Inbox folder is called the source folder, and the Volunteers folder is called the destination folder. A **source folder** is the location of the document or message to be moved or copied. A **destination folder** is the location where you want to move or copy the file or message. The following steps move the message from Julio Alvarez to the Volunteers folder.

1

- Click Home on the Ribbon to display the Home tab.

- In the Inbox folder (source folder), click the message header from Julio Alvarez in the Inbox message list to select the e-mail message.

- Click the Move button (Home tab | Move group) to display the Move menu (Figure 1–49).

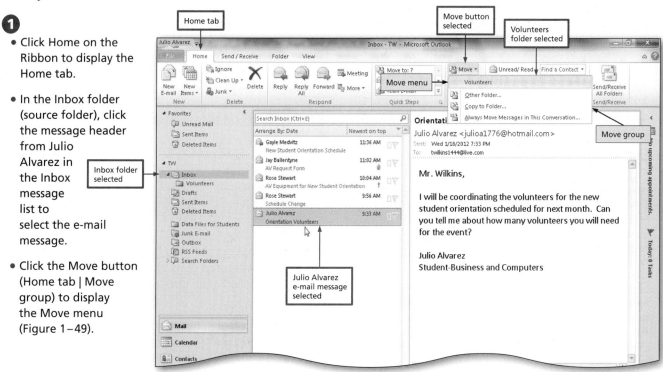

Figure 1–49

2

- Click Volunteers on the Move menu to move the selected message from the source folder (Inbox folder, in this case) to the destination folder (Volunteers folder, in this case).

- In the Navigation Pane, click the Volunteers folder to display its contents (Figure 1–50).

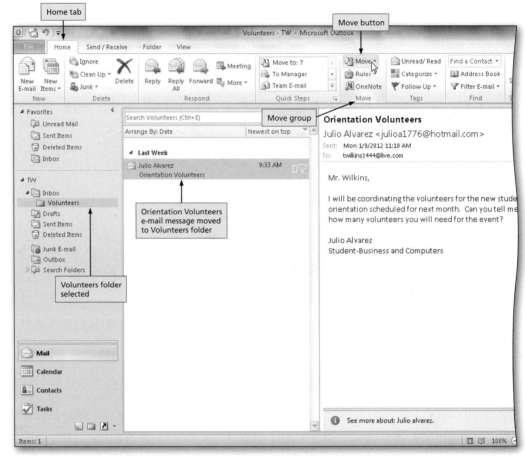

Figure 1–50

Q&A

Can I move more than one message at a time?

Yes. Click the first message to select it. While holding the CTRL key, click additional messages to select them. Click the Move button (Home tab | Move group) and then click the destination folder to select it.

Q&A

Can I copy the e-mail messages instead of moving them?

Yes. Select the message(s) to copy and click the Move button (Home tab | Move group). Click Copy to Folder on the menu to display the Copy Items dialog box. Select the destination folder (the folder you want to copy the e-mail message to) and then click the OK button to copy the selected message to the destination folder.

Other Ways

1 Right-click selected message, point to Move, click folder

BTW

Certification
The Microsoft Office Specialist program provides an opportunity for you to obtain a valuable industry credential — proof that you have the Outlook 2010 skills required by employers. For more information, visit the Outlook 2010 Certification Web page (scsite.com/ out2010/cert).

To Quit Outlook

This project now is complete. The following step quits Outlook. For a detailed example of the procedure summarized below, refer to the Office 2010 and Windows 7 chapter at the beginning of this book.

1 If you have an e-mail message open, click the Close button on the right side of the title bar to close the message window and then click the Close button on the right side of the Inbox – TW – Microsoft Outlook to close the message window and quit Outlook.

Chapter Summary

In this chapter, you learned how to use Outlook to read, open, print, reply to, forward, format, delete, save, and send e-mail messages. You viewed and saved file attachments as well as attached a file to an e-mail message. You learned how to add a courtesy copy to an e-mail message and set the importance of e-mail messages. Finally, you created a folder in the Inbox and moved an e-mail message to the new folder. The items listed below include all the new Outlook skills you have learned in this chapter.

1. Start Outlook (OUT 6)
2. Compose and Send an E-Mail Message (OUT 8)
3. Read an E-Mail Message in the Reading Pane (OUT 14)
4. Open an E-Mail Message in a Window (OUT 14)
5. Close an E-Mail Message (OUT 15)
6. Print an E-Mail Message (OUT 15)
7. Print Multiple Copies of an E-Mail Message (OUT 17)
8. Reply to an E-Mail Message (OUT 17)
9. Forward an E-Mail Message (OUT 19)
10. Change the Message Format and Send the Message (OUT 21)
11. Delete an E-Mail Message (OUT 22)
12. Reply to an E-Mail Message (OUT 24)
13. Check the Spelling of a Correctly Typed Word (OUT 24)
14. Check the Spelling of Misspelled Text (OUT 26)
15. Enter More Text (OUT 27)
16. Save and Close an E-Mail Message without Sending It (OUT 27)
17. Open a Saved E-Mail Message (OUT 29)
18. Include a Courtesy Copy Recipient in an E-Mail Message (OUT 30)
19. Attach a File to an E-Mail Message (OUT 30)
20. Set Message Importance for a Single E-Mail Message and Send the Message (OUT 32)
21. Preview and Save an Attachment (OUT 33)
22. Create a New Folder in the Inbox Folder (OUT 36)
23. Move an E-Mail Message to a Folder (OUT 37)
24. Quit Outlook (OUT 38)

 If you have a SAM 2010 user profile, your instructor may have assigned an autogradable version of this assignment. If so, log into the SAM 2010 Web site at www.cengage.com/sam2010 to download the instruction and start files.

BTW

Quick Reference
For a table that lists how to complete the tasks covered in this book using the mouse, Ribbon, shortcut menu, and keyboard, see the Quick Reference Summary at the back of this book, or visit the Outlook 2010 Quick Reference Web page (scsite.com/out2010/qr).

Learn It Online

Test your knowledge of chapter content and key terms.

Instructions: To complete the Learn It Online exercises, start your browser, click the Address bar, and then enter the Web address **scsite.com/out2010/learn**. When the Outlook 2010 Learn It Online page is displayed, click the link for the exercise you want to complete and then read the instructions.

Chapter Reinforcement TF, MC, and SA
A series of true/false, multiple choice, and short answer questions that test your knowledge of the chapter content.

Flash Cards
An interactive learning environment where you identify chapter key terms associated with displayed definitions.

Practice Test
A series of multiple choice questions that test your knowledge of chapter content and key terms.

Who Wants To Be a Computer Genius?
An interactive game that challenges your knowledge of chapter content in the style of the television quiz show.

Wheel of Terms
An interactive game that challenges your knowledge of chapter key terms in the style of the television show *Wheel of Fortune*.

Crossword Puzzle Challenge
A crossword puzzle that challenges your knowledge of key terms presented in the chapter.

Apply Your Knowledge

Reinforce the skills and apply the concepts you learned in this chapter.

Creating an E-Mail Message with an Attachment

Note: To complete this assignment, you will be required to use the Data Files for Students. See the inside back cover of this book for instructions on downloading the Data Files for Students, or contact your instructor for information about accessing the required files.

Instructions: Start Outlook. You are to send an e-mail addressed to selected customers of Hickory Ridge Day Care for Pets who might be interested in boarding their pets. You also attach a file named Day Care for Pets Flyer from the Data Files for Students.

Perform the following tasks:

1. Create a new e-mail message addressed to your instructor and enter `Hickory Ridge Day Care for Pets Bulletin` as the subject.

2. Enter `Greetings,` as the greeting line, checking spelling as you type.

3. Insert a blank line, and then enter `Hickory Ridge Day Care for Pets would like to acquaint you with our newly upgraded facility. We have expanded our facilities to include a climate controlled playroom and a security system to monitor our facility 24/7. Please stop by with your pet any time between 7 am and 5 pm for a visit. We would love to see you and your pet.` as the message text, checking spelling as you type.

4. Enter your name as the signature.

5. Attach the Day Care for Pets Flyer file to the e-mail message.

6. Save the e-mail message on a USB flash drive using the file name, Day Care for Pets Bulletin. Submit the e-mail message, shown in Figure 1–51, in the format specified by your instructor.

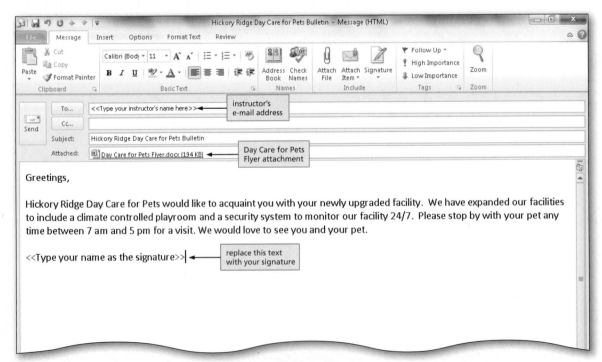

Figure 1–51

Extend Your Knowledge

Extend the skills you learned in this chapter and experiment with new skills. You may need to use Help to complete the assignment.

Managing E-Mail Messages

Note: To complete this assignment, you will be required to use the Data Files for Students. See the inside back cover of this book for instructions on downloading the Data Files for Students, or contact your instructor for information about accessing the required files.

Instructions: Start Outlook. Open the Extend 1-1.pst mailbox file from the Data Files for Students. You will create three folders, rename the folders, and then move messages into the appropriate folders. You also will apply a follow-up flag for the messages in one of the folders. Use Outlook Help to learn about how to add a flag to a message for follow-up and how to create an Outlook Data File (.pst).

Perform the following tasks:

1. Create three new subfolders in the Inbox folder. Name one folder New folder 1, another folder New folder 2, and the third folder New folder 3. Make sure that only mail items are contained in the new folders.

2. In the Navigation Pane, rename the newly created folders. Rename New folder 1 to USB Problems. Rename New folder 2 to Monitor Problems. Rename New folder 3 to Printer Problems. (*Hint:* To rename the folders, right-click the folder you want to rename in the Navigation Pane to open a shortcut menu. Select Rename Folder on the shortcut menu. Type the new name of the folder, and then press the ENTER key).

3. Based on the message headers and content of the e-mail messages in the Extend 1-1 mailbox, move each message to one of the folders you created. Figure 1–52 shows the mailbox with the messages moved to the new folders.

4. In the Monitor Problems folder, assign a flag for follow-up for next week to all messages.

5. Export the Inbox mailbox to an Outlook data file (.pst) on a USB flash drive using the file name, Extend 1-1.pst, and then submit it in the format specified by your instructor.

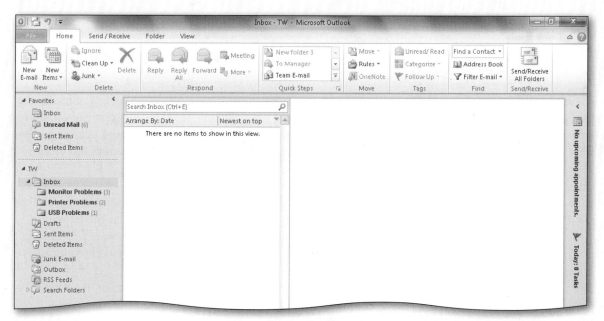

Figure 1–52

Make It Right

Analyze a document and correct all errors and/or improve the design.

Correcting Errors and Changing the Format of an E-Mail Message

Note: To complete this assignment, you will be required to use the Data Files for Students. See the inside back cover of this book for instructions on downloading the Data Files for Students, or contact your instructor for information about accessing the required files.

Instructions: In a folder window, open the message file, Make It Right 1-1.msg, from the Data Files for Students. Outlook starts and opens the message. The Dietary Needs for the Upcoming Conference message contains spelling errors. To see the red wavy line under the misspelled words, click at the end of the message and press the SPACEBAR. The e-mail message was sent using the HTML message format, as shown in Figure 1-53.

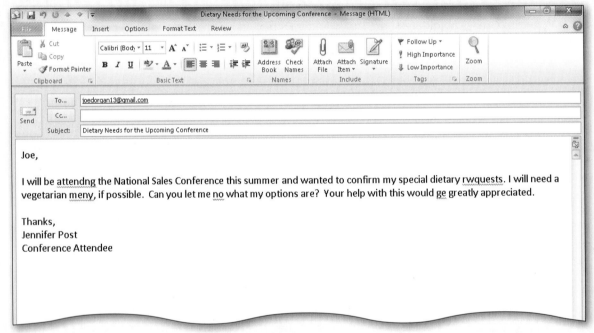

Figure 1-53

If you received the message as Plain Text, change the message format to HTML. Recheck the spelling and grammar errors by pressing F7 to open the Spelling and Grammar dialog box, clicking the Options button, clicking the Recheck E-mail button, and then clicking Yes. Then correct each spelling (red wavy underline) and grammar error (green or blue wavy underlines). In most cases, you can make the correction by right-clicking the flagged text and then clicking the appropriate correction on the shortcut menu. In some cases, however, you may need to make the correction by hand. If your screen does not display the wavy underlines, click the File tab on the Ribbon to open the Backstage view, and then click Options to display the Outlook Options dialog box. In the Compose messages section, click the Editor Options button to display the Editor Options dialog box. Click Proofing in the left pane (Editor Options dialog box). In the 'When correcting spelling in Outlook' section, ensure the 'Check spelling as you type' check box and the 'Mark grammar errors as you type' check box each contains a check mark. Click the OK button two times.

Change the format of the e-mail message to Plain Text, and then send the message to yourself. Save the message on a USB flash drive as Make It Right 1-1.msg, and then submit it in the format specified by your instructor.

In the Lab

Design and/or create an e-mail message using the guidelines, concepts, and skills presented in this chapter. Labs are listed in order of increasing difficulty.

Lab 1: Composing and Saving an E-Mail Message with High Importance

Problem: After returning from an illness that required you to miss a class at school, you need to contact your instructor. Create an e-mail message to your instructor requesting information about missed class assignments and change the message format to Plain Text. Because you need this information immediately, send the e-mail message with high importance. Also, send a Cc (courtesy copy) to yourself. Figure 1–54 shows the completed e-mail message.

Instructions: Perform the following tasks:

1. Open the Untitled – Message window to create a new e-mail message.

2. Address the e-mail message to your instructor and send a Cc (courtesy copy) to yourself.

3. Type **Missed Class Assignments** as the subject.

4. Change the format of the message to Plain Text.

5. Type the message text as shown in Figure 1–54, inserting blank lines where they appear in the figure. Use your name as the signature. If Outlook flags any misspelled words as you type, check their spelling and correct them.

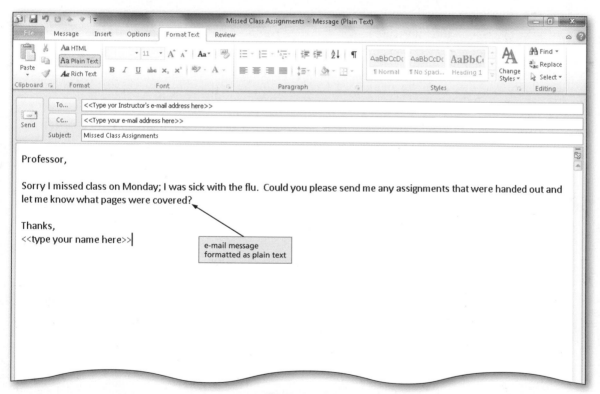

Figure 1–54

6. Apply High Importance to this message and send the message.

7. Save the message in the Drafts folder.

8. Save the message on a USB flash drive as Missed Class Assignments.msg, and then submit it in the format specified by your instructor.

In the Lab

Lab 2: Composing and Sending, and Replying to an E-Mail Message

Problem: As a part-time employee in the Computer Help Center for your school, you have been asked to compile a list of keyboard shortcuts for Outlook 2010. First, you compose the e-mail message shown in Figure 1–55, and then you attach a file. The document to be attached is named Outlook 2010 Keyboard Shortcuts.

Note: To complete this assignment, you may be required to use the Data Files for Students. See the inside back cover of this book for instructions on downloading the Data Files for Students, or contact your instructor for information about accessing the required files.

Instructions: Perform the following tasks:

1. Create a new e-mail message. Address the message to yourself with a courtesy copy to your instructor.

2. Enter the subject, message text, and signature shown in Figure 1–55a. Insert blank lines where they are shown in the figure. If Outlook flags any misspelled words as you type, check their spelling and correct them.

3. Attach the Outlook 2010 Keyboard Shortcuts file to the e-mail message.

4. Send the e-mail message with high importance and use the HTML format for the message.

5. When you receive the Keyboard Shortcuts for Outlook 2010 e-mail message, move it to a new folder in your Inbox named Shortcuts.

6. Open the message in the Shortcuts folder, and then compose the reply. Figure 1–55b shows a reply from a student named Dana Cooper to a student named Heather Moore. Copy the text of the e-mail message shown in Figure 1–55b, but replace Heather's e-mail address with your own. Be sure to remove your instructor's e-mail address from the Cc text box, if necessary. If Outlook flags any misspelled words as you type, check their spelling and correct them.

7. If necessary, change the format of the e-mail message to Plain Text, and then send the message to yourself.

8. When you receive the RE: Keyboard Shortcuts for Outlook 2010 message, move it to the Shortcuts folder in your Inbox folder.

9. Save the e-mail message on a USB flash drive using your last name plus *Lab 2* as the file name. For example, if your last name is Smith, the file name would be Smith Lab 2.msg. Submit the file in the format specified by your instructor.

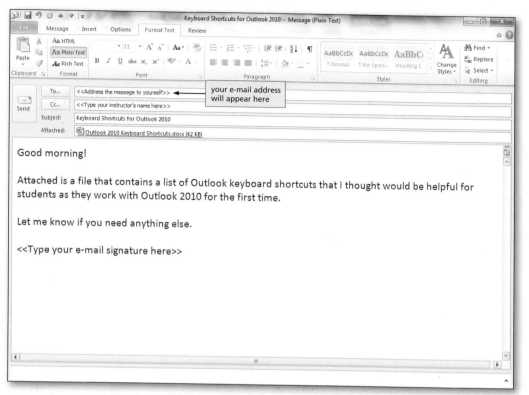

Figure 1–55 (a)

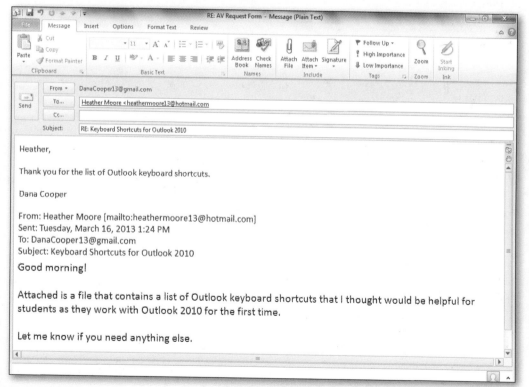

Figure 1–55 (b)

In the Lab

Lab 3: Creating and Sending an E-Mail Message to Several People

Problem: Your boss at Maple Valley Bakery has asked you to send e-mail messages to a few new customers inviting them to a pastry and coffee event the bakery is hosting. For one e-mail message, you need to attach a document named Maple Valley Bakery Flyer. You prepare the e-mail messages shown in Figure 1–56.

Note: To complete this assignment, you may be required to use the Data Files for Students. See the inside back cover of this book for instructions on downloading the Data Files for Students, or contact your instructor for information about accessing the required files.

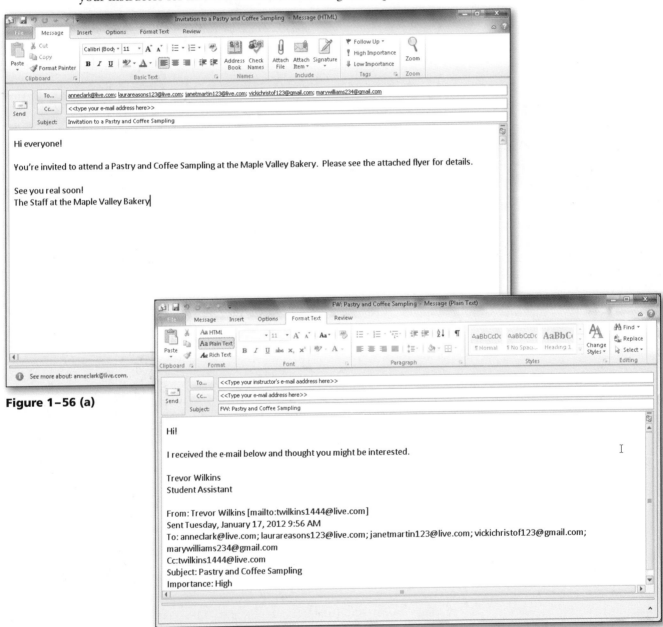

Figure 1–56 (a)

Figure 1–56 (b)

Instructions: Perform the following tasks:

1. Create a new e-mail message. Address the message to the following recipients:

   anneclark@live.com

   laurareasons123@live.com

   janetmartin123@live.com

   vickichristof123@gmail.com

   marywilliams234@gmail.com

2. Enter your e-mail address so that you send a courtesy copy to yourself.

3. Enter the subject, message text, and signature shown in Figure 1–56a. Insert blank lines where they are shown in the figure. If Outlook flags any misspelled words as you type, check their spelling and correct them.

4. Attach the Maple Valley Bakery Flyer document to the e-mail message.

5. Save the e-mail message in the Drafts folder.

6. Send the e-mail message with high importance and use the HTML format for the message.

7. When you receive the Invitation to a Pastry and Coffee Sampling e-mail message, move it to a new folder in your Inbox named Events.

8. Select the message in the Events folder, and then forward to your instructor the message shown in Figure 1–56b. If Outlook flags any misspelled words as you type, check their spelling and correct them.

9. If necessary, change the format of the e-mail message to Plain Text, and then send yourself a courtesy copy.

10. Save the response e-mail message on a USB flash drive using your last name plus *Lab 3* as the file name. For example, if your last name is Smith, the file name would be Smith Lab 3.msg. Submit the file in the format specified by your instructor.

Cases and Places

Apply your creative thinking and problem solving skills to design and implement a solution.

Note: To complete these assignments, you may be required to use the Data Files for Students. See the inside back cover of this book for instructions on downloading the Data Files for Students, or contact your instructor for information about accessing the required files.

1: Compose, Print, and Send a Message for a Campus Event

Academic

As an employee of the student union, you are responsible for creating and sending e-mail messages informing student leaders about upcoming lectures and presentations at the union. This month, the union has two lectures and one presentation scheduled. The presentation is about travel in Washington, DC. The e-mail message should include an attachment of a digital photo. The Data Files for Students contain a photo named DC.jpg or you can use your own digital photo if it is appropriate for the topic of the e-mail message. The e-mail message should be addressed to yourself and your instructor. The subject should contain the text, Spring Lectures at the Union. The message text consists of the following, in any order: The student union is sponsoring three events in its lecture series on our nation's capital this month. Enjoy a panoramic presentation about tourism in Washington, DC.

Continued >

Cases and Places *continued*

Experience the varieties of culinary offerings. Learn about the upcoming festivals and cultural events throughout the Washington, DC, metropolitan area. Use the concepts and techniques presented in this chapter to create this e-mail message. Be sure to check spelling and grammar before you send the message. Submit your assignment in the format specified by your instructor.

2: Compose an E-Mail Message to a Relative or Friend and Attach a File

Personal

Being involved with your studies, extracurricular activities, and college life in general can limit the time you have to communicate with family and friends. Compose and send an e-mail message to a close relative or friend. The e-mail message should contain information about your class schedule, activities, and new friends that you have made. Attach a picture of the school to the message. You can use the file College.jpg or you can use your own digital photo of your school. Compose the message in HTML format. The subject should be Campus Life or you can use your own subject. The message text consists of at least the following information: This semester I am taking 15 credits, so my schedule is very full. I also am involved in the Student Government Association. I met a student who went to high school in a neighboring town, and we found we have many mutual friends. Attached is a picture of one of our buildings so you can get a sense of how beautiful the campus is. Add a greeting line, closing, and other appropriate text. Use the concepts and techniques presented in this chapter to create this e-mail message. Be sure to check spelling and grammar before you send the message. Submit your assignment in the format specified by your instructor.

3: Forward an E-Mail Message to Multiple Recipients Informing Them about an Event

Professional

As an IT recruiter for local executive search firm, you receive many e-mail messages regarding job and career fairs throughout your community. You recently received an e-mail message, IT Recruitment Fair. msg, inviting you to attend an employment fair sponsored by the Chamber of Commerce and held at a local high school. The Career Fair also provides job seekers with a free résumé review service and access to a job search database. More than 100 employers representing various industries will be represented and attending would be a wonderful networking opportunity. Your schedule is full and you cannot attend. The e-mail message asks that you forward the invitation to anyone you think might be interested in attending. In a folder window, open the message file IT Recruitment Fair.msg from the Data Files for Students in the Cases and Places folder. Replace nikitanner123@gmail.com in the To box with your own e-mail address and send the e-mail message to yourself. Now you can forward the e-mail message to your coworkers.

Forward the e-mail message to three coworkers who you think might benefit from attending, telling them about the benefits of such an event. Their e-mail addresses are as follows:

davidclark@live.com

angelareasons123@live.com

marcimartin123@live.com

Send a courtesy copy to your boss, in case she might want to send additional people to the event or perhaps attend the event herself. Her e-mail address is susanwilliams234@gmail.com.

Print the forwarded message and submit it in the format specified by your instructor.

2 | Managing Calendars

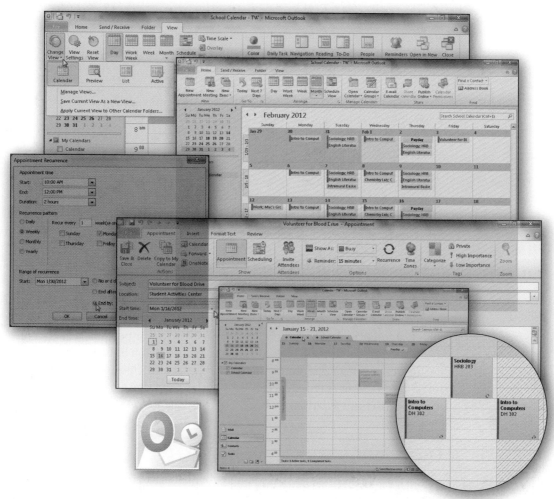

Objectives

You will have mastered the material in this chapter when you can:

- Open the Calendar folder

- Describe the components of the Outlook Calendar

- Navigate the Calendar using the Date Navigator

- View specific dates on the Date Navigator

- Create a personal calendar

- Enter, save, move, edit, and delete appointments

- Set the status of and a reminder for an appointment

- Create and edit events

- Move and delete events

- Create and edit meetings and respond to meeting requests

- Display the calendar in Day, Work Week, Week, and Month views

- Print the calendar in Daily Style

2 | Managing Calendars

Introduction

Whether you are a student at a local college, an activity coordinator in your community, or a business professional, you can take advantage of the Outlook Calendar to schedule and manage appointments, events, and meetings. In particular, you can use Calendar to keep track of your class schedule and appointments, and to schedule meetings. If you are traveling and do not have electronic access to your calendar, you can print a copy to keep with you. You can use Outlook to view or print a daily, weekly, or monthly calendar.

In addition to using Calendar in your academic or professional life, you will find it helpful for scheduling personal time. Most people have multiple appointments to keep each day, week, or month. Calendar can organize activity-related information in a structured, readable manner.

Project — Appointments, Events, and Meetings in Calendar

Time management is a part of everyday life. Many people constantly are rearranging appointments, work schedules, and vacations in an attempt to use their time efficiently. Managing your schedule using a calendar can increase productivity, while maximizing free time. Outlook is the perfect tool to maintain both a professional and a personal schedule. The **Calendar** is the Outlook folder that contains your personal schedule of appointments, events, and meetings. In this project, you use the basic features of Calendar to create a calendar for appointments, classes, work schedules, and extracurricular activities for Trevor Wilkins (Figure 2–1). In addition to creating a calendar for Trevor, you will learn how to print a daily, weekly, or monthly calendar.

Overview

As you read through this chapter, you will learn how to create the calendar shown in Figure 2–1 by performing these general tasks:

- Enter appointments on specific dates.
- Create one-time and recurring appointments.
- Move appointments to new dates.
- Create one-time and recurring events.
- Schedule a meeting with others.
- Respond to a meeting request.
- View and print the calendar.

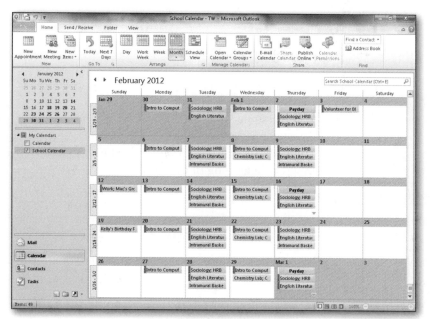

Figure 2–1

General Project Guidelines

When creating a calendar, the actions you perform and decisions you make will affect the appearance and characteristics of the finished calendar. As you create an appointment, event, or meeting to develop a schedule, you should follow these general guidelines:

Plan
Ahead

1. **Determine what you need to schedule.** People use a calendar to keep track of their schedule and to organize and manage their time. For students, a class list with room numbers and class times would be a good start toward managing their school schedule. For business professionals, the calendar is a dynamic tool that requires frequent updating to keep track of appointments and meetings. You also may want to keep track of personal items, such as birthdays and family gatherings.

2. **Determine where to store your calendar items.** Any information you add to the Outlook Calendar is called a calendar item, or item for short. Outlook stores items in a folder named Calendar by default. If you are creating personal, academic, or business items, you may want to create separate calendars for each group.

3. **Determine if an activity is recurring.** A recurring activity is one that happens on a regular basis. Classes most likely recur throughout the semester. Work schedules can change week-by-week or month-by-month. Family events, such as birthdays and anniversaries, also can be recurring events on the calendar.

4. **Create an agenda before scheduling a meeting.** An agenda is a list of items to be discussed in a meeting. A poorly organized meeting may be the least productive tool in the business world, while a carefully planned meeting with a defined agenda can be a productive use of time, helping meeting participants stay focused and on schedule.

5. **Set calendar item options.** When creating items on a calendar, determine how to display the time of an appointment or event, such as busy or out of the office, so that the calendar is an accurate indication of your time. Also, decide whether to set a reminder for the item and how often it recurs, if at all.

6. **Determine the best method for distributing a calendar.** Consider whether you need to share a calendar with others. If you do, you can share calendars electronically in Outlook or print a calendar and distribute printed copies.

When necessary, more specific details concerning the above guidelines are presented at appropriate points in the chapter. The chapter also will identify the actions performed and decisions made regarding these guidelines during the creation of the calendar shown in Figure 2–1.

For an introduction to Windows 7 and instruction about how to perform basic Windows 7 tasks, read the Office 2010 and Windows 7 chapter at the beginning of this book, where you can learn how to resize windows, change screen resolution, create folders, move and rename files, use Windows Help, and much more.

To Start Outlook

If you are using a computer to step through the project in this chapter and you want your screens to match the figures in this book, you should change your screen's resolution to 1024 × 768. For information about how to change a computer's resolution, refer to the Office 2010 and Windows 7 chapter at the beginning of this book.

The following steps, which assume Windows 7 is running, start Outlook based on a typical installation. You may need to ask your instructor how to start Outlook for your computer. For a detailed example of the procedure summarized below, refer to the Office 2010 and Windows 7 chapter at the beginning of this book.

1 Click the Start button on the Windows 7 taskbar to display the Start menu.

2 Type `Microsoft Outlook` as the search text in the 'Search programs and files' text box and watch the search results appear on the Start menu.

3 Click Microsoft Outlook 2010 in the search results on the Start menu to start Outlook with your Inbox as the default Mail folder.

4 If the Outlook window is not maximized, click the Maximize button next to the Close button on its title bar to maximize the window.

5 Click the Calendar button in the Navigation Pane to display the Calendar – TW – Microsoft Outlook window in Day view (Figure 2–2).

Q&A

Why does my title bar not match the title bar in Figure 2–2?

The title bar always displays the name of the Outlook data file, which may include your name or initials.

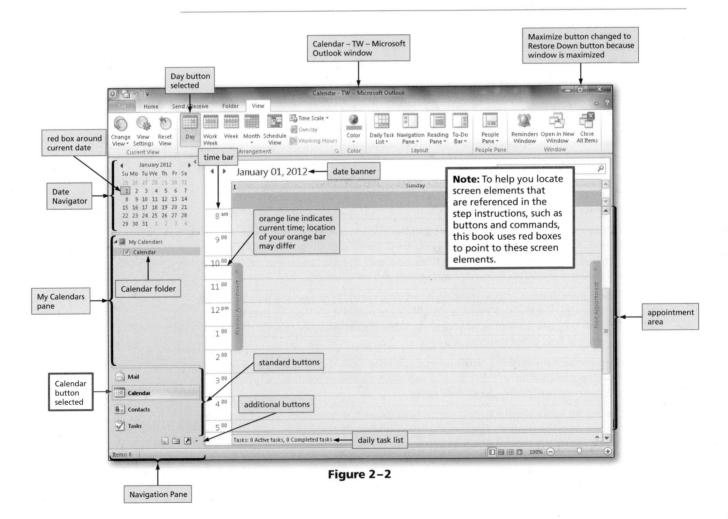

Figure 2–2

Calendar Window

The Calendar – TW – Microsoft Outlook window shown in Figure 2–2 includes a variety of features to help you work efficiently. It contains many elements similar to the windows in other Office programs, as well as some that are unique to Outlook. The main elements of the Calendar window are the Navigation Pane, the appointment area, and the Daily Task List.

The Navigation Pane includes two sets of buttons (standard and additional) and two panes: the Date Navigator and the My Calendars pane. The **Date Navigator** shows a calendar for the current month with a red box around the current date, scroll arrows to advance from one month to another, and any date on which an item is scheduled in bold. The **My Calendars pane** includes a list of available calendars where you can view a single calendar or view additional calendars side by side. The Standard folders represent shortcuts to the standard items that are part of the Microsoft Outlook mailbox: Mail, Calendar, Contacts, and Tasks. Additional folder buttons are displayed below the Standard folder buttons and represent shortcuts to other Outlook functions, such as Notes, Folder List shortcuts, and Configure buttons, which allow you to specify which folders to display. The appointment area contains a date banner, a day heading, and a time bar. The appointment area displays 30-minute time slots by default when viewing Calendar in Day, Work Week, or Week view and is not available in Month view. Similar to the time bar, the task list displays a list of current tasks, appears below the appointment area, and is only visible in Day, Work Week, and Week views.

Calendar Items

An **item** is any element in Outlook that contains information. Examples of calendar items include appointments, events, and meetings. All calendar items start as an appointment. Outlook defines an **appointment**, such as a doctor's appointment, as an activity that does not involve other people or resources, such as conference rooms. Outlook defines an **event**, such as a seminar or vacation, as an activity that occurs at least once and lasts 24 hours or longer. An appointment becomes an event when you schedule it for the entire day. An annual event, such as a birthday, anniversary, or holiday, occurs yearly on a specific date. Events do not occupy time slots in the appointment area and, instead, are displayed in a banner below the day heading when viewing the calendar in Day, Work Week, or Week view. An appointment becomes a **meeting** when people and other resources, such as meeting rooms, are invited.

When you create items on your calendar, it is helpful to show your time using the appointment status information. You set the appointment status for a calendar item using the Show As button, which provides four options for showing your time on the calendar: Free, Tentative, Busy, and Out of Office. For example, if you are studying or working on a project, you might show your time as busy because you are unable to perform other tasks at the same time. On the other hand, a dental appointment or a class would show your time as Out of Office because you need to leave your home or office to attend. Table 2–1 describes the items you can schedule on your calendar and the appointment status option associated with each item. Each calendar item also can be one-time or recurring.

BTW

Using Calendars
Other users can give you access to their calendars. This allows you to make appointments, check free times, schedule meetings, and refer to contact information. This is especially useful when you are scheduling meetings or events that depend on other people's schedules.

Table 2–1 Calendar Items		
Calendar Item	**Description**	**Show As Default**
One-time appointment	Default calendar item, involves only your schedule and does not invite other attendees or require resources such as a conference room	Busy
Recurring appointment	Occurs at regular intervals, such as weekly, biweekly, monthly, or bimonthly	Busy
One-time event	Occurs at least once and lasts 24 hours or longer, such as a vacation or conference	Free
Recurring event	Occurs at regular intervals, such as weekly, biweekly, monthly, or bimonthly, such as holidays	Free
One-time meeting	Includes people and other resources, such as meeting rooms	Busy
Recurring meeting	Occurs at regular intervals, such as weekly, biweekly, monthly, or bimonthly, such as staff meetings or department meetings	Busy

Plan Ahead

Determine where to store your calendar items.
When you schedule an appointment, Outlook adds the appointment to the Calendar folder by default. If you are creating personal, academic, and business items, you may want to create a separate calendar for each group. Users often create multiple calendars to keep personal items separate from academic or business items.

To Create a Personal Folder

As in other Outlook folders, such as the Inbox, you can create multiple folders within the Calendar folder. In certain situations, you may need to keep more than one calendar, such as one for business items and another for personal items.

The following steps create a folder to store your class and school related information, separate from your default folder, Calendar.

1
- With the Calendar – TW – Microsoft Outlook window open, click Folder on the Ribbon to display the Folder tab (Figure 2–3).

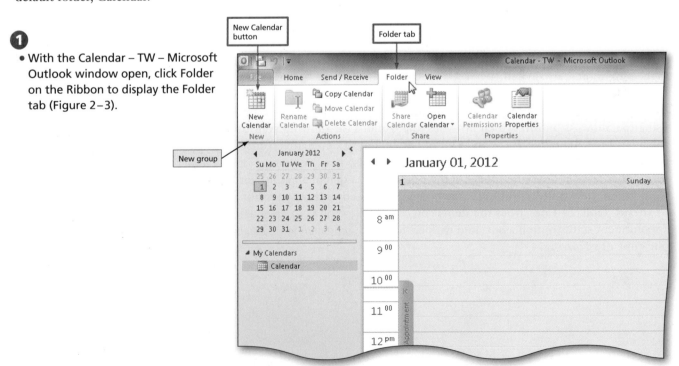

Figure 2–3

2
- Click the New Calendar button (Folder tab | New group) to display the Create New Folder dialog box.

- Type **School Calendar** in the Name text box (Create New Folder dialog box) to enter a name for the new folder.

- If necessary, click the Folder contains button to display a list of items the folder will contain.

- Click Calendar Items to specify what the folder will contain.

- If necessary, click Calendar in the 'Select where to place the folder' list to specify where the folder will be stored (Figure 2–4).

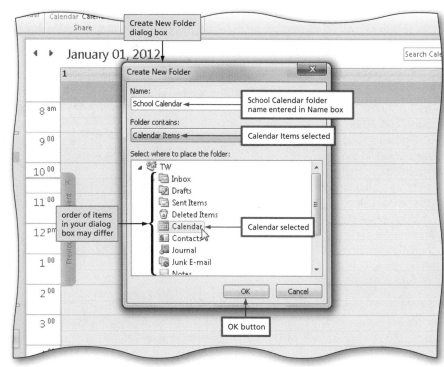

Figure 2–4

3
- Click the OK button to close the Create New Folder dialog box and add the new folder to the My Calendars list (Figure 2–5).

Q&A

The School Calendar folder is not displayed after I create it. Why is that?

Outlook does not automatically display the newly created calendar.

Figure 2–5

Other Ways
1. Press CTRL+SHIFT+E

To Display a Personal Calendar

Now that the School Calendar folder has been created, the next step is to display both calendar folders in the appointment area, so that the default Calendar folder and the School Calendar folder appear side by side. The following step displays the Calendar and the School Calendar folders side by side.

1

- In the My Calendars pane, click School Calendar to place a check mark in the check box, so that both the Calendar and the School Calendar folders are selected in the calendar list and displayed in the appointment area (Figure 2–6).

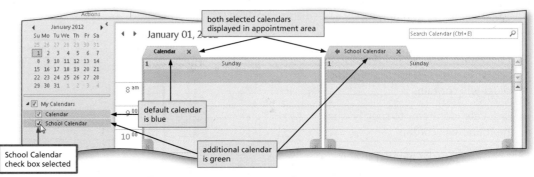

Figure 2–6

Q&A Why is the default calendar displayed in a different color from the School Calendar?

Outlook automatically assigns a different color to each new calendar you create to make it easier to distinguish one calendar from the other. Your calendar colors might be different from those shown in Figure 2–6.

Q&A What does the left pointing arrow mean on the School Calendar tab?

When the calendars are displayed side by side, the arrow allows you to view the School Calendar in overlay mode, which increases the size of the School Calendar while keeping the other calendar open. The appointments on the Calendar folder in the background still are visible on the School Calendar, allowing you to see any appointment conflicts.

To Remove the Default Calendar from the Appointment Area

While working with the School Calendar, you may want to display only that calendar in the Outlook window to avoid entering the information on the wrong calendar. The following step removes the default calendar from the appointment area.

1

- Click Calendar in the My Calendars pane to remove the check mark from the Calendar check box so that the default calendar no longer is displayed in the appointment area (Figure 2–7).

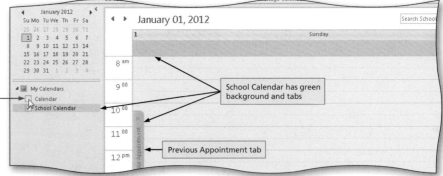

Q&A Why does my view look different from what is shown?

Figure 2–7 shows Day view, which is the default view for Calendar. If this is not the current view, click the Day button (Home tab | Arrange group).

Figure 2–7

Q&A What do the green tabs in the appointment area represent?

The green tabs provide navigation to the previous and next appointments.

Viewing the Calendar

Each Microsoft Outlook 2010 folder displays the items it contains in a layout called a view. You can change the arrangement and format of the folder contents by changing the view. Recall that the default view of the Calendar folder is Day view. Some people may prefer a different view of their calendar, such as weekly or monthly. For instance, you might want to view all the items for a given month at one time, in which case Month view would work best.

In this section, you will navigate to a specific date and then examine the different ways to view a calendar. Although the Outlook window looks different in each view, you can accomplish the same tasks in each view: you can add, edit, or delete appointments, events, and meetings.

BTW

Q&As
For a complete list of the Q&As found in many of the step-by-step sequences in this book, visit the Outlook 2010 Q&A Web page (scsite.com/out2010/qa).

To Go to a Specific Date

The next step in this project is to display a date that is not visible in the current view so that you can view that date in the appointment area. One option is to use the Go To Dialog Box Launcher, which allows you to navigate to a specific date and display that date in the appointment area. The following steps display a specific date, in this case January 15, 2012, in the appointment area in a calendar.

1

- If necessary, display the Home tab, and then click the Go To Dialog Box Launcher (Home tab | Go To group) to display the Go To Date dialog box (Figure 2–8).

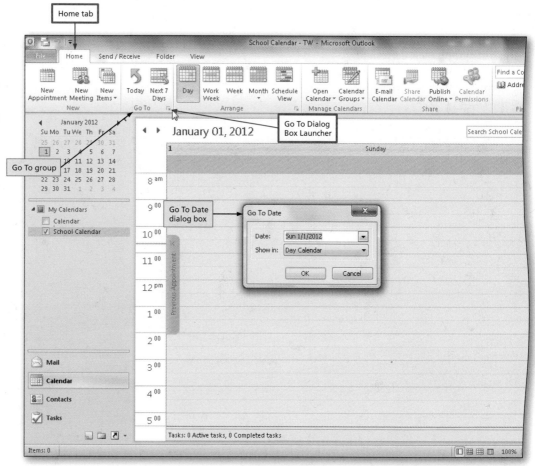

Figure 2–8

2

• Type **1/15/2012** in the Date box (Go To Date dialog box) to enter the date you want to display in the current calendar.

• If necessary, click the Show in button to display the list of calendar views.

• Click Day Calendar to show the calendar in Day view (Figure 2–9).

Q&A

Why did 'Sun' appear next to the date in the Date box?

Outlook automatically includes the day of the week (Sunday, in this case) when you enter a date in the Date box.

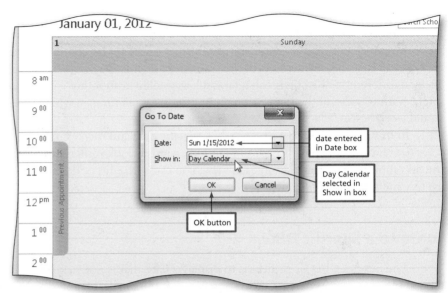

Figure 2–9

3

• Click the OK button to close the Go To Date dialog box and display the current calendar with the entered date as the selected date (Figure 2–10).

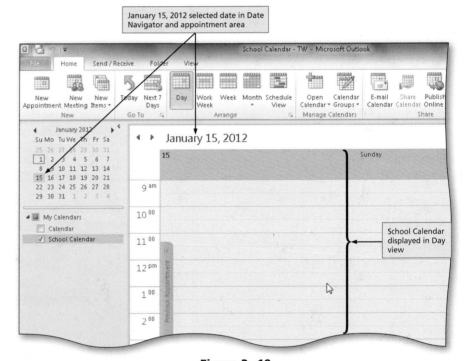

Figure 2–10

Other Ways
1. Press CTRL+G

To Display the Calendar in Work Week View

In Outlook, you can display several calendar days at once so that you can see multiple appointments at the same time. **Work Week view** shows five workdays (Monday through Friday) in a columnar style. Hours that are not part of the default workday (8:00 AM – 5:00 PM) appear shaded when viewing the calendar in Day, Work Week, and Week view. The following step displays the calendar in Work Week view.

1

- Click the Work Week button (Home tab | Arrange group) to display the work week in the appointment area for the selected date (Figure 2–11).

Experiment

- Scroll up and down in Day view to see how the color changes to reflect hours outside the default workday.

Q&A

Why is Monday, January 16, through Friday, January 20, highlighted on the Date Navigator?

The calendar days displayed in the appointment area are highlighted on the Date Navigator.

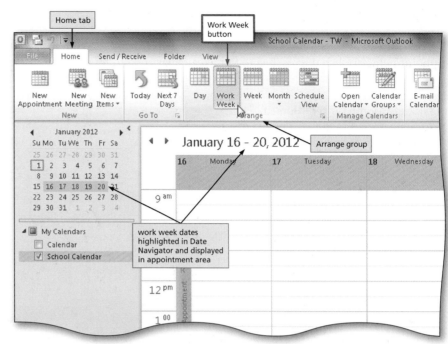

Figure 2–11

Other Ways
1. Press CTRL+ALT+2

To Display the Calendar in Week View

The advantage of displaying a calendar in **Week view** is to see how many appointments are scheduled for any given week, including weekends. In Week view, the seven days of the selected week appear in the appointment area. The following step displays the calendar in Week view.

1

- Click the Week button (Home tab | Arrange group) to display the full week, including weekends, in the appointment area (Figure 2–12).

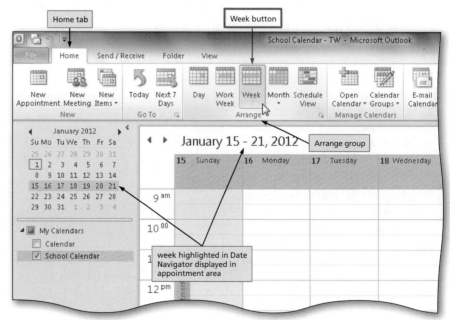

Figure 2–12

Other Ways
1. Press CTRL+ALT+3

To Display the Calendar in Month View

Month view resembles a standard monthly calendar page and displays a schedule for an entire month. Appointments are listed in each date in the calendar. The following step displays the calendar in Month view.

- Click the Month button (Home tab | Arrange group) to display one full month in the appointment area (Figure 2–13).

**Experiment**

- By default, Month view displays dates from the beginning to the end of a calendar month. To select several weeks across two calendar months, click the Date Navigator and then drag to select the weeks you want to view.

Q&A

What if I accidentally click the Month button arrow instead of the Month button?

Click the Month button arrow again to remove the list of options displayed when you clicked the Month button arrow.

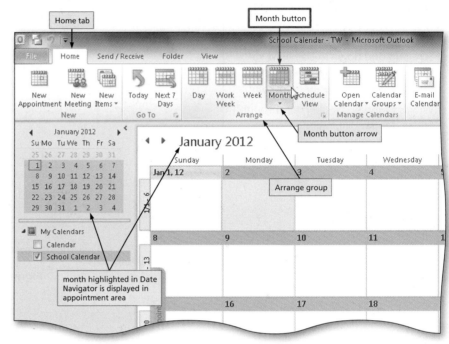

Figure 2–13

Other Ways

1. Press CTRL+ALT+4

To Display the Calendar in Schedule View

Schedule View, new to Outlook 2010, displays multiple calendars at the same time in a horizontal layout of the daily calendar. The following steps display the default Calendar and the School Calendar in Schedule View so that you can check for overlapping items.

- Click Calendar in the Navigation Pane to place a check mark in the check box and to display both the Calendar and the School Calendar in the appointment area (Figure 2–14).

Q&A

Why are both calendars displayed in Month view?

Outlook displays the newly displayed Calendar in the same view that the existing Calendar was displayed. In this case, the School Calendar was displayed in Month view, so the default Calendar also is displayed in Month view.

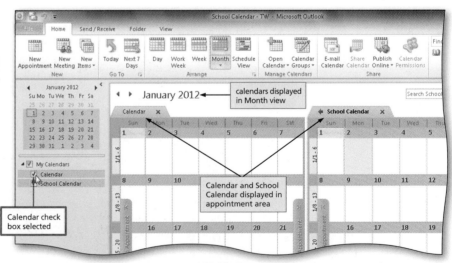

Figure 2–14

2

- Click the Schedule View button (Home tab | Arrange group) to display both calendars in Schedule View (Figure 2–15).

Q&A Why does Schedule View show a single day instead of multiple days?

Schedule View only displays one day at a time.

Q&A What does the dark blue shaded area in the calendar represent?

The dark blue shaded area represents the selected time in Day view.

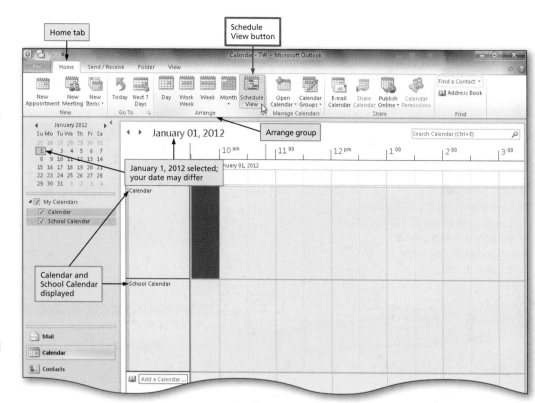

Figure 2–15

Other Ways

1. Press CTRL+ALT+5

Creating and Editing Appointments

Recall that every item you schedule in Outlook Calendar begins as an appointment. In Outlook, you easily can change an appointment to an event or a meeting. This section describes how to navigate to a specific date, schedule a dental visit as a one-time appointment, and enter classes in a class schedule as recurring appointments, starting with January 1, 2012.

Determine what you need to schedule.

As mentioned previously, you can schedule appointments, events, and meetings using Outlook Calendar. You can create appointments either directly in the appointment area or use the New Appointment dialog box. One method may be more efficient than the other, depending on the item you are scheduling and how much detail you need to enter for the calendar item you are creating.

Plan Ahead

Creating Appointments in the Appointment Area

A one-time appointment, such as a lunch date, doctor's appointment, or conference call, is an appointment that occurs only once on a calendar. A recurring appointment, such as a class in a class schedule, repeats on the calendar at regular intervals. Appointments can be created in two ways: using the appointment area, where you enter the appointment directly in the appropriate time slot, or the Untitled – Appointment window, where you can enter more specific details about the appointment. This chapter examines each method.

BTW

Keeping Appointments Private
Besides setting the status of an appointment, you can designate an appointment as private so that other users cannot view or access the appointment. Use the Private button (Calendar Tools Appointment tab | Tags group) to mark an appointment as private.

To Display One Calendar in Day View

When working with your school schedule, you may want to display only the calendar with which you are working. The following step closes the Calendar folder and displays the School Calendar folder in Day view.

1

- In the My Calendars pane, click Calendar to remove the check mark from the check box, remove the Calendar from the appointment area, and display the School Calendar in Day view (Figure 2–16).

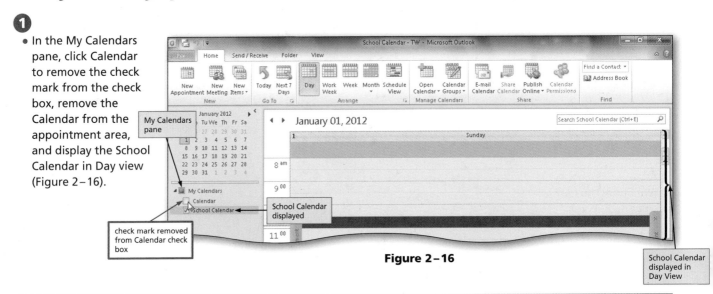

Figure 2–16

To Create a One-Time Appointment Using the Appointment Area

When you click a day on the calendar in the Navigation Pane, Outlook displays the calendar for the date selected in Day view in the appointment area. Day view shows a daily view of a specific date in half-hour increments. As mentioned previously, one way to create an appointment is to enter the information directly in the appointment area. The following steps create a one-time conference call appointment on January 16 using the appointment area.

1

- If necessary, click the Day button (Home tab | Arrange group) to display the daily view of the calendar in the appointment area.

- Click 16 in the January calendar on the Date Navigator to display the selected date in the appointment area (Figure 2–17).

Experiment

- View several dates that are not consecutive by clicking a date in the Date Navigator, holding down the CTRL key, and then clicking additional days.

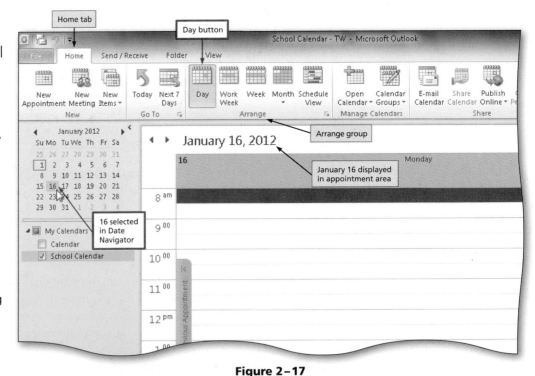

Figure 2–17

2

● Drag to select the three half-hour increments from the 10:00 AM to the 11:30 AM time slots in the appointment area (Figure 2–18).

Q&A What if I select more or fewer half-hour increments?

If you incorrectly select the appointment time, simply repeat this step to try again.

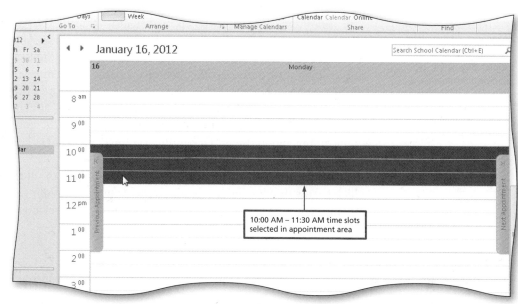

10:00 AM – 11:30 AM time slots selected in appointment area

Figure 2–18

3

● Type **Conference Call** as the appointment subject and then press the ENTER key to enter the conference call appointment in the appointment area (Figure 2–19).

Q&A What are the white dots on the selected appointment, in this case, the conference call?

The white dots indicate that the appointment is selected.

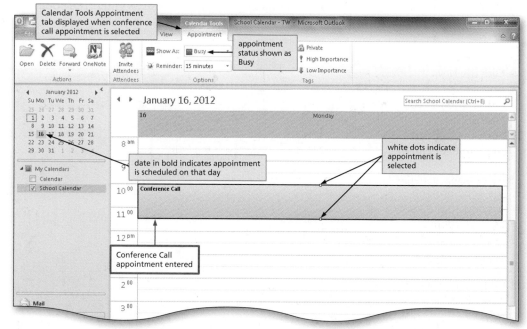

Calendar Tools Appointment tab displayed when conference call appointment is selected

appointment status shown as Busy

white dots indicate appointment is selected

date in bold indicates appointment is scheduled on that day

Conference Call appointment entered

Figure 2–19

Q&A Do I have to save the appointment entry?

No, the appointment entry is saved automatically when you press the ENTER key.

Q&A Why is Busy showing in the Show As box?

When you create an appointment, Outlook assigns your time as busy by default.

Q&A Why does the date of the conference call appointment appear in bold on the Date Navigator?

Outlook displays in bold any date with a time allocated on your calendar as busy to indicate that you have something scheduled on that day.

Other Ways

1. Select beginning time slot, hold down SHIFT, click ending time slot, type appointment name, press ENTER.

Creating Appointments Using the Appointment Window

Recognizing Recurring Appointments
The Recurrence symbol appears on recurring appointments and events. You can double-click an item with a Recurrence symbol to edit one or more occurrences of the appointment or event.

Another way to create an appointment is by using the Appointment window, which lets you enter more details than the appointment area. The Appointment window provides additional options for entering an appointment, such as the location of the appointment and a **recurrence pattern.** The recurrence pattern schedules the Outlook appointment on the calendar at regular intervals for a designated period of time.

Outlook also allows you to configure a **reminder**, similar to an alarm clock reminder, which is an alert window that briefly appears on your screen as a reminder of an upcoming appointment. Depending on how Outlook Calendar is configured, you may hear a chime or other sound as part of the reminder.

Another option when creating an appointment is to set the **appointment status**, which is how the time for a calendar item is marked on your calendar. The default appointment status setting is Busy, as indicated in the previous steps, but you can change the status to more accurately reflect your time.

To Create a One-Time Appointment Using the Appointment Window

You volunteered to work at the annual blood drive from 11:00 AM until 4:00 PM on Tuesday, January 17. Because this appointment has more detailed information than the conference call appointment, you decide to use the Appointment window to create this appointment. The following steps enter the blood drive appointment using the Appointment window.

1
- Click the New Appointment button (Home tab | New group) to open the Untitled – Appointment window.

- If necessary, maximize the appointment window to provide as much room as possible to work in the calendar.

- Type **Volunteer for Blood Drive** in the Subject text box as the appointment subject.

- Press the TAB key to move the insertion point to the Location box (Figure 2–20).

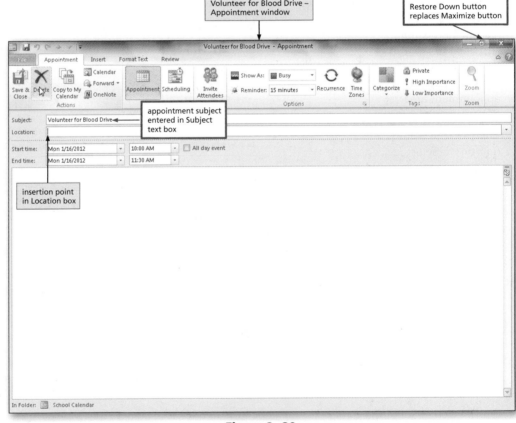

Figure 2–20

Q&A
Why did the title of the window change from Untitled – Appointment to Volunteer for Blood Drive – Appointment?

The title bar displays the name of the appointment. Because the name of the appointment has changed, the name on the title bar also changes.

2

- Type **Student Activities Center** in the Location text box as the location of the event (Figure 2–21).

Q&A Why are the date and time already specified?

When you start to create a new appointment, Outlook configures the start and end times using the time selected in the appointment area.

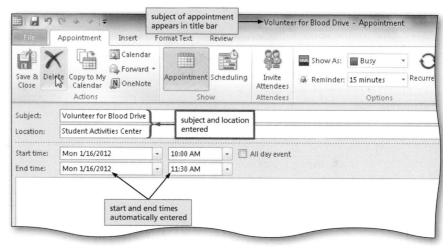

Figure 2–21

3

- Click the first Start time box arrow to display a calendar for the current month (Figure 2–22).

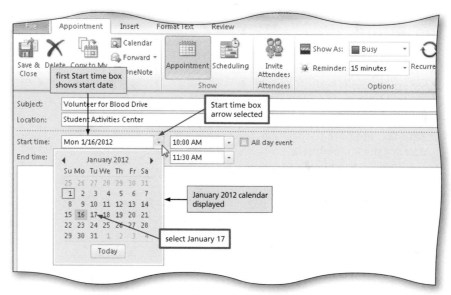

Figure 2–22

4

- Click 17 to select the start date, in this case, January 17.

- Click the second Start time box arrow to display a list of time slots (Figure 2–23).

Q&A Why did the end time in the first Start time box change to the same date as the end time in the first End time box?

Outlook automatically sets appointments to occur during a single day.

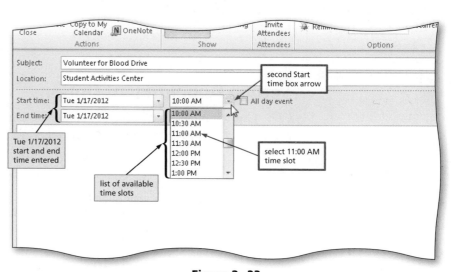

Figure 2–23

5

- Click 11:00 AM to select it as the Start time for the appointment.

- Click the second End time box arrow and then scroll to display 4:00 PM (5 hours) in the list of time slots (Figure 2–24).

Q&A Why does the second end time list have a duration next to it?

Outlook automatically sets the duration in half-hour increments next to the end time so that you know how long the appointment will take.

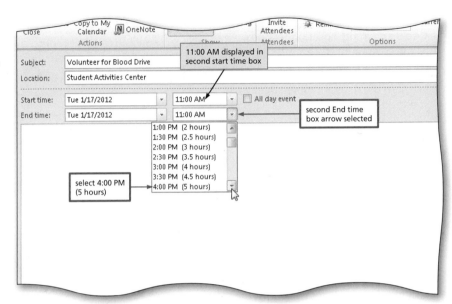

Figure 2–24

6

- Click 4:00 PM (5 hours) to select it as the End time for the appointment (Figure 2–25).

Q&A Why did I not have to specify an End date for the appointment?

When you specify a Start date, Outlook uses the same date for the End date by default.

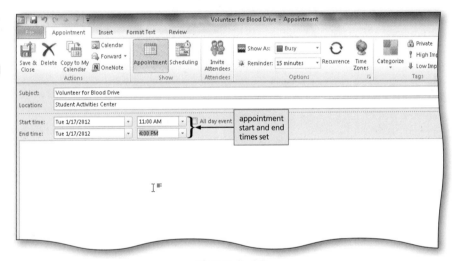

Figure 2–25

Other Ways

1 CTRL+SHIFT+A

Setting Appointment Options

One advantage to creating appointments using the Appointment window is the ability to set options for an appointment.

Plan
Ahead

Set Calendar item options.

When creating items on your calendar, you can set a number of options that determine how the Calendar is displayed and how it handles an appointment. Table 2–2 lists the options available when creating an item on your calendar. Consider setting one or all of the options shown in Table 2–2.

Table 2–2 Main Elements of the Calendar Window

Option	Description
Show As	Indicates your availability on a specific date and time; if you want to show others your availability when they schedule a meeting with you during a specific time, this must be set accurately
Reminder	Alerts you at a specific time prior to the item's occurrence
Recurrence	If an item on your calendar repeats at regularly scheduled intervals, set the recurring options so that you only have to enter the item once on your calendar

Outlook provides four options for indicating your availability on the Calendar, as described in Table 2–3.

Table 2–3 Calendar Item Status Options

Calendar Item Status Options	Description
Free	Shows time with a white bar in Day, Week, Work Week, or Month view
Tentative	Shows time with a slashed bar in Day, Week, Work Week, or Month view
Busy	Shows time in Day, Week, Work Week, or Month view
Out of Office	Shows time with a purple bar in Day, Week, Work Week, or Month view

The following pages illustrate how to set these various appointment options.

To Change the Status of an Appointment

To make sure your time is displayed accurately on the calendar, you change the appointment status from the default of Busy to Out of Office, meaning you are not in the office for the time of the blood drive appointment. The following steps change the status of an appointment.

1

- Click the Show As box arrow (Appointment tab | Options group) to display the list of appointment status options (Figure 2–26).

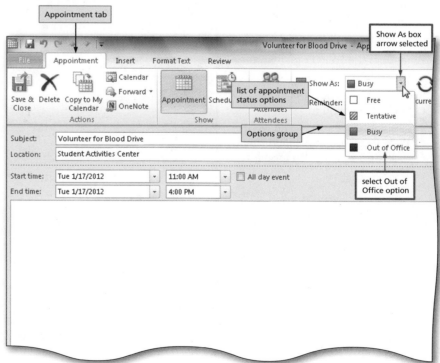

Figure 2–26

2

- Click Out of Office to change the appointment status from Busy to Out of Office (Figure 2–27).

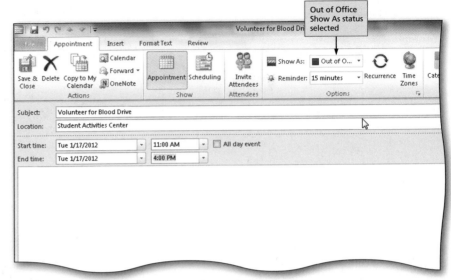

Figure 2–27

To Set a Reminder for the Appointment

With the start and end date and time for the blood drive appointment set and the appointment status selected, you want to schedule a reminder so that you do not forget the appointment. Recall that a reminder works similar to an alarm clock with options such as snooze and dismiss. When the reminder is displayed, you also can open the item for further review. The following steps set a 30-minute reminder for the blood drive appointment.

1

- Click the Reminder box arrow (Appointment tab | Options group) to display a list of available reminder intervals (Figure 2–28).

Q&A

What does the Sound option in the reminder list do?

In addition to a visual reminder, Outlook allows you to set an auditory alarm, much like an alarm clock. You can use the default sound or click the Sound option to select your own.

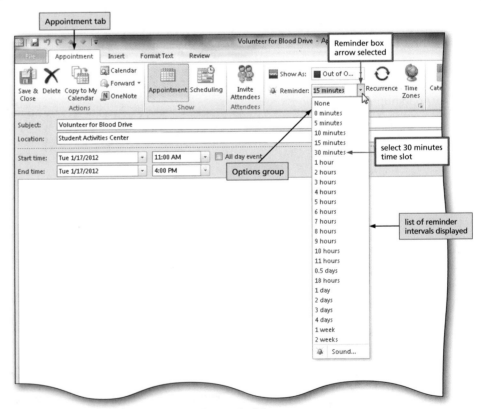

Figure 2–28

2
- Click 30 minutes to set a reminder for 30 minutes prior to the start time of the appointment (Figure 2–29).

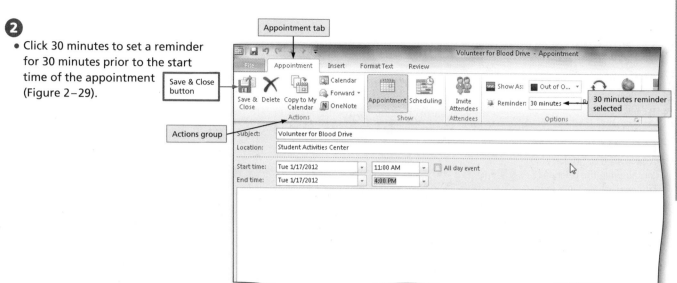

Figure 2–29

To Save the Appointment

Recall that appointments created directly in the appointment area are saved when you press the ENTER key. When you create an appointment using the New Appointment window, you must save it manually. The following step saves the Volunteer for Blood Drive – Appointment and closes the Volunteer for Blood Drive – Appointment window.

1
- Click the Save & Close button (Appointment tab | Actions group) to save and close the Volunteer for Blood Drive – Appointment window and place the appointment on the calendar.

- Click 17 on the Date Navigator to display January 17, 2012 in the appointment area (Figure 2–30).

Q&A
Do I have to click the date in the appointment area when I save an appointment?

It is not necessary to click the date in the appointment area, but it is good practice to verify your appointments to ensure the details are accurate.

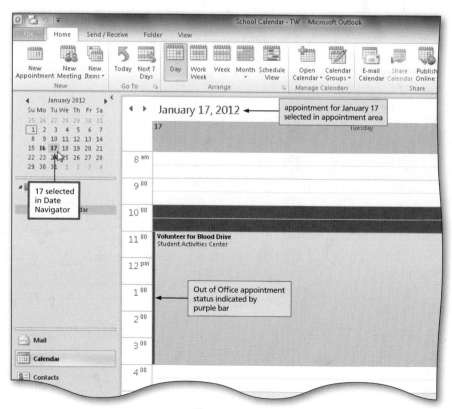

Figure 2–30

To Create the Remaining One-Time Appointments and View the Calendar

With the Volunteer for Blood Drive appointment created, the next step is to add the other appointments listed in Table 2–4, which shows appointments for various student activities on campus. The following steps create the remaining one-time appointments in the Appointment window.

Table 2–4 Additional One-Time Appointments						
Subject	Location	Start Date	Start Time	End Time	Show As	Reminder
Interview for student activity position	Activity Center	1/18/2012	9:00 AM	10:30 AM	Out of Office	10 minutes
International Student Fundraiser	RFB 400	1/19/2012	11:00 AM	12:00 PM	Tentative	30 minutes
Internship Opportunities	DH 100	1/20/2012	9:30 AM	11:00 AM	Tentative	5 minutes

1 Click the New Appointment button (Home tab | New group) to open the Untitled – New Appointment window.

2 Enter the subject for the first appointment in Table 2–4 in the Subject text box and then press the TAB key to move the insertion point to the Location text box.

3 Enter the location for the first appointment in Table 2–4.

4 Click the first Start time box arrow to display a calendar of available dates, and then click the date listed in Table 2–4 to select it.

5 Click the second Start time box arrow to display a list of time slots, and then click the time the class starts.

6 Click the second End time box arrow to display a list of available time slots and then select the time the class ends.

7 Click the Show As box arrow option to change the appointment status for the first appointment as indicated in Table 2–4.

8 Click the Reminder box arrow to change the reminder for the first appointment as indicated in Table 2–4.

9 Click the Save & Close button (Appointment tab | Actions group) to save the appointment.

10 Repeat Steps 1 through 9 for the two remaining one-time appointments in Table 2–4.

11 Click the Week button (Home tab | Arrange group) to view the completed calendar (Figure 2–31).

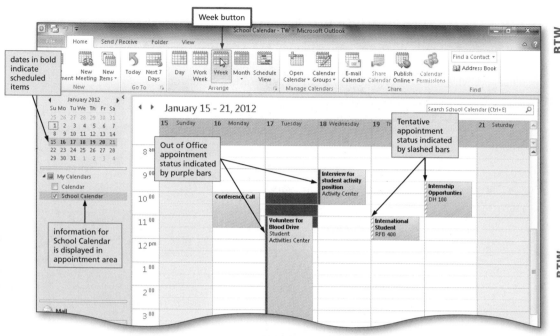

Figure 2–31

BTW

The Ribbon and Screen Resolution
Outlook may change how the groups and buttons within the groups appear on the Ribbon, depending on the computer's screen resolution. Thus, your Ribbon may look different from the ones in this book if you are using a screen resolution other than 1024 × 768.

BTW

Changing the Color
Outlook 2010 provides 15 colors for your calendar. Click the Color button (View tab | Color group) to display the list of available colors, and then click the color you want to apply to the calendar.

Creating Recurring Appointments

Many appointments are **recurring appointments**, meaning they happen at regular intervals for a designated period of time. For example, a class held every Monday and Wednesday from 9:00 AM to 11:00 AM is a recurring appointment. Your college classes occur two times per week, at regular weekly intervals during the semester, and entering these recurring appointments for each occurrence during the semester would be time-consuming. You want to add the classes to the calendar as recurring appointments so that you can keep track of time throughout the entire semester. Adding these classes as recurring appointments enables you to enter the appointment information one time, with it automatically recurring at a set interval for a specified period of time. You will create the appointment only once and configure the recurrence pattern to designate the rate of recurrence, in this case weekly, and on what day(s) of the week the class occurs.

To Create an Appointment Using the Appointment Window

The following steps create an appointment for the Introduction to Computers class.

1 Click the New Appointment button (Home tab | New group) to open the Untitled – Appointment window.

2 Type `Intro to Computers` in the Subject text box and then press the TAB key to move the insertion point to the Location text box.

3 Type `DH 302` in the Location text box as the location for the class.

4 Click the Start time box arrow to display a calendar of available dates, and then click 23 to select Mon 1/23/2012 as the day the first class meets.

5 Click the second Start time box arrow to display a list of time slots, and then click 10:00 AM as the time the class starts.

6 Click the second End time box arrow to display a list of available time slots, scroll through the list, and then click 12:00 PM (2 hours) to set the End time to 12:00 PM.

To Set Recurrence Options for an Appointment

Now that the appointment for the first class is created, you will establish a recurring pattern so that you do not have to enter the class schedule every week. The following steps configure a recurring pattern for the Introduction to Computers class, which meets every Monday and Wednesday until the end of the semester.

1

- Click the Recurrence button (Appointment tab | Options group) to display the Appointment Recurrence dialog box (Figure 2–32).

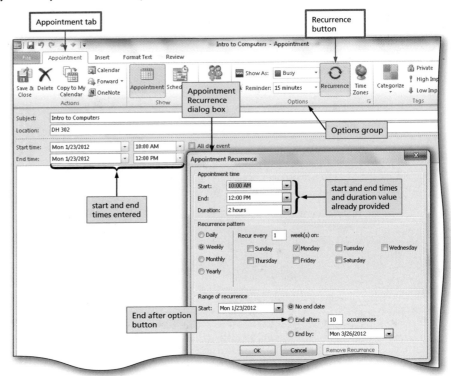

Figure 2–32

2

- If necessary, in the Recurrence pattern area, click Weekly (Appointment Recurrence dialog box) to set the recurrence pattern.

- In the Recur every text box (Appointment Recurrence dialog box), type 1 if it does not already appear in the text box to schedule the frequency of the recurrence pattern.

- Click Wednesday to place a check mark in the check box and to schedule the class two times per week (Mondays and Wednesdays) (Figure 2–33).

Q&A

Why is the Monday check box already selected in the Recurrence pattern area?

Monday is already selected because that was the date you entered for the day the class starts. If the class started on Tuesday, then the Tuesday check box would be selected when you set the recurrence pattern.

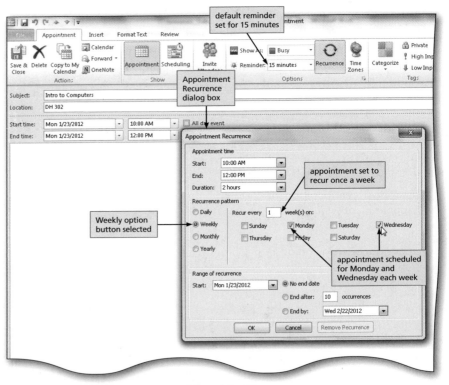

Figure 2–33

Q&A Why does the Start box in the 'Range of recurrence' area contain a date?

When you display the Appointment Recurrence dialog box, Outlook automatically sets the range of recurrence with the date the appointment starts.

3

- In the 'Range of recurrence' area, click End by and then press the TAB key two times to select the End by box.

- Type **5/9/2012** as the day the class ends to replace the displayed end date with a new date (Figure 2–34).

Q&A What if I do not know the end date, but I know how many times the class meets?

You can click the End after option button and then type the number of times the class meets in the End after text box.

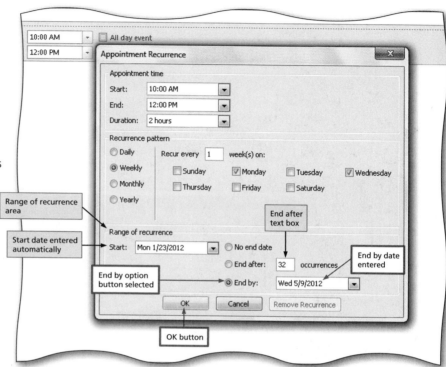

Figure 2–34

4

- Click the OK button to close the Appointment Recurrence dialog box and set the recurrence pattern (Figure 2–35).

Q&A Why is the value in the Reminder box (Appointment Series tab | Options group) set for 15 minutes?

The default reminder time for all calendar items is 15 minutes.

Q&A Why did the Appointment tab change to the Appointment Series tab?

When you set a recurring pattern, the tab name changes to reflect a series.

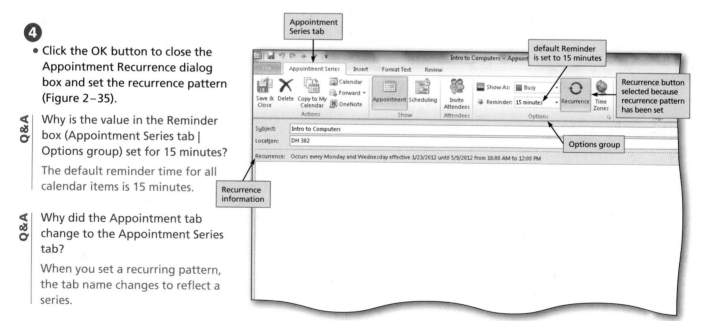

Figure 2–35

To Set a Reminder and Show As Options for an Appointment

Next, you will set a reminder 30 minutes prior to the class and mark your time as Out of Office because you will be in class during this time. The following steps set the Show As and Reminder options.

1 Click the Show As box arrow (Appointment Series tab | Options group) to display the list of appointment status options.

2 Click Out of Office to change the appointment status from Busy to Out of Office.

3 Click the Reminder box arrow (Appointment Series tab | Options group) to display a list of available reminder intervals.

4 Click 30 minutes to set a reminder for 30 minutes prior to the start time of the appointment (Figure 2–36).

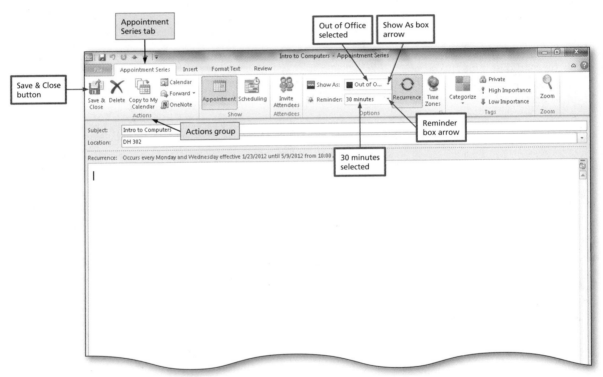

Figure 2–36

To Save the Appointment

With all the information about the Introduction to Computers class entered, you must save the appointment. The following steps save the Intro to Computers – Appointment Series and close the window.

1 Click the Save & Close button (Appointment Series tab | Actions group) to save the recurring appointment on the calendar and close the window.

2 Click 23 on the Date Navigator to display the January 23, 2012 recurring appointment in the appointment area in Week view (Figure 2–37).

Q&A Do I need to display the appointment after I save it?

No, this step was included to view the appointment on the calendar.

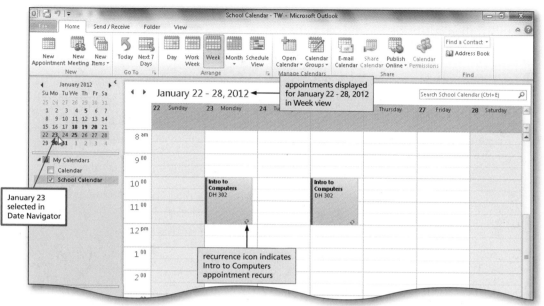

Figure 2–37

To Create the Recurring Appointments

With the Intro to Computers class appointment series created, the next step is to create recurring class appointments for the remainder of your class schedule using the appointment information in Table 2–5. The following steps create the remaining class schedule.

Table 2–5 Recurring Appointments

Appointment (Class)	Location	Start Date	End Date	Start Time	End Time	Show As	Reminder	Recurrence
Sociology	HRB 203	1/24/2012	Set in Recurrence	8:00 AM	10:00 AM	Out of Office	30 minutes	Weekly, every Tuesday and Thursday; end by Thursday, 5/3/2012
English Literature	Library 105	1/24/2012	Set in Recurrence	11:00 AM	1:00 PM	Out of Office	15 minutes	Weekly, every Tuesday and Thursday; end by Thursday, 5/3/2012

1 If necessary, click the Day button (Home tab | Arrange group) to display the daily view of the calendar in the appointment area.

2 Click 24 in the January calendar on the Date Navigator to display the selected date in the appointment area.

3 Drag to select a two-hour increment from the 8:00 AM to the 10:00 AM time slot in the appointment area.

4 Type `Sociology` as the appointment subject and then press the ENTER key to enter the appointment in the appointment area.

5 Select the appointment to display the Calendar Tools Appointment tab on the Ribbon.

6 Select the Show as box arrow to display the list of appointment status options and then click the option shown Table 2–5.

7 Select the Reminder box arrow to display the list of time slots and then click the option shown in Table 2–5.

8 Double-click the Sociology appointment to open the Appointment window, and then type the location in Table 2–5 in the Location box.

9 Click the Save & Close button to close the Appointment window.

10 Click the Recurrence button (Calendar Tools Appointment tab | Options group) and set the recurrence pattern shown in Table 2–5, and then click the OK button to close the Appointment Recurrence window.

11 Repeat Steps 1 through 10 to add the information in the second row of Table 2–5 (Figure 2–38).

Q&A What if I have appointments that recur other than weekly?

You can set daily, weekly, monthly, or yearly recurrence patterns in the Appointment Recurrence dialog box. A recurring appointment can be set to have no end date, to end after certain number of occurrences, or to end by a certain date.

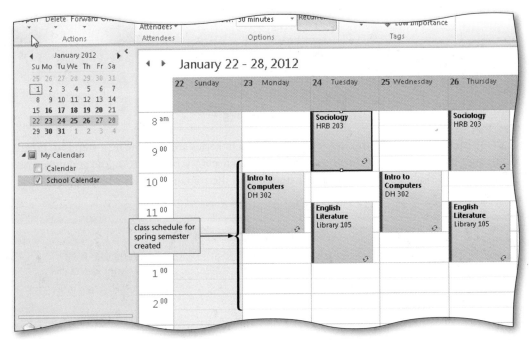

Figure 2–38

Using Natural Language Phrasing

In the previous steps, you entered dates and times in the Appointment window using standard numeric entries, such as 1/31/2012. You also can specify appointment dates and times using natural language. A **natural language phrase** is a phrase closely resembling how people speak during normal conversation. For example, you can type a phrase, such as "next Tuesday," "two weeks from yesterday," or a single word, such as "midnight," and Outlook will calculate the correct date and time, relative to the current date and time on the computer's system clock.

In addition to these natural language phrases, Outlook can convert abbreviations and ordinal numbers into complete words and dates. For example, you can type "Feb" instead of "February" or "the first of May" instead of "5/1". Outlook's Calendar also can convert words such as "yesterday" and "tomorrow" and the names of holidays that occur on the same date each year, such as Valentine's Day. Table 2–6 lists various natural language options.

Table 2–6 Natural Language Options

Category	Examples
Dates Spelled Out	• July twenty-third, March 29th, first of December • This Fri, next Sat, two days from now • Three weeks ago, next week • One month from today
Times Spelled Out	• Noon, midnight • Nine o'clock AM, five-twenty • 7 PM
Descriptions of Times and Dates	• Now • Yesterday, today, tomorrow • Next, last
Holidays	• Cinco de Mayo • Christmas Day, Christmas Eve • Halloween • Independence Day • New Year's Day, New Year's Eve • St. Patrick's Day • Valentine's Day • Veteran's Day
Formulas for dates and times	3/14/2012 + 12d converts the date to 3/26/2012; use *d* for day, *m* for month, or *y* or year and add that amount of time to any date

To Enter an Appointment Date and Time Using Natural Language Phrases

You signed up for a college trip to New York this coming Saturday and need to enter the trip information on your calendar. Buses leave from the front parking lot at 7:00 AM and will return by 11:00 PM the same day. The following steps create an appointment using natural language phrases for the date and time of the New York trip.

- Click the New Appointment button (Home tab | New group) to open the Untitled – Appointment window.

- Type **New York Trip** in the Subject text box, and then press the TAB key to move the insertion point to the Location text box.

- Type **Bus pickup in front parking lot** in the Location text box, and then press the TAB key to select the first Start time box (Figure 2–39).

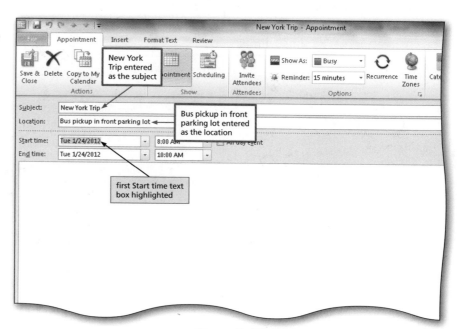

Figure 2–39

2

- Type **next saturday** in the Start time box to enter the start date.

- Press the TAB key to select the second Start time box.

- Type **seven am** as the time in the second Start time box to enter the start time (Figure 2–40).

Q&A Do I need to use proper capitalization when entering natural language phrases?

No, Outlook converts the text to the proper date or time, regardless of the capitalization.

Q&A Why did the text change to a numeric date when I pressed the TAB key?

When you enter the date using natural language phrasing, Outlook converts typed text to the correct date format when you click or move the insertion point to a different box.

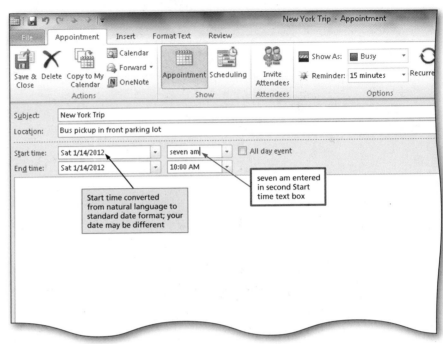

Figure 2–40

3

- Press the TAB key two times to convert the Start time entry to 7:00 AM and to select the entry in the second End time box.

- Type **eleven pm** as the time in the second End time box (Figure 2–41).

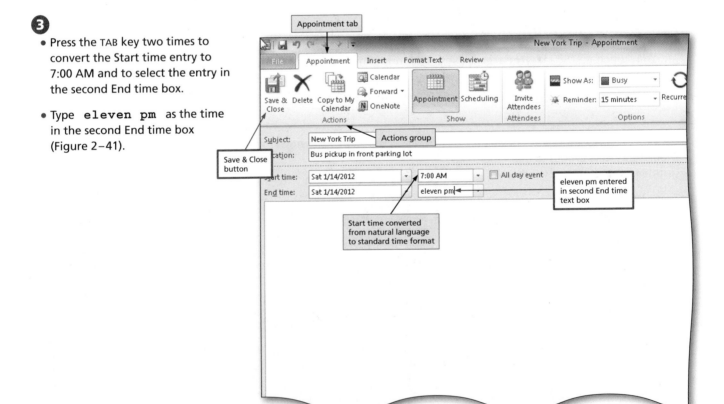

Figure 2–41

④

- Press the ENTER key to convert the end time text to 11:00 PM.

- Click the Save & Close button (Appointment tab | Actions group) to save the appointment and close the window.

- Scroll to find the date that corresponds to next Saturday's date (Figure 2–42).

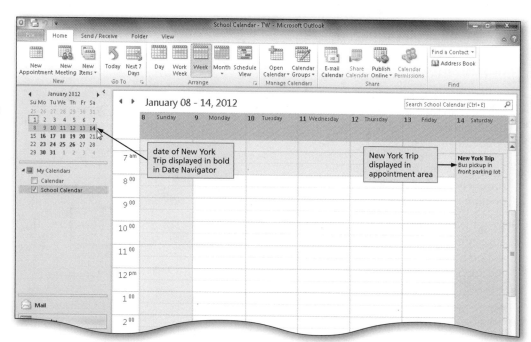

date of New York Trip displayed in bold in Date Navigator

New York Trip displayed in appointment area

New York Trip
▸ Bus pickup in front parking lot

Figure 2–42

Q&A

Why is it important to verify the appointment?

It is important to verify that you did not make inadvertent mistakes while adding the appointment to your calendar. Errors might cause you to miss an important appointment.

Q&A

Why is the New York trip appointment scheduled for January 14 and not January 7?

In Outlook, next Saturday means the Saturday in the next full week. This Saturday means the Saturday in the current week.

Editing Appointments

Schedules often need to be rearranged, and Outlook provides several ways to edit appointments. You can change the subject and location by clicking the appointment and editing the information directly in the appointment area, or by double-clicking the appointment and making corrections using the Appointment window. You can specify whether all occurrences in a series of recurring appointments need to be changed, or a single occurrence should be altered.

To Move an Appointment to a Different Time on the Same Day

Outlook provides several ways to move appointments. Suppose, for instance, that you cannot attend the conference call appointment at 10:00 AM on Monday, January 16, 2012. The appointment needs to be rescheduled to 1:00 PM for the same amount of time (two hours, in this case). Instead of deleting and then retyping the appointment, you can drag it to a new time slot. The following step moves the conference call appointment to a new time slot.

BTW

Moving a Recurring Appointment
If you move a recurring appointment, you move only the selected instance of the appointment. To move all instances of a recurring appointment, open the appointment, click the Recurrence button (Appointment tab | Options group), and then change the recurrence pattern.

1

- If necessary, click a scroll arrow on the Calendar in the Navigation Pane until January 2012 is displayed in the calendar on the Date Navigator.

- Click 16 in the January 2012 calendar on the Date Navigator to display the selected date in the appointment area.

- Position the mouse pointer on the conference call appointment to prepare to move the appointment.

- Drag the conference call appointment to the 1:00 PM time slot on the same day to reschedule the appointment (Figure 2–43).

Other Ways

1. Double-click appointment, change time

2. Press CTRL+O, change time

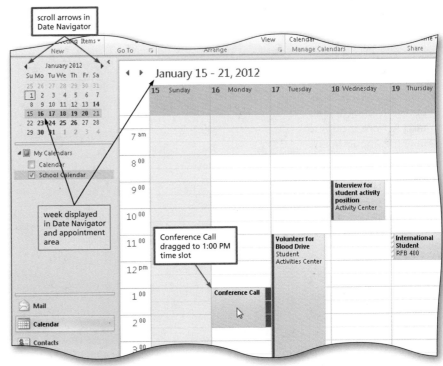

Figure 2–43

To Move an Appointment to a Different Date

If you are moving an appointment to a new date but remaining in the same time slot, you can drag the appointment to the new date on the Date Navigator. The following step moves an appointment to a new date in the same time slot.

1

- Drag the selected appointment on January 16, 2012 to the 25 in the January 2012 calendar on the Date Navigator and then release the mouse button to move the appointment to a new date (Figure 2–44).

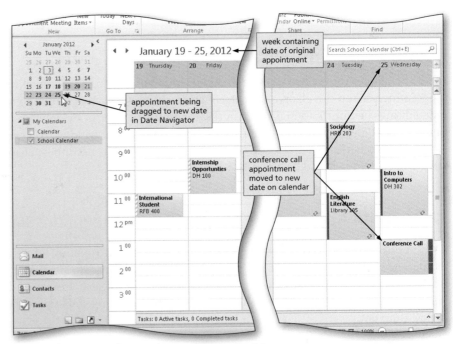

Figure 2–44

To Move an Appointment to a Different Month

The blood drive, originally scheduled for January 17, 2012, has been rescheduled to February 3, 2012. To move an appointment to another month, you must open the Appointment window. The following steps open the Volunteer for Blood Drive appointment and move it to February 3, 2012.

1

- Click 17 in the January 2012 calendar on the Date Navigator to display the selected date in the appointment area (Figure 2–45).

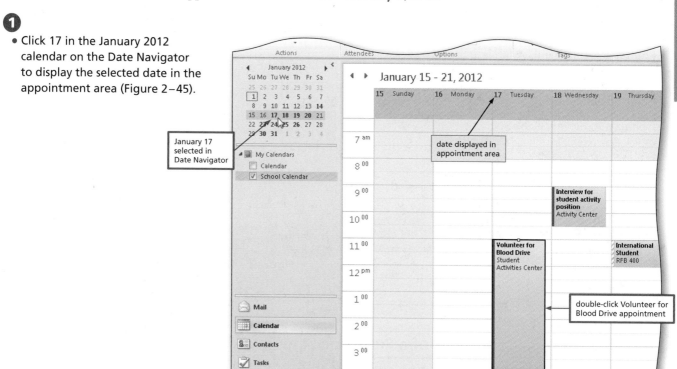

Figure 2–45

2

- Double-click the Volunteer for Blood Drive appointment in the appointment area to open the appointment window.

- Click the first Start time box arrow to display the calendar for selecting a start date.

- Click the right scroll arrow to display the calendar for February 2012 (Figure 2–46).

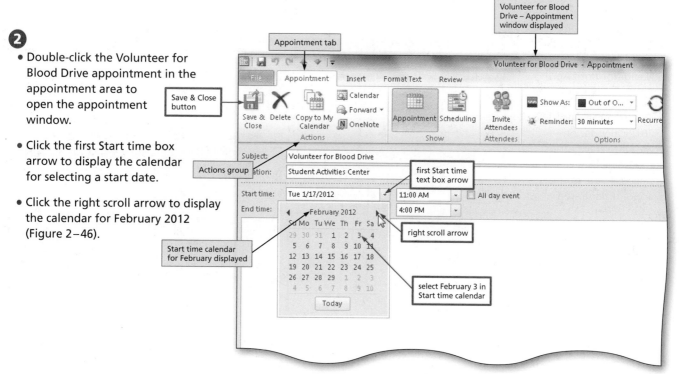

Figure 2–46

3

• Click 3 in the February calendar to display the selected date in both the first Start time and first End time boxes.

• Click the Save & Close button (Appointment tab | Actions group) to save the change to the appointment and close the window.

• Click February 3 in the Date Navigator to verify the appointment change (Figure 2–47).

Other Ways

1. Click appointment, press CTRL+O, set appointment options, click Save & Close

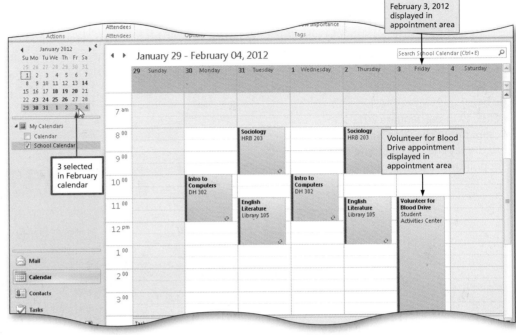

Figure 2–47

To Delete a Single Occurrence of a Recurring Appointment

Appointments sometimes are canceled and must be deleted from the schedule. For example, the schedule created thus far in this project contains class appointments during the spring semester. The college is closed for Spring Break from April 9 – 13, 2012 and no classes will meet during that time. The classes scheduled during Spring Break need to be deleted. The following steps delete only the classes scheduled during Spring Break.

1

• Click the right scroll arrow on the Date Navigator until April 2012 is displayed.

• Click 9 in the April 2012 calendar on the Date Navigator to display the selected date in the appointment area.

• Click the first appointment to be deleted, Intro to Computers, scheduled for April 9, 2012, to select the appointment and display the Calendar Tools Appointment Series tab (Figure 2–48).

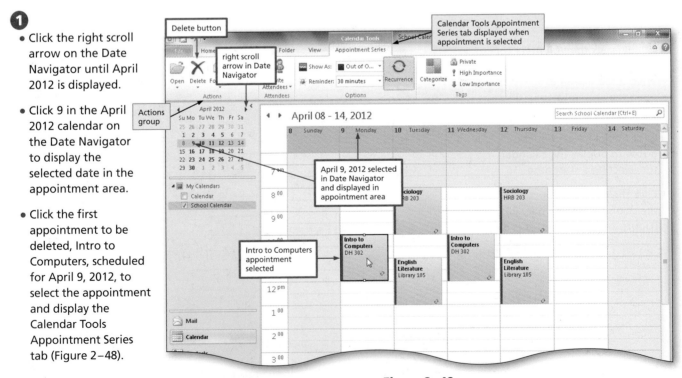

Figure 2–48

2

• Click the Delete button (Calendar Tools Appointment Series tab | Actions group) to display the Delete menu (Figure 2–49).

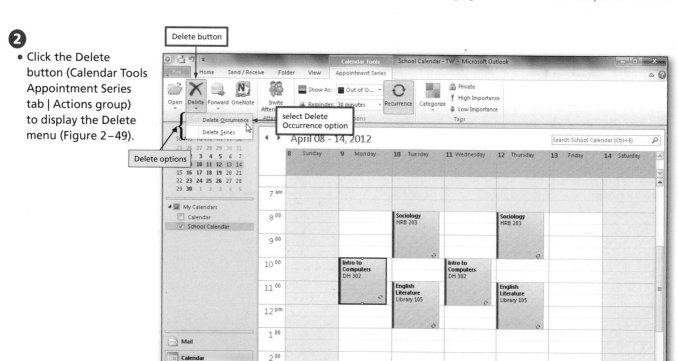

Figure 2–49

3

• Click Delete Occurrence on the Delete menu to delete only the selected occurrence from the calendar.

4

• Repeat Steps 1 through 3 to delete the remaining classes from the week of April 9, 2012 (Figure 2–50).

Other Ways

1. Click appointment, press DELETE, click Delete Occurrence, click OK

2. Right–click appointment, click Delete on shortcut menu, click Delete Occurrence, click OK

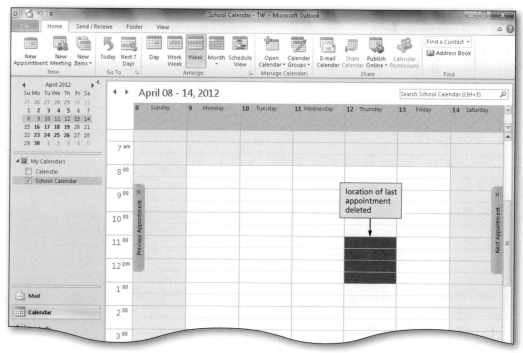

Figure 2–50

Break Point: If you wish to take a break, this is a good place to do so. To resume at a later time, start Outlook and continue following the steps from this location forward.

Creating and Editing Events

BTW

Adding Holidays to the Calendar
To add holidays to your calendar, click the File tab, click Options, and then click Calendar. In the Calendar Options section, click the Add Holidays button. Your country is selected by default. Click the OK button.

Outlook's Calendar folder allows you to keep track of important events. Recall that events are activities that last 24 hours or longer. Examples of events include conferences, vacations, and holidays. Events can be one-time or recurring. In Outlook, events differ from appointments in one primary way — they do not appear in individual time slots in the appointment area. Instead, when you schedule an event, its description appears in a small banner below the day heading. Similar to an appointment, the event status can be indicated as time that is free, busy, tentative, or out of the office during the event. See Table 2–3 on page OUT 67 for a complete description of these options.

To Create a One-Time Event in the Appointment Window

A Computer Expo is being held at the Convention Center from May 9, 2012 through May 11, 2012 that you want to attend. Because the conference will last for several days, Outlook will schedule the conference as an event. You begin to schedule an event by creating an appointment. Because you are not certain you can attend the event, you decide to show your time as Tentative. The following steps create an event for the convention on the calendar.

1
- Click the New Appointment button (Home tab | New group) to open the Untitled – Appointment window.

- Type **Computer Expo** in the Subject text box, and then press the TAB key to move the insertion point to the Location text box.

- Type **Convention Center** as the location of the event (Figure 2–51).

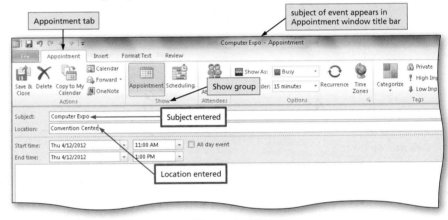

Figure 2–51

2
- Click the first Start time box arrow to display the Start time calendar.

- Click the right scroll arrow until the May 2012 calendar is displayed.

- Click 9 in the May calendar to display Wed 5/9/2012 as the day the Computer Expo starts.

- Click All day event to place a check mark in the 'All day event' check box and change the appointment to an event (Figure 2–52).

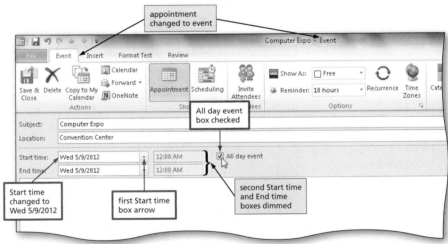

Figure 2–52

Q&A Can I create an event without using the Untitled – Appointment window?

Yes. Click the New Items button (Home tab | New group) to display a list of items and then click All Day Event to open the Untitled – Event window.

Q&A Why did the second Start and End time boxes become dimmed when the 'All day event' check box was checked?

An event occurs during a 24-hour time period, so the hourly time slot option is not needed.

3

- Click the first End time box arrow to display the End time calendar.

- Click 11 in the May calendar as the end date to set the end date (Figure 2–53).

Q&A

Why does the Show As box display the time as Free?

The default Show As appointment status for events is Free because events do not occupy blocks of time during the day on the calendar.

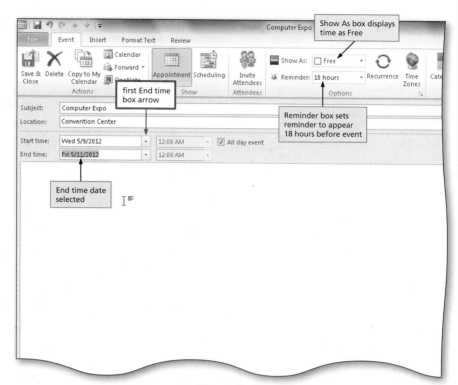

Figure 2–53

4

- Click the Show As box arrow to display a list of appointment status options.

- Click Tentative to set the appointment status.

- Click the Reminder box arrow to display the list of reminder time slots.

- Click None to set no reminder (Figure 2–54).

Q&A

Why does the appointment area display dashes in the time slots?

When you show the time for an event as Tentative, the appointment displays dashes to indicate the tentative status of the time on your calendar.

Q&A

Why is the event reminder set for 18 hours?

The default reminder for events is 18 hours.

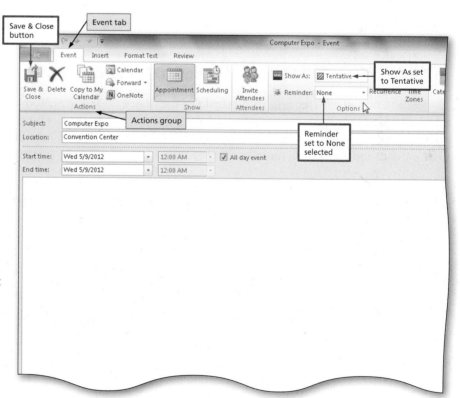

Figure 2–54

5

- Click the Save & Close button (Event tab | Actions group) to save the event and close the window.

- If necessary, click the right scroll arrow on the Date Navigator to scroll to May 2012.

- Click 9 to display May 9, 2012 in the appointment area and to view the Computer Expo event banner (Figure 2–55).

Q&A

Why is the Computer Expo event displayed at the top of the Day view of the calendar?

Events do not occupy time slots on the Day view of the calendar, so they appear as banners at the top of the calendar on the day they occur.

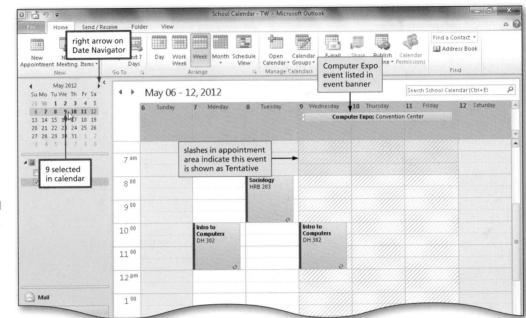

Figure 2–55

To Move a One-Time Event to a New Date and Change the Event Status

The Computer Expo, originally scheduled for May 9, has been postponed to a later date. You need to move the Computer Expo event to a new date. Because you will be off campus for the Computer Expo, you also want the calendar to show your time for the Computer Expo as Out of Office. The following steps move the one-time event to a new date and change the status to Out of Office.

1

- Double-click the Computer Expo event to open the window for the selected event (Figure 2–56).

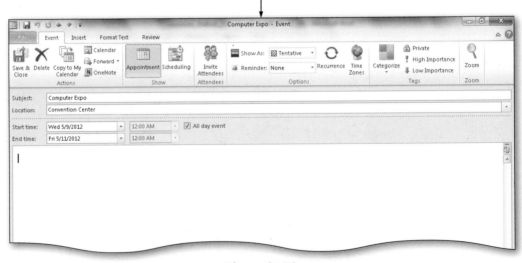

Figure 2–56

2

- Click the first Start time box arrow to display a calendar.

- Click 11 to change the Computer Expo start time.

- Click the Show As box arrow (Event tab | Options group) to display the list of appointment status options and then click Out of Office to change the event status from Tentative to Out of Office (Figure 2–57).

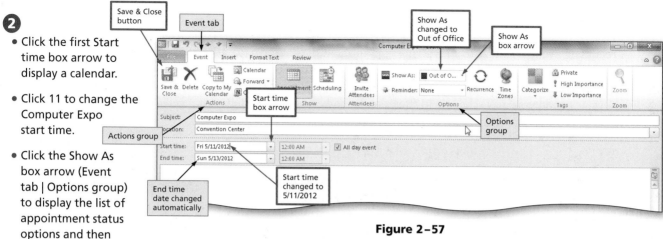

Figure 2–57

Q&A Why did the end time change when I changed the start time?

Outlook automatically calculates the new end time when you change the start time.

3

- Click the Save & Close button (Event tab | Actions group) to save the changes to the selected event and close the window.

- If necessary, click 11 on the Date Navigator to display May 11, 2012 in the appointment area and view the Computer Expo event banner.

Q&A Why did the reminder not change when I changed the appointment status?

When the appointment status changes after you create the appointment, the reminder does not automatically change as it does when you create the appointment for the first time.

To Delete a One-Time Event

Because your schedule has changed, you no longer can attend the Computer Expo event. You need to delete the Computer Expo event from your calendar. The following step deletes the Computer Expo event from your calendar.

1

- If necessary, click the Computer Expo event banner in the appointment area of the calendar to select it and display the Calendar Tools Appointment tab on the Ribbon.

- Click the Delete button (Calendar Tools Appointment tab | Actions group) to delete the Computer Expo event from the calendar, and then click the 8:00 AM box for May 11 (Figure 2–58).

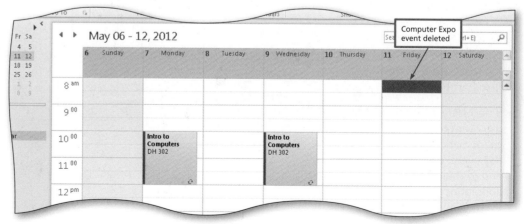

Figure 2–58

Other Ways
1. Select appointment, press DELETE

To Create a Recurring Event Using the Appointment Window

A recurring event is similar to a recurring appointment in that it occurs at regular intervals on your calendar. However, editing a recurring event is slightly different from editing one-time events. You can specify whether all occurrences in a series of recurring events need to be changed or if a single occurrence should be altered.

You want to add your pay schedule to the calendar to keep track of when you receive a paycheck. The following steps create a recurring event for your pay schedule.

1
- Click Home on the Ribbon to display the Home tab.

- Click the New Appointment button (Home tab | New group) to display the Untitled – Appointment window.

- If necessary, click the Maximize button on the title bar to maximize the window.

- In the Subject text box, type **Payday** as the subject.

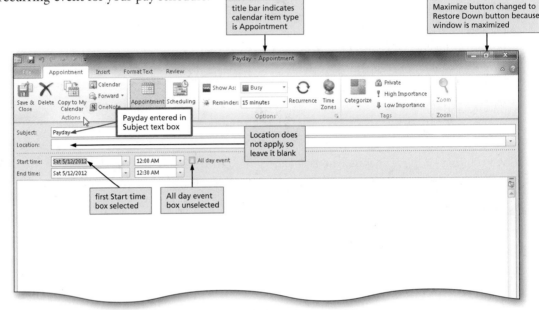

Figure 2–59

- Press the TAB key two times to select the time in the first Start time box (Figure 2–59).

Q&A Do I need to add a location to the Payday event?

No, an event such as a payday, birthday, or anniversary does not have a location.

Q&A Why does the title bar indicate that this is an Appointment window?

The title bar and Appointment tab on the Ribbon will display the item as an appointment until you place a check mark in the 'All day event' check box. When you change the appointment to an all-day event, the title bar identifies the item as an event.

2
- Type **1/6/2012** as the first payday in the first Start time box.

- If necessary, click All day event to place a check mark in the 'All day event' check box and to change the appointment to an event (Figure 2–60).

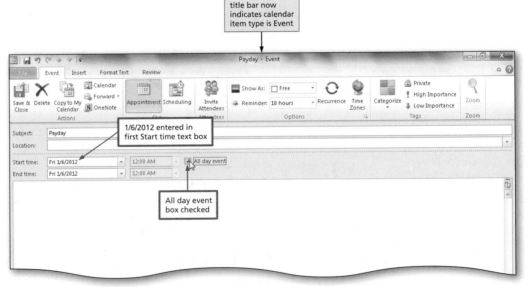

Figure 2–60

- Click the Recurrence button (Event tab | Options group) to display the Appointment Recurrence dialog box (Figure 2–61).

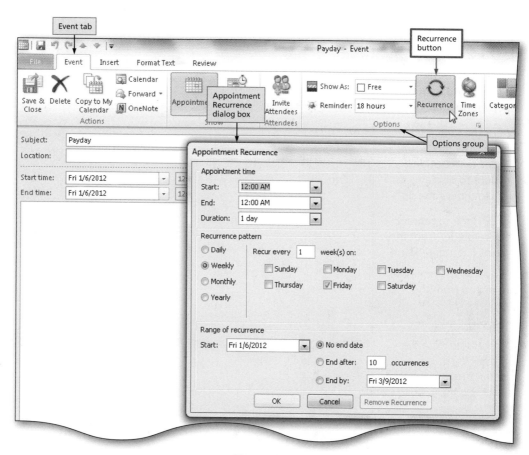

Figure 2–61

- If necessary, in the Recurrence pattern section, click Weekly (Appointment Recurrence dialog box) to set the Recurrence pattern to Weekly.

- In the Recur every text box, type 2 to have the event appear on the calendar every two weeks.

- If necessary, click the Friday check box to schedule the day for this event.

- If necessary, click any other selected check box in the Recur every section to remove the check marks so that only Friday is selected.

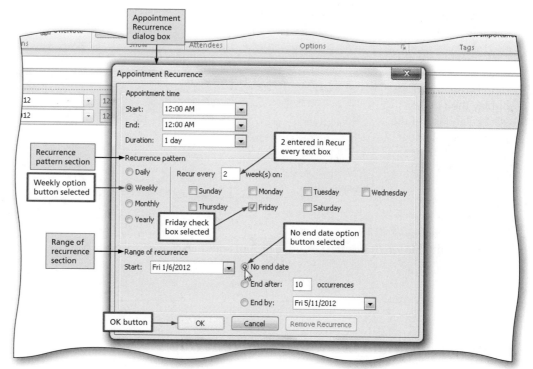

Figure 2–62

- In the 'Range of recurrence' section, click the 'No end date' option button so that the event remains on the calendar indefinitely (Figure 2–62).

5

• Click the OK button to accept the recurrence settings and close the Appointment Recurrence dialog box.

• Click the Reminder box arrow (Recurring Event tab | Options group) to display a list of reminder time slots.

• Click None to remove the reminder from the event (Figure 2–63).

Why was the reminder removed from the event?

The Payday event does not require a reminder.

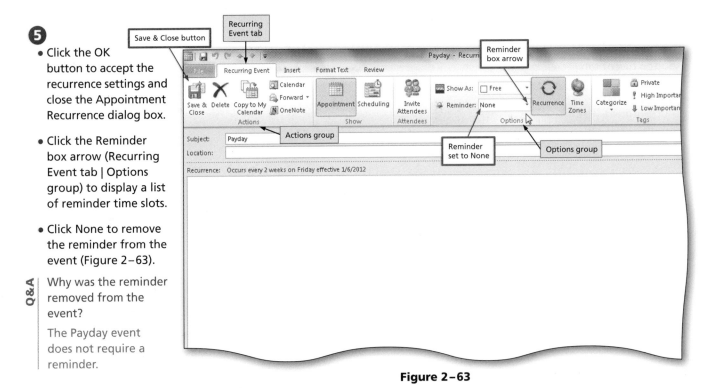

Figure 2–63

6

• Click the Save & Close button (Recurring Event tab | Actions group) to save the event and close the window.

• Click the appropriate scroll arrow on the Date Navigator to display the January 2012 calendar and the Payday event banner in the appointment area (Figure 2–64).

Experiment

• To view more pay dates at one time, click the Month button (Home tab | Arrange group) and then change the view to Week view.

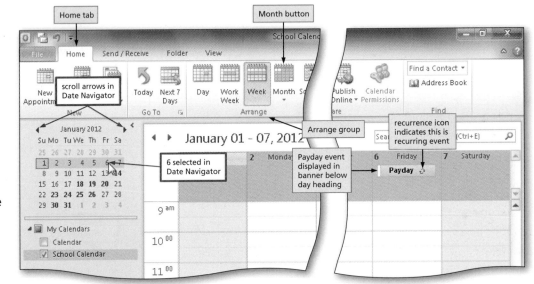

Figure 2–64

To Move a Recurring Event to a Different Day

Your school is changing the day it pays employees from Friday to Thursday. Because this will affect all Payday events in the series, you will change the date in the Payday event series from Friday to Thursday. The following steps change the date for all occurrences in a series.

1

• Click 6 to display January 6, 2012 and the Payday event banner in the appointment area.

• In the appointment area, click the Payday event banner to display commands for changing the appointment series on the Calendar Tools Appointment Series tab (Figure 2–65).

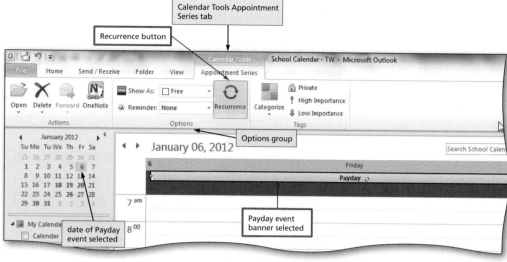

Figure 2–65

2

• Click the Recurrence button (Calendar Tools Appointment Series tab | Options group) to display the Appointment Recurrence dialog box.

• Click Thursday to place a check mark in the check box.

• Click Friday to remove the check mark from the check box.

• Click the Start box arrow in the Range of Recurrence area to change the start date to Thu 1/5/2012 (Figure 2–66).

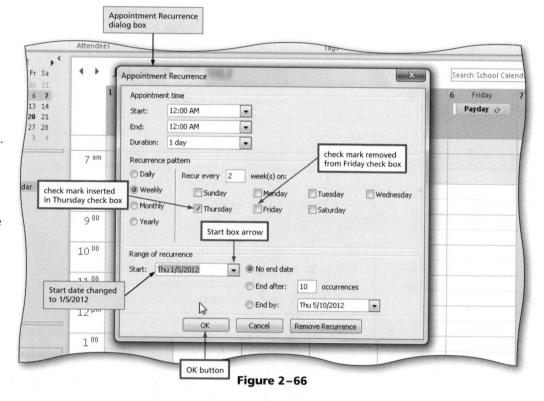

Figure 2–66

3

• Click the OK button to close the Appointment Recurrence dialog box and change the event day.

• Click 19 in the Date Navigator to view the event in the banner (Figure 2–67).

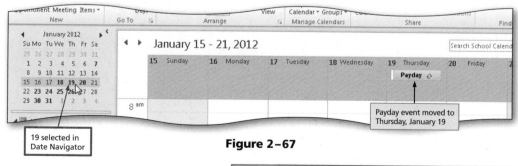

Figure 2–67

Other Ways
1. Double-click event, open series, click Recurrence button	2. Click event, press CTRL+O, click Recurrence button

BTW

Deleting Items Permanently
Items you delete, including events and e-mail messages, are stored in the Deleted Items folder until you empty this folder by right-clicking the Deleted Items folder and then clicking Empty Folder on the shortcut menu.

To Delete a Recurring Event

Deleting a recurring event is similar to deleting a recurring appointment. If you choose to delete a recurring event, you would use the following steps.

1. Click the scroll arrow on the Date Navigator to display the date of the event.
2. Click the event to display the Calendar Tools Appointment Series tab.
3. Click the Delete button (Calendar Tools Appointment Series tab | Actions group) to display the Delete menu.
4. Click Delete Series on the Delete menu to delete the event from the calendar.

Creating and Editing Meetings

BTW

Entering Locations
As you enter appointments, events, and meetings, you can include location information by entering it in the Location box. After entering one or more locations, you can click the Location box arrow and select a location from the list.

Outlook Calendar includes many items that help you manage your time in a given day, week, or month. In addition to appointments and events, you likely will have to schedule meetings with other people or reply to a meeting invitation you received indicating to the sender whether you can attend. As defined earlier, a meeting is an appointment that includes people to whom you send an invitation. A meeting also can include resources such as conference rooms. The person who creates the meeting and sends the invitations is known as the **meeting organizer**. The meeting organizer schedules a meeting by creating a **meeting request**, which is an e-mail invitation to the meeting and arrives in each attendee's Inbox. Responses to a meeting request arrive in the Inbox of the meeting organizer. The Untitled – Meeting request window is similar to the Untitled – Appointment window with a few exceptions. The meeting request window includes the To text box, where you enter an e-mail address for **attendees**, who are people invited to the meeting, and the Send button, which sends the invitation for the meeting to the attendees. When a meeting request arrives in the attendee's Inbox, it displays an icon different from an e-mail message icon.

Plan Ahead

Create an agenda before scheduling a meeting.
Have a list of topics for discussion prepared and estimate the time for each item and an ending time. When creating the agenda, consider who will attend the meeting and where it will be held.

- **Be sure you include everyone you need to attend the meeting.** Invite only those people whose attendance is absolutely necessary to ensure that all of the agenda items can be addressed at the meeting.

- **Be sure you have a location for the meeting.** Confirm that the location of the meeting is available and that the room is the appropriate size for the number of people invited. Also, make sure the room can accommodate any multimedia equipment that might be needed for the meeting, such as a projector or telephone and video conferencing capabilities.

To View the School Calendar in Overlay Mode

Before you schedule a meeting on your main calendar, you want to make sure no scheduling conflicts exist on the School Calendar. Outlook provides overlay mode, which allows you to view one calendar folder in front of another. The following steps display both calendars in overlay mode and make the Calendar folder the active folder.

1
- Click the Calendar check box to display the Calendar.

- If necessary, click the School Calendar arrow on the School Calendar tab to view the School Calendar in Overlay Mode (Figure 2–68).

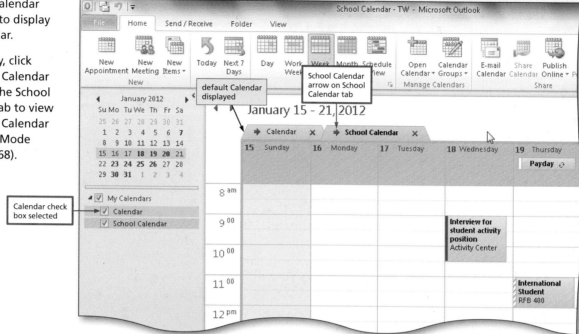

Figure 2–68

2
- Click the Calendar tab to display the Calendar in front of the School Calendar (Figure 2–69).

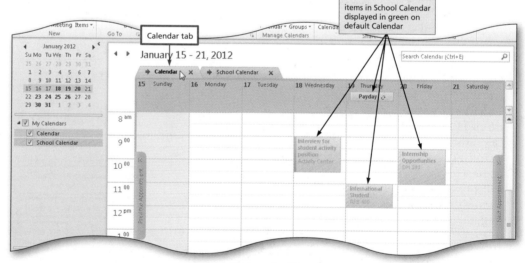

Figure 2–69

To Create and Send a Meeting Request

You want to meet with your advisor, Jay Ballentyne, to discuss your course selection for the next semester. Rather than send an e-mail message requesting the meeting, you decide to use Outlook Calendar to create this meeting. Meetings can be scheduled on your main calendar or supplemental calendars, even though meetings scheduled on your secondary calendars will be not be tallied. The following steps display the main calendar, create a meeting request, and send an invitation to your advisor. You will also use overlay mode to see if any conflicts appear on your schedule. If you are completing this project on a personal computer, use the e-mail address of your instructor instead of Jay Ballentyne's e-mail address.

1

- Click the New Meeting button (Home tab | New group) to open the Untitled – Meeting window.

- If necessary, maximize the Untitled – Meeting window to provide as much room as possible to work (Figure 2–70).

Why does the message header include the text, "Invitations have not been sent for this meeting"?

When scheduling a meeting with other people, invitations are sent to them. This notice reminds you that you have not yet sent the invitation to the meeting.

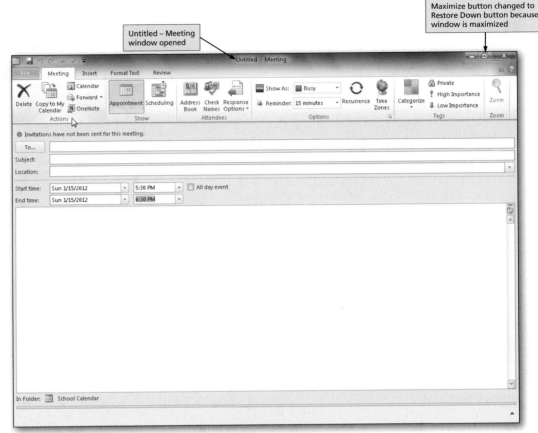

Untitled – Meeting window opened

Maximize button changed to Restore Down button because window is maximized

Figure 2–70

2

- Click the To text box and then type **jay .ballentyne@ hotmail.com** (substitute your instructor's e-mail address for Jay Ballentyne's e-mail address) as the invitee to this meeting.

- Press the TAB key to move the insertion point to the Subject text box.

- Type **Course Selection for Next Semester** as the subject of the meeting.

- Press the TAB key to move the insertion point to the Location text box.

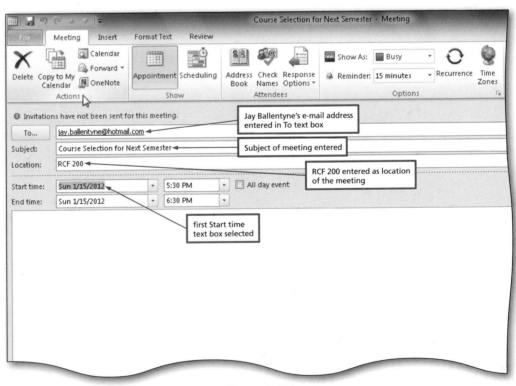

Jay Ballentyne's e-mail address entered in To text box

Subject of meeting entered

RCF 200 entered as location of the meeting

first Start time text box selected

Figure 2–71

- Type **RCF 200** as the location of the meeting.

- Press the TAB key to select the date in the first Start time text box (Figure 2–71).

3

- Type `4/23/2012` as the start date of the meeting, and then press the TAB key to select the time in the second Start time box.

- Type `12:30 pm` as the start time for the meeting, and then press the TAB key two times to select the time in the second End time box.

- Type `1:30 pm` as the end time for the meeting (Figure 2–72).

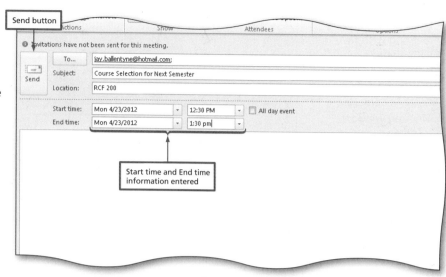

Figure 2–72

4

- Click the Send button to send the invitation to Jay Ballentyne (or your instructor) and add the meeting to the calendar.

- Click the appropriate scroll arrow on the Date Navigator to display the April 2012 calendar.

- Click April 23, 2012 on the Date Navigator to display the date in the meeting area and view the meeting (Figure 2–73).

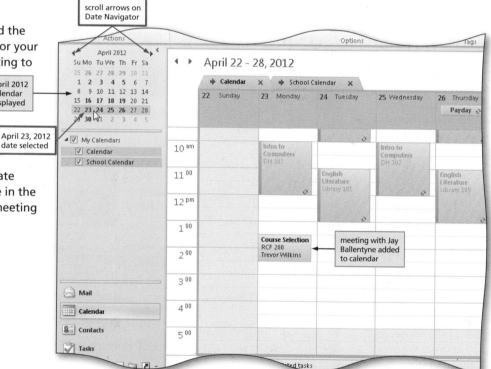

Figure 2–73

To Change the Time of a Meeting and Send an Update

Your schedule has changed, which means you need to change the time of the meeting with Jay Ballentyne and send an update to inform her of the change. Though the invitee can propose a new time, only the originator can change or delete the meeting. Other reasons to update a meeting request may be that you have added or removed attendees or resources, changed the meeting to a recurring series, or moved the meeting to a different date or time. The following steps change the time of the meeting and send an update to the attendee.

1

- Double-click the meeting with Jay Ballentyne (or your instructor) to open the Course Selection for Next Semester – Meeting window.

- Click the second Start time box arrow to display a list of times.

- Click 1:30 PM as the new start time for the meeting (Figure 2–74).

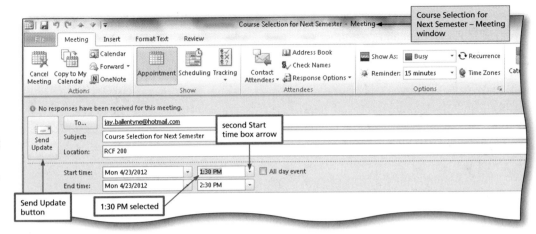

Figure 2–74

2

- Click the Send Update button in the message header to send the new information, close the meeting request, and view the updated meeting in the appointment area (Figure 2–75).

Q&A

What if I need to cancel the meeting?

Click the meeting in the appointment area to display the Calendar Tools Meeting tab on the Ribbon, click the Cancel Meeting button (Cancel Meeting button | Actions group), and then click the Send Cancellation button to send the cancellation notice and remove the meeting from the calendar.

Figure 2–75

Other Ways

1. Drag meeting to new time, click 'Save changes and send update', click OK, click Send Update

To Reply to a Meeting Request

You and another student, Gillian Winston, are working on a project for your social studies class. Using Outlook Calendar, Gillian has sent you a meeting request to meet and work on the project together. You accept the invitation by replying to the meeting request from Gillian. Outlook allows you to choose from four response options: Accept, Tentative, Decline, or Propose New Time. The following steps accept the meeting request from Gillian Winston. If you do not have a meeting request from Gillian Winston, substitute another meeting request in your Inbox. If you do not have any meeting requests, read these steps without performing them.

1

- If necessary, click the Mail button in the Navigation Pane to display the Inbox folder.

- Open a folder window displaying the data files for this chapter to retrieve the message from Gillian Winston.

- Arrange the window so you can see both the folder window and the Outlook window.

- Drag the Work on project message from the folder window to the Inbox to import the message into the Inbox.

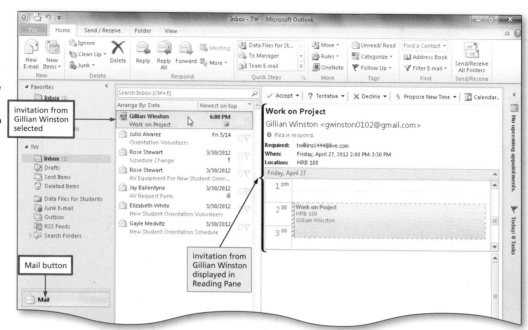

Figure 2–76

- If necessary, click the invitation from Gillian Winston in the message list to select the invitation (Figure 2–76).

2

- Double-click the Gillian Winston message header to open the invitation.

- Click the Accept button (Meeting tab | Respond group) to display the options for accepting the meeting, and then point to Send the Response Now (Figure 2–77).

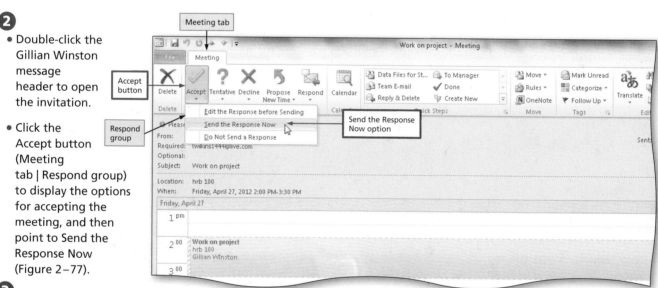

Figure 2–77

3

- Click Send the Response Now to send the accept response and add the meeting to the calendar.

Q&A What happened to the meeting invitation in the Inbox?

When you accept or tentatively accept a meeting request, the invitation is deleted from the Inbox and the meeting is added to your calendar. The meeting response is in the Sent Items folder.

Q&A What happens when I decline a meeting request?

When a meeting request is declined, the meeting request is removed from your Inbox and the meeting is not added to your calendar. The reply is placed in the Sent Items folder.

To Propose a New Meeting Time

BTW

BTWs
For a complete list of the BTWs found in the margins of this book, visit the Outlook 2010 BTW Web page (scsite.com/out2010/btw).

When you receive a meeting invitation, one thing you can do is propose a new time. When you propose a new time, a proposal is sent to the meeting originator via e-mail, indicating that you tentatively accept the request, but propose the meeting be held at a different time or on a different date. To propose a new time for a meeting, you would perform the following steps.

1. Click the appropriate meeting request to display the Calendar Tools Meeting Occurrence tab on the Ribbon.

2. Click the Propose New Time button (Calendar Tools Meeting Occurrence tab | Respond group) to display the Occurrence menu.

3. Click the Tentative and Propose New Time option to display the Propose New Time dialog box for the selected meeting.

4. Drag through the time slot that you want to propose or enter the appropriate information in the Meeting start and Meeting end boxes (Propose New Time dialog box).

5. Click the Propose time button to open the New Time Proposed – Meeting Response window.

6. Click the Send button.

To Change the Time of a One-Time Meeting and Send an Update

BTW

E-Mailing Calendar Items
To send a calendar item to someone else, click the item, such as an appointment, and then click the Forward button (Calendar Tools Appointment tab | Actions group). Enter the e-mail address of the recipient and send the message.

When someone proposes a new meeting time, it may be necessary to update the meeting request to the other potential attendees. Other reasons to update a meeting request may be that you have added or removed attendees, changed the meeting to a recurring series, or moved the meeting to a different date. To change the time of a meeting and send an update, you would perform the following steps.

1. With the Calendar window open, drag the meeting to its new time.

2. When the Microsoft Outlook dialog box is displayed, select the 'Save changes and send an update' option button.

3. Click the OK button. If the appointment opens, click the Send button.

To Cancel a Meeting

You no longer need to meet with Jay Ballentyne and want to cancel the meeting. The following steps cancel a meeting.

- Click the Course Selection for Next Semester meeting in the appointment area to select the meeting and display the Calendar Tools Meeting tab on the Ribbon (Figure 2–78).

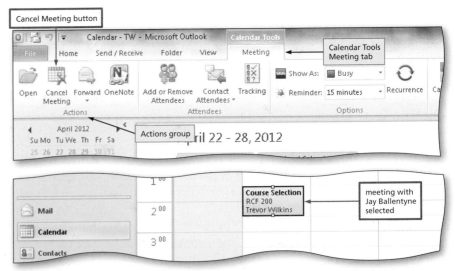

Figure 2–78

2

• Click the Cancel Meeting button (Calendar Tools Meeting tab | Actions group) to open the window for the selected meeting (Figure 2–79).

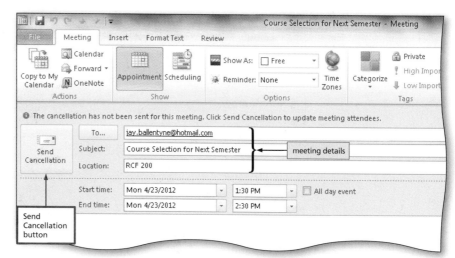

Figure 2–79

3

• Click the Send Cancellation button in the message header to send the cancellation notice and delete the meeting from your calendar (Figure 2–80).

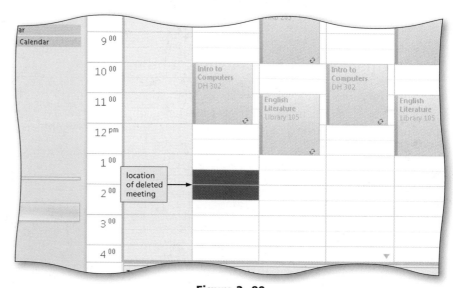

Figure 2–80

Other Ways

1. Click Delete button (Calendar Tools Meeting tab | Actions group), select option

Printing Calendars in Different Views

All or part of a calendar can be printed in a number of different views, or **print styles**. Printing a calendar enables you to distribute the calendar to others in a form that can be read or viewed, but cannot be edited. You can print a monthly, daily, or weekly view of your calendar and select options such as the date range and fonts used. You also can view your calendar in a list by changing the current view from Calendar view to List view. This section prints your calendar from Calendar view in the Weekly Calendar style, and then changes the current view to List view and prints the calendar in Table style. Table 2–7 lists the print styles available for printing your calendar from Calendar view.

Table 2–7 Print Styles for Calendar View	
Print Style	**Description**
Daily	Prints a daily appointment schedule for a specific date including one day per page, a daily task list, an area for notes, and a two-month calendar
Weekly Agenda	Prints a seven-day weekly calendar with one week per page and a two-month calendar
Weekly Calendar	Prints a seven-day weekly calendar with one week per page and an hourly schedule, similar to the Daily style
Monthly	Prints five weeks per page of a particular month or date range
Tri–fold	Prints a page for each day, including a daily task list and a weekly schedule
Calendar Details	Prints a list of calendar items and supporting details

Plan Ahead

Determine the best method for distributing a calendar.
The traditional method of distributing a calendar uses a printer to produce a hard copy. A **hard copy** or **printout** is information that exists on a physical medium such as paper. Hard copies can serve as reference material if your storage medium is lost or becomes corrupted and you need to re-create the calendar.

To Print the Calendar in Weekly Calendar Style

In this exercise, you will be working with the School Calendar, so you need to make that the active calendar and close the default calendar. Also, you want a hard copy of your first week of classes so that you can see all your appointments for the first week of the semester. The following steps display the School Calendar, and then print the calendar for the first week of classes.

1
- Click the Calendar check box to close the default Calendar and display only the School calendar.

- Click the Go To Dialog Box Launcher to display the Go To Date dialog box.

- Type 1/29/2012 to display that date in the appointment area, and then click the OK button to close the Go To Date dialog box.

- Click File on the Ribbon to open the Backstage view.

- Click the Print tab in the Backstage view to display the Print gallery.

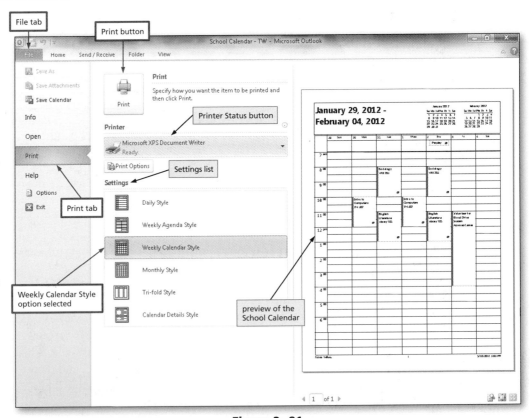

Figure 2–81

- Select Weekly Calendar Style in the Settings list to preview how the printed calendar will look in Weekly Calendar Style (Figure 2–81).

Experiment

- Click the other settings to preview the different print styles. When finished, select Weekly Calendar Style.

2

- Verify the printer name that appears on the Printer Status button will print a hard copy of the calendar. If necessary, click the Printer Status button to display a list of available printer options and then click the desired printer to change the currently selected printer.

- Click the Print button in the Print gallery to print the calendar on the currently selected printer.

- When the printer stops, retrieve the hard copy (Figure 2–82).

Q&A How can I print multiple copies of my calendar?

Click the Print Options button to display the Print dialog box, increase the number in the Number of Copies box, and then click the Print button to send the calendar to the printer and return to the calendar.

Q&A What if I decide not to print the calendar at this time?

Click File on the Ribbon to close the Backstage view and return to the calendar window.

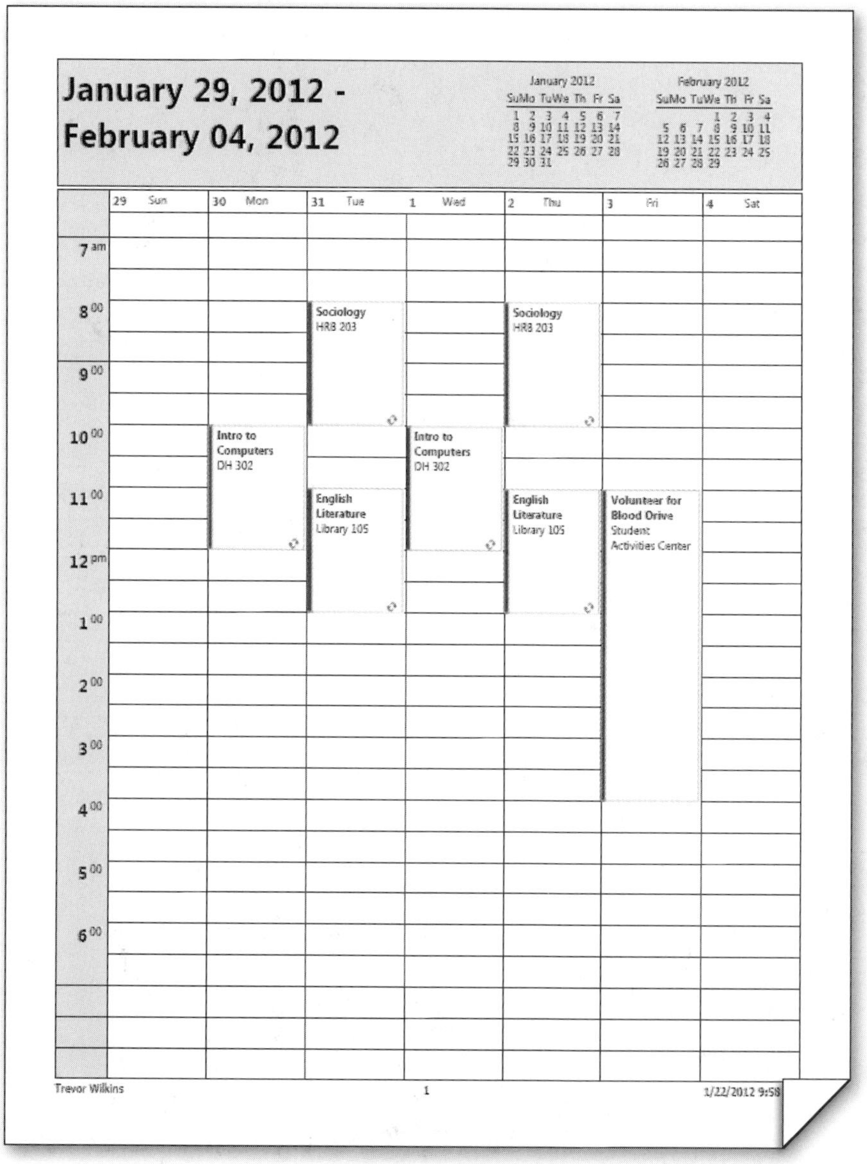

Figure 2–82

Other Ways

1. Press CTRL+P, press ENTER

BTW

Shortcut Keys
To print a complete list of shortcut keys in Outlook, click the Microsoft Outlook Help button near the upper-right corner of the Outlook window, type **shortcut keys** in the search text box at the top of the Outlook Help window, press the ENTER key, click the Keyboard shortcuts for Microsoft Outlook link, click the Show All link in the upper-right corner of the Help window, click the Print button in the Help window, and then click the Print button in the Print dialog box.

To Change the Current View to List View

You can print a list of all your calendar items using Table style, which prints your calendar in a table format. To print a calendar in this view, you must change the current view to List view, which only is available when you change the current view from the View tab. The following steps change the view from Calendar view to List view and then print the calendar in the Table style.

1

- With the Calendar button selected in the Navigation Pane, click View on the Ribbon to display the View tab.

- Click the Change View button (View tab | Current View group) to display the Change View gallery (Figure 2–83).

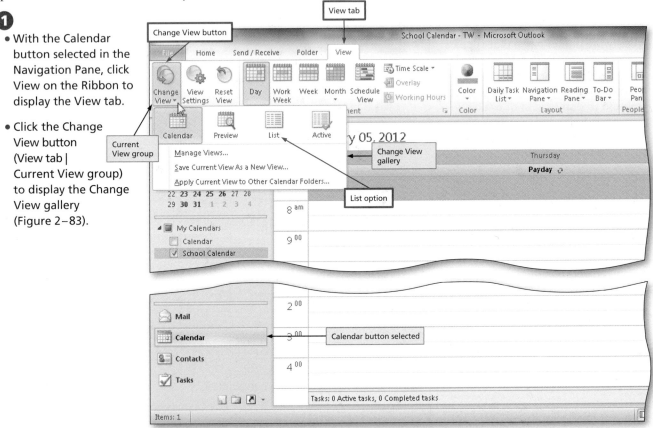

Figure 2–83

2

- Click List in the Change View gallery to display a list of calendar items in the appointment area (Figure 2–84).

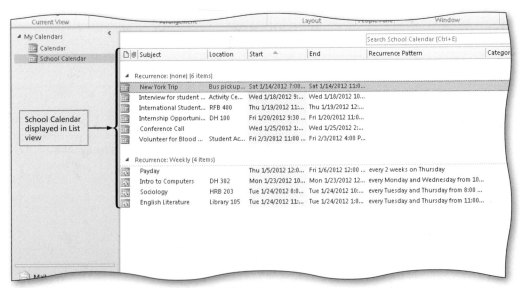

Figure 2–84

To Print the Calendar from List View

Now that the calendar view is displaying all your calendar items in a list, you want to print the calendar in this format. The following steps print the calendar in Table style.

1 Click File on the Ribbon to open the Backstage View.

2 Click the Print tab in the Backstage view to display the Print gallery.

3 Click the Table style option in the Settings list to preview the calendar in Table Style.

4 Verify the printer name in the Printer box will print a hard copy of the calendar in Table Style. If necessary, click the Printer box to display a list of available printer options and then click the desired printer to change the currently selected printer.

5 Click the Print button to send the list of appointments to the selected printer.

6 When the printer stops, retrieve the hard copy (Figure 2–85).

Q&A How can I modify what is included on the hard copy?

Click the Print Options button to display the Print dialog box for additional print options.

Q&A When I changed the view from List view to Calendar view, why did the Calendar display the current date and not the date I printed?

The calendar always displays the current date when you change from List view to Calendar view.

BTW

Changing Settings before Printing
To change the margins, page orientation, or paper size before printing, click the Print Options button in the Print dialog box and then click the Page Setup button to display the Page Setup dialog box.

🗋	Ⓤ	Subject	Location	Start	End	Recurrence Pattern	
Recurrence: (none) (6 items)							
		Volunteer for Blood ...	Student Ac...	Fri 2/3/2012 11:0...	Fri 2/3/2012 4:00 ...		
		Conference Call		Wed 1/25/2012 1...	Wed 1/25/2012 2:...		
		Internship Opportun...	DH 100	Fri 1/20/2012 9:3...	Fri 1/20/2012 11:0...		
		International Studen...	RFB 400	Thu 1/19/2012 11...	Thu 1/19/2012 12:...		
		Interview for studen...	Activity Ce...	Wed 1/18/2012 9...	Wed 1/18/2012 1...		
		New York Trip	Bus pickup ...	Sat 1/14/2012 7:0...	Sat 1/14/2012 11:...		
Recurrence: Weekly (4 items)							
		English Literature	Library 105	Tue 1/24/2012 11...	Tue 1/24/2012 1:0...	every Tuesday and Thursday from 11:00 AM to 1:00 PM	
		Sociology	HRB 203	Tue 1/24/2012 8:...	Tue 1/24/2012 10:...	every Tuesday and Thursday from 8:00 AM to 10:00 AM	
		Intro to Computers	DH 302	Mon 1/23/2012 1...	Mon 1/23/2012 1...	every Monday and Wednesday from 10:00 AM to 12:00 PM	
		Payday		Thu 1/5/2012 12:...	Fri 1/6/2012 12:00...	every Thursday	

Trevor Wilkins · 1 · 1/22/2012 10:17 AM

Figure 2–85

Other Ways

1. Press CTRL+P, click Print

Exporting and Importing Folders

The calendar now is ready to be saved on a USB flash drive. Saving your work on an external storage device allows you to take your schedule to another computer where you will import the calendar for use on a secondary computer.

With many programs, a single file, such as a letter or spreadsheet, can be saved directly on an external storage device. With Outlook, each appointment, task, or contact is a separate file. Rather than saving numerous individual files, Outlook uses the **Import and Export Wizard** to guide you through the process of saving an entire folder including any subfolders, which are folders within another folder. Transferring a subfolder to a USB flash drive is called **exporting**. Adding a subfolder to your Outlook mailbox is called **importing**. Subfolders can be imported and exported from any Outlook item. When you export a folder, Outlook saves the folder and its subfolders to a USB flash drive, adding the extension **.pst** to the exported file. A .pst file is a data file that stores all Outlook items in a specific location.

To Export a Subfolder to a USB Flash Drive

The following steps export a Calendar subfolder to a USB flash drive.

1
- Connect the USB flash drive containing the Data Files for Students to one of the computer's USB ports.

- Click File on the Ribbon to display the Backstage view and then click the Open tab to display the Open options (Figure 2–86).

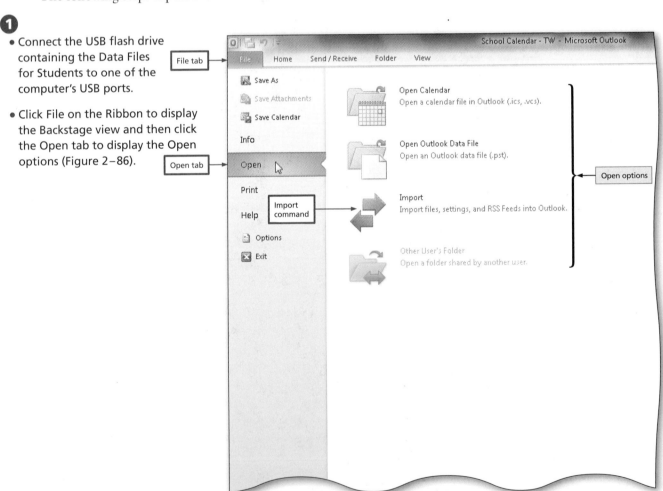

Figure 2–86

2

- Click Import to display the Import and Export Wizard dialog box (Figure 2–87).

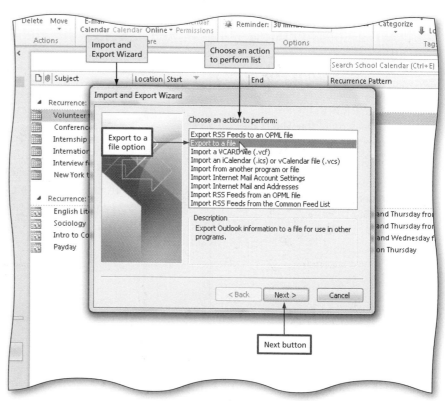

Figure 2–87

3

- Click 'Export to a file' in the 'Choose an action to perform' list to indicate you want to export an item.

- Click the Next button to display the Export to a File dialog box.

- In the Export to a File dialog box, click Outlook Data File (.pst) to select .pst as the file type for exporting (Figure 2–88).

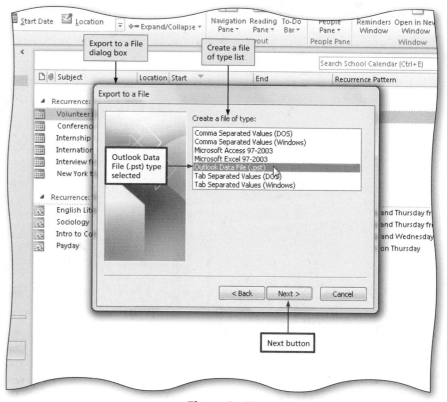

Figure 2–88

4

- Click the Next button to display the first Export Outlook Data File dialog box.

- If necessary, scroll until the Calendar folder is displayed, and then click the expand arrow to the left of the Calendar icon in the 'Select the folder to export from' list to view School Calendar in the list.

- Click School Calendar to select it as the folder to export from (Figure 2–89).

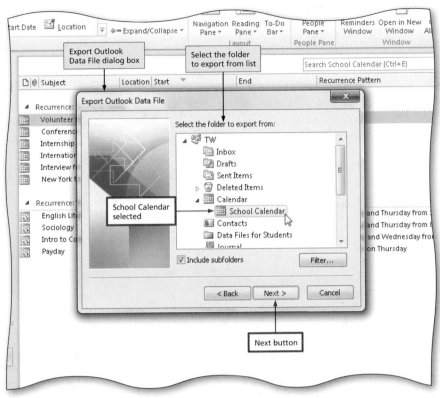

Figure 2–89

5

- Click the Next button to display the next Export Outlook Data File dialog box.

- Click the Browse button to display the Open Outlook Data Files dialog box (Figure 2–90).

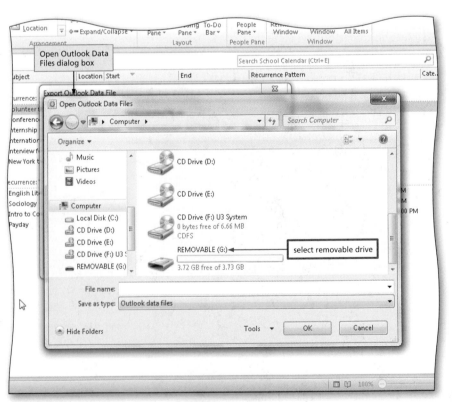

Figure 2–90

- If necessary, click Computer in the Navigation pane to display the list of possible locations, and then double-click the drive where you store your data files, such as the REMOVABLE (G:) USB flash drive.

- Type **School Calendar** in the File name text box (Figure 2–91).

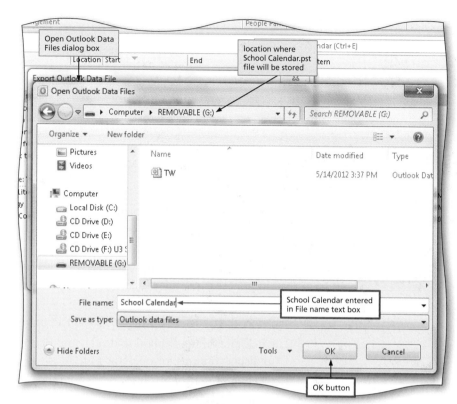

Figure 2–91

- Click the OK button to specify the name and location of the file, close the Open Outlook Data Files dialog box, and return to the Export Outlook Data File dialog box.

- Click the 'Replace duplicates with items exported' option button to replace any duplicate information in the School Calendar with the information in the School Calendar you are exporting (Figure 2–92).

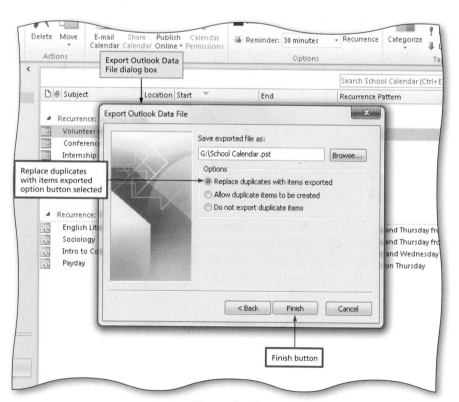

Figure 2–92

8

• Click the Finish button to export the School Calendar subfolder to a .pst file.

◄ What should I do if I am prompted for a password?
Q&A Click the OK button to avoid associating a password with this file.

◄ What programs can I use to view the exported subfolder (.pst file)?
Q&A Exported subfolders (.pst files) can be viewed only in Outlook and must be opened from within Outlook.

TO IMPORT A PERSONAL SUBFOLDER

You may want to transfer your school calendar from one computer to another. For example, you may want to have your calendar on a notebook computer and a desktop computer. To do this, you need to export your calendar, as shown earlier, and then import that calendar to another computer. To import a calendar, you would perform the following steps.

1. Select the folder into which you want to import the data file.
2. Click File on the Ribbon to display the Backstage view, and then click the Open tab to display options for opening a file.
3. Click the Import button to start the Import and Export Wizard.
4. Click 'Import from another program or file' and then click the Next button.
5. Select Outlook Data File (.pst) and then click the Next button.
6. Click the Browse button in the Import Outlook Data File dialog box and then navigate to the location where the data file is stored.
7. Select the file to import and click the Open button.
8. In the Options section, select the desired option regarding duplicates and then click the Next button.
9. In the 'Select the folder to import from' box, select the appropriate folder and include subfolders if desired.
10. Select the 'Import items into the current folder' option button.
11. Click the Finish button.

To Delete a Personal Subfolder

The School Calendar subfolder now has been exported to a USB flash drive. A copy of the School Calendar.pst file still is stored on the hard disk of your computer, and appears in Outlook's Folder List. To delete a subfolder from the computer entirely, use the Delete command. The following steps delete a personal subfolder. If you did not complete the previous set of steps, do not delete the School Calendar subfolder.

1

- Click the School Calendar button in the Navigation Pane to display the School Calendar in the appointment area.

- Click the Delete Calendar button (Folder tab | Actions group) to display the Microsoft Outlook dialog box (Figure 2–93).

Q&A

Is there a way to retrieve a deleted folder?

Yes. Outlook sends the deleted folder to the **Deleted Items** folder. If you accidentally delete a folder without first exporting it to an external storage device, you still can open the folder by double-clicking it in the Deleted Items folder in the Folder List.

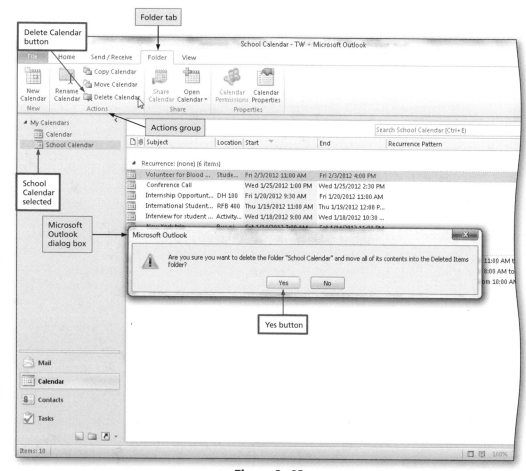

Figure 2–93

Q&A

Can I delete the Calendar folder below My Calendars?

The Calendar folder is the default Calendar and cannot be deleted.

2

- Click the Yes button in the Microsoft Outlook dialog box to delete the folder.

Other Ways
1. Right-click folder to delete, click Delete Calendar
2. Click folder to delete, press DELETE

To Quit Outlook

With the project complete, the final step is to quit the Outlook program and return to the Windows desktop. The following step quits Outlook.

1 Click the Close button on the right side of the title bar to quit Outlook.

BTW

Quick Reference

For a table that lists how to complete the tasks covered in this book using the mouse, Ribbon, shortcut menu, and keyboard, see the Quick Reference Summary at the back of this book, or visit the Outlook 2010 Quick Reference Web page (scsite.com/out2010/qr).

BTW

Certification

The Microsoft Office Specialist program provides an opportunity for you to obtain a valuable industry credential — proof that you have the Outlook 2010 skills required by employers. For more information, visit the Outlook 2010 Certification Web page (scsite.com/out2010/cert).

Chapter Summary

In this chapter, you have learned how to use Outlook to create a personal schedule by entering appointments, creating recurring appointments, moving appointments to new dates, and scheduling events. You also learned how to invite attendees to a meeting, accept a meeting request, and propose and change the time of a meeting. To review your schedule, you learned to view and print your calendar in different views and print styles. Finally, you learned how to export your personal folder to an external storage device. The following list includes all the new Outlook skills you have learned in this chapter.

1. Create a Personal Folder (OUT 54)
2. Display a Personal Calendar (OUT 56)
3. Remove the Default Calendar from the Appointment Area (OUT 56)
4. Go to a Specific Date (OUT 57)
5. Display the Calendar in Work Week View (OUT 58)
6. Display the Calendar in Week View (OUT 59)
7. Display the Calendar in Month View (OUT 60)
8. Display the Calendar in Schedule View (OUT 60)
9. Create a One-Time Appointment Using the Appointment Area (OUT 62)
10. Create a One-Time Appointment Using the Appointment Window (OUT 64)
11. Change the Status of an Appointment (OUT 67)
12. Set a Reminder for an Appointment (OUT 68)
13. Save the Appointment (OUT 69)
14. Create a Recurring Appointment Using the Appointment Window (OUT 71)
15. Set Recurrence Options for a Recurring Appointment (OUT 72)
16. Set a Reminder and Show As Options for an Appointment (OUT 74)
17. Enter an Appointment Date and Time Using Natural Language Phrases (OUT 77)
18. Move an Appointment to a Different Time on the Same Day (OUT 79)
19. Move an Appointment to a Different Date (OUT 80)
20. Move an Appointment to a Different Month (OUT 81)
21. Delete a Single Occurrence of a Recurring Appointment (OUT 82)
22. Create a One-Time Event in the Appointment Window (OUT 84)
23. Move a One-Time Event to a New Date and Change the Event Status (OUT 86)
24. Delete a One-Time Event (OUT 87)
25. Create a Recurring Event Using the Appointment Window (OUT 88)
26. Move a Recurring Event to a Different Day (OUT 90)
27. Delete a Recurring Event (OUT 92)
28. View the School Calendar in Overlay Mode (OUT 92)
29. Create and Send a Meeting (OUT 93)
30. Change the Time of a Meeting and Send an Update (OUT 95)
31. Reply to a Meeting Request (OUT 96)
32. Cancel a Meeting (OUT 98)
33. Print the Calendar in Weekly Calendar Style (OUT 100)
34. Change the Current View to List View (OUT 102)
35. Export a Subfolder to a USB Flash Drive (OUT 104)
36. Delete a Personal Subfolder (OUT 108)

Learn It Online

Test your knowledge of chapter content and key terms.

Instructions: To complete the Learn It Online exercises, start your browser, click the Address bar, and then enter the Web address `scsite.com/out2010/learn`. When the Outlook 2010 Learn It Online page is displayed, click the link for the exercise you want to complete and then read the instructions.

Chapter Reinforcement TF, MC, and SA
A series of true/false, multiple choice, and short answer questions that test your knowledge of the chapter content.

Flash Cards
An interactive learning environment where you identify chapter key terms associated with displayed definitions.

Practice Test
A series of multiple choice questions that test your knowledge of chapter content and key terms.

Who Wants To Be a Computer Genius?
An interactive game that challenges your knowledge of chapter content in the style of a television quiz show.

Wheel of Terms
An interactive game that challenges your knowledge of chapter key terms in the style of the television show *Wheel of Fortune*.

Crossword Puzzle Challenge
A crossword puzzle that challenges your knowledge of key terms presented in the chapter.

Apply Your Knowledge

Reinforce the skills and apply the concepts you learned in this chapter.

Editing a Calendar
Note: To complete this assignment, you will be required to use the Data Files for Students. See the inside back cover of this book for instructions on downloading the Data Files for Students, or contact your instructor for information about accessing the required files.

Instructions: Start Outlook. Edit the calendar provided in the file called Apply Your Knowledge 2-1 Calendar, located on the Data Files for Students. The Apply Your Knowledge 2-1 Calendar is a personal calendar with appointments for personal activities, class schedules, and events in 2012. Many of the scheduled items have changed and you now need to revise these scheduled items.

Perform the following tasks:
1. Create a folder called Apply Your Knowledge and import the Apply Your Knowledge 2-1 Calendar folder into the newly created folder.
2. Display only the Apply Your Knowledge 2-1 Calendar in the Outlook Calendar window. Use Week view to display the calendar.
3. Change Kelly's Birthday Party from February 17 to February 19. The party is at the same time.
4. Reschedule the work on February 9 to February 12. The work starts at 12:00 PM and continues until 4:00 PM.
5. Reschedule the two-hour Chemistry Study Lab on Wednesday evenings from 5:00 PM – 7:00 PM to 6:00 PM – 8:00 PM in CHM 225.
6. Change Intramural Basketball from Mondays and Wednesdays to Tuesdays and Thursdays at the same time.

Continued >

Apply Your Knowledge *continued*

7. Print the final calendar in Month view, shown in Figure 2–94, and then submit the printout to your instructor.

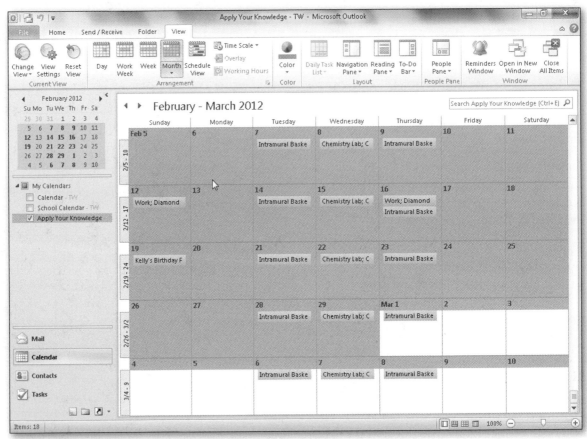

Figure 2–94

8. Export the Apply Your Knowledge 2–1 Calendar folder to a USB flash drive and then delete the folder from the hard disk.

Extend Your Knowledge

Extend the skills you learned in this chapter and experiment with new skills. You may need to use Help to complete the assignment.

Sharing and Publishing Calendars

Instructions: Start Outlook. Create a new blank calendar and then add appointments to the new calendar. You will also share the calendar with others.

Perform the following tasks:

1. Start Outlook and create a new blank calendar named Extend Your Knowledge 2-1.

2. Add three appointments to the new calendar. At least one appointment should be a weekly recurring appointment and end after six occurrences.

3. Use Help to learn about e-mailing calendars, creating a Windows Live account, and publishing a calendar online.

4. Using the E-mail Calendar button (Home tab | Share group), e-mail the calendar to your instructor. The calendar should include only the dates containing the three appointments added in Step 2. Change the e-mail layout to 'List of events.'

5. Create a Windows Live account, and then publish the calendar to Office.com (Figure 2–95). (If you are unable to create a Windows Live account, contact your instructor.) In an e-mail message, write three reasons that someone might choose to publish their calendar online.

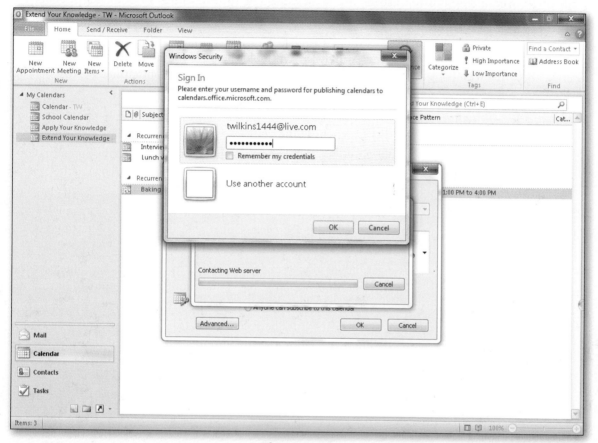

Figure 2–95

6. Share your calendar with your instructor. When you share your calendar, request permission to view your instructor's calendar. In the e-mail message, include the answers to the following questions: What is the difference between sending a calendar as an e-mail message and sharing a calendar? What steps are required to designate who can view the calendar, as well as who can edit the calendar?

7. You decide that it no longer is necessary to share your calendar or publish it online. Configure your calendar so that it no longer is shared with anyone or published online.

8. Remove the three appointments added in Step 2.

9. Submit your answers in the format specified by your instructor.

Make It Right

Analyze a calendar and correct all errors and/or improve the design.

Correcting Appointment Times

Note: To complete this assignment, you may be required to use the Data Files for Students. See the inside back cover of this book for instructions on downloading the Data Files for Students, or contact your instructor for information about accessing the required files.

Instructions: Start Outlook. Import the Make It Right 2-1 Calendar folder in the Data Files for Students folder into Outlook. While reviewing your Outlook calendar, you realize that you created several appointments incorrectly. You will identify and open the incorrect appointments, edit them so that they reflect the correct information, and then save all changes.

Perform the following tasks:

1. Display only the Make It Right 2–1 Calendar in the Outlook Calendar window.

2. While adding a dentist appointment to the Calendar, you inadvertently recorded the appointment time as 2:00 AM instead of 2:00 PM. Edit the appointment on April 2, 2012, and change the Start time to 2:00 PM. The appointment still will last one hour.

3. The Yoga class scheduled for Wednesday, April 25, 2012 is a recurring appointment on your calendar. Change the appointment to reflect the Yoga class meeting every Thursday starting April 19, 2012 through the end of June from 7:00 PM until 9:00 PM.

4. Your monthly homeowner's association board meeting has modified their meeting schedule to meet on the second Tuesday of each month instead of on the thirteenth of each month. Update the calendar to reflect this change.

5. An appointment during the week of April 16, 2012, has been added to your calendar two times with the same start time and end time. Remove one of these appointments from the calendar.

6. Print the calendar using the Monthly style for April 8, 2012 to May 12, 2012 (Figure 2–96).

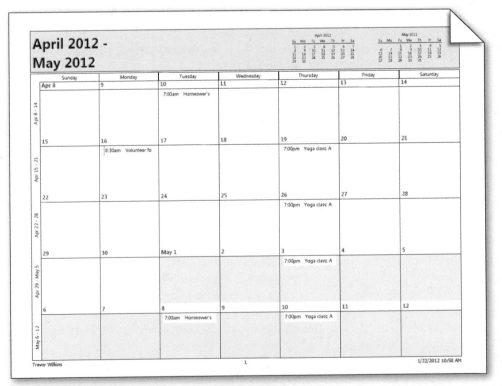

Figure 2–96

7. Export the Make It Right 2–1 Calendar folder to a USB flash drive and then delete the folder from the hard disk.

8. Submit the calendar in a format specified by your instructor.

In the Lab

Design, create, modify, and/or use a document using the guidelines, concepts, and skills presented in this chapter. Labs are listed in order of increasing difficulty.

Lab 1: Creating Recurring Events

Problem: You are a graduate assistant for the English Department at your college and have been asked to create a list of faculty birthdays. Table 2–8 lists each faculty member's birthday. Enter the birthdays as recurring events (these events should occur one time per year).

Perform the following tasks:

1. Create a personal Calendar subfolder named English Department Birthdays.

2. Create the events in the calendar, using the information listed in Table 2–8.

Table 2–8 Employee Birthday Information	
Employee Name	**Birthday**
Shannon Brown	1/6/1952
Brett Lipinski	2/17/1980
Sloan McLoughlin	3/29/1975
Joseph Kelly	5/6/1963
Emma Thompson-Wright	6/5/1979
Madelyn Judowski	8/26/1968

3. For each event, show the time as Free.

4. For each event, set the reminder to one day.

5. Set each event to recur yearly on the same day.

6. Each event should be an all-day event.

7. Print the English Department Birthdays calendar using the Calendar Details style, and submit it in a format specified by your instructor.

In the Lab

Lab 2: Creating a Calendar

Problem: You are the owner of a small hardware store. Your store has experienced rapid growth during the last several months, and with spring approaching, you need to change to regular from seasonal stock. As the owner, you also have administrative duties to perform, such as staff meetings, payroll, advertising, and sales campaigns. To make your schedule even more hectic, you coach your child's spring soccer team. You need to create a schedule of appointments to help you keep track of your various jobs and responsibilities each day (Figure 2–97).

Continued >

In the Lab *continued*

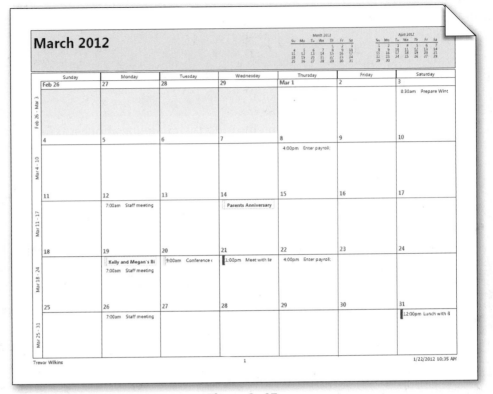

Figure 2–97

Perform the following tasks:

1. Create a personal Calendar subfolder named A-1 Hardware.

2. Enter the calendar items in the calendar, using the information listed in Table 2–9.

Table 2–9 Calendar Appointment Information

Description	Location	Date	Time	Show As	Reminder	Recurrence
Staff meeting	Lunchroom	Every Monday from March 12, 2012 – June 12, 2012	7:00 AM – 8:00 AM	Busy	30 minutes	Weekly, end by June 12, 2012
Prepare Winter Closeout Sale	Manager's Office	March 3, 2012	8:30 AM – 10:30 AM	Busy	10 minutes	None
Enter payroll	Manager's Office	Start March 8, 2012, every Thursday	4:00 PM – 5:00 PM	Busy	15 minutes	Every two weeks, no end date
Kelly & Megan's birthday		March 19, 2012	All-day event	Free	None	Yearly
Parents Anniversary		March 14, 2012	All-day event	Free	1 day	Yearly
Conference call with Liz and Greg		March 20, 2012	9:00 AM – 10:00 AM	Tentative	15 minutes	None
Meet with lawn care supplier		March 21, 2012	1:00 PM – 2:00 PM	Out of Office	30 minutes	None
Lunch with Beth		March 31, 2012	12:00 PM – 1:00 PM	Out of Office	15 minutes	None

3. Print the Appointment calendar for the month of March, and then submit the printout in the format specified by your instructor.

In the Lab

Lab 3: Creating a Schedule

Problem: Start Outlook. Create a new Calendar folder using your name as the name of the new folder. You are to create a schedule of classes and other appointments using the information in Table 2–10. This calendar is for the spring semester that begins Monday, January 30, 2012, and ends Friday, May 11, 2012. The calendar you create is shown in Figure 2–98.

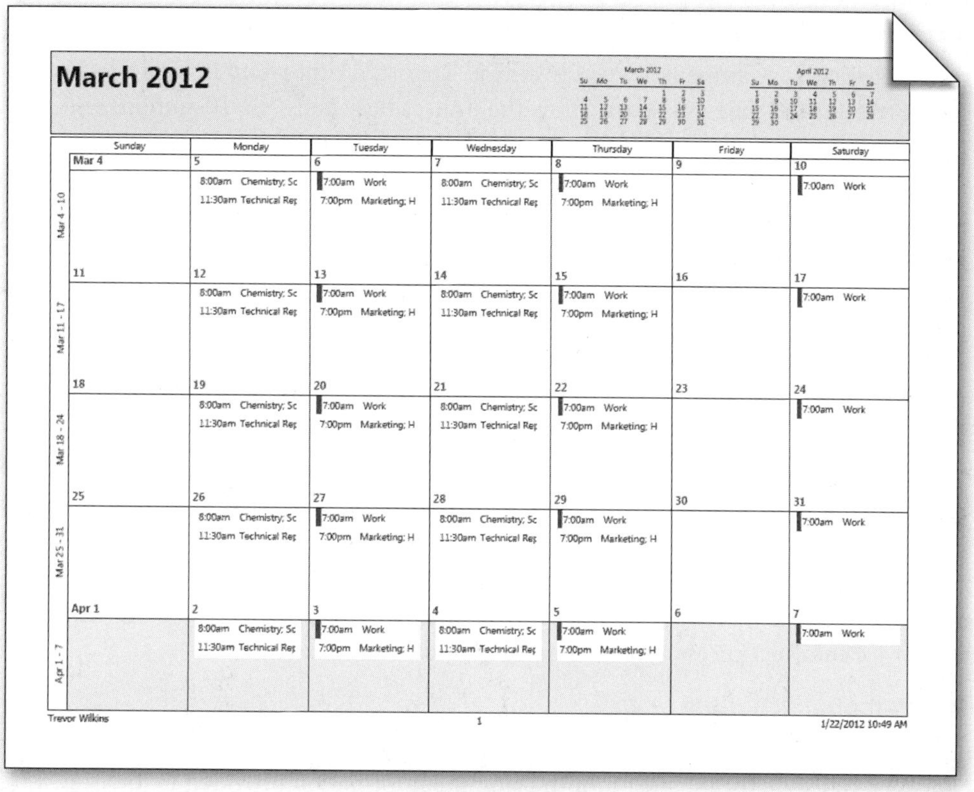

Figure 2–98

Table 2–10 Appointment Information

Subject	Location	Start Date	Time	Show As	Reminder	Recurrence	End After
Doctor Appointment	Drs. office	2/3/2012	2:00 PM – 3:00 PM	Out of Office	30 minutes	None	
Work		1/31/2012	7:00 AM – 3:30 PM	Out of Office	1 hour	Weekly, T, Th, Sa	No end date
Volunteer for New Student Orientation	Student Union	1/21/2012	8:30 AM – 12:00 PM	Out of Office	15 minutes	None	
Chemistry	Science 300	1/30/2012	8:00 AM – 9:30 AM	Busy	15 minutes	Weekly, M, W	30 classes
Technical Report Writing	HRB 201	1/30/2012	11:30 AM – 1:00 PM	Busy	10 minutes	Weekly, M, W	30 classes
Marketing	HRB 300	1/31/2012	7:00 PM – 8:30 PM	Busy	30 minutes	Weekly, T, Th	30 classes

Perform the following tasks:

1. Create a one-time appointment for the first item in Table 2–10. Enter the text in the Subject column, Doctor Appointment, as the appointment subject. Enter the location, start date, and time as shown in Table 2–10. Show the time as Out of Office in your calendar and set a 30-minute reminder.

Continued >

In the Lab continued

2. Create a recurring appointment for the Work item in Table 2–10. Enter the subject, start date, and time as shown. Show the time as Out of Office in your calendar and set a one-hour reminder. Set the appointment to recur weekly on Tuesdays, Thursdays, and Saturdays with no end date.

3. Create a one-time appointment for the Volunteer for New Student Orientation item in Table 2–10. Enter the subject, start date, and time as shown. Show the time as Out of Office in your calendar and set a 15-minute reminder.

4. Create a recurring appointment for the Chemistry item in Table 2–10. Enter the subject, start date, and time as shown. Show the time as busy and set a 15-minute reminder. Set the appointment to recur weekly on Mondays and Wednesdays for 30 occurrences.

5. Create a recurring appointment for the Technical Report Writing item in Table 2–10. Enter the subject, start date, and time as shown. Show the time as busy and set a 10-minute reminder. Set the appointment to recur weekly on Mondays and Wednesdays for 30 occurrences.

6. Create a recurring appointment for the Marketing item in Table 2–10. Enter the subject, start date, and time as shown. Show the time as busy and set a 30-minute reminder. Set the appointment to recur weekly on Tuesdays and Thursdays for 30 occurrences.

7. Print the February 2012 calendar in Month view, and then submit it in the format specified by your instructor.

Cases and Places

Apply your creative thinking and problem solving skills to design and implement a solution.

Note: To complete these assignments, you may be required to use the Data Files for Students. See the inside back cover of this book for instructions on downloading the Data Files for Students, or contact your instructor for information about accessing the required files.

1: Create a Personal Schedule

Academic

Create a personal schedule for the next month using the information provided in Table 2–11. Include your appointments for work, classes, and study time. You also can include any extracurricular activities in which you participate. Use recurring appointments when possible. Schedule all-day activities as events. Print the calendar in Monthly Style and submit it in the format specified by your instructor.

Table 2–11 Academic Calendar Items						
Description	**Location**	**Date**	**Time**	**Show As**	**Reminder**	**Recurrence**
Financial Planning Workshop	Columbia Inn	March 11, 2012	1:00 PM – 4:00 PM	Busy	30 minutes	None
Spring Fling	Quad	March 3, 2012	12:00 PM – 2:00 PM	Out of Office	10 minutes	None
Department Meeting		Every Monday	2:00 PM – 3:00 PM	Busy	5 minutes	Weekly, end after 12 occurrences
Petition to Graduate		March 15, 2012	All Day Event	Free	1 day	None
Parents Anniversary		October 20, 2012	All Day Event	Free	1 day	Yearly
NJCAA D3 Women's Lacrosse Nationals		March 6, 2012 – March 8, 2012	All Day Event	Tentative	None	None
SGA Meeting		March 21, 2012	11:30 PM – 12:30 PM	Out of Office	30 minutes	None
Work Schedule		2/28/2012	2:00 PM – 5:30 PM	Out of Office	15 minutes	Tuesdays and Thursdays

2: Create a Work Schedule for Employees

Professional

At work, you are in charge of scheduling snack bar coverage for your local athletic club for the month of May. Create a schedule of work times for four employees. Brett works Mondays, Wednesdays, and Fridays from 9:00 AM to 5:00 PM; Megan works Tuesdays, Thursdays, and Saturdays from 9:00 AM to 5:00 PM; Joe works from 12:00 PM until 9:00 PM on Mondays, Wednesdays, and Fridays. Pat completes the schedule working from 12:00 PM until 9:00 PM on Tuesdays, Thursdays, and Saturdays. Print the calendar in Monthly Style and submit it in the format specified by your instructor.

3: Create Meeting Invitations

Personal

Create a personal calendar to keep track of several items relating to your schedule outside of class or work. Use Table 2–12 to add these items to your personal calendar.

Table 2–12 Personal Calendar Items						
Description	Location	Date	Time	Show As	Reminder	Recurrence
Open House at your child's new school	Jenna's School	April 3, 2012	1:00 PM – 4:00 PM	Out of Office	30 minutes	None
Annual Physical	Medical Plan	April 5, 2012	12:00 PM – 2:00 PM	Out of Office	10 minutes	None
Air Conditioning Yearly Service	Home	April 4, 2012	2:00 PM – 3:00 PM	Busy	5 minutes	Yearly, on the first Wednesday in April
Performance Evaluation	Manager's Office	April 16, 2012	All Day Event	Free	1 day	None
Car Payment Due		April 15, 2012	All Day Event	Free	1 day	Monthly, 15th day of every month

3 Managing Contacts and Personal Contact Information with Outlook

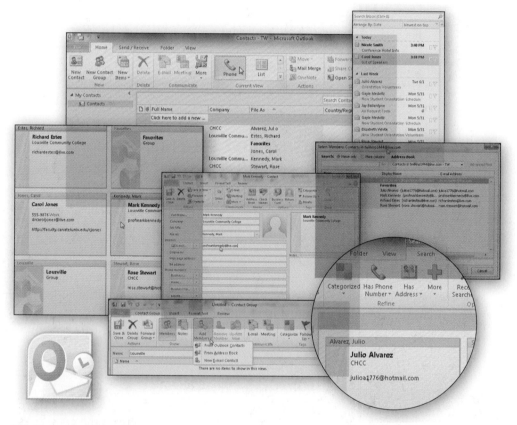

Objectives

You will have mastered the material in this chapter when you can:

- Create a new contact
- Create a contact from an e-mail message
- Modify a contact
- Manipulate attachments to contacts
- Display your contacts in different views
- Find contacts using complete or partial information

- Find contacts from any Outlook folder
- Create a contact group
- Modify a contact group
- Add and remove names in a contact group
- Preview a contact list
- Print a contact list

3 | Managing Contacts and Personal Contact Information with Outlook

Introduction

To keep track of your friends, business partners, family, and others with whom you communicate, you can use Outlook to create contact lists and contact groups. A **contact list** lets you record information about people, such as their e-mail address, phone number, birthday, and physical address. Each person's information is recorded in a contact record in the contact list. If you have several colleagues at work that you e-mail frequently, you can add them to a contact group. You then can send e-mail messages to the group using the contact group rather than having to select each contact individually.

Project — Contact List with Groups

People and businesses create contact lists to keep track of people that are important to them or their business. A contact list may contain groups so that several contacts can be using the group name rather than each individual contact. Managing your contacts using a contact list can increase productivity greatly.

The project in this chapter follows general guidelines and uses Outlook to create the contact list shown in Figure 3 – 1. This contact list in the TW mailbox includes individual contacts and contact groups displayed in a view that presents the contact information in a business card layout. In this layout, the individual contacts display essential information only, such as the name, affiliation, and e-mail address of the contact. The contact groups display the name of the group, have a Group label, and include a different border graphic than the individual contacts.

Overview

As you read this chapter, you will learn how to create the contact list shown in Figure 3 – 1 by performing these general tasks:

- Create a new contact.
- Edit a contact.
- Change the view of the contact folder.
- Find a contact.
- Create a contact group.
- Print the contact list.

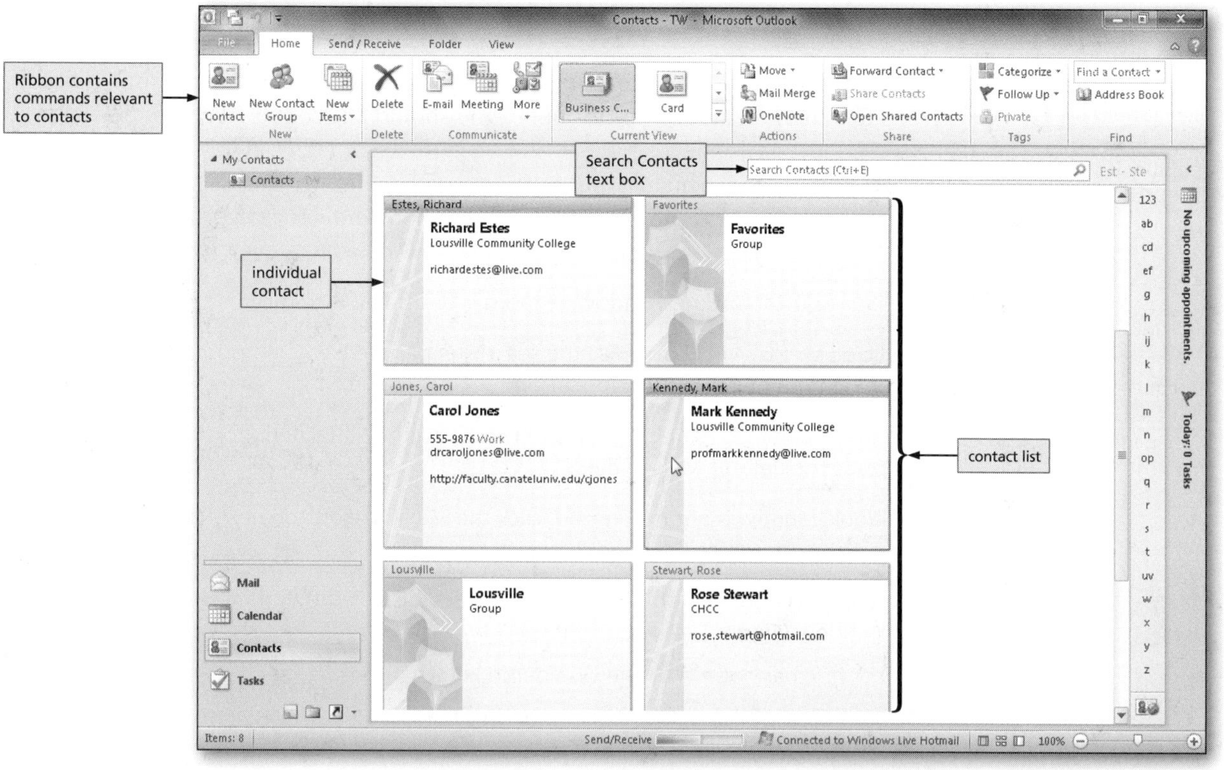

Figure 3–1

General Project Guidelines

Plan
Ahead

When creating and organizing contacts, the actions you perform and decisions you make will affect the appearance and characteristics of your contact list. As you create and group your contacts, such as those shown in Figure 3–1, you should follow these general guidelines:

1. **Determine whom you want to have as contacts.** People use contacts to keep track of the people with whom they interact the most. For example, students may add study partners as contacts and business professionals may add customer and colleagues as contacts. It also is common for people to add their family and friends as contacts.

2. **Determine the information you want to store for a contact.** For any contact, you can use many contact fields for tracking contact information. In addition to name and e-mail address, you can record information such as phone numbers, Web page addresses, and mailing addresses. You also can attach files such as Word documents to a contact record.

3. **Determine how you would like to view your contacts.** Select a view to display contact information you refer to often, such as phone numbers or business names.

4. **Determine what groups you may need.** Adding contacts to a group allows you to e-mail and work with the group as a whole. For example, you can send advertisements and event information to a group containing clients. Students might create a class project group to communicate with other students working with them on a project.

5. **Determine the best method for distributing a contact list.** Consider whether you need to share a contact with others. If you do, you can share contacts electronically in Outlook or print a contact list and distribute printed copies.

When necessary, more specific details concerning the above guidelines are presented at appropriate points in the chapter. The chapter also will identify the actions performed and decisions made regarding these guidelines during the creation of the contact list shown in Figure 3–1.

To Start Outlook

BTW

BTWs
For a complete list of the BTWs found in the margins of this book, visit the Outlook 2010 BTW Web page (scsite.com/out2010/btw).

BTW

Q&As
For a complete list of the Q&As found in many of the step-by-step sequences in this book, visit the Outlook 2010 Q&A Web page (scsite.com/out2010/qa).

If you are using a computer to step through the project in this chapter and you want your screens to match the figures in this book, you should change your screen's resolution to 1024 × 768.

The following steps, which assume Windows 7 is running, start Outlook based on a typical installation. You may need to ask your instructor how to start Outlook for your computer.

1 Click the Start button on the Windows 7 taskbar to display the Start menu.

2 Type `Microsoft Outlook` as the search text in the 'Search programs and files' text box and watch the search results appear on the Start menu.

3 Click Microsoft Outlook 2010 in the search results on the Start menu to start Outlook with your Inbox as the default Mail folder.

4 If the Outlook window is not maximized, click the Maximize button next to the Close button on its title bar to maximize the window.

5 Click the Contacts button in the Navigation Pane to display the Contacts – TW – Microsoft Outlook window (Figure 3–2).

Q&A Why does my title bar not match the title bar in Figure 3–2?
The title bar always displays the name of the Outlook data file, which may include your name or initials instead of "TW."

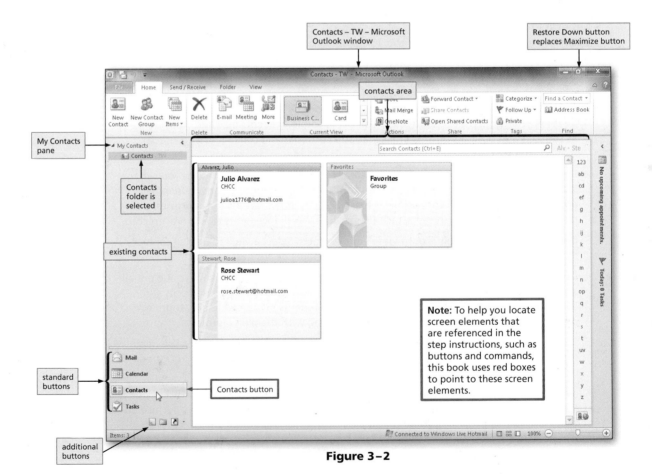

Figure 3–2

Contacts Window

The Contacts – TW – Microsoft Outlook window shown in Figure 3–2 includes a variety of features to help you work efficiently. It contains many elements similar to the windows in other Office programs, as well as some that are unique to Outlook. The main elements of the Contacts window are the Navigation Pane, the contacts area, and the To-Do bar.

The Navigation Pane includes two sets of buttons (standard and additional) and the My Contacts pane. The **My Contacts pane** displays the available contact lists, each of which is stored in its own folder. The standard buttons represent shortcuts to the standard items that are part of Microsoft Outlook mailbox: Mail, Calendar, Contacts, and Tasks. Additional buttons are displayed below the standard buttons and represent shortcuts to other Outlook functions, such as Notes, Folder List shortcuts, and Configure buttons, which allow you to specify which folders to display.

Creating a Contact List

The first step in creating a contact list is to select a folder for storing your contacts. By default, Outlooks stores contacts in the Contacts folder, but you also can create a personal folder to store your contacts using the technique presented in Chapter 2. In this chapter, you will create contacts and groups in the Contacts folder.

> **Determine who you want to have as contacts.**
> You can make contacts for nearly everyone you know or who has sent you an e-mail message. However, not everyone should be added to your contacts. Only create contacts for those people with whom you plan to interact on a regular basis, such as your friends, family, and co-workers. Adding too many contacts can make it difficult to manage your contact list.
>
> **Determine the information you want to store for a contact.**
> In addition to name and e-mail address, you can record information such as phone numbers, Web page addresses, and mailing addresses. Attach one or more files to a contact to store documents, tables, pictures, or clip art, for example, along with contact information.

Plan Ahead

To Create a New Contact

To create the contact list in this chapter, you will start by adding the first contact, Mark Kennedy. He is coming to a lecture series that you will be holding, so you want to create a contact record for him to make sure he receives updates and relevant information. The steps on the next pages create a new contact for Mark Kennedy.

BTW

Contacts Window
By default, clicking the Contacts button in the Navigation Pane displays the contacts in the Microsoft Outlook window. To display the contacts in a new window, right-click the Contacts button in the Navigation Pane, and then click Open in New Window on the shortcut menu.

BTW

The Ribbon and Screen Resolution
Outlook may change how the groups and buttons within the groups appear on the Ribbon, depending on the computer's screen resolution. Thus, your Ribbon may look different from the ones in this book if you are using a screen resolution other than 1024 × 768.

1

- If the Home tab is not the active tab, click Home on the Ribbon to display the Home tab.

- Click the New Contact button (Home tab | New group) to display the Untitled – Contact window (Figure 3–3).

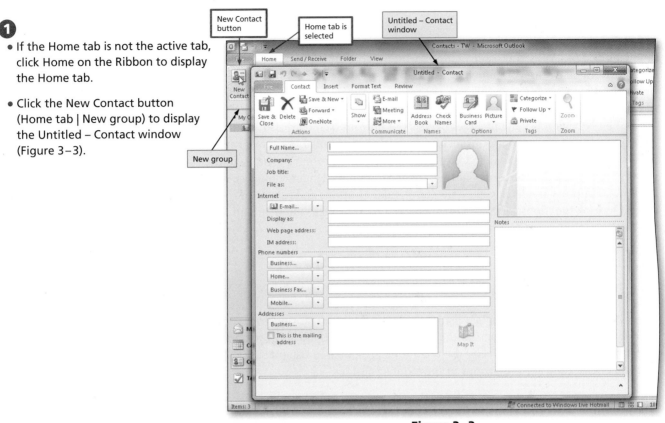

Figure 3–3

2

- Type **Mark Kennedy** in the Full Name text box to enter a name for the contact.

- Type **Lousville Community College** in the Company text box to enter a company for the contact.

- Type **profmarkkennedy@ live.com** in the E-mail text box to enter an e-mail address for the contact (Figure 3–4).

Q&A Why did the title of the Contact window change after I entered the name?

As soon as you enter the name, Outlook updates the Contact window title to reflect the information you have entered. Outlook also displays the name in the File as text box. The contact is not saved, however; only the window title and File as text boxes are updated.

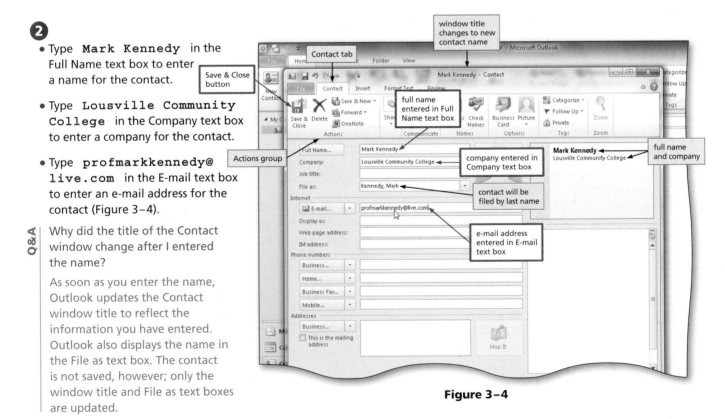

Figure 3–4

Q&A Can I add information to other fields for a contact?

Certainly. As long as you have the information, you can fill out the fields accordingly. You even can add fields besides those listed.

3

- Click the Save & Close button (Contact tab | Actions group) to save the contact and close the Contact window (Figure 3–5).

Q&A Can I send contact information to someone else?

Yes. To forward a contact, select the contact, click Forward Contact (Home tab | Share group), and then click the method you want to use to forward the contact.

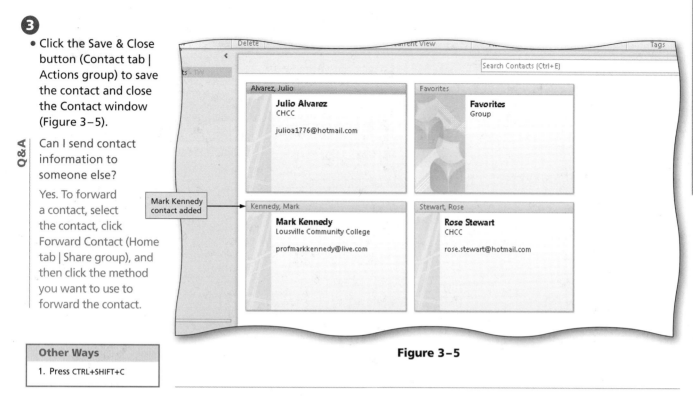

Figure 3–5

Other Ways

1. Press CTRL+SHIFT+C

To Create a Contact from an E-Mail Message

Carol Jones frequently e-mails you about your work. You want to add her to your contact list to better keep track of her information. Outlook can create a contact based on the information located in the e-mail message. The following steps create a contact from an e-mail message from Carol Jones.

1

- Click the Mail button in the Navigation Pane to display your mailbox.

- Click the Carol Jones message header to preview the e-mail message in the Reading Pane (Figure 3–6).

Q&A What if I do not have an e-mail message from Carol Jones?

If you did not import the data file for this chapter, you might not have an e-mail message from Carol Jones. In that case, perform these steps using another e-mail message in your mailbox.

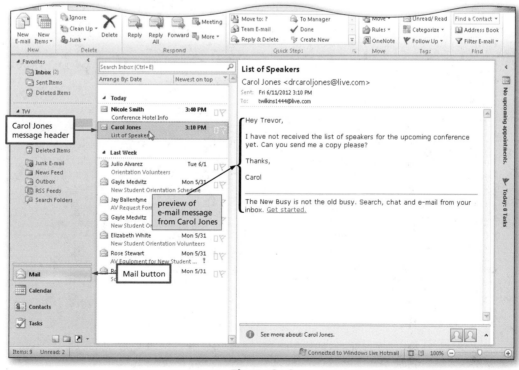

Figure 3–6

- Right-click Carol Jones's e-mail address to display a shortcut menu (Figure 3–7).

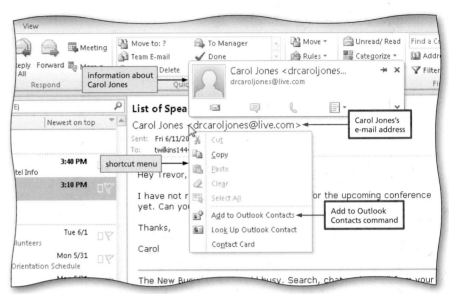

Figure 3–7

- Click Add to Outlook Contacts to display the Carol Jones – Contact window (Figure 3–8).

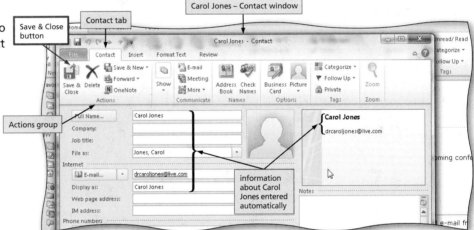

Figure 3–8

- Click the Save & Close button (Contact tab | Actions group) to save the contact and close the Contact window.

- Click the Contacts button in the Navigation Pane to display your contacts, including the new contact for Carol Jones (Figure 3–9).

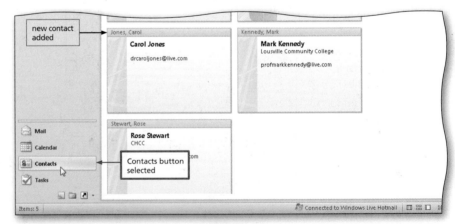

Figure 3–9

To Create a Contact from an Existing Contact

Mark asked his colleague, Richard Estes, to accompany him to the upcoming lecture series. You want to add Richard Estes as a new contact. When a new contact shares information with an existing contact, you can create a new contact from the existing contact, and then edit only the information unique to the new contact. The following steps copy the Mark Kennedy contact to create a contact for Richard Estes.

- Click the Mark Kennedy contact to select it (Figure 3–10).

Q&A Why is the top bar of the Mark Kennedy contact orange?

The orange bar indicates that the contact is selected.

Figure 3–10

- Click the New Items button (Home tab | New group) to display the New Items menu (Figure 3–11).

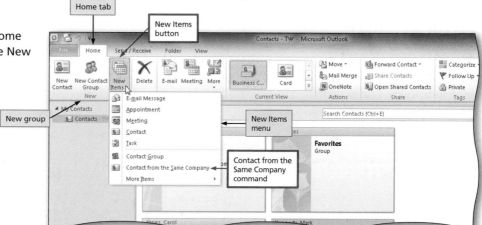

Figure 3–11

- Click Contact from the Same Company to display a new Contact window with selected information from the previously selected contact, in this case, Mark Kennedy (Figure 3–12).

Q&A Why does the title of the Contact window show the company name?

Until you enter a name for the contact, Outlook uses the company name as the title of the window. When you enter the contact's name, Outlook changes the title of the window accordingly.

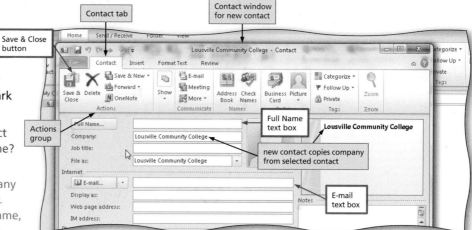

Figure 3–12

4

- Type `Richard Estes` in the Full Name text box to enter a name for the contact.

- Type `richardestes@live.com` in the E-mail text box to enter an e-mail address for the contact.

- Click the Save & Close button (Contact tab | Actions group) to save the contact and close the Contact window (Figure 3–13).

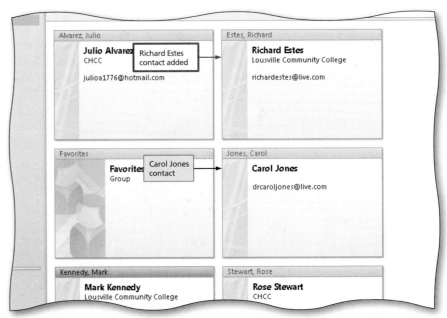

Figure 3–13

To Edit a Contact

When you created a contact record for Carol Jones, it did not include her work phone number and e-mail address. She now has given you her work phone number and e-mail address, and you want to edit her contact record to include the new information. The following steps edit the Carol Jones contact.

1

- Double-click the Carol Jones contact to display the Carol Jones – Contact window (Figure 3–14).

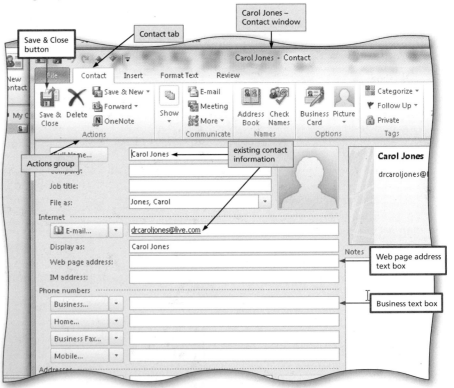

Figure 3–14

2

- Type `http://faculty
  .canateluniv.edu/cjones`
  in the 'Web page address' text box
  to enter a Web page address for the
  contact.

- Type `555-9876` in the Business
  text box to enter a business phone
  number for the contact.

- Click the Save & Close button
  (Contact tab | Actions group)
  to save the contact and close
  the Contact window
  (Figure 3–15).

Q&A Why did the title of the
contact icon change?

When you edit the contact, the
contact icon updates to display
the new information.

Q&A Why did the area code appear after entering the business phone number?

Depending on the configuration of your computer and its programs,
Outlook might insert the local area code automatically.

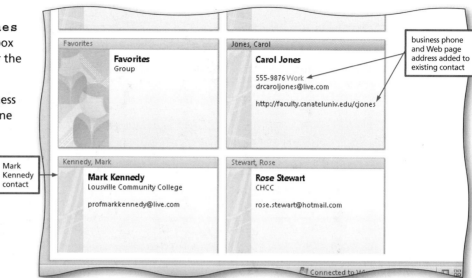

Figure 3–15

To Add an Attachment to a Contact

Mark Kennedy has sent you a document listing the hours he will be available in the tutoring center. You decide
to include this document as part of his contact record so that you can find this schedule easily. Any files you attach to
a contact are displayed in the Notes section of the Contact window. You also can insert items such as tables, pictures,
and clip art to the Notes section. The following steps add Mark's tutoring hours to his contact information.

1

- Double-click the Mark Kennedy
  contact to display the Mark
  Kennedy – Contact window
  (Figure 3–16).

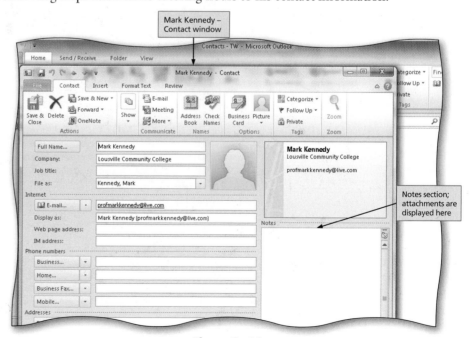

Figure 3–16

• Click Insert on the Ribbon to display the Insert tab.

• Click the Attach File button (Insert tab | Include group) to display the Insert File dialog box (Figure 3–17).

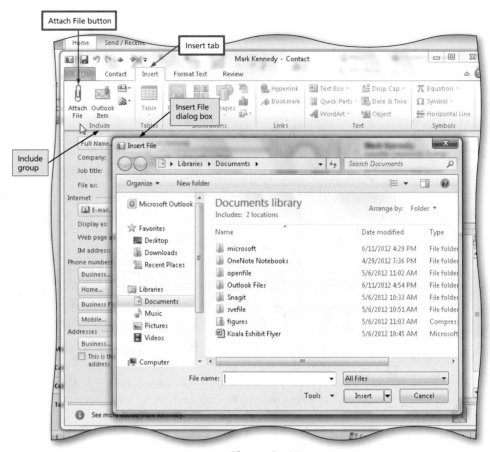

Figure 3–17

• Navigate to the file location (in this case, the Chapter 03 folder in the Outlook folder in the Data Files for Students folder on a USB flash drive).

• Click the Tutoring Schedule document to select it (Figure 3–18).

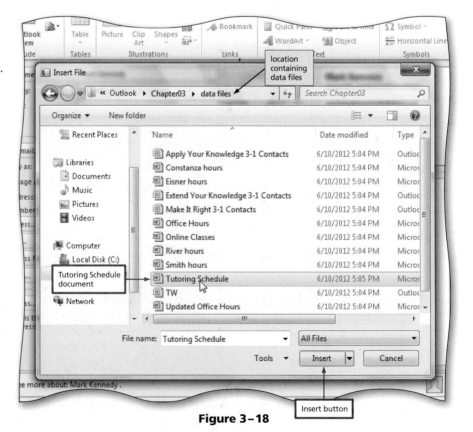

Figure 3–18

4

- Click the Insert button (Insert File dialog box) to attach the document to the contact (Figure 3–19).

Q&A Can I add more than one attachment?

Yes; you can add as many attachments as you want.

Q&A How do I view an attachment after I have added it?

Open the contact and then double-click the attachment to open it.

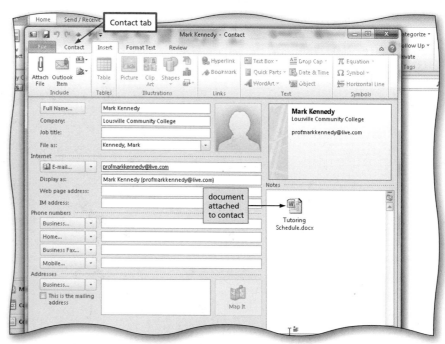

Figure 3–19

5

- Click Contact on the Ribbon to display the Contact tab.

- Click the Save & Close button (Contact tab | Actions group) to save the contact and close the Contact window (Figure 3–20).

Q&A Can I send a meeting request to a contact?

Yes. To send a meeting request to a contact, click the contact to select it, click Meeting (Home tab | Communicate group), enter the details of the meeting in the Untitled – Meeting window, and then click the Send button.

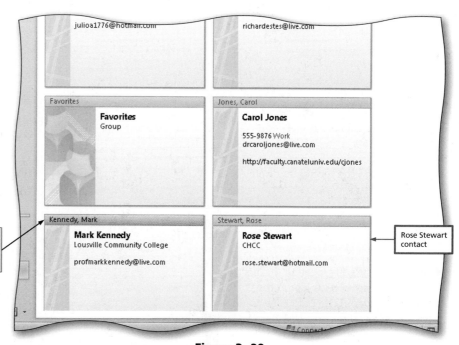

Figure 3–20

To Change an Attachment to a Contact

Rose Stewart has sent you updated office hour information. You need to replace the attachment in her contact with the document containing the updated office hours. The steps on the next pages change the attachment for the Rose Stewart contact.

1

- Double-click the Rose Stewart contact to display the Rose Stewart – Contact window (Figure 3–21).

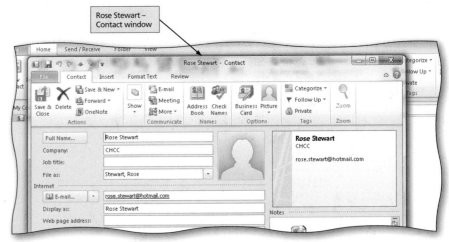

Figure 3–21

2

- Click the Office Hours document to select it (Figure 3–22).

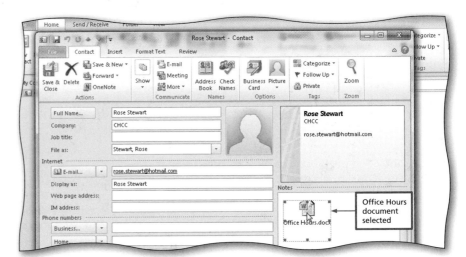

Figure 3–22

3

- Click Insert on the Ribbon to display the Insert tab.

- Click the Attach File button (Insert tab | Include group) to display the Insert File dialog box.

- Navigate to the file location (in this case, the Chapter 03 folder in the Outlook folder in the Data Files for Students folder on a USB flash drive).

- Click the Updated Office Hours document to select it.

- Click the Insert button (Insert File dialog box) to change the attachment for the contact (Figure 3–23).

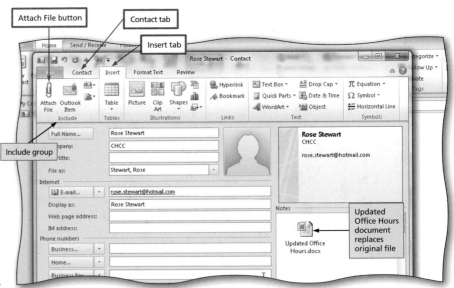

Figure 3–23

Q&A

Why did the new file replace the original file?

Because the original file was selected before attaching the new file, the new file replaced the original file. If the original file were not selected, Outlook would add the new file while keeping the original file.

4

- Click Contact on the Ribbon to display the Contact tab.

- Click the Save & Close button (Contact tab | Actions group) to save the contact and close the Contact window (Figure 3–24).

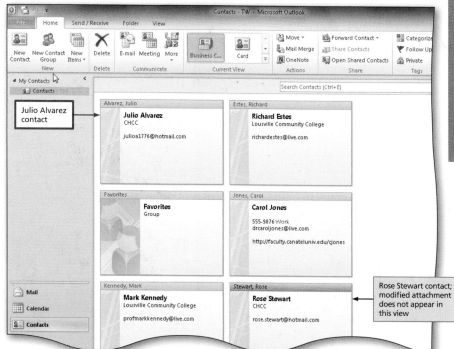

Figure 3–24

To Remove an Attachment to a Contact

Sometimes you need to remove attachments that you have added to a contact. Julio Alvarez was teaching online classes for the previous semester but now is not teaching any online classes. You need to remove the list of online classes from his contact. The following steps remove the attachment from the Julio Alvarez contact.

1

- Double-click the Julio Alvarez contact to display the Julio Alvarez – Contact window (Figure 3–25).

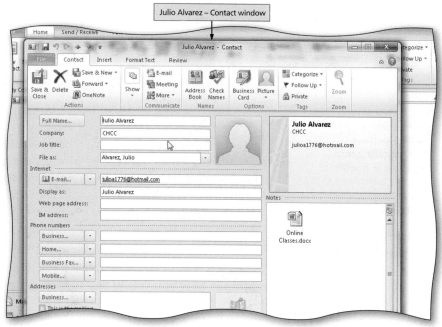

Figure 3–25

2

- Click the Online Classes document to select it (Figure 3–26).

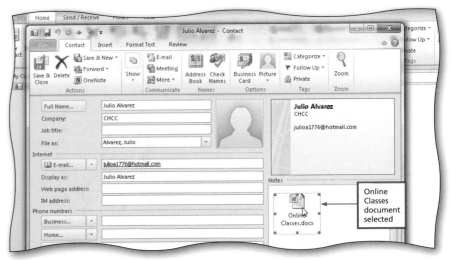

Figure 3–26

3

- Press the DELETE key to remove the attachment (Figure 3–27).

4

- Click the Save & Close button (Contact tab | Actions group) to save the contact and close the Contact window.

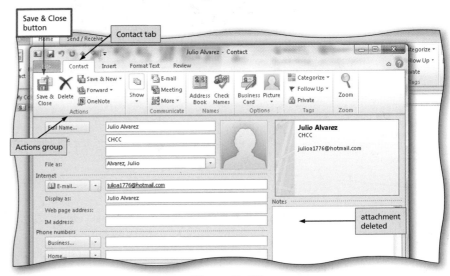

Figure 3–27

Viewing and Sorting Your Contact List

Filing Contacts
When creating a new contact, Outlook automatically inserts in the File as box the contact's full name, usually in LastName, FirstName format. Outlook sorts contacts on the value stored in the File as box for each contact.

Outlook supports several ways for you to view your contact list. **Business Card view** is the default view; it displays the contacts as if they were business cards. **Card view** shows the contacts as cards but much smaller than Business Card view, with most information being only partially visible. In **Phone view**, you see the contacts in a list displaying phone information. Finally, in **List view**, the contacts are arranged in a list according to businesses. You also can create custom views to display your contacts in a way that suits a particular purpose.

When working with contacts in any view, you can sort the contacts to display them in a different order. Each view provides different sort options. For example, in Phone view, you can sort the list using any of the column heading buttons that are displayed.

Plan
Ahead

Determine how you would like to view your contacts.
Before determining a view or sort order to use for your contacts, consider what you are trying to find in your contacts, as well as your preferred way to view information. This can help you quickly find the information for which you are looking.

To Change the Current View

While Business Card view provides useful information, you want to explore the other views. Phone view, for example, is very helpful when you are looking for a contact's phone number in a long list. Changing the view sometimes can help you find a contact's information more quickly. The following steps change the current view to Phone view and then back to the default Business Card view.

1
• Click the Phone button (Home tab | Current View group) to switch to Phone view (Figure 3–28).

Q&A What if the Phone button is not displayed in the Current View group?

Click the More button or Change View button (Home tab | Current View group) to display a list of available views, and then click Phone.

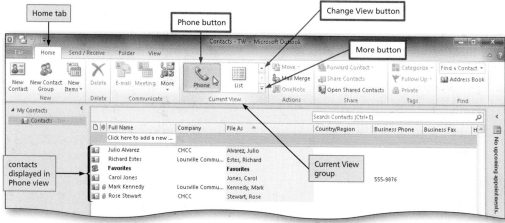

Figure 3–28

2
• Click the More button (Home tab | Current View group), and then click Business Card to switch to Business Card view (Figure 3–29).

Q&A What if the More button is not displayed in the Current View group?

You likely are using a higher resolution than 1024 × 768, so the Ribbon can display additional buttons. Click the Business Card button in the Current View group to switch to Business Card view.

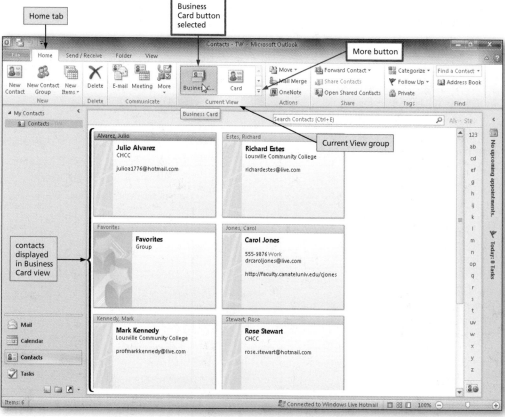

Figure 3–29

🔍 Experiment

• Click the other views in the Current View group to view the contacts in other arrangements. When you are finished, click Business Card to return to Business Card view.

To Sort Contacts

Business Card view displays the contacts in alphabetical order by default; however, you can sort them to view the contacts in reverse order, which is especially helpful if you want to quickly open a record for a contact at the end of a long contact list. The following steps sort the contact list in reverse order, and then switch back to alphabetical order.

1

- Click View on the Ribbon to display the View tab.

- Click the Reverse Sort button (View tab | Arrangement group) to display the contact list in reverse alphabetical order (Figure 3–30).

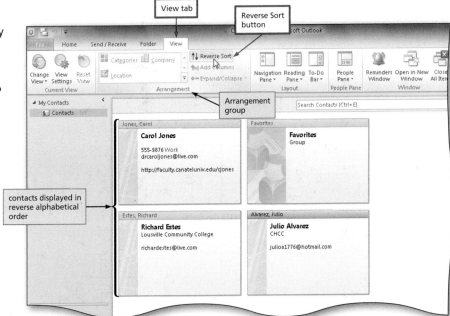

Figure 3–30

2

- Click the Reverse Sort button (View tab | Arrangement group) to display the contact list in the original order (Figure 3–31).

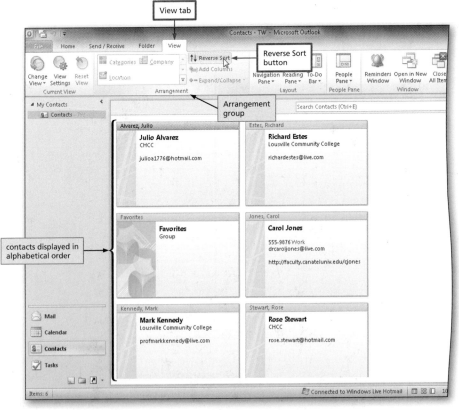

Figure 3–31

Break Point: If you wish to take a break, this is a good place to do so. To resume at a later time, start Outlook and continue following the steps from this location forward.

Using Search to Find a Contact

Over time, contact lists can grow quite large, making them difficult to navigate. In addition, you sometimes may not remember details about a contact you want to find. For example, you may remember that someone works for a particular company, but not their name. Alternatively, you may remember a phone number but nothing else. If this happens, you can use the Search Contacts text box to search your contact list.

BTW

Start Menu Search Box
In addition to using the search features in Outlook to locate a contact, you also can search for a contact using the Search box on the Start menu.

You also can find contacts using the Find a Contact search box in the Find group on the Home tab. This works no matter which folder you are using (such as Mail, Calendar, Contacts, or Tasks). This means that anytime you need to find your contacts, you quickly can look them up.

You can maximize your search efforts if you create a list of keywords that you can assign to contacts. The more general the keyword, the more results you will find. Using more specific keywords will reduce the number of results.

To Find a Contact by Searching for an E-Mail Address

If you only know partial information such as the area code in a phone number, the first word in a school name, or the domain name in an e-mail address, you can use it to find matching contacts. Note that you might find many contacts that contain the text for which you are searching. The text you are using as the search term could be part of an e-mail address or a name, for example. Therefore, you may have to examine the results further. The following steps find all contacts that contain the text, hotmail.

1

• Click the Search Contacts text box to display the Search Tools Search tab (Figure 3–32).

Q&A Why is the Search Tools Search tab displayed when I click the Search Contacts text box?

The Search Tools Search tab is a tool tab that contains buttons and commands that can help you search contacts.

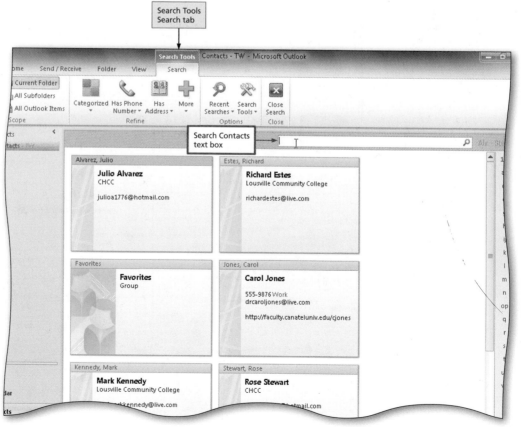

Figure 3–32

2

- Type **hotmail** in the Search Contacts text box to search for all contacts containing the text, hotmail (Figure 3–33).

Q&A

Can I modify a search further after getting the initial results?

Certainly. You can use the Search Tools Search tab to refine your search by specifying a phone number or address, for example. You also can expand the search to include all of the Outlook folders.

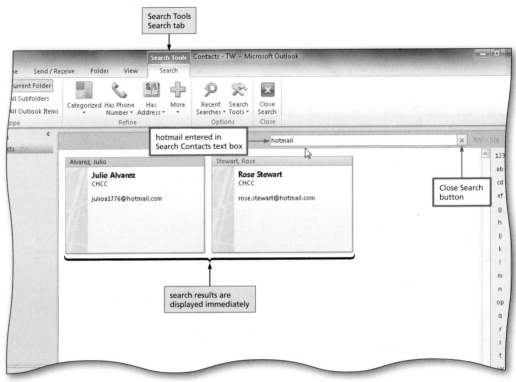

Figure 3–33

3

- Click the Close Search button in the Search Contacts text box to close the search and return to the Contact folder (Figure 3–34).

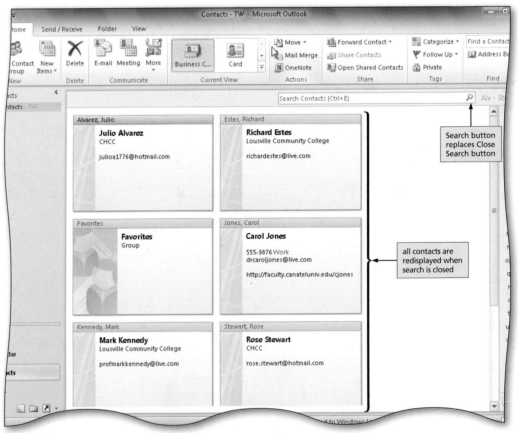

Figure 3–34

Other Ways

1. Press CTRL+E

To Refine a Search

If you type a full name or e-mail address in the Search Contacts text box, you will find your contact, but the information need not be in only the Full Name field or the E-mail field. The results might contain contacts where the name or e-mail address is part of the Notes field, for example. Instead, you can find a contact by searching only a particular field. The results will contain only contacts that contain the search term in the specified field. No contacts will appear that contain the search term in a different field.

You want to update the Richard Estes contact record by searching only the Full Name field. The following steps search for the Richard Estes contact.

1

- Click the Search Contacts text box to display the Search Tools Search tab.

- Click the More button (Search Tools Search tab | Refine group) to display a list of common properties for refining a search (Figure 3–35).

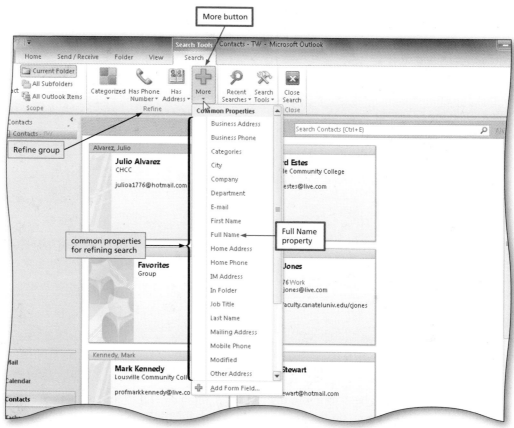

Figure 3–35

2

- Click Full Name to display the Full Name text box.

- Type **Richard Estes** in the Full Name text box to search for the Richard Estes contact (Figure 3–36).

Q&A Why might Outlook display search results that do not appear to contain the search text?

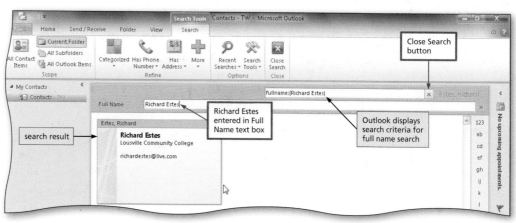

Figure 3–36

When you perform a search, Outlook searches all specified fields for a match. However, the matching fields might not be displayed in the list of search results, although the contact record does contain the search text.

3

- Double-click the Richard Estes contact to open it.

- Type **Manages Seminar Blog** in the Notes field to update the contact.

- Click the Save & Close button (Contact tab | Actions group) to save the contact and close the Contact window.

- Click the Close Search button in the Search Contacts text box to close the search and return to the Contact folder (Figure 3–37).

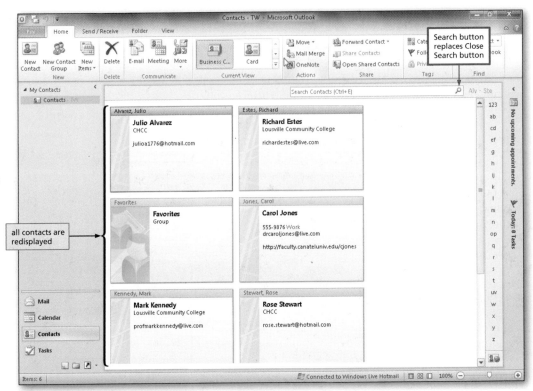

all contacts are redisplayed

Figure 3–37

Other Ways

1. Press CTRL+E, type search criteria

To Find a Contact from any Outlook Folder

You do not have to be working in the Contacts folder to search for contacts. You can use the Find a Contact search box in the Find group on the Home tab to search for contacts no matter which folder you are viewing. If what you type in the search box matches a single contact, that entry will be displayed in a contact window. If what you type matches more than one entry, you will be asked to select the contact that you want to view. For example, if you search for a contact using part of the company name, more than one contact may appear in the search results. You then can select a single contact from the results.

The following steps search for the Mark Kennedy contact from the Mail folder using only part of the company name, Lousville.

1

- Click the Mail button in the Navigation Pane to display your mailbox (Figure 3–38).

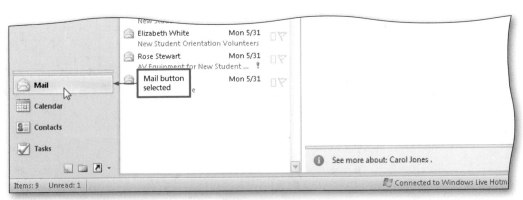

Mail button selected

Figure 3–38

2

- Type `Lousville` in the Find a Contact search box (Home tab | Find group) to search for contacts containing the search text (Figure 3–39).

Figure 3–39

3

- Press ENTER to display the Choose Contact dialog box (Figure 3–40).

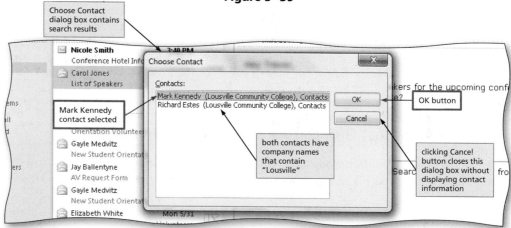

Figure 3–40

4

- If necessary, click Mark Kennedy to select the contact.

- Click the OK button (Choose Contact dialog box) to display the contact record (Figure 3–41).

Figure 3–41

5

- Click the Close button to close the window.

- Click the Contacts button in the Navigation Pane to return to the Contacts folder (Figure 3–42).

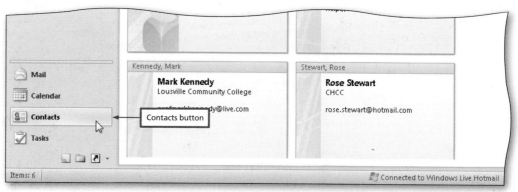

Figure 3–42

Create and Edit a Contact Group

When you have several contacts that you frequently e-mail or work with as a group, you can create a contact group and add the contacts to it. A **contact group** provides a single name for you to use when working with contacts. You are not creating subfolders, but rather another way to reference multiple contacts at one time. For example, you could create a group called Family and then add all your family members to the group. Whenever you want to send an e-mail message to your entire family at one time, you could enter the contact group name, Family, as the recipient of the e-mail message and every contact in the group would receive the e-mail message.

**Plan
Ahead**

> **Determine what groups you may need.**
> When thinking about the groups you need, keep in mind that the names of the groups should relate to the contacts that are organized under the group name. Choosing good names will make it easier for you to remember the purpose of the group.

To Create a Contact Group from Existing Contacts

When creating contact groups, you choose the name for your contact group and then add the contacts you want to have in the group. The following steps create a Lousville contact group and then add the Lousville-related contacts to the group.

1
- Click the New Contact Group button (Home tab | New group) to display the Untitled – Contact Group window (Figure 3–43).

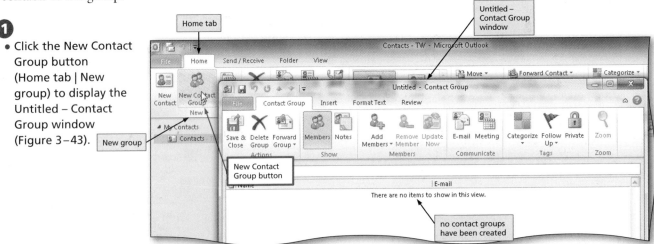

Figure 3–43

2
- Type **Lousville** in the Name text box to enter a name for the group (Figure 3–44).

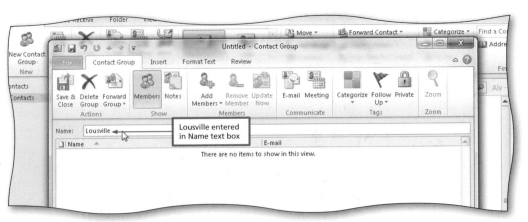

Figure 3–44

3

• Click the Add Members button (Contact Group tab | Members group) to display the Add Members menu (Figure 3–45).

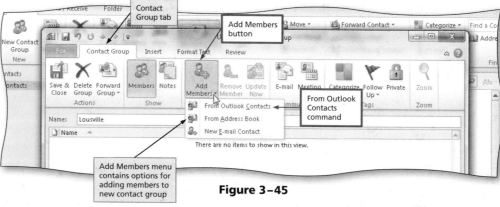

Figure 3–45

4

• Click From Outlook Contacts to display the Select Members dialog box (Figure 3–46).

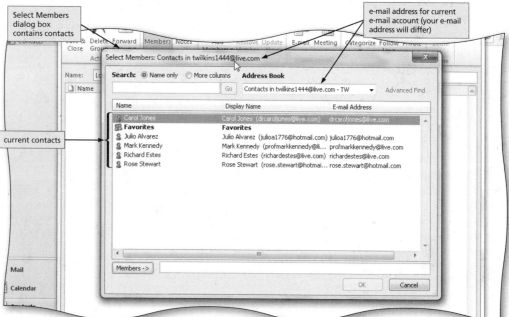

Figure 3–46

5

• Click the Mark Kennedy contact to select it, press and hold the CTRL key, and then click the Richard Estes contact to select both contacts.

• Click the Members button (Select Members dialog box) to move the information to the Members text box (Figure 3–47).

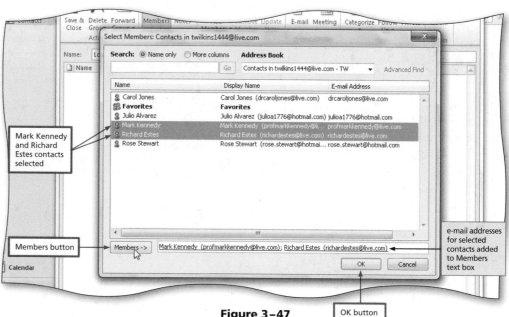

Figure 3–47

6

- Click the OK button to add the contacts to the group (Figure 3–48).

What if I add the wrong member(s)?

In the Contact Group window, select the member you want to remove, and then click the Remove Member button (Contact Group tab | Members group). Next, repeat Steps 3 – 6 to add any missing members.

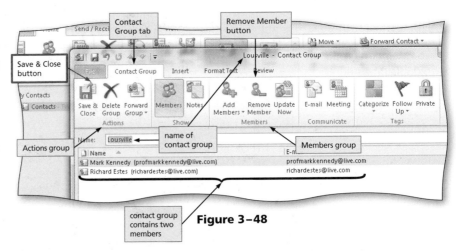

Figure 3–48

7

- Click the Save & Close button (Contact Group tab | Actions group) to save the contact group and close the window (Figure 3–49).

Why are the contacts and the group displayed in the Contacts window?

You use a contact group to send e-mail messages to a set of contacts using the group name; it does not replace or move the existing contacts.

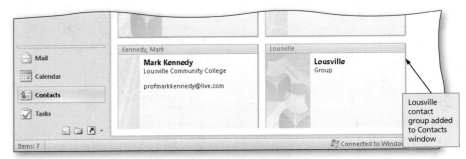

Figure 3–49

To Create a Contact Group from an Existing E-Mail Message

Outlook allows you to create a group for individuals who are not in your contact list yet, but who have sent you an e-mail message. To do this, you copy a name from an e-mail message and then paste the name in the Select Members dialog box when creating the group. The following steps create a contact group named Conference and then add a member by using information in an e-mail message from Nicole Smith.

1

- Click the Mail button in the Navigation Pane to display your mailbox (Figure 3–50).

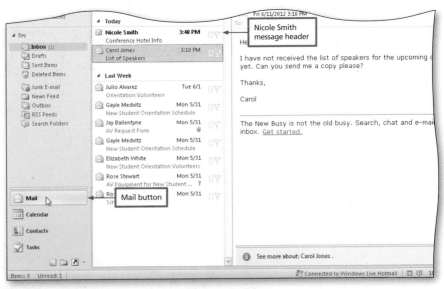

Figure 3–50

2

- Click the Nicole Smith message header to preview the e-mail message in the Reading Pane.

- In the Reading Pane, right-click the e-mail address to display a shortcut menu (Figure 3–51).

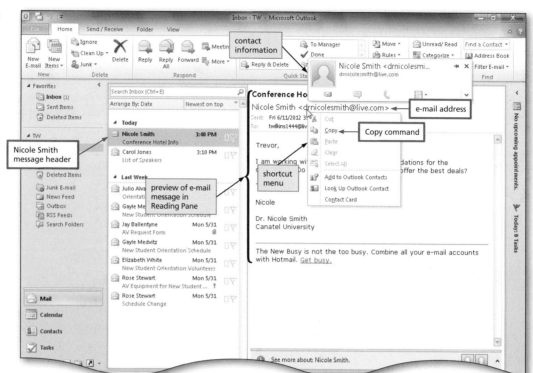

Figure 3–51

3

- Click Copy to copy the name and e-mail address.

- Click the New Items button (Home tab | New group) to display the New Items menu.

- Click More Items to display the More Items submenu (Figure 3–52).

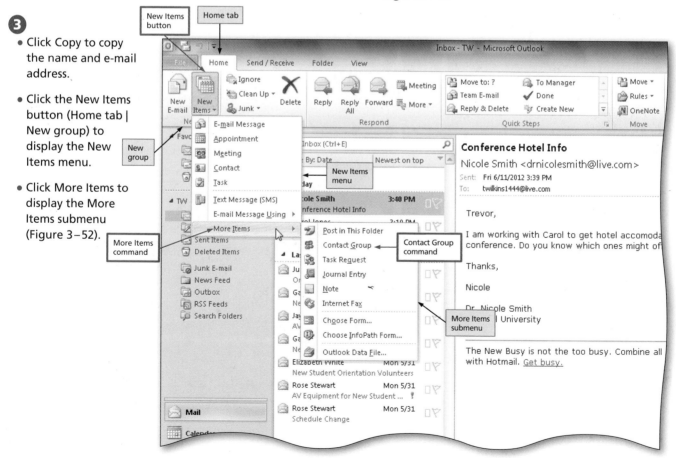

Figure 3–52

4

- Click Contact Group to display the Untitled – Contact Group window.

- Type **Conference** in the Name text box to enter a name for the group.

- Click the Add Members button (Contact Group tab | Add Members group) to display the Add Members menu.

- Click From Outlook Contacts to display the Select Members dialog box (Figure 3–53).

Q&A

Why did I click From Outlook Contacts?

You need to display the Select Members dialog box, and the From Outlook Contacts menu option opens it. You also could have clicked From Address Book to display the dialog box.

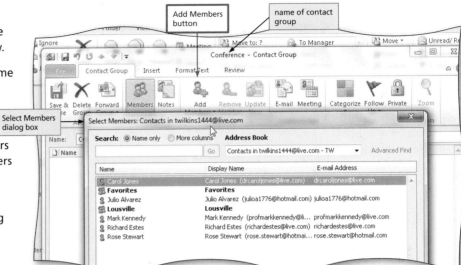

Figure 3–53

5

- Right-click the Members text box to display a shortcut menu.

- Click Paste to paste the copied name and e-mail address (Figure 3–54).

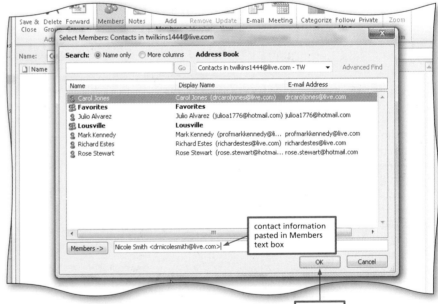

Figure 3–54

6

- Click the OK button (Select Members dialog box) to add the contact to the group (Figure 3–55).

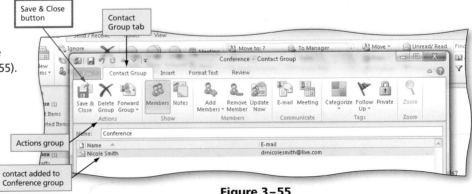

Figure 3–55

- Click the Save & Close button (Contact Group tab | Actions group) to save the contact and close the window.

- Click the Contacts button in the Navigation Pane to display your contacts (Figure 3–56).

Q&A Can I forward a contact group to someone else?

Yes. You can forward a contact group by selecting the contact group, clicking Forward Contact (Home tab | Share group), and then selecting the option you want to use to forward the contact group.

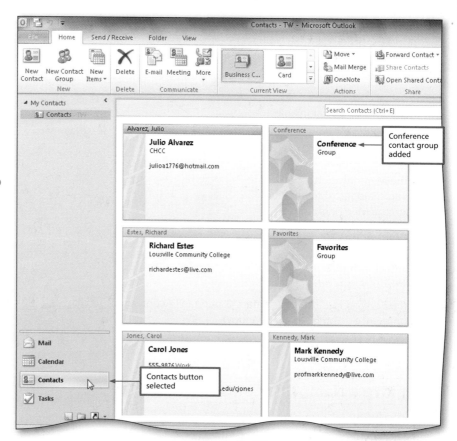

Figure 3–56

To Add a Name to a Contact Group

As you meet and work with people, you can add them to one or more contact groups. Carol Jones indicated that she will be attending the upcoming conference, and you want to add her to the Conference contact group so that she receives e-mail messages regarding the conference. The following steps add Carol Jones to the Conference contact group.

1

- Double-click the Conference contact group to display the Conference – Contact Group window (Figure 3–57).

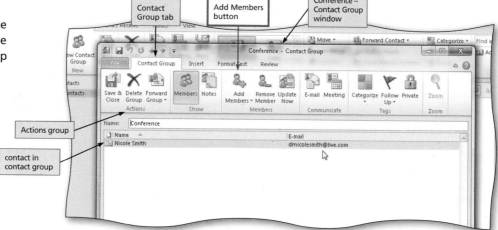

Figure 3–57

2

- Click the Add Members button (Contact Group tab | Add Members group) to display the Add Members menu.

- Click From Outlook Contacts to display the Select Members dialog box.

- Click Carol Jones to select her contact record.

- Click the Members button (Select Members dialog box) to add Carol Jones to the Members text box.

- Click the OK button (Select Members dialog box) to add Carol Jones to the contact group (Figure 3–58).

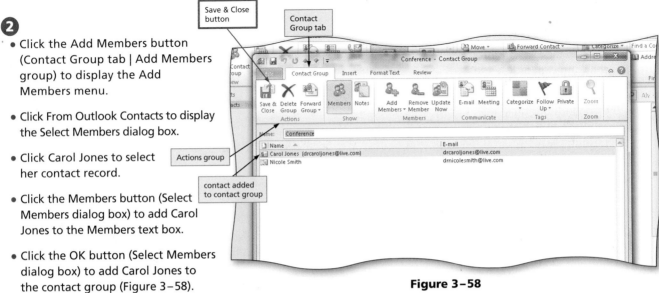

Figure 3–58

3

- Click the Save & Close button (Contact Group tab | Actions group) to save the contact and close the Conference – Contact Group window.

To Remove a Name in a Contact Group

Periodically, you may need to remove someone from a contact group. For example, contacts may switch jobs or ask to be removed from your list as they no longer are working on a particular project. Mark Kennedy is going on a sabbatical for one year and you have decided to remove him from the Lousville contact group so that he will not receive e-mail messages sent to the group. The following steps remove Mark Kennedy from the Lousville group.

1

- If necessary, scroll in the Contacts window until the Lousville contact group is visible.

- Double-click the Lousville contact group to display the Lousville – Contact Group window (Figure 3–59).

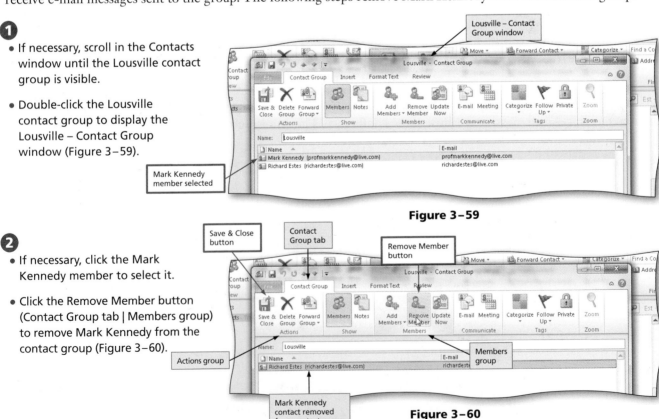

Figure 3–59

2

- If necessary, click the Mark Kennedy member to select it.

- Click the Remove Member button (Contact Group tab | Members group) to remove Mark Kennedy from the contact group (Figure 3–60).

Figure 3–60

3

- Click the Save & Close button (Contact Group tab | Actions group) to save the changes to the contact group and close the window (Figure 3–61).

Q&A When you remove a contact from a contact group, does it also remove the contact from Outlook?

No. The contact remains in Outlook, even after removing it from a contact group.

Q&A How can I delete a contact group?

To delete a contact group, select the contact group to delete, and then click Delete (Home tab | Delete group).

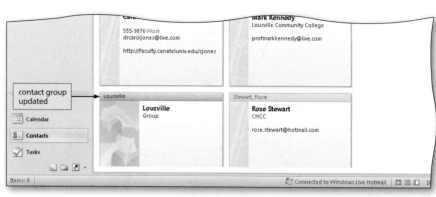

Figure 3–61

Printing Your Contacts

All or part of your contacts can be printed in a number of different views, or **print styles**. You can distribute a printed contact or contact list to others in a form that can be read or viewed, but cannot be edited. You can choose to print only one contact or the entire list. To print only part of your contacts, select one or more contacts and then change the print options so that you print your selection. This section previews the entire contact list and then prints the selected contacts in Card style. Table 3–1 lists the print styles available for printing your contacts from Contact view.

Table 3–1 Print Styles for Contact View	
Print Style	**Description**
Card	Prints a list of contacts separated by alphabet dividers and with a sheet for adding more contact information
Small Booklet	Prints a list of contacts similar to Card style but designed so that it can be folded into a small booklet
Medium Booklet	Prints a list of contacts similar to Card style but designed so that it can be folded into a medium-sized booklet
Memo	Prints a page for each contact, each page formatted to look like a memo
Phone Directory	Prints a list of contacts showing phone numbers only

BTW

Conserving Ink and Toner
If you want to conserve ink or toner, you can instruct Outlook to print draft quality documents by clicking File on the Ribbon to open the Backstage view, clicking the Print tab in the Backstage view to display the Print gallery, clicking the Print Options button, and then clicking the Properties button (Print dialog box). The Properties dialog box will vary depending on the type of printer you are using, but look for and select fast, economical options for the print quality. Then, use the Backstage view to print the document as usual.

Plan Ahead

Determine the best method for distributing a contact list.
The traditional method of distributing a contact list uses a printer to produce a hard copy. A **hard copy** or **printout** is information that exists on a physical medium such as paper. Hard copies can serve as reference material if your storage medium is lost or becomes corrupted and you need to re-create the contact list.

BTW

Certification
The Microsoft Office Specialist program provides an opportunity for you to obtain a valuable industry credential — proof that you have the Outlook 2010 skills required by employers. For more information, visit the Outlook 2010 Certification Web page (scsite.com/out2010/cert).

BTW

Quick Reference
For a table that lists how to complete the tasks covered in this book using the mouse, Ribbon, shortcut menu, and keyboard, see the Quick Reference Summary at the back of this book, or visit the Outlook 2010 Quick Reference Web page (scsite.com/out2010/qr).

To Preview a Contact List

Unless you change the print options, you will see all your contacts when you preview the list before printing. The following steps preview the contact list in various print styles.

- In the Contacts window, select the Richard Estes and Mark Kennedy contacts (Figure 3–62).

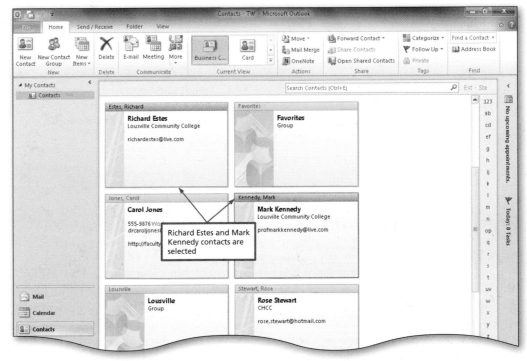

Figure 3–62

- Click File on the Ribbon to open the Backstage view.

- Click the Print tab in the Backstage view to display the Print gallery (Figure 3–63).

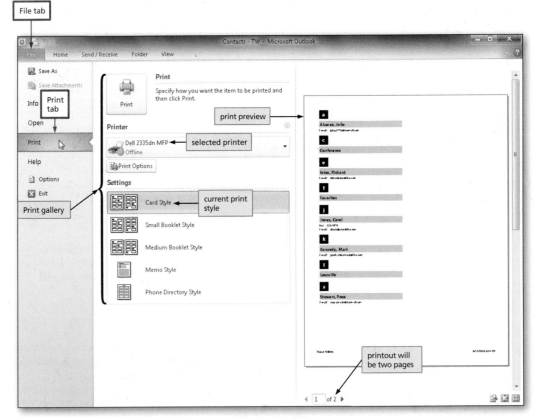

Figure 3–63

3

• Click Medium Booklet Style in the Settings area to change the print style (Figure 3–64).

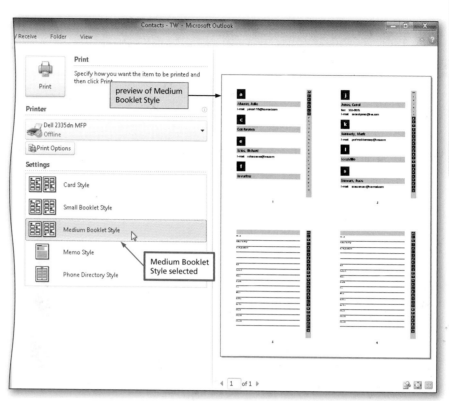

Figure 3–64

4

• Click Phone Directory Style in the Settings area to change to Phone Directory Style (Figure 3–65).

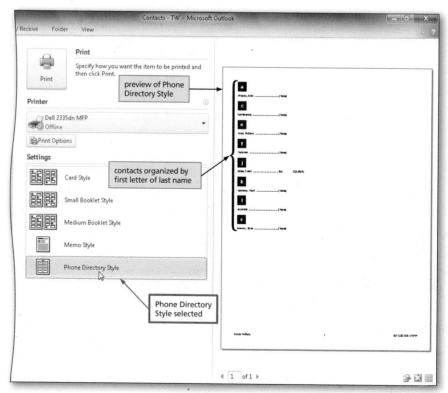

Figure 3–65

5
- Click Card Style in the Settings area to change to Card Style (Figure 3–66).

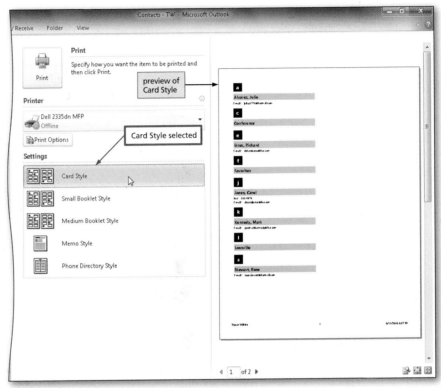

Figure 3–66

6
- Click the Print Options button to display the Print dialog box (Figure 3–67).

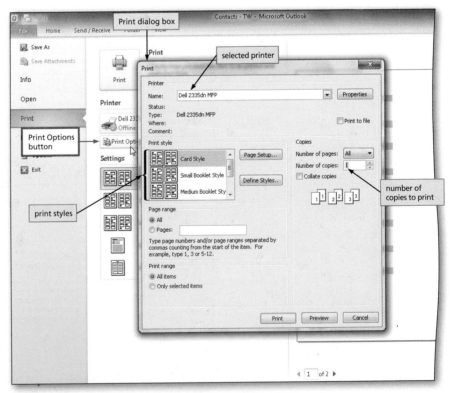

Figure 3–67

7

• Click the 'Only selected items' option button (Print dialog box) to preview only the selected contacts (Figure 3–68).

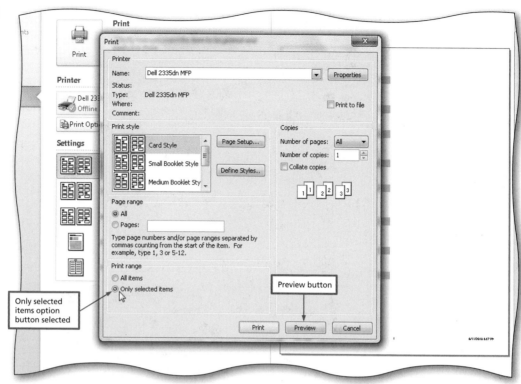

Figure 3–68

8

• Click the Preview button (Print dialog box) to close the dialog box and preview only the selected contacts (Figure 3–69).

If I click the other styles, will they only show selected contacts?

No. If you change the style, the preview returns to showing all contacts. To see the selected contacts in a particular style, you select the style and then change the print options.

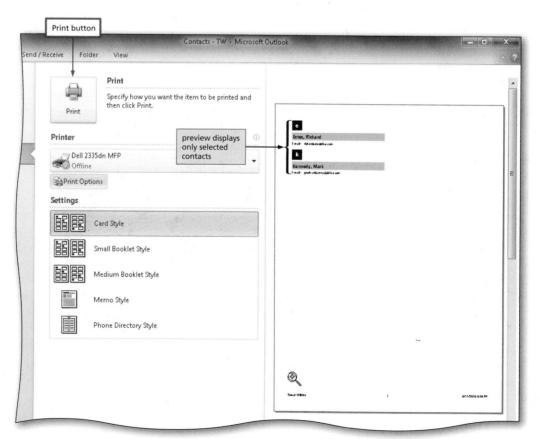

Figure 3–69

To Print the Contact List

The following step prints the selected contacts in Card style.

1

● Click the Print button to print the selected contacts (Figure 3–70).

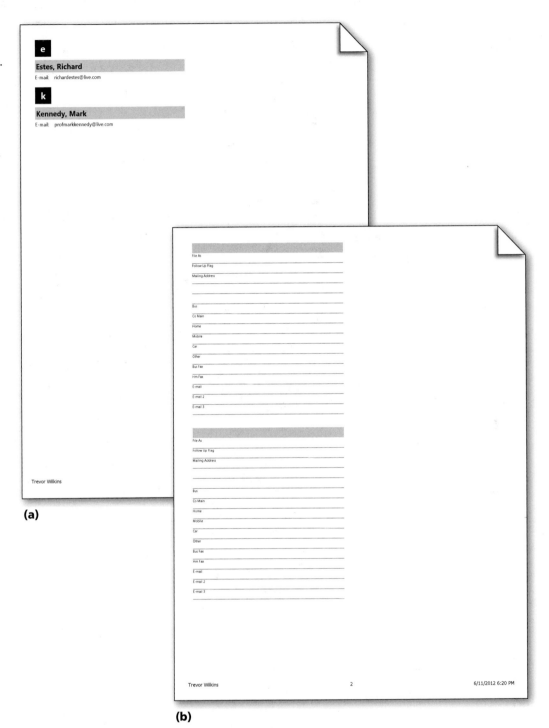

(a)

(b)

Figure 3–70

To Quit Outlook

The project is complete. Thus, the following step quits Outlook.

 Click the Close button on the right side of the title bar to quit Outlook.

Chapter Summary

In this chapter, you have learned how to create a contact list, view and sort contacts, search for contacts, create and edit a contact group, and print contacts. The items listed below include all the new Outlook skills you have learned in this chapter.

1. Create a New Contact (OUT 125)
2. Create a Contact from an E-Mail Message (OUT 127)
3. Create a Contact from an Existing Contact (OUT 129)
4. Edit a Contact (OUT 130)
5. Add an Attachment to a Contact (OUT 131)
6. Change an Attachment to a Contact (OUT 133)
7. Remove an Attachment to a Contact (OUT 135)
8. Change the Current View (OUT 137)
9. Sort Contacts (OUT 138)
10. Find a Contact by Searching for an E-Mail Address (OUT 139)
11. Refine a Search (OUT 141)
12. Find a Contact from any Outlook Folder (OUT 142)
13. Create a Contact Group from Existing Contacts (OUT 144)
14. Create a Contact Group from an Existing E-Mail Message (OUT 146)
15. Add a Name to a Contact Group (OUT 149)
16. Remove a Name in a Contact Group (OUT 150)
17. Preview a Contact List (OUT 152)
18. Print the Contact List (OUT 156)

 If you have a SAM 2010 user profile, your instructor may have assigned an autogradable version of this assignment. If so, log into the SAM 2010 Web site at www.cengage.com/sam2010 to download the instruction and start files.

Learn It Online

Test your knowledge of chapter content and key terms.

Instructions: To complete the Learn It Online exercises, start your browser, click the Address bar, and then enter the Web address `scsite.com/out2010/learn`. When the Outlook 2010 Learn It Online page is displayed, click the link for the exercise you want to complete and then read the instructions.

Chapter Reinforcement TF, MC, and SA
A series of true/false, multiple choice, and short answer questions that test your knowledge of the chapter content.

Flash Cards
An interactive learning environment where you identify chapter key terms associated with displayed definitions.

Practice Test
A series of multiple choice questions that test your knowledge of chapter content and key terms.

Who Wants To Be a Computer Genius?
An interactive game that challenges your knowledge of chapter content in the style of a television quiz show.

Wheel of Terms
An interactive game that challenges your knowledge of chapter key terms in the style of the television show *Wheel of Fortune*.

Crossword Puzzle Challenge
A crossword puzzle that challenges your knowledge of key terms presented in the chapter.

Apply Your Knowledge

Reinforce the skills and apply the concepts you learned in this chapter.

Editing a Contact List

Note: To complete this assignment, you will be required to use the Data Files for Students. See the inside back cover of this book for instructions on downloading the Data Files for Students, or contact your instructor for information about accessing the required files.

Instructions: Start Outlook. Edit the contact list provided in the file called Apply Your Knowledge 3-1 Contacts, located on the Data Files for Students. The Apply Your Knowledge 3-1 Contacts is a contacts folder containing the contacts of Dr. Carol Jones. Many of the contacts have changed and some are incomplete. You now need to revise these contacts and print them in Card view (Figure 3–71).

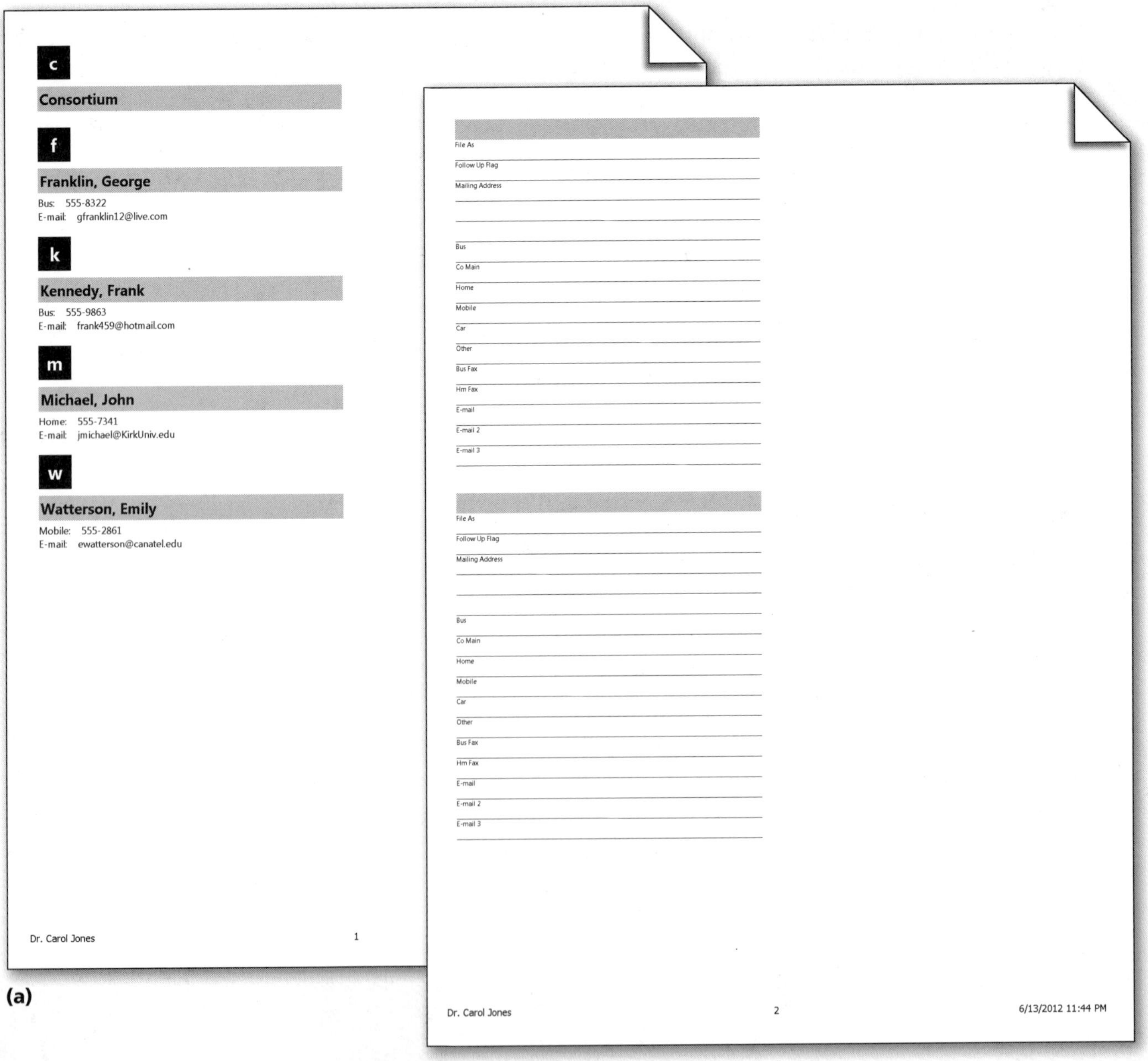

c

Consortium

f

Franklin, George
Bus: 555-8322
E-mail: gfranklin12@live.com

k

Kennedy, Frank
Bus: 555-9863
E-mail: frank459@hotmail.com

m

Michael, John
Home: 555-7341
E-mail: jmichael@KirkUniv.edu

w

Watterson, Emily
Mobile: 555-2861
E-mail: ewatterson@canatel.edu

Dr. Carol Jones   1

(a)

File As
Follow Up Flag
Mailing Address

Bus
Co Main
Home
Mobile
Car
Other
Bus Fax
Hm Fax
E-mail
E-mail 2
E-mail 3

File As
Follow Up Flag
Mailing Address

Bus
Co Main
Home
Mobile
Car
Other
Bus Fax
Hm Fax
E-mail
E-mail 2
E-mail 3

Dr. Carol Jones   2   6/13/2012 11:44 PM

(b)

Figure 3–71

Perform the following tasks:

1. Import the Apply Your Knowledge 3-1 Contacts folder.

2. Change Frank Kennedy's company to Smyrna CC. Move the Home phone number to the Business phone number text box. Add the Job title of Professor.

3. Change George Franklin's Job title to adjunct. Add the company name, CHCC, to the contact. Type `gfranklin12@live.com` as the e-mail address. The Business phone should be 555-8322.

4. Change John Michael's e-mail address to jmichael@KirkUniv.edu. Change the Web page address to http://www.KirkUniv.edu/jmichael. Add a Home phone of 555-7341.

5. Enter the company name, Canatel University, for Emily Watterson. Type `ewatterson@canatel.edu` for the e-mail address. Enter a mobile phone number of 555-2861.

6. Change the Consort contact group name to Consortium. Add all the contacts to the contact group.

7. Print the final contact list in Card view, as shown in Figure 3–71, and then submit the printout to your instructor.

8. Export the Apply Your Knowledge 3-1 Contacts folder to a USB flash drive and then delete the folder from the hard disk.

Extend Your Knowledge

Extend the skills you learned in this chapter and experiment with new skills. You may need to use Help to complete the assignment.

Creating a Contact Folder

Note: To complete this assignment, you will be required to use the Data Files for Students. See the inside back cover of this book for instructions on downloading the Data Files for Students, or contact your instructor for information about accessing the required files.

Instructions: Start Outlook. Edit the contact list provided in the file called Extend Your Knowledge 3-1 Contacts, located on the Data Files for Students. The Extend Your Knowledge 3-1 Contacts folder has no contacts. You will create a new contacts folder, add contacts to the new contacts folder, and print the contact list. You also will share the contact folder with others.

Perform the following tasks:

1. Use Help to learn about creating a contacts folder and sharing a contact list.

2. Start Outlook and create a new contacts folder named Marketing Department.

3. Create the contacts displayed in Table 3–2.

Table 3–2 Marketing Department Information				
Full Name	**Company**	**Job Title**	**E-Mail Address**	**Work Phone**
Bob McCornly	Music Oddities	Advertising	mccornly@musicoddities.com	555-1278
Max Vindo	Music Oddities	Research	vindo@musicoddities.com	555-1290
Susie Wells	Music Oddities	Planning	wells@musicoddities.com	555-1358
Tammi Townsend	Music Oddities	Purchasing	townsend@musicoddities.com	555-2751
Vicki Wickers	Music Oddities	Research	wickers@musicoddities.com	555-2776
Al Sanders	Music Oddities	Research	sanders@musicoddities.com	555-2689

Continued >

Extend Your Knowledge *continued*

4. Create a contact group called Everyone. Add all of the contacts to this group.

5. Create a contact group called Research Group. Add all the employees with Research as their job title to this group.

6. Print the contact list in Phone Directory view, as shown in Figure 3–72, and then submit the printout to your instructor.

7. Use the Share Contacts button (Home tab | Share group) to e-mail the contact list to your instructor.

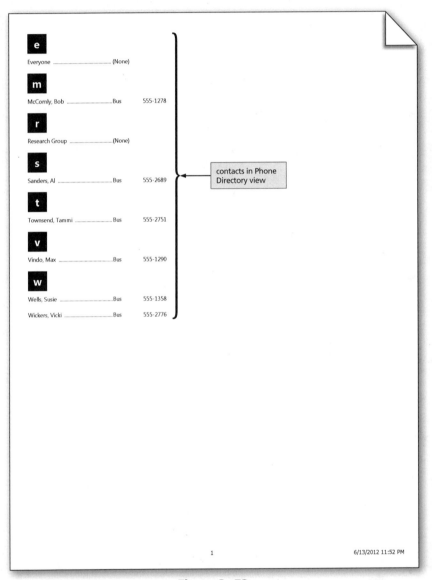

Figure 3–72

Make It Right

Analyze contacts and correct all errors and/or improve the design.

Correcting Contacts and Contact Groups

Note: To complete this assignment, you will be required to use the Data Files for Students. See the inside back cover of this book for instructions on downloading the Data Files for Students, or contact your instructor for information about accessing the required files.

Instructions: Start Outlook. Import the Make It Right 3-1 Contacts folder in the Data Files for Students folder into Outlook. While reviewing your Outlook contacts, you realize that you created several contacts incorrectly, failed to add a contact, and incorrectly added contacts to your contact group. You will identify and open the incorrect contacts, edit them so that they reflect the correct information, add the missing contact, edit the contact group, and then save all changes. You will also print the contacts in Small Booklet style (Figure 3–73).

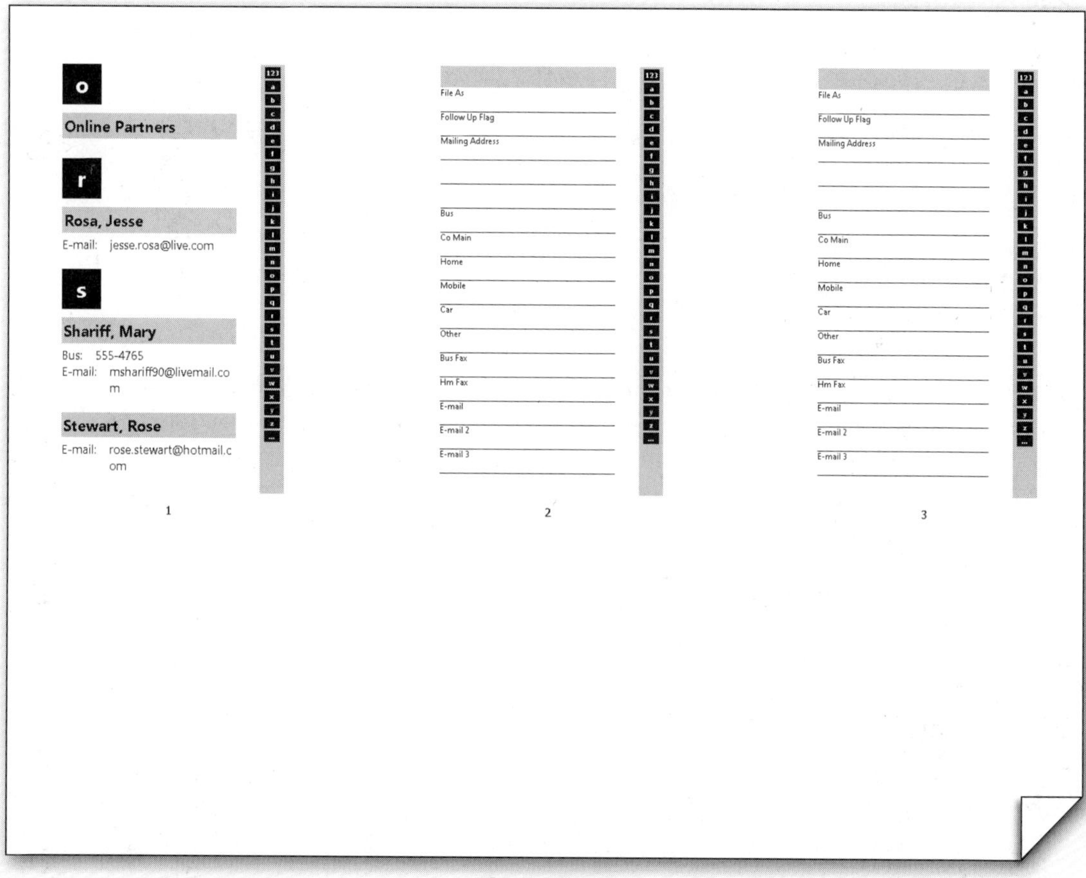

Figure 3–73

Continued >

Make It Right *continued*

Perform the following tasks:

1. Display only the Make It Right 3-1 Contacts folder in the Outlook Contacts window.

2. While adding the Jesse Rosa contact, you inadvertently recorded the e-mail address as jesse.rosa@ com.live.edu. Change the e-mail address to jesse.rosa@live.com. If necessary, press the F5 key to update the change.

3. Mary Shariff works for Alentawn Bakery with a work phone of 555-4765. Edit the contact to show the correct information.

4. You were supposed to add Rose Stewart, who had sent you an e-mail message, to your contacts. Add her now as a contact, using the e-mail message she sent you.

5. Your online partners only include Jesse Rosa and Rose Stewart; however, your Online Partners contact group includes Mary Shariff instead of Rose Stewart. Edit the group to include the correct members.

6. Print the contacts using the Small Booklet style (Figure 3–73).

7. Export the Make It Right 3-1 Contacts folder to your USB flash drive and then delete the folder from the hard disk.

8. Submit the Contacts folder in a format specified by your instructor.

In the Lab

Design, create, modify, and/or use a document using the guidelines, concepts, and skills presented in this chapter. Labs are listed in order of increasing difficulty.

Lab 1: Creating Departmental Contacts

Problem: You are a graduate assistant for the provost at South Landis Community College (SLCC) and have been asked to create a contact list of the departmental offices on campus. Each department now has an e-mail address, so that e-mail messages can be sent there and then forwarded by the dean of each department as necessary. Table 3–3 lists each department's contact information. Enter the contacts into the contacts list. The contact list you create will look like that in Figure 3–74.

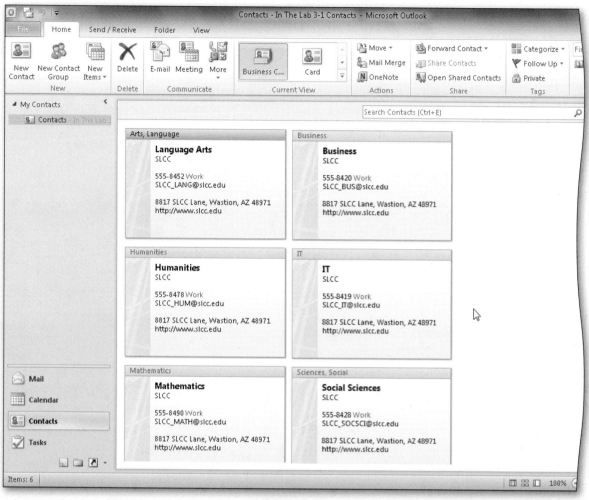

Figure 3–74

Perform the following tasks:

1. Create the contacts in the Contacts folder, using the information listed in Table 3–3.

Table 3–3 Departmental Information			
Department	**E-Mail Address**	**Phone**	**Fax**
IT	SLCC_IT@slcc.edu	555-8419	555-8513
Social Sciences	SLCC_SOCSCI@slcc.edu	555-8428	555-8529
Humanities	SLCC_HUM@slcc.edu	555-8478	555-8578
Business	SLCC_BUS@slcc.edu	555-8420	555-8525
Language Arts	SLCC_LANG@slcc.edu	555-8452	555-8554
Mathematics	SLCC_MATH@slcc.edu	555-8490	555-8593

2. For each contact, list the full name using the department name.

3. For each contact, list the company as SLCC.

4. For each contact, list the Web page address as http://www.slcc.edu.

5. For each contact, list the business address as 8817 SLCC Lane, Wastion, AZ 48971.

6. Print the contacts list using Memo style, and submit it in a format specified by your instructor.

In the Lab

Lab 2: Creating an Employee Contact List

Problem: You are the owner of PetExotic, a small pet store. Your store has decided to e-mail reminders to employees such as weekly schedules, store specials to memorize, and other information. You have two shifts in your store, morning and afternoon. You need to create a list of all your contacts, and also add contact groups, so that you send specific information just to the morning and afternoon employees (Figure 3–75).

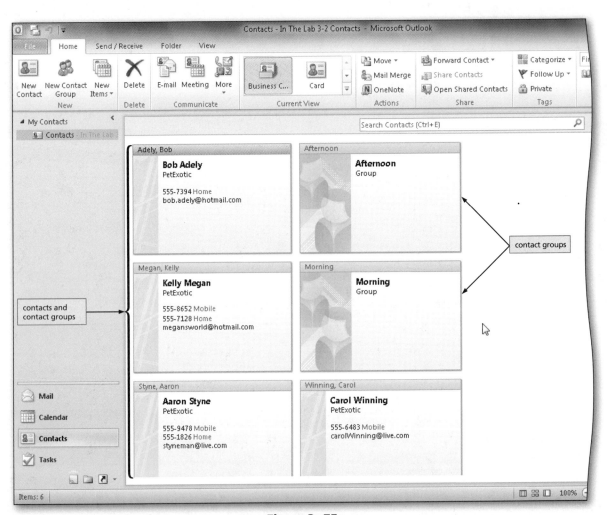

Figure 3–75

Perform the following tasks:

1. Create two contact groups called Morning and Afternoon.

2. Enter the contacts in the Contacts folder, using the information listed in Table 3–4. Do not add the shift information to the contacts. Use the shift information to determine in which contact group you should place the contacts. Add the contacts to the appropriate contact group.

Table 3–4 PetExotic Store Employee Information

Full Name	E-Mail Address	Home Phone	Mobile Phone	Shift
Bob Adely	bob.adely@hotmail.com	555-7394		Morning
Aaron Styne	styneman@live.com	555-1826	555-9478	Morning
Carol Winning	carolwinning@live.com		555-6483	Afternoon
Kelly Megan	megansworld@hotmail.com	555-7128	555-8652	Afternoon

3. Print the contacts list in Small Booklet style, and then submit it in the format specified by your instructor.

In the Lab

Lab 3: Creating Contacts with Attachments

Note: To complete this assignment, you will be required to use the Data Files for Students. See the inside back cover of this book for instructions on downloading the Data Files for Students, or contact your instructor for information about accessing the required files.

Problem: Start Outlook. You are to create a contact list for Lattel's Hardware Store using Table 3–5. The contact list you create is shown in Figure 3–76. Each employee will have an attachment of the hours they work weekly, which you will add to their contact information.

You will need the documents from the Data Files for Students folder to attach to the contacts.

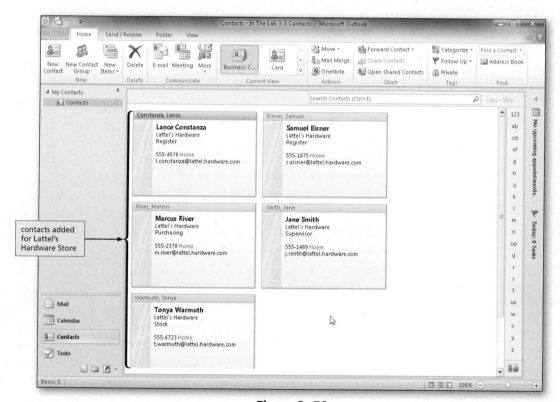

Figure 3–76

Continued >

In the Lab *continued*

Perform the following tasks:

1. Create contacts for each employee using the information in Table 3–5. Create the first contact including the company name, and then create the rest from that contact.

Table 3–5 Lattel's Hardware Information			
Employee	**Position**	**E-Mail Address**	**Home**
Jane Smith	Supervisor	j.smith@lattel.hardware.com	555-1489
Marcus River	Purchasing	m.river@lattel.hardware.com	555-2378
Tonya Warmuth	Stock	t.warmuth@lattel.hardware.com	555-6723
Lance Constanza	Register	l.constanza@lattel.hardware.com	555-4578
Samuel Eisner	Register	s.eisner@lattel.hardware.com	555-1875

2. Edit the Jane Smith contact. Add the Smith hours document from the data files as an attachment to the contact.

3. Edit the Marcus River contact. Add the River hours document from the data files as an attachment to the contact.

4. Edit the Tonya Warmuth contact. Add the Warmuth hours document from the data files as an attachment to the contact.

5. Edit the Lance Constanza contact. Add the Constanza hours document from the data files as an attachment to the contact.

6. Edit the Samuel Eisner contact. Add the Eisner hours document from the data files as an attachment to the contact.

7. Print the contacts list in Medium Booklet style, and then submit it in the format specified by your instructor.

Cases and Places

Apply your creative thinking and problem solving skills to design and implement a solution.

Note: To complete these assignments, you may be required to use the Data Files for Students. See the inside back cover of this book for instructions on downloading the Data Files for Students, or contact your instructor for information about accessing the required files.

1: Create a Study Group List

Academic

Create contacts for a study group at Canatel University using the information in Table 3–6. Use Canatel University as the company name. You should create the first contact and then create the rest as contacts from the same company. Print the list in Card style and in Phone Directory style. Submit it in the format specified by your instructor.

Table 3–6 Study Group Members			
Full Name	E-Mail Address	Home Phone	Mobile Phone
Marge Jones	mjones@live.com	555-7812	
Juan Escobar	gocanatel@hotmail.com	555-8772	555-9871
April Kent	April.Kent@live.com		555-2145
Addison Hu	addison9871@live.com		555-8912
Larry Honda	SuperHonda@hotmail.com	555-7728	555-3476
Kim Young	Kim.Young@live.com	555-5874	

2: Create a Team List

Professional

At Hank's Handheld Mobile, you are in charge of scheduling your team of employees. The business is located at 9821 South End Dr, Tarnnel, IN 33389. Whenever you create a schedule, you need to e-mail it to your entire team. You also use e-mail to send your team important information they should know. Create contacts for each member of your team using the information in Table 3–7. Create a contact group called Team and add the contacts to the group. Print the contact list in Card style and submit it in the format specified by your instructor.

Table 3–7 Hank's Handheld Mobile Information		
Full Name	E-Mail Address	Home Phone
Carla Angel	angel@hankshandheld.com	555-1278
Angel Esposita	esposita@hankshandheld.com	555-8221
Abigail Shin	shin@hankshandheld.com	555-9856
Nina Montgomery	montgomery@hankshandheld.com	555-3846
Stan Applebaum	applebaum@hankshandheld.com	555-2877
Josiah Bell	bell@hankshandheld.com	555-8745

Continued >

Cases and Places *continued*

3: Create a Family List

Personal

Create a list of family contacts. Use Table 3–8 to add these items to your contacts. After you have made the contacts, your sister Emily sends you an e-mail message and reminds you that she has recently gotten married to Benjamin Genius and has moved to 1789 Willow Lane, Soonerville, OH 44218. The home phone has changed to 555-8319 and Ben's mobile phone number is 555-7811. He does not have an e-mail address yet. She asks if you could update the information since you often print and mail the contact list to the rest of the family. Edit the entry and print the contacts list in Medium Booklet style.

Table 3–8 Marion Family Information				
Name	**Address**	**E-Mail Address**	**Home Phone**	**Mobile Phone**
Emily Marion	1289 Oak Ave Soonerville, OH 44218	EmilyBlogs@live.com	555-8744	555-7412
Susan Marion	8871 South Dr. Soonerville, OH 44218		555-2977	
Peter Marion	8871 South Dr. Soonerville, OH 44218	MarionFamily@hotmail.com	555-2977	
Lance Marion	89201 Central Ave. Soonerville, OH 44218	lmarion@hotmail.com	555-8863	555-1799
Katelyn Marion	2821 Oak Ave Soonerville, OH 44218	katelynmarion@canateluniv.edu		555-2859

4 | Creating and Managing Tasks

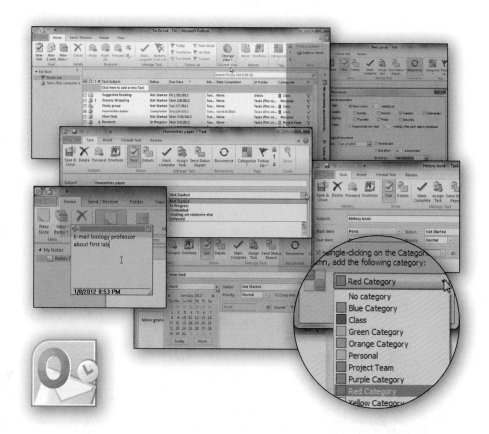

Objectives

You will have mastered the material in this chapter when you can:

- Create a new task
- Customize a task
- Categorize a task
- Create a recurring task
- Attach items to a task
- Categorize and flag e-mail messages

- Configure Quick Clicks
- Assign a task
- Send a status report
- Print tasks
- Create a note
- Change the view of notes

4 | Creating and Managing Tasks

Introduction

Creating and managing tasks in Outlook allows you to keep track of projects, which might include school projects, work projects, or personal projects. A **task** lets you record information about a project such as start date, due date, status, priority, and percent complete. Outlook also can remind you about the task so that you do not forget to complete it. If you are managing a project, for example, you can assign tasks to people so that everyone can complete their portion of the project.

Project — Managing Tasks

People and businesses create tasks to keep track of projects that are important to them or their organizations. Tasks can be categorized and monitored to ensure that all projects are completed in a timely fashion. You can track one-time tasks as well as tasks that recur over a period of time. Tasks can be prioritized so that you can decide which ones must be completed first.

The project in this chapter follows general guidelines and uses Outlook to create the task list shown in Figure 4–1. The task list in the TW mailbox includes tasks that are organized using class, personal, and project team categories.

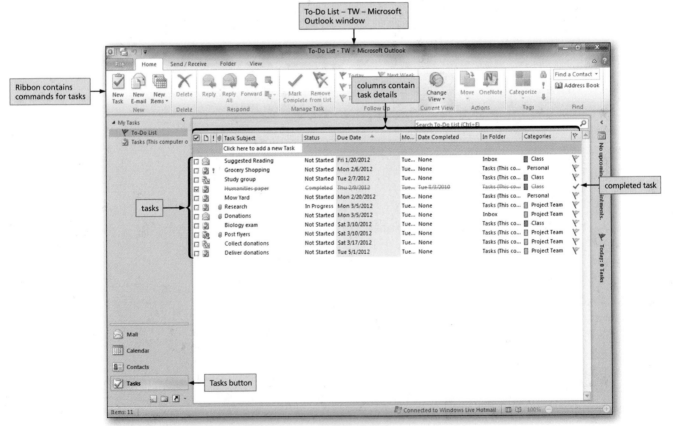

Figure 4–1

Overview

As you read this chapter, you will learn how to create the task list shown in Figure 4–1 by performing these general tasks:

- Create a new task.
- Categorize a task.
- Flag and categorize an e-mail message.
- Assign a task.
- Print tasks.
- Create and use notes.

Plan
Ahead

General Project Guidelines

When creating and working with tasks, the actions you perform and decisions you make will affect the appearance and characteristics of your task list. As you create your tasks, such as those shown in Figure 4–1, you should follow these general guidelines:

1. **Determine what projects you want to track.** People use tasks to keep track of the projects that are most important to them. For example, students may track their class projects, study group sessions, or exams. You also can track activities such as volunteering for a charity.

2. **Determine the information you want to store for a task.** For any task, you can store basic information, add attachments, and add detailed instructions. For example, you might attach a list of meeting rooms used for a particular project.

3. **Plan categories for tasks.** To identify and group tasks and other Outlook items easily, assign the items to categories. For example, if you assign certain tasks, notes, and e-mail messages to the same category, you can see at a glance that they are related, which helps you keep track of your tasks and other obligations.

4. **Determine which tasks may need to be assigned to others.** When managing a large project involving several people, tasks can be assigned to members of the group so that the project is completed on time. You should determine which team member of the project is best suited for completing each task.

5. **Determine how you want to view your tasks.** Select a view to display task information, such as a detailed list or prioritized list. Selecting the right view can help you be more efficient in managing your tasks.

When necessary, more specific details concerning the above guidelines are presented at appropriate points in the chapter. The chapter also will identify the actions performed and decisions made regarding these guidelines during the creation of the task list shown in Figure 4–1.

To Start Outlook

If you are using a computer to step through the project in this chapter and you want your screens to match the figures in this book, you should change your screen's resolution to 1024 × 768.

The following steps, which assume Windows 7 is running, start Outlook based on a typical installation. You may need to ask your instructor how to start Outlook for your computer.

1 Click the Start button on the Windows 7 taskbar to display the Start menu.

2 Type `Microsoft Outlook` as the search text in the 'Search programs and files' text box and watch the search results appear on the Start menu.

3 Click Microsoft Outlook 2010 in the search results on the Start menu to start Outlook with your Inbox as the default Mail folder.

4 If the Outlook window is not maximized, click the Maximize button next to the Close button on its title bar to maximize the window.

5 Click the Tasks button in the Navigation Pane to display the To-Do List TW – Microsoft Outlook window (Figure 4–2).

Q&A Why does my title bar not match the title bar in Figure 4–2?

If you did not import the data file for this chapter, your title bar will be different. The title bar always displays the name of the Outlook data file.

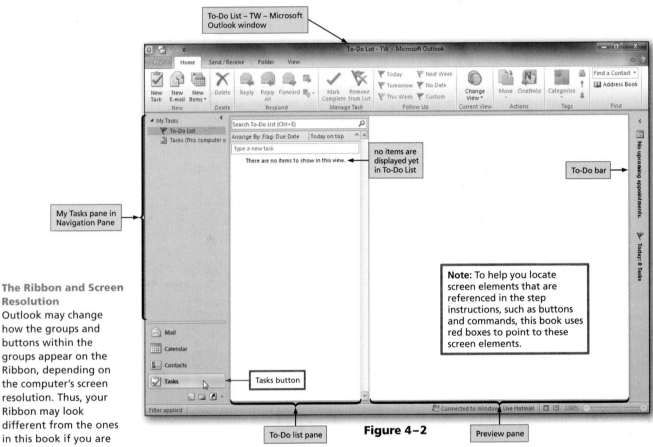

Figure 4–2

BTW

The Ribbon and Screen Resolution
Outlook may change how the groups and buttons within the groups appear on the Ribbon, depending on the computer's screen resolution. Thus, your Ribbon may look different from the ones in this book if you are using a screen resolution other than 1024 × 768.

BTW

Q&As
For a complete list of the Q&As found in many of the step-by-step sequences in this book, visit the Outlook 2010 Q&A Web page (scsite.com/out2010/qa).

To-Do List Window

The To-Do list – TW – Microsoft Outlook window shown in Figure 4–2 includes a variety of features to help you manage your tasks. It contains many elements similar to the windows in other Office programs, as well as some that are unique to Outlook. The main elements of the To-Do List window are the Navigation Pane, the To-Do list pane, the Preview pane, and the To-Do bar.

The Navigation Pane includes two sets of buttons (standard and additional) and the My Tasks pane. The **My Tasks pane** displays the To-Do list link and Tasks folder. Clicking the To-Do list link displays the tasks in the To-Do list view, and clicking Tasks displays the tasks in the task folder in Simple List view. The standard buttons represent shortcuts to the standard items that are part of Microsoft Outlook mailbox: Mail, Calendar, Contacts, and Tasks. Additional buttons are displayed below the standard buttons and represent shortcuts to other Outlook functions, such as Notes, Folder List shortcuts, and Configure buttons, which allow you to specify which folders to display.

Creating a To-Do List

The first step in creating a To-Do list is to select a folder for storing your tasks. By default, Outlook stores tasks in the Tasks folder, but you also can create a personal folder in which to store your tasks, using the technique presented in Chapter 2. In this chapter, you will create tasks in the Tasks folder.

Determine what projects you want to track. You can make tasks for nearly everything you do, but not everything should be added to the task list. Only create tasks for those projects that you want to track. For example, you do not need to track what time you get up every day; however, you might add a task about getting up on time to catch a flight. Adding too many tasks can make it difficult to manage your task list. **Determine the information you want to store for a task.** In addition to time, date, and task description, you can record information such as status, priority, and category. Attach one or more files to a task to store documents, tables, pictures, or clip art, for example, along with task information.	**Plan** **Ahead**

To Create a New Task

To create the tasks in this chapter, you will start by adding the first task, which is to help your grandmother by mowing her yard. Your uncle normally mows the yard, but he is going on vacation for two weeks. You volunteered to mow the yard in his absence, so you want to add the task so that you do not forget about it. The following steps create a new task.

1

- If necessary, display the Home tab.

- Click the New Task button (Home tab | New group) to display the Untitled – Task window (Figure 4–3).

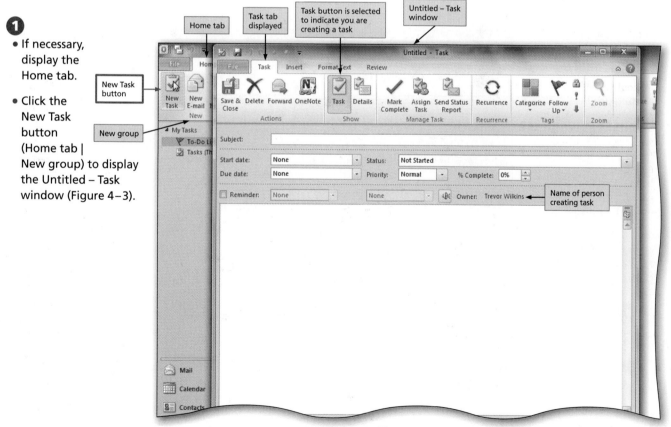

Figure 4–3

②

- Type **Mow Yard** in the Subject text box to enter a subject for the task.

- Type **Mow grandmother's yard** in the task body area to enter a description for the task (Figure 4–4).

Q&A

Why did the title of the Task window change after I entered the subject?

As soon as you enter the subject, Outlook updates the Task window title to reflect the information you entered. The task is not saved, however; only the window title is updated.

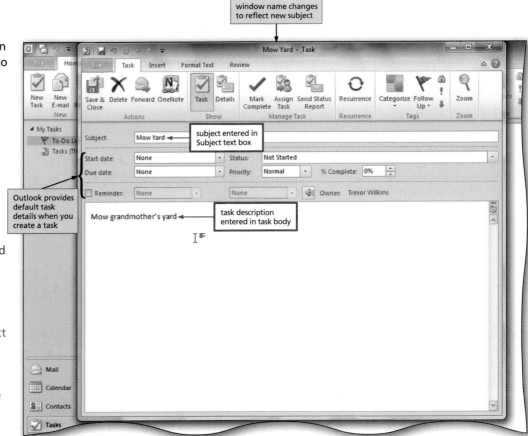

Figure 4–4

③

- Click the Start date box arrow to display a calendar for the current month (Figure 4–5).

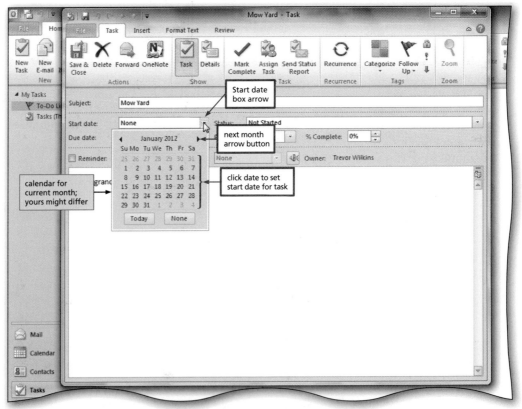

Figure 4–5

4

- Click the next month arrow button an appropriate number of times to advance to February 2012.

- Click 17 to select Fri 2/17/2012 as the start date (Figure 4–6).

Q&A Why did the due date change?

If you enter a start date, the due date automatically changes to match the start date. You can change the due date if needed.

Q&A Can I just type in the date?

Yes, you can just type in the date. Using the calendar allows you to avoid potential errors due to typing mistakes.

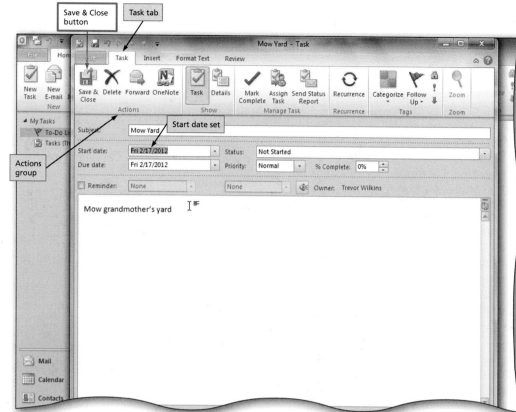

Figure 4–6

Q&A What if February 2012 is in the past?

If February 2012 is in the past, click the previous month arrow an appropriate number of times until you reach February 2012.

5

- Click the Save & Close button (Task tab | Actions group) to save the task and close the Task window (Figure 4–7).

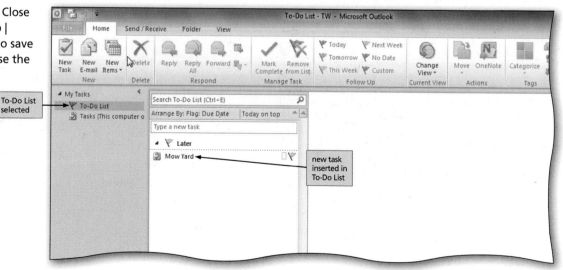

Figure 4–7

Other Ways

1. Press CTRL+SHIFT+K

To Create a Task with a Due Date

When you created the first task, the due date was automatically set when you entered the start date. If you have a specific due date, you can enter it when you create a task. You have a biology exam on March 10 that you would like to add as a task. The following steps create a biology exam task due on March 10.

1
- Click the New Task button (Home tab | New group) to display the Untitled – Task window.

- Type **Biology exam** in the Subject text box to enter a subject for the task (Figure 4–8).

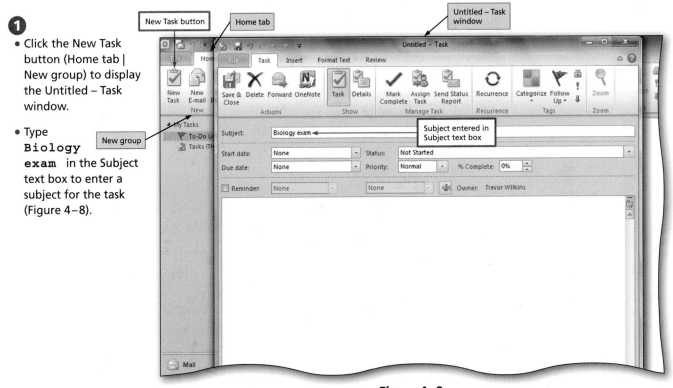

Figure 4–8

2
- Click the Due date box arrow to display a calendar for the current month.

- Click the next month arrow button an appropriate number of times to advance to March 2012.

- Click 10 to select Sat 3/10/2012 as the due date (Figure 4–9).

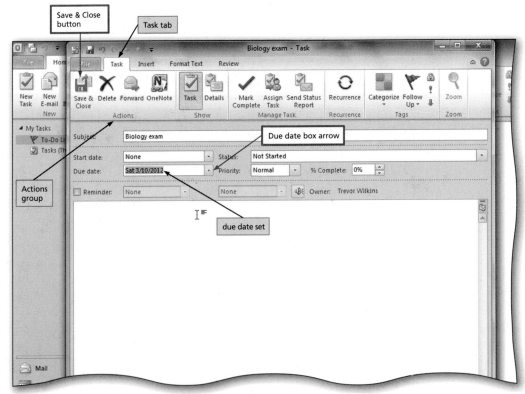

Figure 4–9

- Click the Save & Close button (Task tab | Actions group) to save the task and close the Task window (Figure 4–10).

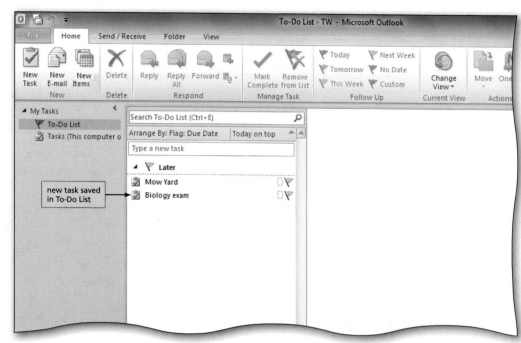

Figure 4–10

Other Ways
1. Press CTRL+SHIFT+K

To Create a Task with a Status

You have been working on a paper for your humanities class that is due February 9. Outlook allows you to assign a status to any task you create. You can assign one of five status indicators: Not Started, In Progress, Completed, Waiting on someone else, and Deferred. Because you already have started working on your humanities paper, you will add the task and set the status to In Progress.

- Click the New Task button (Home tab | New group) to display the Untitled – Task window.

- Type **Humanities paper** in the Subject text box to enter a subject for the task.

- Click the Due date box arrow to display a calendar for the current month.

- Click the next month arrow button an appropriate number of times to advance to February 2012.

- Click 9 to select Thu 2/9/2012 as the due date (Figure 4–11).

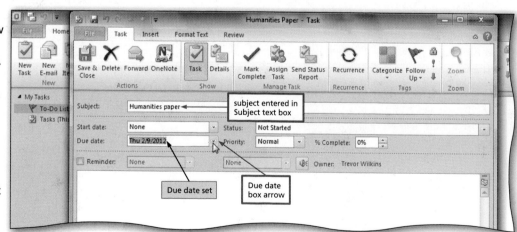

Figure 4–11

2

- Click the Status box arrow to display the status options (Figure 4–12).

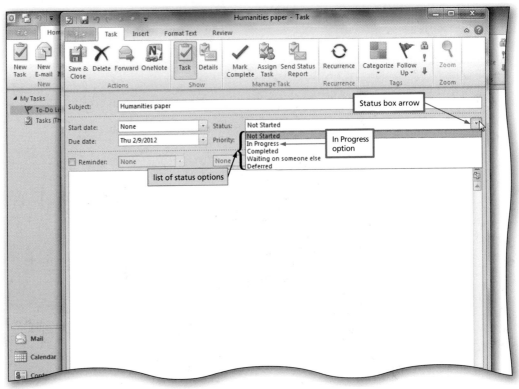

Figure 4–12

3

- Click In Progress to change the status to In Progress (Figure 4–13).

4

- Click the Save & Close button (Task tab | Actions group) to save the task and close the Task window.

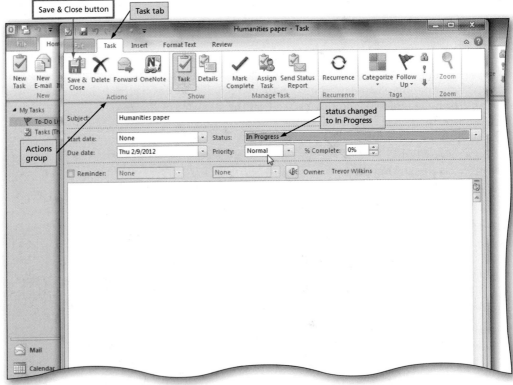

Figure 4–13

Other Ways

1. Press CTRL+SHIFT+K

To Create a Task with a Priority

You are hosting an event at work on February 11, but you know that you will have to shop for groceries and supplies at least five days in advance. You decide that you should enter the event as a task in Outlook and set the priority appropriately. Outlook allows for three priority levels: Low, Normal, and High. The following steps add a grocery shopping task and set the priority to High.

1

- Click the New Task button (Home tab | New group) to display the Untitled – Task window.

- Type **Grocery Shopping** in the Subject text box to enter a subject for the task.

- Click the Due date box arrow to display a calendar for the current month.

- Click the next month arrow button an appropriate number of times to advance to February 2012.

- Click 6 to select Mon 2/6/2012 as the due date (Figure 4–14).

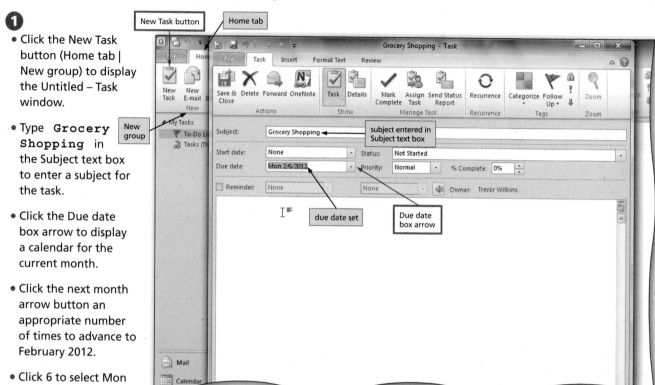

Figure 4–14

2

- Click the Priority box arrow to display the priority options (Figure 4–15).

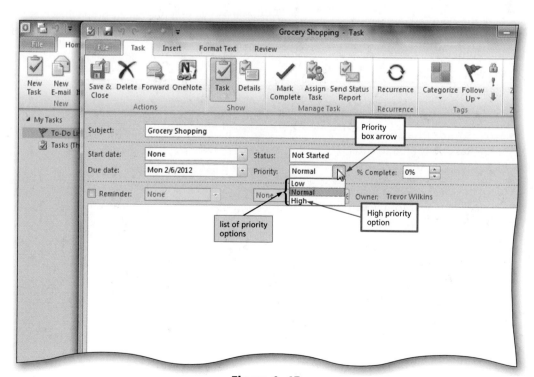

Figure 4–15

- Click High to set the priority (Figure 4–16).

- Click the Save & Close button (Task tab | Actions group) to save the task and close the Task window.

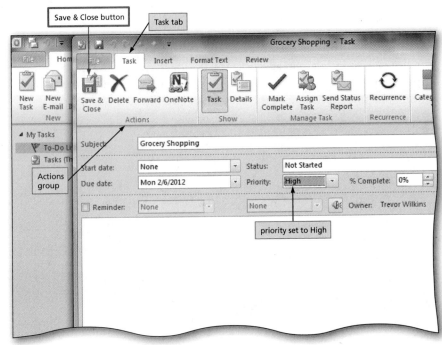

Figure 4–16

To Create a Task with a Reminder

For your history class, you have been asked to read Chapters 1 – 5 by February 17. You want to add the reading assignment as a task in Outlook because Outlook can remind you about the task automatically. You decide that if you are reminded the week before, you will have enough time. The following steps add a history book task and set the reminder option so that you are reminded to read the chapters on February 10.

- Click the New Task button (Home tab | New group) to display the Untitled – Task window.

- Type **History book** in the Subject text box to enter a subject for the task.

- Type **Read Chapters 1–5** in the task body area to enter a description for the task.

- Click the Due date box arrow to display a calendar for the current month.

- Click the next month box arrow an appropriate number of times to advance to February 2012.

- Click 17 to select Fri 2/17/2012 as the due date (Figure 4–17).

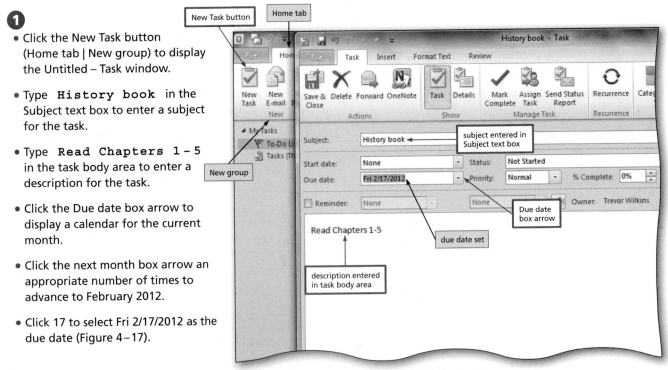

Figure 4–17

2

• Click the Reminder check box to insert a check mark, enable the Reminder boxes, and configure Outlook to display a reminder (Figure 4–18).

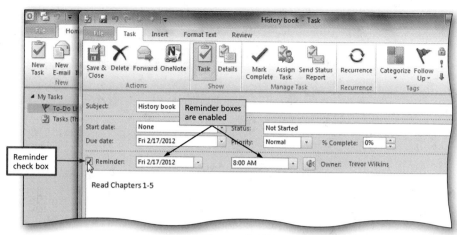

Figure 4–18

3

• Click the Reminder date box arrow to display a calendar for February.

• Click 10 to select Fri 2/10/2012 as the Reminder date (Figure 4–19).

Q&A Can I change the time that Outlook displays the reminder as well?

Yes. When you set a reminder, Outlook automatically sets the time for the reminder to 8:00 AM; however, you can use the Outlook Options dialog box to change the time to whatever time you desire.

4

• Click the Save & Close button (Task tab | Actions group) to save the task and close the Task window.

Q&A How does Outlook remind me of a task?

If you selected a reminder for a task, Outlook displays the Task window for the task. If you used the Sound icon to set an alarm for the reminder, Outlook also plays the sound when it displays the Task window.

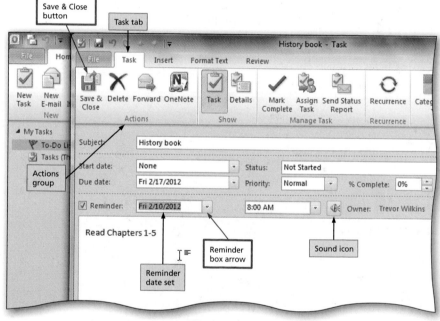

Figure 4–19

Other Ways
1. Press CTRL+SHIFT+K

To Create More Tasks

You have a few more tasks that follow the style of the tasks you have made already. These include three more tasks to enter regarding your work on a project team that is collecting donations for a Youth Summer Camp where you plan to volunteer during the summer. You need to create a research task to track when you have gathered all the information for the project. You also need a task for posting flyers advertising for donations, and a delivery task for when donations are to be delivered to the camp.

Table 4–1 displays the other tasks with their due dates. The following steps create these remaining tasks in the Task window.

Table 4–1 Additional Tasks	
Subject	**Due Date**
Research	3/5/2012
Post flyers	3/10/2012
Deliver donations	5/1/2012

1 Click the New Task button (Home tab | New group) to display the Untitled – Task window.

2 Enter the subject in the Subject text box for the first appointment in Table 4–1.

3 Click the Due date arrow to display a calendar for the current month and then select the due date for the task as shown in Table 4–1.

4 Click the Save & Close button (Task tab | Actions group) to save the task and close the Task window.

5 Repeat Steps 1 through 4 for the two remaining tasks in Table 4–1 (Figure 4–20).

BTW

Task Details
While creating a task, you can modify the task details. Click the Details button (Task tab | Show group), and then enter the desired details in the Date completed box, as well as the Total work, Actual work, Company, Mileage, and Billing information text boxes. To save the task details, click the Save & Close button (Task tab | Actions group).

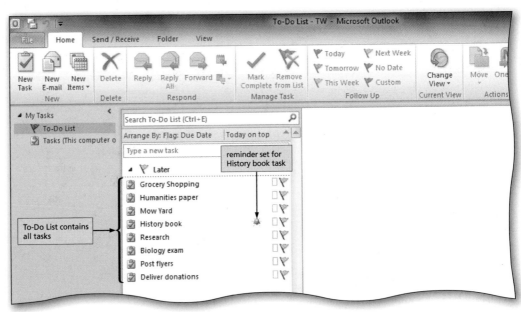

Figure 4–20

To Create a Recurring Task

So far, the tasks you have created have had a specific date for completion. Sometimes, a task occurs repeatedly until the due date. For example, you have joined a study group for your Java programming class that meets every Tuesday night from 6:00 – 8:00 PM in the Learning Center from February 7 until April 24. The task will be considered complete on April 24, but occurs every week until then.

When you create a task, Outlook allows you to specify if it is a recurring task. You can select whether the task recurs daily, weekly, monthly or yearly. For each of those options, you can provide specifics. For example, if it is a monthly task, you can specify the day of the month it occurs. You also can choose to have a task automatically regenerate itself to keep the task from ending. If you know the ending date, you can specify the exact end date.

The following steps add your study group as a recurring task that occurs every Tuesday night from February 7 until April 24.

1

- Click the New Task button (Home tab | New group) to display the Untitled – Task window.

- Type **Study group** in the Subject text box to enter a subject for the task.

- Type **Meet 6:00 – 8:00 pm in the Learning Center** in the task body area to enter a description for the task.

- Click the Start date box arrow to display a calendar for the current month.

- Click the next month arrow button an appropriate number of times to advance to February 2012.

- Click 7 to select Tue 2/7/2012 as the start date (Figure 4–21).

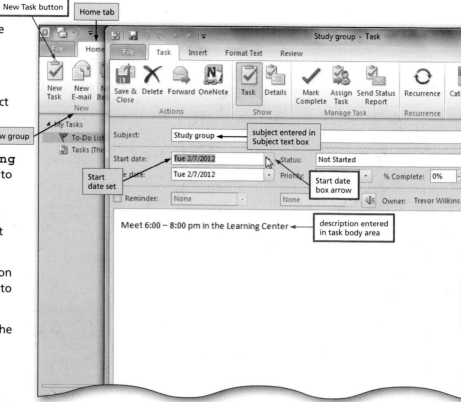

Figure 4–21

2

- Click the Recurrence button (Task tab | Recurrence group) to display the Task Recurrence dialog box (Figure 4–22).

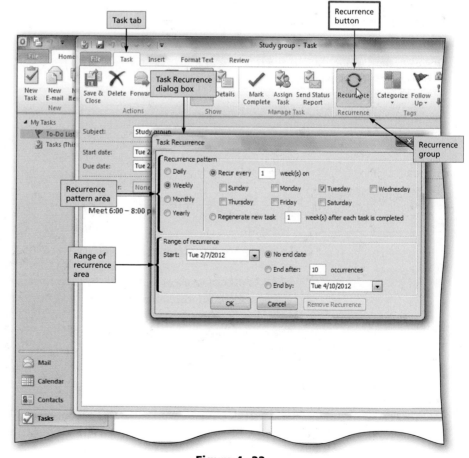

Figure 4–22

3

- Click the End by option button to select it.

- Click the End by box arrow to display a calendar.

- If necessary, click the next month arrow button an appropriate number of times to advance to April 2012.

- Click 24 to select Tue 4/24/2012 as the End by date (Figure 4–23).

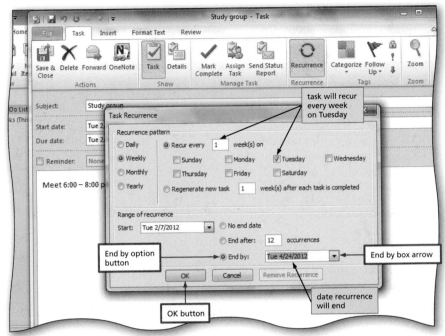

Figure 4–23

4

- Click the OK button (Task Recurrence dialog box) to accept the recurrence settings (Figure 4–24).

5

- Click the Save & Close button (Task tab | Actions group) to save the task and close the Task window.

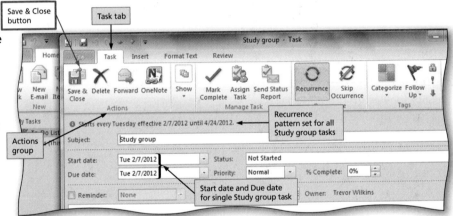

Figure 4–24

Other Ways

1. Press CTRL+SHIFT+K

To Create Another Recurring Task

As part of your work for the Youth Summer Camp, you need to set up a recurring task for collecting the donations. You and your team plan to collect the donations from the donation bins placed around campus every Saturday from March 17 until April 28. The collected donations will be delivered on May 1, as your Deliver donations task already indicates.

The following steps add a new Collect donations task as a recurring task that occurs every Saturday from March 17 until April 28.

1 Click the New Task button (Home tab | New group) to display the Untitled – Task window.

2 Type **Collect donations** in the Subject text box to enter a subject for the task.

3 Click the Start date box arrow to display a calendar for the current month.

④ Click the next month arrow button an appropriate number of times to advance to March 2012.

⑤ Click 17 to select Sat 3/17/2012 as the start date.

⑥ Click the Recurrence button (Task tab | Recurrence group) to display the Task Recurrence dialog box.

⑦ Click the End by option button to select it.

⑧ Click the End by box arrow to display a calendar.

⑨ Click the previous month arrow button an appropriate number of times to return to April 2012.

⑩ Click 28 to select Sat 4/28/2012 as the End by date.

⑪ Click the OK button to accept the recurrence settings.

⑫ Click the Save & Close button (Task tab | Actions group) to save the task and close the Task window (Figure 4–25).

Other Ways
1. Press CTRL+SHIFT+K

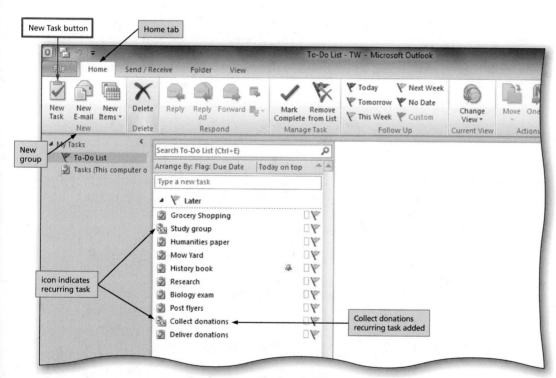

Figure 4–25

TO ADD A TASK USING THE TO-DO BAR

You sometimes need to add a task quickly. You can do this using the To-Do bar. The To-Do bar lets you create quick tasks that normally are due the day you add them. If you wanted to add a task using the To-Do bar, you would use the following steps.

1. Click the To-Do bar to expand the To-Do bar.
2. Click the 'Type a new task' box to select the text box.
3. Type a description to enter a description of the task.
4. Press the ENTER key to finish adding the task and display it in the To-Do list with the current date.

BTW

Task Options
You can modify options for tasks, such as changing the default reminder time for tasks with due dates, changing default colors for overdue and completed tasks, and setting the Quick Click flag. To access task options, open the Backstage view and then click Tasks.

Categorizing Tasks

BTW

BTWs
For a complete list of the BTWs found in the margins of this book, visit the Outlook 2010 BTW Web page (scsite.com/out2010/btw).

Outlook allows you to categorize e-mail messages, contacts, tasks, and calendar items so that you can identify which ones are related to each other as well as quickly identify the items by their color. By default, Outlook provides six categories: blue category, green category, orange category, purple category, red category, and yellow category. The first time you use one of these categories, you will be given an opportunity to rename them; otherwise, their names will remain the same until you rename them later.

You also can create your own categories and select one of 25 colors to associate with them. After you create a category, you can set it as a Quick Click. The **Quick Click** category is the category that will be applied by default if you click an item's category column in the list pane. For example, the default Quick Click category is the red category. If you clicked a task's category column in the To-Do list pane, the red category automatically is assigned to it.

Plan Ahead

> **Plan categories for tasks.**
> Assign tasks and other Outlook items to color categories so that you can find, sort, and manage related items. If necessary, you can assign a task to more than one category. Use the default color categories or create custom categories to suit your needs.
>
> To determine which categories you want to add to Outlook, look over your task list to identify tasks that relate to each other. Build a list of categories based on these relationships. If you have five tasks related to playing in a football league, for example, you could create a Football category so that you easily can identify the tasks related to the football league.

To Create a New Category

You decide to create custom categories to organize the tasks listed in Outlook. The first category you want to create is Personal. You intend to use the Personal category for all tasks that are not work or school related. To create a category, you select a task first and then create the category. Outlook applies the category to the selected task. After you create a category, you can apply it to other tasks as necessary.

The following steps create the Personal category and apply it to the Grocery Shopping task.

1

- Click the Grocery Shopping task to select it.

- Click the Categorize button (Home tab | Tags group) to display the Categorize menu (Figure 4–26).

Q&A

Why did I have to select the Grocery Shopping task?

To activate the Categorize button, you first need to select a task or group of tasks.

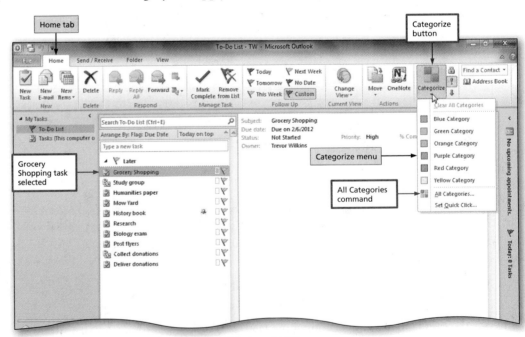

Figure 4–26

2

- Click All Categories to display the Color Categories dialog box (Figure 4–27).

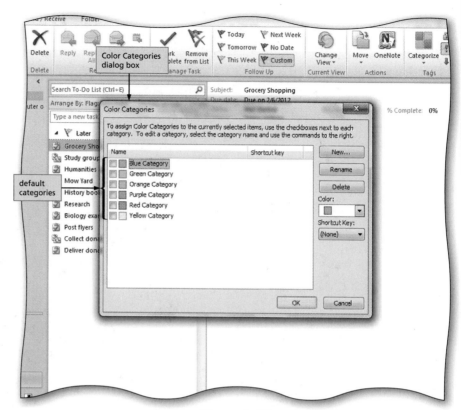

Figure 4–27

3

- Click the New button (Color Categories dialog box) to display the Add New Category dialog box (Figure 4–28).

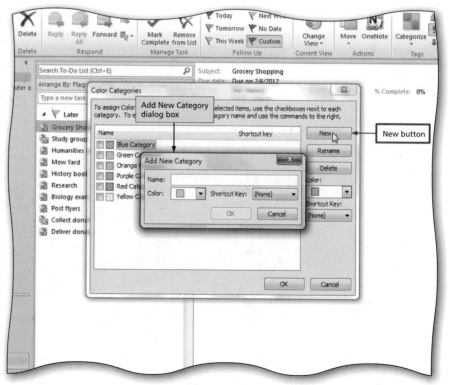

Figure 4–28

4

- Type **Personal** in the Name text box to enter a name for the category.

- Click the Color box arrow to display a list of colors (Figure 4–29).

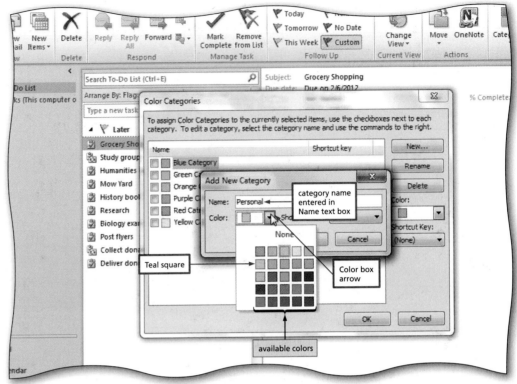

Figure 4–29

5

- Click the Teal square (column 1, row 2) to select Teal as the category color.

- Click the OK button (Add New Category dialog box) to create the new category (Figure 4–30).

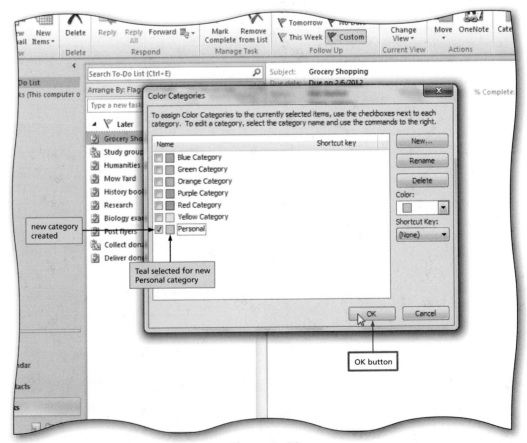

Figure 4–30

- Click the OK button (Color Categories dialog box) to categorize the Grocery Shopping task as Personal (Figure 4–31).

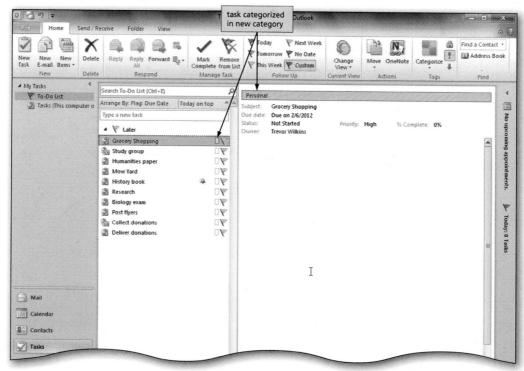

Figure 4–31

Other Ways

1. Right-click task's category column, click All Categories

To Categorize a Task

Now that you have created the Personal category for the Grocery Shopping task, you can apply it to any other task that is related to the category. The following steps categorize the Mow Yard task as personal.

- Click the Mow Yard task to select it.

- Click the Categorize button (Home tab | Tags group) to display the Categorize menu (Figure 4–32).

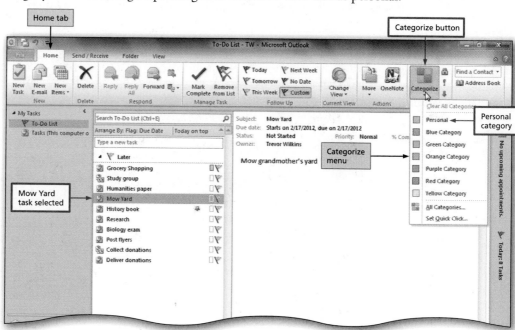

Figure 4–32

2

- Click Personal to categorize the Mow Yard task (Figure 4–33).

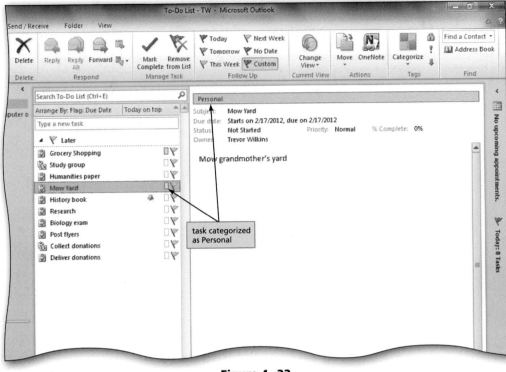

Figure 4–33

Other Ways

1. Right-click task's category column, click category

To Categorize Multiple Tasks

Outlook allows you to categorize multiple tasks at the same time. You decide to categorize all of your class-related tasks in a new category called Class. The tasks to assign to the Class category include the Study group, Humanities paper, History book, and Biology exam tasks.

The following steps create the Class category and apply it to the class-related tasks.

1

- Select the Study group, Humanities paper, History book, and Biology exam tasks.

Q&A

How do I select more than one task?

Click the first task, press and hold the CTRL key, and then click the other tasks to select them.

- Click the Categorize button (Home tab | Tags group) to display the Categorize menu (Figure 4–34).

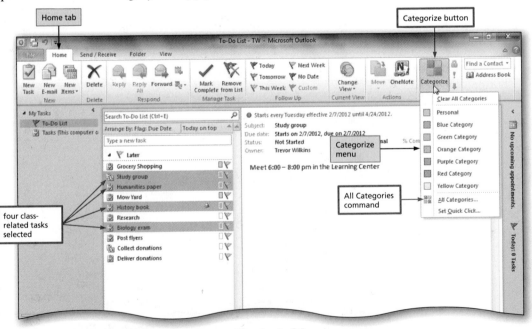

Figure 4–34

2

- Click All Categories to display the Color Categories dialog box.

- Click the New button (Color Categories dialog box) to display the Add New Category dialog box (Figure 4–35).

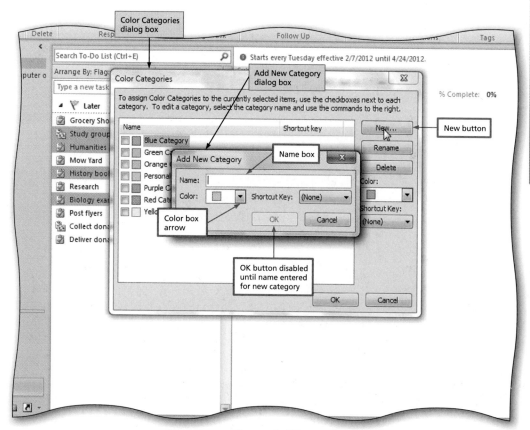

Figure 4–35

3

- Type `Class` in the Name text box to enter a name for the category.

- Click the Color box arrow to display a list of colors.

- Click the Dark Orange square (column 2, row 4) to select dark orange as the category color.

- Click the OK button (Add New Category dialog box) to create the Class category (Figure 4–36).

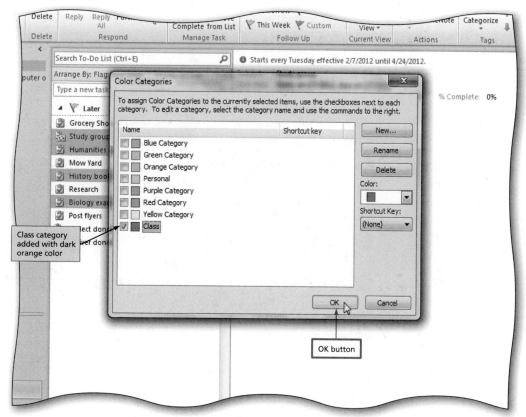

Figure 4–36

4

- Click the OK button (Color Categories dialog box) to categorize the selected tasks as Class (Figure 4–37).

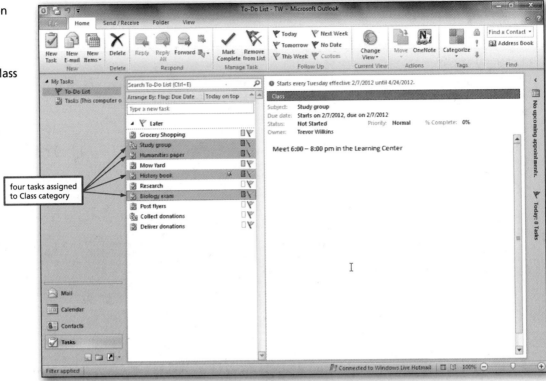

four tasks assigned to Class category

Figure 4–37

To Categorize Remaining Tasks

Now that you know how to categorize multiple tasks at once, you decide to categorize the remaining tasks using Project as the category name. The following steps create the Project category and apply it to the project-related tasks.

1 Select the Research, Post flyers, Collect donations, and Deliver donations tasks.

2 Click the Categorize button (Home tab | Tags group) to display the Categorize menu.

3 Click All Categories to display the Color Categories dialog box.

4 Click the New button (Color Categories dialog box) to display the Add New Category dialog box.

5 Type `Project` in the Name text box to enter a name for the category.

6 Click the Color box arrow to display a list of colors.

7 Click the Maroon square (column 5, row 2) to select maroon as the category color.

8 Click the OK button (Add New Category dialog box) to create the new category.

9 Click the OK button (Color Categories dialog box) to categorize the selected tasks as Project (Figure 4–38).

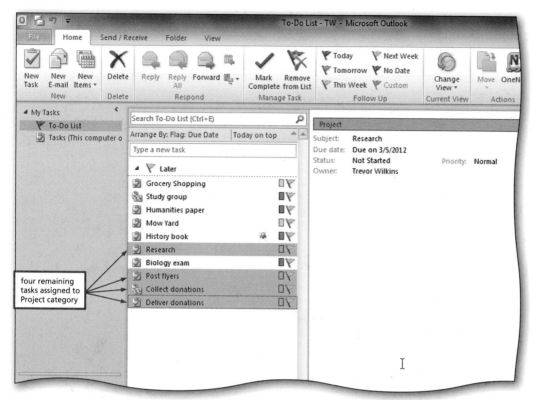

Figure 4–38

To Rename a Category

After categorizing your project tasks, you realize that the other members of your project had agreed to use Project Team as the category name. You decide to rename your Project category to reflect the name used by the rest of the members.

The following steps rename the Project category.

1
- Click the Categorize button (Home tab | Tags group) to display the Categorize menu.

- Click All Categories to display the Color Categories dialog box (Figure 4–39).

Q&A

Do the Project tasks have to be selected?

No, any task can be selected. When you change the name, Outlook will update every task in that category.

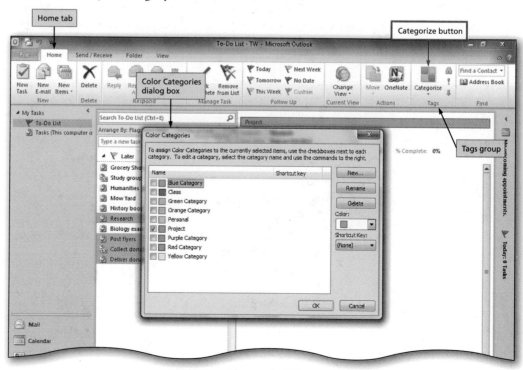

Figure 4–39

2

- Click the Project category to select it.

- Click the Rename button (Color Categories dialog box) to select the category name for editing.

- Type **Project Team** and press ENTER to change the category name (Figure 4–40).

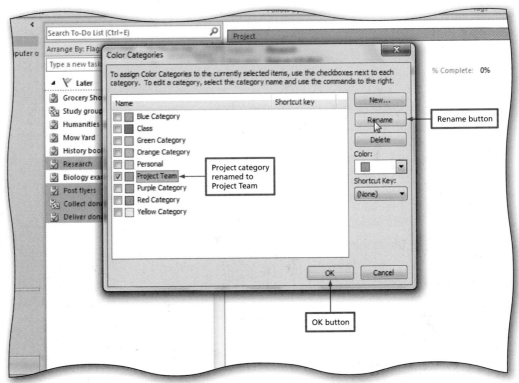

Figure 4–40

3

- Click the OK button (Color Categories dialog box) to apply the changes (Figure 4–41).

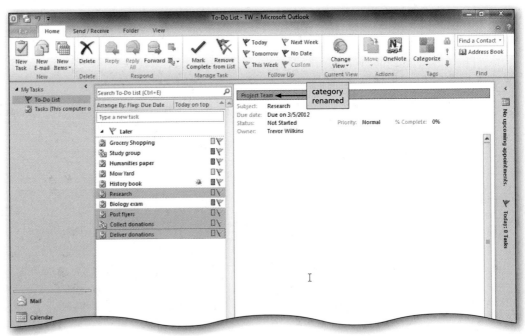

Figure 4–41

Other Ways

1. Right-click task's category column, click All Categories, select category, click Rename button

To Set a Quick Click

So far, you have been categorizing tasks using the Categorize menu options. You could have applied a category by clicking the category box next to each task in the To-Do list pane. If you click the category box, the default category is applied.

If you have a particular category that you know you will use frequently, you can set it as the default category. Outlook allows you to do this by setting the category as a Quick Click.

You decide that as the semester progresses, more of your tasks will be class related, so you decide to set the default category to Class. The following steps make Class the default category.

1

- Click the Categorize button (Home tab | Tags group) to display the Categorize menu.

- Click Set Quick Click to display the Set Quick Click dialog box (Figure 4–42).

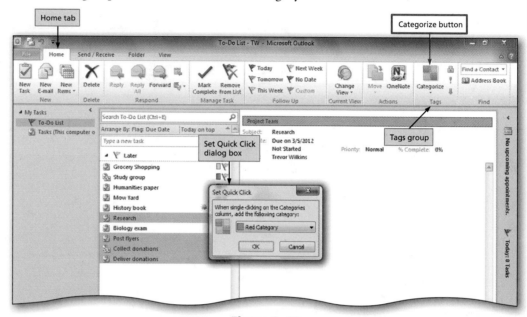

Figure 4–42

2

- Click the category button arrow to display the list of categories (Figure 4–43).

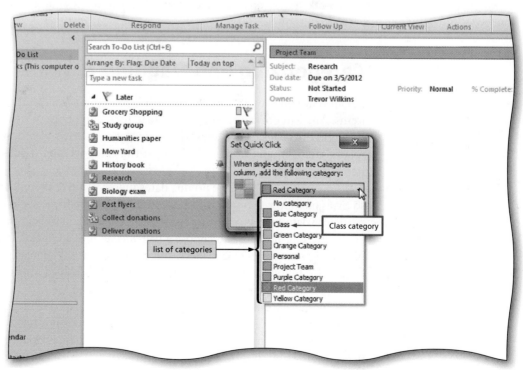

Figure 4–43

- Click Class to set it as the Quick Click category (Figure 4–44).

- Click the OK button (Set Quick Click dialog box) to apply the changes.

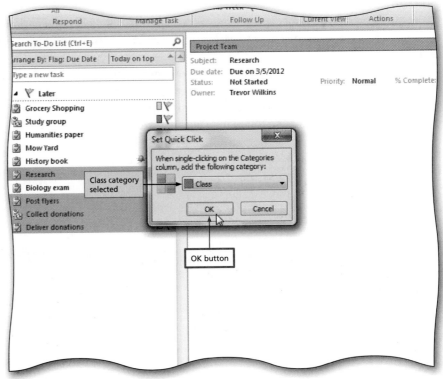

Figure 4–44

Other Ways
1. Right-click any task's category column, click Set Quick Click

Break Point: If you wish to take a break, this is a good place to do so. To resume at a later time, start Outlook and continue following the steps from this location forward.

Categorizing and Flagging E-Mail Messages

Recall that you can use categories with e-mail messages, contacts, tasks, and calendar items. Any category you create for a task then can be used for your e-mail messages. Categorizing your e-mail messages allows you to create a link between them and other related items in Outlook. By looking at the category, you quickly can tell which Outlook items go together.

E-mail messages have no due dates unless you flag them. You can flag e-mail messages so that you follow them up within a certain amount of time such as within a week or on a particular date such as Saturday, April 5. This helps you to be more efficient in prioritizing your activities. You also can choose a flag and set it as a Quick Click for the flag column of e-mail messages, contacts, tasks, and calendar items. When an e-mail message has been flagged for follow-up, the e-mail message will be displayed in your To-Do List as a task for you to complete, as well as remain in your mailbox.

Not every e-mail message needs to be categorized or flagged. An e-mail message from your sister saying she is home, for example, does not need to be categorized or flagged. An e-mail message from your sister saying she is home from a meeting and will need you to baby sit next week while she is at another meeting, on the other hand, could be flagged so that you remember to complete the task.

To Categorize an E-Mail Message

You have received a couple of e-mail messages from your Youth Summer Camp project team. You would like to flag those e-mail messages with the Project Team category. The following steps categorize the Rose Stewart and Julio Alvarez e-mail messages as Project Team messages.

1

- Click the Mail button in the Navigation Pane to switch to your Inbox.

Q&A What should I do if my Inbox is not displayed?

Click the Inbox folder in the Navigation Pane for your mailbox.

- Select the Rose Stewart and Julio Alvarez e-mail messages.

- Click the Categorize button (Home tab | Tags group) to display the Categorize menu (Figure 4–45).

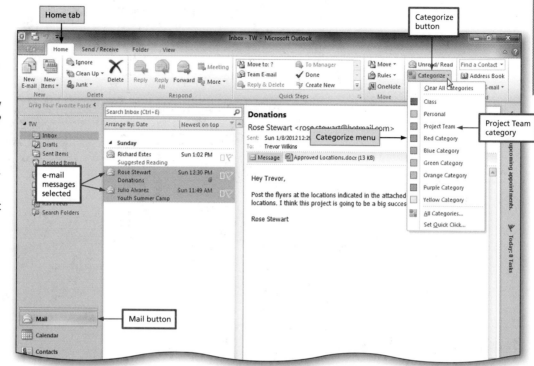

Figure 4–45

2

- Click Project Team to categorize the selected e-mail messages in the Project Team category (Figure 4–46).

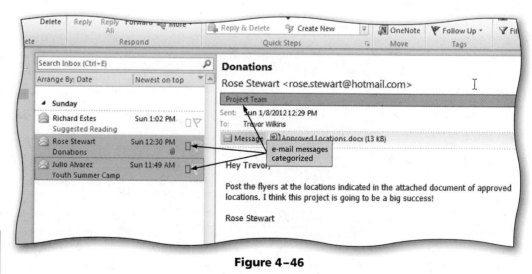

Figure 4–46

Other Ways

1. Right-click e-mail messages category column, click category

To Categorize an E-Mail Message Using a Quick Click

You have set the Class category as a Quick Click, so you now can categorize your class-related e-mail messages directly in the message list. You decide to categorize the e-mail message from Richard Estes as Class because it has information about suggested reading for your Java programming class. The step on the next page categorizes the e-mail message from Richard Estes as Class.

1

• Click the category column for the Richard Estes e-mail message in the message list to change its category to Class (Figure 4–47).

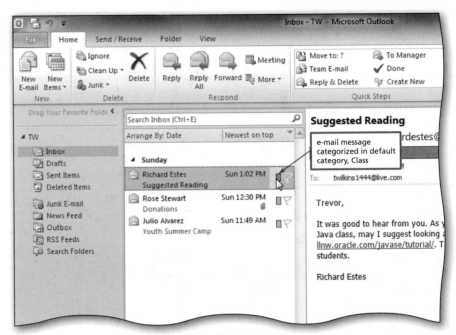

Figure 4–47

To Flag an E-Mail Message

To get a head start on work for your Java programming class, you decide that you should flag the e-mail message from Richard Estes for follow-up within a week. The following steps flag the Richard Estes e-mail message for follow-up within one week.

1

• If necessary, click the Richard Estes e-mail message to select it.

• Click the Follow Up button (Home tab | Tags group) to display the Follow Up menu (Figure 4–48).

Q&A

What do the different colors of the Follow Up flags represent?

The flag colors correspond to the follow-up date. Dark flags are for today, tasks with no date, and custom flags. Medium-colored flags are for follow-up tomorrow. Light-colored flags are for follow-up this week or next week.

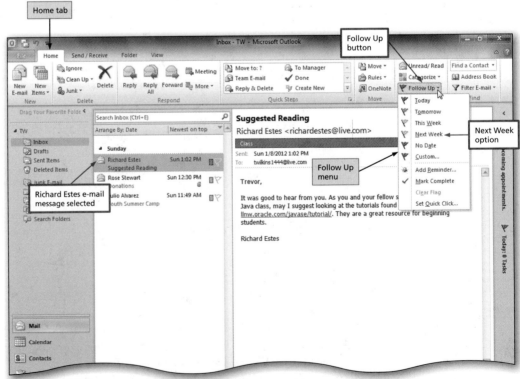

Figure 4–48

2

- Click Next Week to flag the e-mail message for follow-up (Figure 4–49).

Figure 4–49

Other Ways

1. Right-click e-mail's flag column, click Next Week

To Flag an E-Mail Message with a Custom Date

You sometimes might know the exact start date and end date that you want to use when flagging an e-mail message, in which case you can create a custom flag. For example, you know that you have to post the Youth Summer Camp donation flyers by March 10. You have received an e-mail message from Rose Stewart with approved locations for posting flyers, so you estimate that you can verify all these locations by March 5. You decide to flag her e-mail message so that you follow up between February 27 and March 5.

The following steps flag the Rose Stewart e-mail for follow-up between February 27 and March 5.

1

- Click the Rose Stewart e-mail message to select it.

- Click the Follow Up button (Home tab | Tags group) to display the Follow Up menu (Figure 4–50).

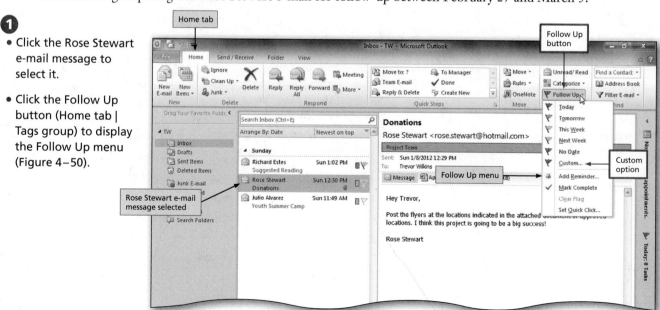

Figure 4–50

- Click Custom to display the Custom dialog box (Figure 4–51).

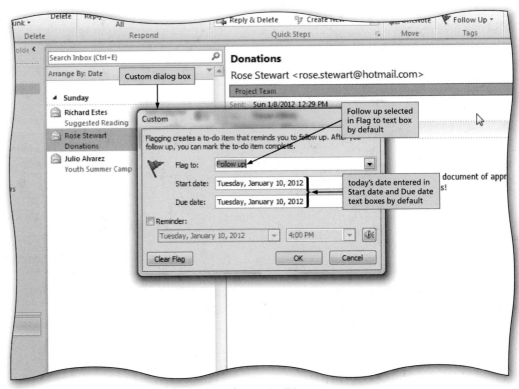

Figure 4–51

- Click the Start date box arrow to display a calendar for the current month.

- Click the next month box arrow an appropriate number of times to advance to February 2012.

- Click 27 to select Monday, February 27, 2012 as the start date (Figure 4–52).

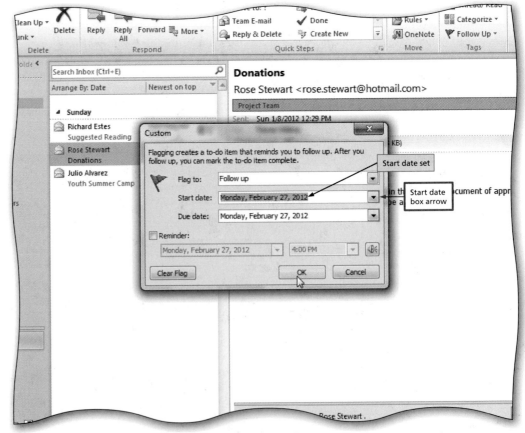

Figure 4–52

- Click the Due date box arrow to display a calendar.

- Click the next month box arrow an appropriate number of times to advance to March 2012.

- Click 5 to select Monday, March 05, 2012 as the due date (Figure 4–53).

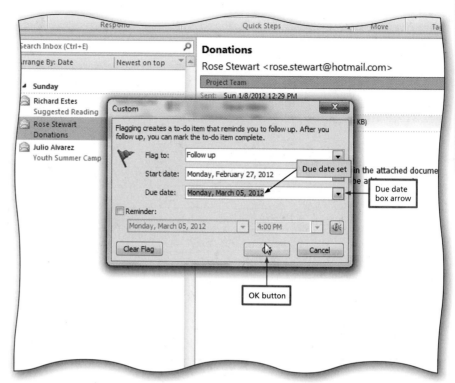

Figure 4–53

- Click the OK button (Custom dialog box) to flag the e-mail message with the custom dates (Figure 4–54).

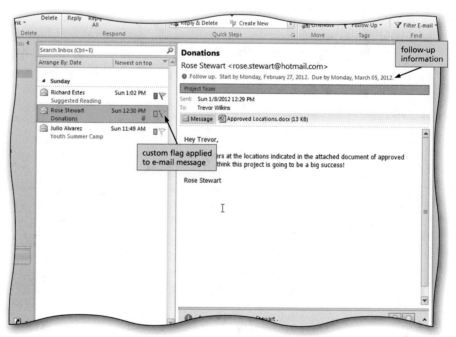

Figure 4–54

Other Ways

1. Right-click e-mail messages flag column, click Custom

BTW

Copying and Moving Tasks

If you want to move or copy an existing task to another folder, select the task, and then click the Move button (Home tab | Actions group). Click the Other Folder command if you want to move the task, or click the Copy to Folder command if you want to copy the task. Next, select the folder to which you want to move or copy the task, and then click the OK button.

Managing Tasks

After creating one or more tasks in your To-Do list, you can perform maintenance on your tasks to manage them. Maintenance can include marking tasks complete when you finish them, updating them, assigning some of them to other people, adding attachments to them, and even removing them. Outlook allows you to manage your tasks and modify them as necessary while you are tracking them.

People sometimes create a To-Do list and never look at it again. To make the best use of your To-Do list, you should review it often to identify tasks that can be marked as complete, removed, or updated. For example, when you finish the reading assignment in your history book, mark the task as complete. That way, you will not have to remember later whether you completed the assignment.

Plan Ahead

> **Determine which tasks may need to be assigned to others.**
> In the professional world, you typically work on projects as a member of a group or team. As you organize the large and small tasks required to complete the project, you can assign each task to members of your team and track the progress of the entire project.

When you are working on a project with others, you sometimes may want to assign tasks to them. Outlook allows you to assign tasks to other people and still monitor the tasks. When a task has been assigned to another person, that person can accept or reject the task. If the task is rejected, it comes back to you. If it is accepted, then the task belongs to that person to complete. When you assign a nonrecurring task, you can retain a copy and request a status report when the task is completed. If the task is a recurring task, you cannot retain a copy, but can request a status report when the task is completed.

To Update a Task

Your grandmother called and asked you to mow her yard on February 20 instead of on February 17. The following steps change the start date for the Mow Yard task to February 20.

1
- Click the Tasks button in the Navigation Pane to display the To-Do list.

- Double-click the Mow Yard task to display the Mow Yard – Task window (Figure 4–55).

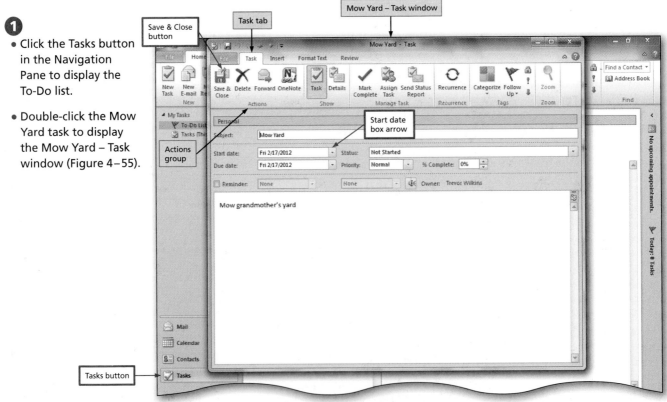

Figure 4–55

2

- Click the Start date box arrow to display a calendar for February.

- Click 20 to select Mon 2/20/2012 as the start date.

- Click Save & Close (Task tab | Actions group) to save the changes (Figure 4–56).

Q&A

How would I change the task name only?

Click the task name in the task list to select it, and then click it again to edit the name.

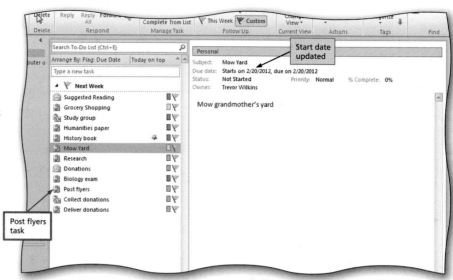

Figure 4–56

To Attach a File to a Task

Outlook allows you to attach a file to a task. This is helpful if you want quick access to information when you are looking at a task. Rose Stewart has e-mailed you a list of approved locations for flyers, which you already have saved to your computer. You decide that you should attach it to the Post flyers task so that you can access the list of locations easily.

The following steps attach the Approved Locations document to the Post flyers task.

1

- Double-click the Post flyers task to display the Post flyers – Task window.

- Display the Insert tab.

- Click the Attach File button (Insert tab | Include group) to display the Insert File dialog box.

- Navigate to the Chapter04 folder on your USB flash drive (Figure 4–57).

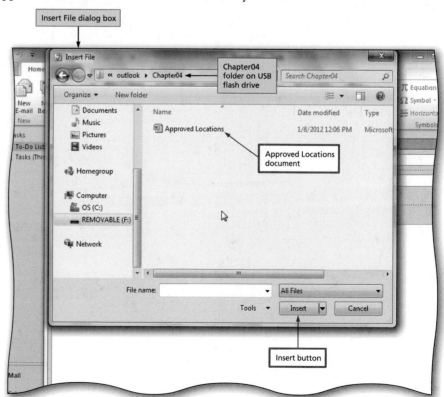

Figure 4–57

2
- Click Approved Locations to select the document.
- Click the Insert button (Insert File dialog box) to attach the file (Figure 4–58).

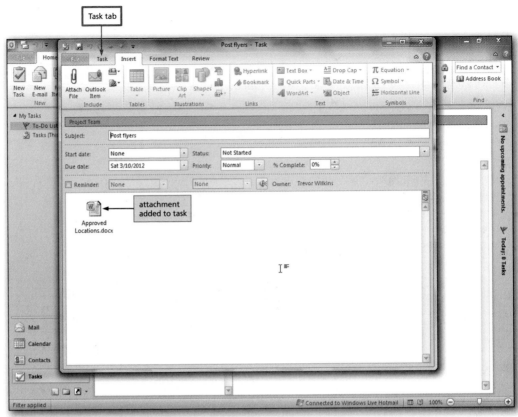

Figure 4–58

3
- Display the Task tab.
- Click Save & Close (Task tab | Actions group) to save the changes (Figure 4–59).

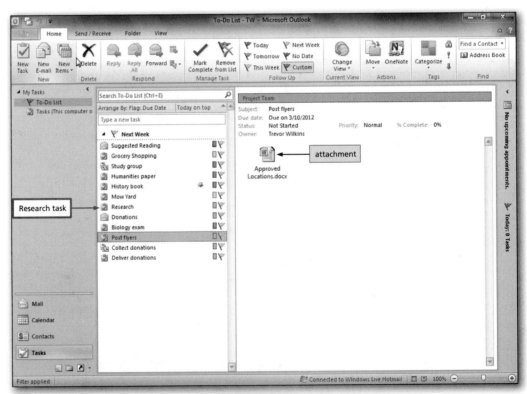

Figure 4–59

To Attach an Outlook Item to a Task

In addition to files, you can attach other Outlook items to a task such as e-mail messages, contacts, or journal entries. You decide that you want to include the e-mail message from Julio Alvarez in your Research task so that you can remember to talk to him about what you need for the Youth Summer Camp project.

The following steps attach the Julio Alvarez e-mail message to the Research task.

1

• Double-click the Research task to display the Research – Task window.

• Display the Insert tab.

• Click the Outlook Item button (Insert tab | Include group) to display the Insert Item dialog box (Figure 4–60).

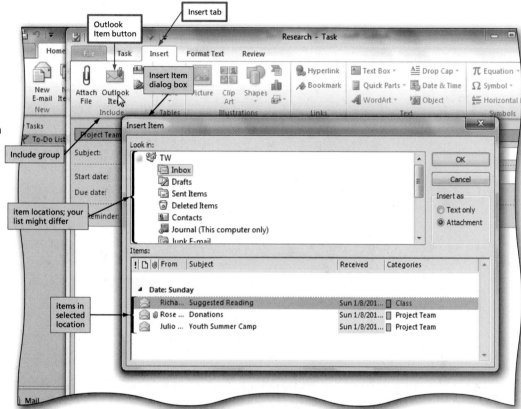

Figure 4–60

2

• Click the Julio Alvarez Youth Summer Camp e-mail message in the Items list box to select it (Figure 4–61).

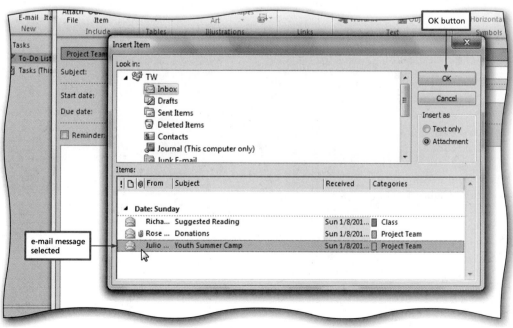

Figure 4–61

3

- Click the OK button (Insert Item dialog box) to attach the e-mail message to the task (Figure 4–62).

4

- Display the Task tab.

- Click Save & Close (Task tab | Actions group) to save the changes.

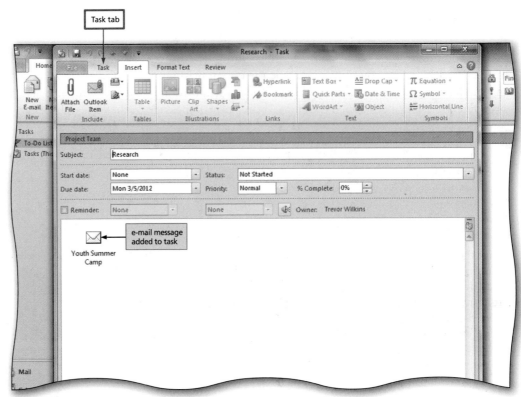

Figure 4–62

To Assign a Task

Gayle Medvitz is on your project team for volunteering for the Youth Summer Camp. She has told you that because you will be collecting and delivering the donations, she is willing to post the flyers. You decide to assign the Post flyers task to her while ensuring that you retain a copy of the task and receive a status report once she has completed the task.

The following steps assign the Post flyers task to Gayle Medvitz.

1

- Double-click the Post flyers task to display the Post flyers – Task window.

- Click the Assign Task button (Task tab | Manage Task group) to display the Assign Task options (Figure 4–63).

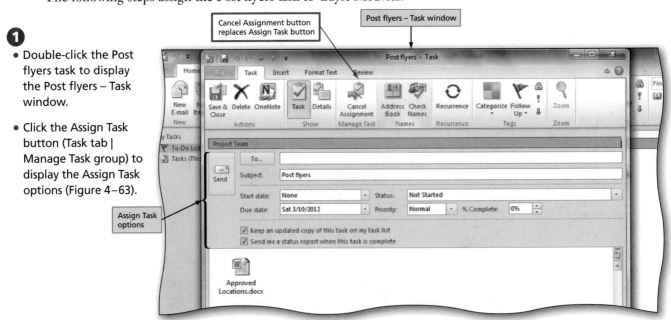

Figure 4–63

2

- Type `gayle
.medvitz@gmail
.com` in the To text
box to enter a recipient
(Figure 4–64).

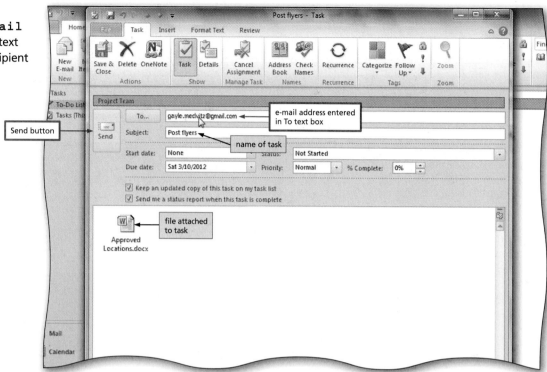

Figure 4–64

3

- Click the Send button
to send the task to
Gayle Medvitz
(Figure 4–65).

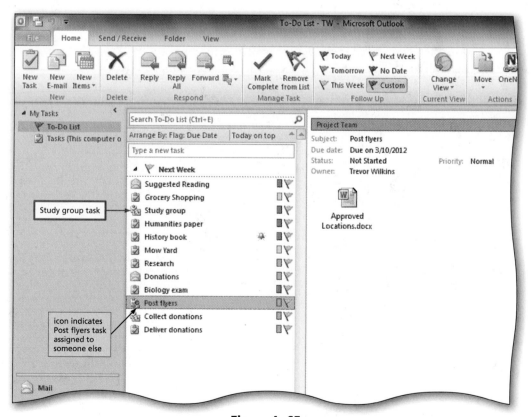

Figure 4–65

To Forward a Task

In addition to assigning a task to a person, you can forward a task to a person. When you forward a task, you are forwarding a copy of the task to the person who can add it to their To-Do list for tracking.

Your study group has added a new member, Jay Ballentyne. You decide to forward your Study group task to him so that he can add it and track it on his own. The following steps forward the Study group task to Jay Ballentyne.

1

- Double-click the Study group task to display the Study group – Task window.

- Click the Forward button (Task tab | Actions group) to display the FW: Study group – Message (HTML) window (Figure 4–66).

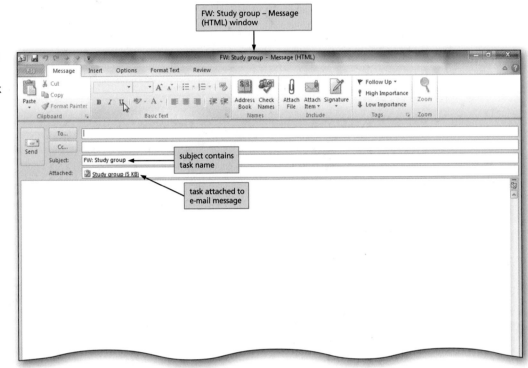

Figure 4–66

2

- Type **jay .ballentyne @gmail.com** in the To text box to enter a recipient.

- Type **Attached is the Study group task for you to add to your To-Do list.** in the message body area to enter a message.

- Press ENTER two times and then type **Trevor** to complete the message (Figure 4–67).

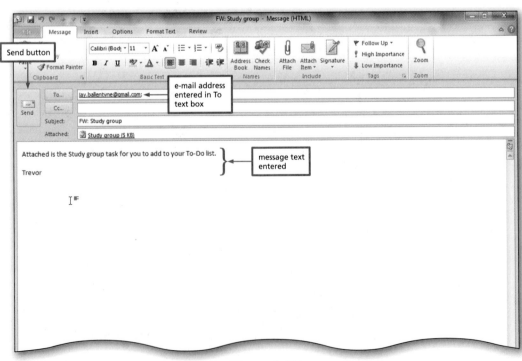

Figure 4–67

3

- Click the Send button to forward the task to Jay Ballentyne.

- Click the Close button to close the Study group – Task window (Figure 4–68).

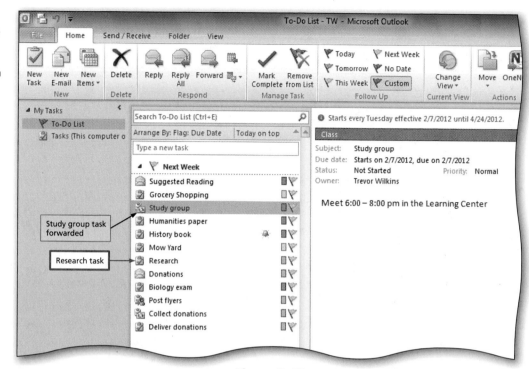

Figure 4–68

To Send a Status Report

While a task is in progress, you can send status reports to other people. The status reports indicate the status and completion percent of the task. Julio Alvarez has requested that you keep him informed about the research you have done for the Youth Summer Camp. You already have completed 25 percent of the work and want to inform him that the task is in progress. The following steps create and send a status report to Julio Alvarez for the Research task.

1

- Double-click the Research task to display the Research – Task window.

- Click the Status box arrow to display a status list.

- Click In Progress to change the status to In Progress (Figure 4–69).

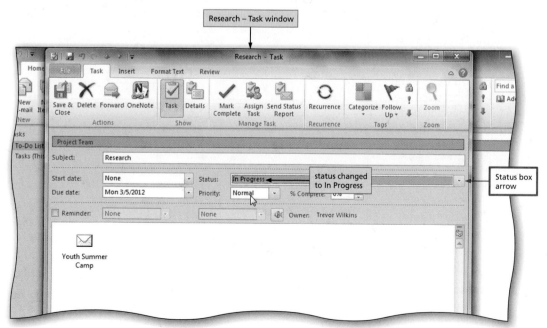

Figure 4–69

2

• Click the Up arrow button to change the % Complete to 25% (Figure 4–70).

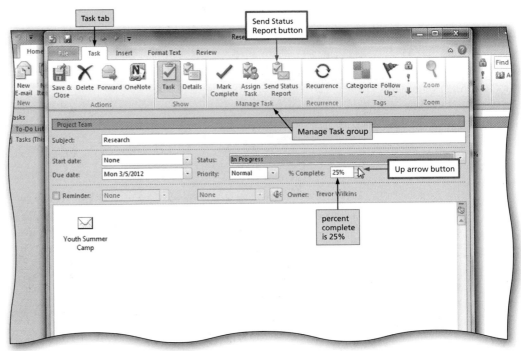

Figure 4–70

3

• Click the Send Status Report button (Task tab | Manage Task group) to display the Task Status Report: Research – Message (Rich Text) window.

• Type `julioa1776 @hotmail.com` in the To text box to enter a recipient.

• Type `Julio,` and press ENTER two times in the message body area to enter the greeting line of the message.

• Type `Here is my first update on this task.` in the message body area to enter the next line of the message.

• Press ENTER two times and then type `Trevor` to complete the message (Figure 4–71).

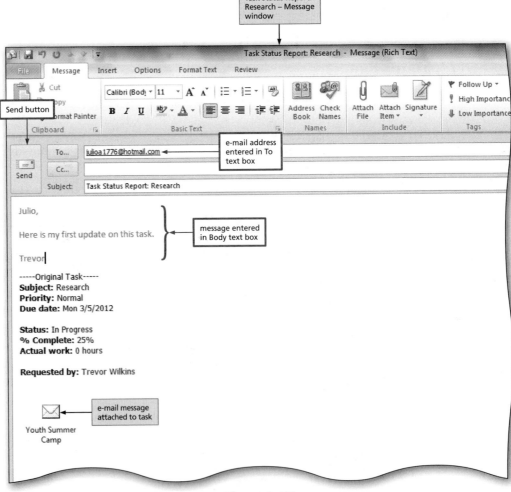

Figure 4–71

- Click the Send button to send the status report to Julio Alvarez.

- Click the Save & Close button (Task tab | Actions group) to save the changes to the task (Figure 4–72).

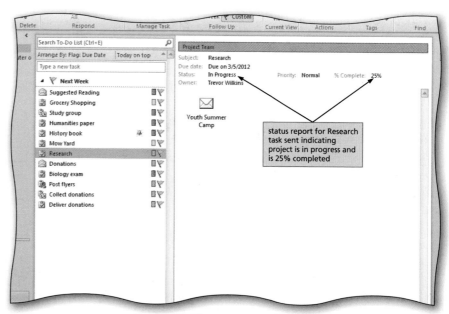

Figure 4–72

To Mark a Task Complete

When you accomplish a task, you should mark it as complete so that you know it is finished. You have just completed your humanities paper; therefore, you can mark it as complete so that you no longer have to worry about it. The following steps mark the Humanities paper task as complete.

1
- Click the Humanities paper task to select it (Figure 4–73).

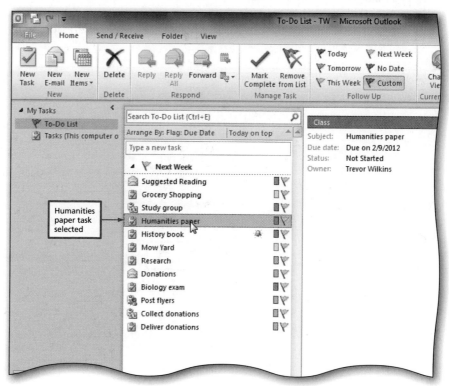

Figure 4–73

2

- Click the Mark Complete button (Home tab | Manage Task group) to mark the Humanities paper task as being completed (Figure 4–74).

Q&A

Why was the Humanities paper task removed from the To-Do list?

Once you mark a task as complete, Outlook removes it from the To-Do list and places it in the Completed list. You can see the Completed list by changing your view to Complete using the Change View button (Home tab | Current View group).

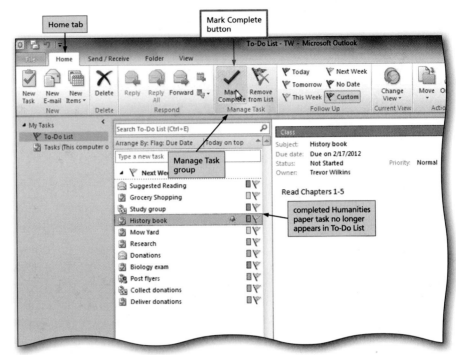

Figure 4–74

Other Ways

1. Right-click task, click Mark Complete

To Remove a Task

You sometimes may need to remove a task. When you remove a task, it no longer is displayed in your To-Do List. For example, you have realized that with your work schedule and volunteer work, that you cannot handle taking seven classes this semester. You have dropped your history class, as you can take it during the summer online; therefore, you have no need for the History book task anymore. The following steps remove the History book task.

1

- Click the History book task to select it (Figure 4–75).

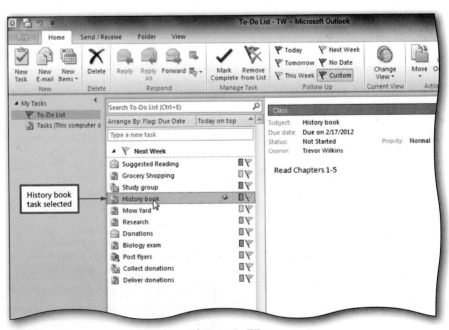

Figure 4–75

2

- Click the Remove from List button (Home tab | Manage Task group) to remove the task (Figure 4–76).

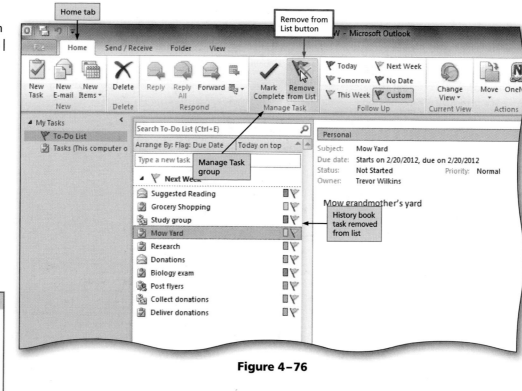

Figure 4–76

Other Ways

1. Right-click task, click Delete
2. Display task, click Delete button (Home tab | Delete group)
3. Display task, press DELETE

To Delete a Category

When you no longer need a category, you can delete it. Deleting a category removes the category from the category list but not from the tasks that already have been assigned to it.

You have decided that since you only have a few personal tasks, you do not really need the Personal category. The following steps delete the Personal category from the category list.

1

- Click the Grocery Shopping task to select it.

- Click the Categorize button (Home tab | Tags group) to display the Categorize menu.

- Click All Categories to display the Color Categories dialog box (Figure 4–77).

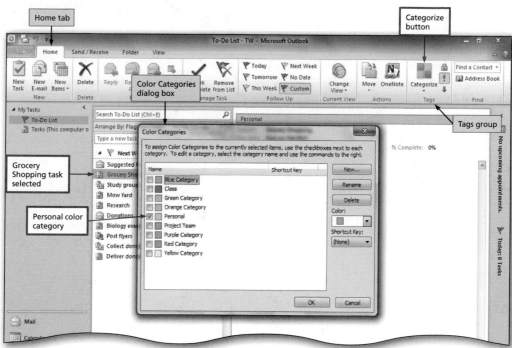

Figure 4–77

2

● Click the Personal color category to select it.

● Click the Delete button (Color Categories dialog box) to delete the color category (Figure 4–78).

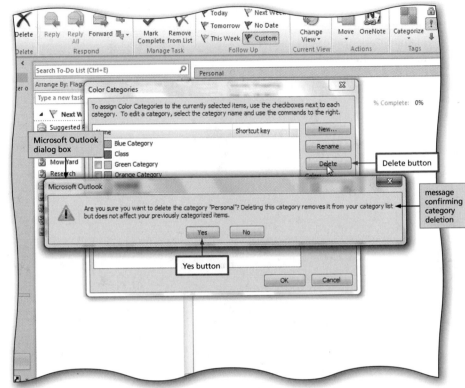

Figure 4–78

3

● Click the Yes button (Microsoft Outlook dialog box) to confirm the deletion (Figure 4–79).

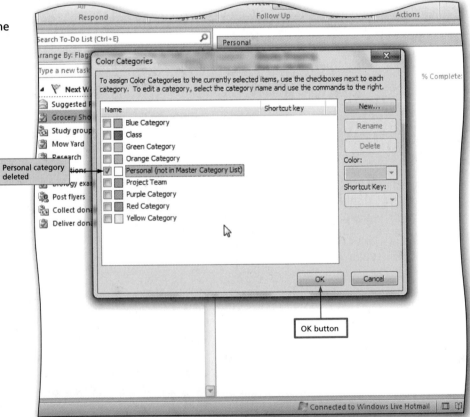

Figure 4–79

4

• Click the OK button (Color Categories dialog box) to close the dialog box (Figure 4–80).

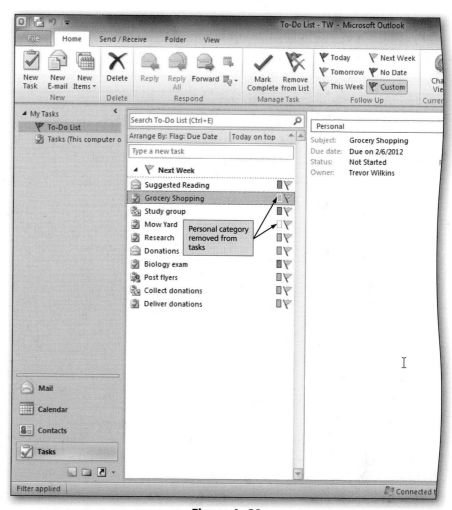

Figure 4–80

Other Ways

1. Right-click task's category column, click All Categories

Choosing Display and Print Views

When working with your tasks, you can change the view to see your tasks better. For instance, you can view your tasks as a detailed list, simple list, priority list, or a complete list. You also can print tasks in a summarized list or include the details for each task.

Determine how you want to view your tasks.

Change the view of your tasks to fit your current needs. For example, if you want to see tasks listed according to their priority (High, Normal, or Low), you can display the tasks in the Prioritized view. The Detailed view provides all the task details, including task subject, status, due date, and categories.

Plan
Ahead

To Change the Task View

You decide that you want to see your tasks in Detailed view because it displays all tasks, including completed tasks. The following steps change the view to Detailed view.

1

• Click the Change View button (Home tab | Current View group) to display the Change View gallery (Figure 4–81).

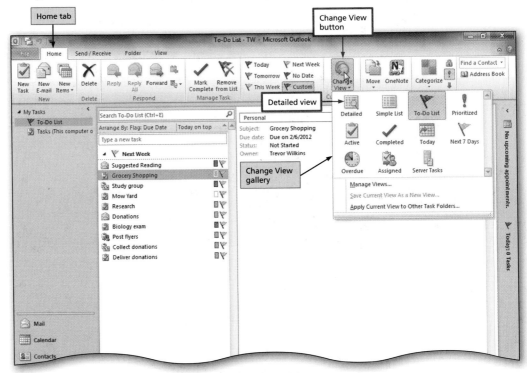

Figure 4–81

2

• Click Detailed to change the view to Detailed view (Figure 4–82).

 Experiment

• Click the other views in the Current View gallery to view the tasks in other arrangements. When you are finished, click Detailed to return to Detailed view.

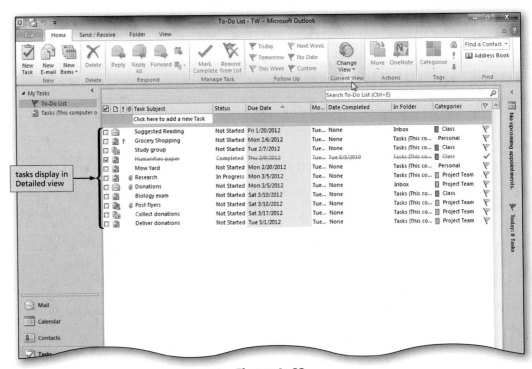

Figure 4–82

To Print Tasks

If you need to print your tasks, Outlook provides printing options based upon the view and tasks you have selected. For example, in the To-Do List view, you can select a single task and print in Table Style or Menu Style. In Detailed view, which is the current view, you can print only in Table Style. The following steps print the tasks using Table Style.

1

- Click File on the Ribbon to open the Backstage view.

- Click the Print tab in the Backstage view to display the Print gallery (Figure 4–83).

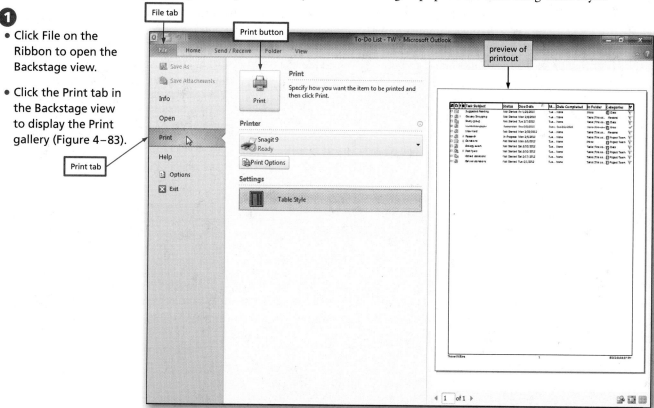

Figure 4–83

2

- Click the Print button to print the tasks in Table Style (Figure 4–84).

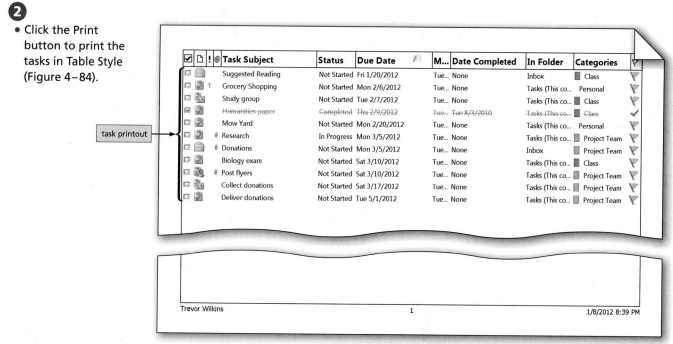

☑	🗋	!	📎	**Task Subject**	**Status**	**Due Date**	**M...**	**Date Completed**	**In Folder**	**Categories**	
☐	🖼			Suggested Reading	Not Started	Fri 1/20/2012	Tue...	None	Inbox	▪ Class	🏱
☐	🖼	!		Grocery Shopping	Not Started	Mon 2/6/2012	Tue...	None	Tasks (This co...	Personal	🏱
☐	🖼			Study group	Not Started	Tue 2/7/2012	Tue...	None	Tasks (This co...	▪ Class	🏱
☑	🖼			~~Humanities paper~~	~~Completed~~	~~Thu 2/9/2012~~	~~Tue...~~	~~Tue 8/3/2010~~	~~Tasks (This co...~~	▪ ~~Class~~	✔
☐	🖼			Mow Yard	Not Started	Mon 2/20/2012	Tue...	None	Tasks (This co...	Personal	🏱
☐	🖼		📎	Research	In Progress	Mon 3/5/2012	Tue...	None	Tasks (This co...	▪ Project Team	🏱
☐	🖼		📎	Donations	Not Started	Mon 3/5/2012	Tue...	None	Inbox	▪ Project Team	🏱
☐	🖼			Biology exam	Not Started	Sat 3/10/2012	Tue...	None	Tasks (This co...	▪ Class	🏱
☐	🖼		📎	Post flyers	Not Started	Sat 3/10/2012	Tue...	None	Tasks (This co...	▪ Project Team	🏱
☐	🖼			Collect donations	Not Started	Sat 3/17/2012	Tue...	None	Tasks (This co...	▪ Project Team	🏱
☐	🖼			Deliver donations	Not Started	Tue 5/1/2012	Tue...	None	Tasks (This co...	▪ Project Team	🏱

Trevor Wilkins   1   1/8/2012 8:39 PM

Figure 4–84

BTW

Certification
The Microsoft Office Specialist program provides an opportunity for you to obtain a valuable industry credential – proof that you have the Outlook 2010 skills required by employers. For more information, visit the Outlook 2010 Certification Web page (scsite.com/out2010/cert).

Using Notes

Outlook allows you to create the equivalent of paper notes using the Notes feature. Use notes to record ideas, spur-of-the-moment questions, and even words that you would like to recall or use at a later time. You can leave notes open on the screen while you continue using Outlook, or you can close them and view them in the Notes window. The Notes window contains the Navigation Pane and Notes Pane.

When working with notes, the Navigation Pane includes two sets of buttons (standard and additional) and the My Notes pane. The **My Notes pane** displays the Notes folder. The standard buttons represent shortcuts to the standard items that are part of the Microsoft Outlook mailbox: Mail, Calendar, Contacts, and Tasks. Additional buttons are displayed below the standard buttons and represent shortcuts to other Outlook functions, such as Notes, Folder List shortcuts, and Configure buttons, which allow you to specify which folders to display.

BTW

Quick Reference
For a table that lists how to complete the tasks covered in this book using the mouse, Ribbon, shortcut menu, and keyboard, see the Quick Reference Summary at the back of this book, or visit the Outlook 2010 Quick Reference Web page (scsite.com/out2010/qr).

To Create a Note

You just received a call that you should e-mail your biology professor for information about the first lab project. You do not have time right now to e-mail him, so you decide to create a note to remind yourself to e-mail him later. When you enter text into a note, it is saved automatically; therefore, you do not have to click a Save button. The following steps create a biology note reminder.

1
• Click the Notes button in the Navigation Pane to display the Notes (This computer only) – TW – Microsoft Outlook window (Figure 4–85).

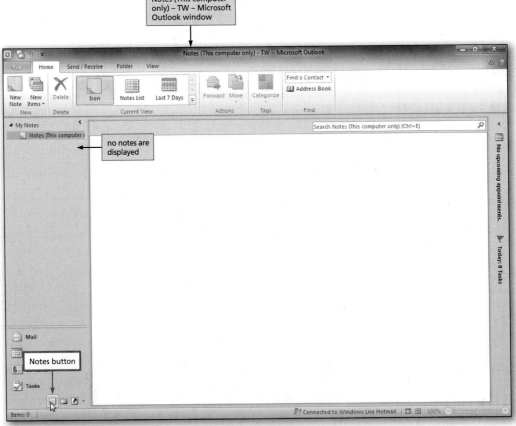

Figure 4–85

2

• Click New Note (Home tab | New group) to display a new blank note (Figure 4–86).

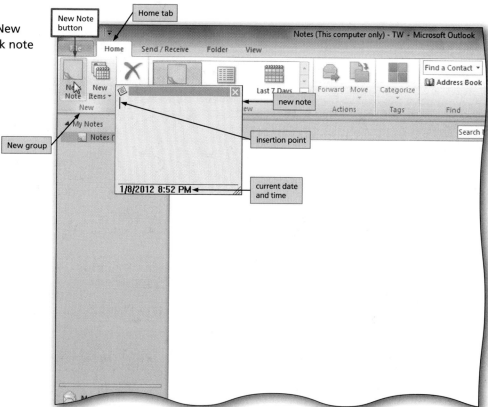

Figure 4–86

3

• Type **E-mail biology professor about first lab** as the note text to enter a note (Figure 4–87).

Q&A

Can I change options for notes?

Yes. Outlook allows you to change the note color, size, font, and the date and time the note was modified. To access these options, open the Backstage view, and then click Notes and Journal.

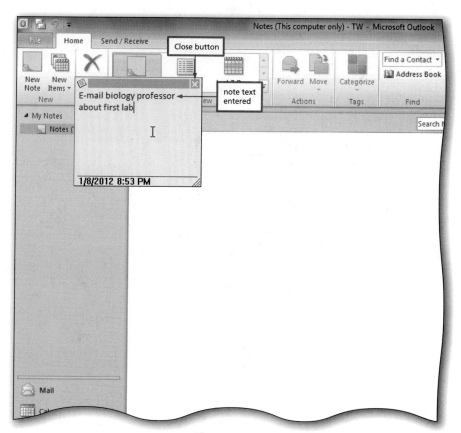

Figure 4–87

4

- Click the Close button to save and close the note (Figure 4–88).

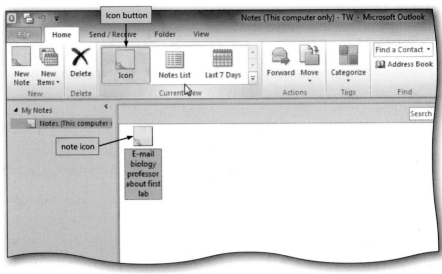
Figure 4–88

Q&A Why is my Notes view different?

There are three basic Notes views: Icon, Notes List, and Last 7 Days. In Figure 4–88, the note is displayed in Icon view. To switch to Icon view, click the Icon button (Home tab | Current View group).

Q&A Can I print notes?

Yes. First, select the note(s) you want to print. To select multiple notes, hold the CTRL key while clicking the notes to print. Next, open the Backstage view, click the Print tab, and then click the Print button.

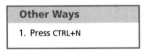

Other Ways

1. Press CTRL+N

To Change the Notes View

As with tasks, you can change the view of your notes. You decide to change your notes view to Notes List. The following step changes the view to Notes List view.

1

- Click the Notes List button (Home tab | Current View group) to change the view to Notes List (Figure 4–89).

 Experiment

- Click the other views in the Current View group to view the notes in other arrangements. When you are finished, click Notes List to return to Notes List view.

Q&A Can I categorize a note?

Yes. To categorize a note, select the note, click the Categorize button (Home tab | Tags group), and then click the desired category.

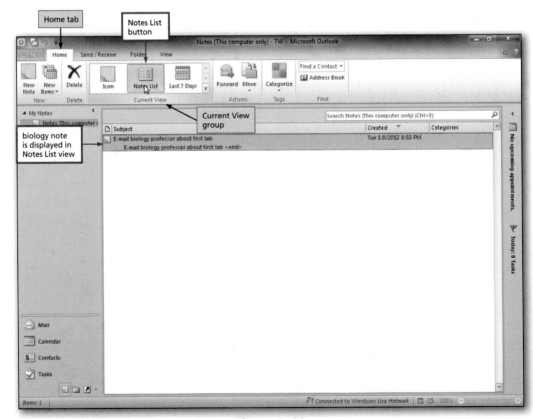
Figure 4–89

To Delete a Note

After sending the e-mail message to your biology professor, you decide to delete the note because you no longer need it. The following step deletes the biology note.

1
- If necessary, click the biology note to select it.

- Click the Delete button (Home tab | Delete group) to delete the note (Figure 4–90).

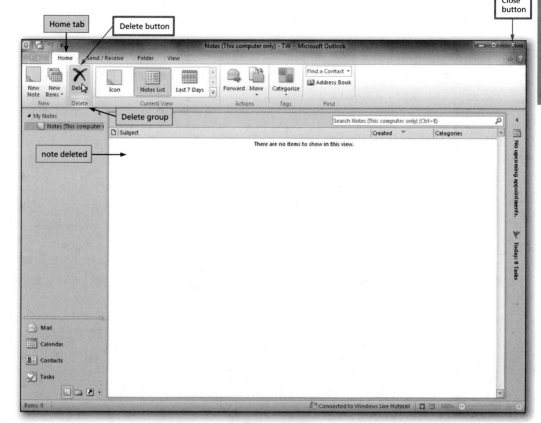

Figure 4–90

To Quit Outlook

The project is complete. Thus, the following step quits Outlook.

1 Click the Close button on the right side of the title bar to quit Outlook.

Chapter Summary

In this chapter, you have learned how to create a task list, categorize tasks, categorize and tag e-mail messages, manage tasks, print tasks, create notes, and print notes. The items listed below include all the new Outlook skills you have learned in this chapter.

1. Create a New Task (OUT 173)
2. Create a Task with a Due Date (OUT 176)
3. Create a Task with a Status (OUT 177)
4. Create a Task with a Priority (OUT 179)
5. Create a Task with a Reminder (OUT 180)
6. Create a Recurring Task (OUT 182)
7. Create a New Category (OUT 186)
8. Categorize a Task (OUT 189)
9. Categorize Multiple Tasks (OUT 190)
10. Rename a Category (OUT 193)
11. Set a Quick Click (OUT 195)
12. Categorize an E-Mail Message (OUT 197)
13. Categorize an E-Mail Message Using a Quick Click (OUT 197)
14. Flag an E-Mail Message (OUT 198)
15. Flag an E-Mail Message with a Custom Date (OUT 199)
16. Update a Task (OUT 202)
17. Attach a File to a Task (OUT 203)
18. Attach an Outlook Item to a Task (OUT 205)
19. Assign a Task (OUT 206)
20. Forward a Task (OUT 208)
21. Send a Status Report (OUT 209)
22. Mark a Task Complete (OUT 211)
23. Remove a Task (OUT 212)
24. Delete a Category (OUT 213)
25. Change the Task View (OUT 216)
26. Print Tasks (OUT 217)
27. Create a Note (OUT 218)
28. Change the Notes View (OUT 220)
29. Delete a Note (OUT 221)

 If you have a SAM 2010 user profile, your instructor may have assigned an autogradable version of this assignment. If so, log into the SAM 2010 Web site at www.cengage.com/sam2010 to download the instruction and start files.

Learn It Online

Test your knowledge of chapter content and key terms.

Instructions: To complete the Learn It Online exercises, start your browser, click the Address bar, and then enter the Web address `scsite.com/out2010/learn`. When the Outlook 2010 Learn It Online page is displayed, click the link for the exercise you want to complete and then read the instructions.

Chapter Reinforcement TF, MC, and SA
A series of true/false, multiple choice, and short answer questions that test your knowledge of the chapter content.

Flash Cards
An interactive learning environment where you identify chapter key terms associated with displayed definitions.

Practice Test
A series of multiple choice questions that test your knowledge of chapter content and key terms.

Who Wants To Be a Computer Genius?
An interactive game that challenges your knowledge of chapter content in the style of a television quiz show.

Wheel of Terms
An interactive game that challenges your knowledge of chapter key terms in the style of the television show *Wheel of Fortune*.

Crossword Puzzle Challenge
A crossword puzzle that challenges your knowledge of key terms presented in the chapter.

Apply Your Knowledge

Reinforce the skills and apply the concepts you learned in this chapter.

Editing a Task List

Note: To complete this assignment, you will be required to use the Data Files for Students. See the inside back cover of this book for instructions on downloading the Data Files for Students, or contact your instructor for information about accessing the required files.

Instructions: Start Outlook. Import the Apply Your Knowledge 4-1 Tasks folder from the Data Files for Students folder into Outlook. The Apply Your Knowledge 4-1 Tasks file contains tasks for Dr. Carol Jones. Many of the tasks have changed and some are incomplete. You need to revise the tasks and then create categories for them. You also will categorize and tag a recent e-mail message Carol received. Then, you will print the resulting task list (Figure 4–91).

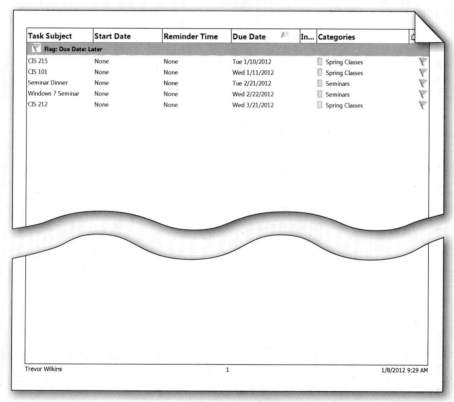

Task Subject	Start Date	Reminder Time	Due Date	In...	Categories	
▼ Flag: Due Date: Later						
CIS 215	None	None	Tue 1/10/2012		Spring Classes	▼
CIS 101	None	None	Wed 1/11/2012		Spring Classes	▼
Seminar Dinner	None	None	Tue 2/21/2012		Seminars	▼
Windows 7 Seminar	None	None	Wed 2/22/2012		Seminars	▼
CIS 212	None	None	Wed 3/21/2012		Spring Classes	▼

Trevor Wilkins   1   1/8/2012 9:29 AM

Figure 4–91

Perform the following tasks:

1. Display the Apply Your Knowledge 4-1 Tasks folder in the Outlook To-Do List window.
2. Change the due date of the Windows 7 Seminar task to February 22, 2012.
3. Change the due date of the Seminar Dinner task to February 21, 2012. In the Task body, type **Welcoming reception dinner for all speakers**.
4. Change the task name of CIS 315 to CIS 215. Configure the task as a recurring task that occurs every Tuesday and Thursday from January 10, 2012 until May 1, 2012.

Continued >

Apply Your Knowledge *continued*

5. Make CIS 212 a recurring task that occurs every Wednesday from March 21, 2012 until May 1, 2012.

6. Make CIS 101 a recurring task that occurs every Monday, Wednesday, and Saturday from January 11, 2012 until May 1, 2012.

7. Create two color categories. Name the first one Spring Classes and the second one Seminars. Use the colors of your choice.

8. Categorize CIS 215, CIS 212, and CIS 101 using the Spring Classes category. Categorize the Windows 7 Seminar and Seminar Dinner tasks using the Seminars category.

9. Categorize the e-mail message from Nicole Smith using the Seminars category. Tag the e-mail message for follow-up using the custom start date of February 11, 2012 and due date of February 15, 2012. Configure a reminder for February 11.

10. Print the final task list, as shown in Figure 4–91 on the previous page, and then submit it in the format specified by your instructor.

11. Export the Apply Your Knowledge 4-1 Tasks folder to a USB flash drive and then delete the folder from the hard disk.

Extend Your Knowledge

Extend the skills you learned in this chapter and experiment with new skills. You may need to use Help to complete the assignment.

Creating Notes

Note: To complete this assignment, you will be required to use the Data Files for Students. See the inside back cover of this book for instructions on downloading the Data Files for Students, or contact your instructor for information about accessing the required files.

Instructions: Start Outlook. Import the Extend Your Knowledge 4-1 Notes folder from the Data Files for Students folder into Outlook. The Extend Your Knowledge 4-1 Notes folder has no notes. You will create new notes, categorize the notes, and then print the notes.

Perform the following tasks:

1. Use Help to learn about customizing notes.

2. Display the Extend Your Knowledge 4-1 Notes folder in the Outlook Notes window.

3. Create the following notes:
   - E-mail John Durant concerning upcoming network upgrade
   - Remember to input data for the new company Web site
   - Fill out necessary paperwork for spring break trip
   - Get copy of mission statement for the company Web site
   - Contact Professor Martin about spring break trip
   - Set up secondary e-mail account to handle work e-mails

4. Select the E-mail John Durant note, and then create the color category, Work. Categorize the remaining work notes using the Work category.

5. Select the 'Fill out necessary paperwork' note, and then create a color category, Trip. Categorize the remaining spring break trip notes using the Trip category.

6. Change the view to Notes List. Print the notes in Table view, as shown in Figure 4–92, and then submit them in the format specified by your instructor.

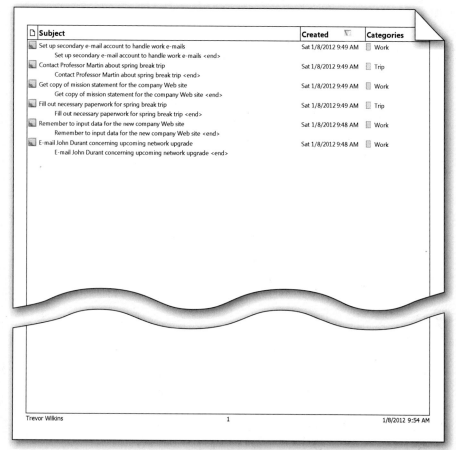

Subject	Created ▽	Categories
Set up secondary e-mail account to handle work e-mails	Sat 1/8/2012 9:49 AM	Work
Set up secondary e-mail account to handle work e-mails <end>		
Contact Professor Martin about spring break trip	Sat 1/8/2012 9:49 AM	Trip
Contact Professor Martin about spring break trip <end>		
Get copy of mission statement for the company Web site	Sat 1/8/2012 9:49 AM	Work
Get copy of mission statement for the company Web site <end>		
Fill out necessary paperwork for spring break trip	Sat 1/8/2012 9:49 AM	Trip
Fill out necessary paperwork for spring break trip <end>		
Remember to input data for the new company Web site	Sat 1/8/2012 9:48 AM	Work
Remember to input data for the new company Web site <end>		
E-mail John Durant concerning upcoming network upgrade	Sat 1/8/2012 9:48 AM	Work
E-mail John Durant concerning upcoming network upgrade <end>		

Trevor Wilkins   1   1/8/2012 9:54 AM

Figure 4–92

7. Export the Extend Your Knowledge 4-1 Notes folder to a USB flash drive and then delete the folder from the hard disk.

Make It Right

Analyze tasks and correct all errors and/or improve the design.

Correcting Tasks and Task Groups

Note: To complete this assignment, you will be required to use the Data Files for Students. See the inside back cover of this book for instructions on downloading the Data Files for Students, or contact your instructor for information about accessing the required files.

Instructions: Start Outlook. Import the Make It Right 4-1 Tasks folder from the Data Files for Students folder into Outlook.

While reviewing your Outlook tasks, you realize that you created several tasks incorrectly, failed to add a task, and categorized some tasks inappropriately. You will identify and open the incorrect tasks, edit them so that they reflect the correct information, add the missing task, apply the right categories, and then save all changes. You also will print the tasks.

Continued >

Make It Right *continued*

Perform the following tasks:

1. Display the Make It Right 4-1 Tasks in the Outlook To-Do List window.

2. The House Renovations task should be displayed as In Progress and 10% completed. Edit the task to show the correct information.

3. The Yoga Class is supposed to be a recurring task that runs from January 1, 2012 to December 27, 2012, occurring weekly on Thursdays. Edit the task to correct the mistakes.

4. The Deliver Presentation task is incorrectly categorized as Home when it should be categorized as Professional. Its priority also should be set to High, with a reminder being sent two days before the due date. Edit the task to correct the mistakes.

5. The Workshops task should include `Teach system to fellow employees` in the task body and include an attached document named roster from the data files. Edit the task to correct the mistakes.

6. Print the tasks (Figure 4–93), and then submit the task list in the format specified by your instructor.

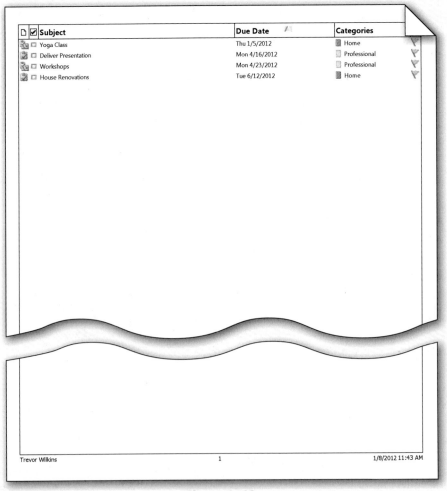

☐ ☑ Subject	Due Date	Categories	
☐ Yoga Class	Thu 1/5/2012	Home	
☐ Deliver Presentation	Mon 4/16/2012	Professional	
☐ Workshops	Mon 4/23/2012	Professional	
☐ House Renovations	Tue 6/12/2012	Home	

Trevor Wilkins	1	1/8/2012 11:43 AM

Figure 4–93

7. Export the Make It Right 4-1 Tasks folder to your USB flash drive and then delete the folder from the hard disk.

Outlook Chapter 4

STUDENT ASSIGNMENTS

In the Lab

Design, create, modify, and/or use tasks and notes using the guidelines, concepts, and skills presented in this chapter. Labs are listed in order of increasing difficulty.

Lab 1: Creating Departmental Tasks

Note: To complete this assignment, you will be required to use the Data Files for Students. See the inside back cover of this book for instructions on downloading the Data Files for Students, or contact your instructor for information about accessing the required files.

Problem: You are an assistant for the Marketing department at A-1 Electronics. Your team is working on a marketing campaign and must complete several tasks to make the campaign a success. Table 4–2 lists the regular tasks and Table 4–3 lists the recurring tasks for the Marketing department. Enter the tasks into the To-Do list. The task list you create will look like the one in Figure 4–94.

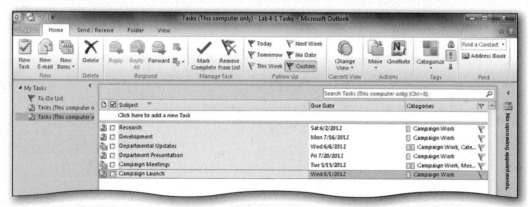

Figure 4–94

Perform the following tasks:

1. Create a Tasks folder named Lab 4-1 Tasks.

2. Create the regular tasks in the Lab 4-1 Tasks folder using the information listed in Table 4–2.

Table 4–2 Marketing Tasks

Task	Start Date	Due Date	Status	Priority
Research	5/14/2012	6/2/2012	In Progress	Normal
Development	6/3/2012	7/16/2012		Normal
Department Presentation	7/20/2012	7/20/2012		High
Campaign Launch		8/1/2012		High

3. Create the recurring tasks in the Lab 4-1 Tasks folder using the information listed in Table 4–3.

Table 4–3 Marketing Recurring Tasks

Task	Start Date	Due Date	Recurrence
Campaign Meetings	5/15/2012	8/1/2012	Weekly, Tuesdays
Departmental Updates	6/6/2012	7/20/2012	Monthly, first Wednesday

4. Create a color category called Meetings, using a color of your choice. Classify the Campaign Meetings, Departmental Updates, and Department Presentation tasks using the Meetings category.

5. Create a color category called Campaign Work, using a color of your choice. Categorize all tasks with this category.

Continued >

In the Lab *continued*

6. Attach the Stakeholders document from the data files to the Research task.

7. Attach the Marketing Group document from the data files to the Department Presentation task.

8. Print the Lab 4-1 Tasks list in Table Style, and then submit it in a format specified by your instructor (Figure 4–94).

9. Export the Lab 4-1 Tasks folder to your USB flash drive and then delete the folder from the hard disk.

In the Lab

Lab 2: Creating a Music Store Task List

Problem: You are the owner of Tiarpin Music store and decide to enter your various tasks into Outlook for your first year of business. You need to create a list of all your tasks and categorize them appropriately (Figure 4–95).

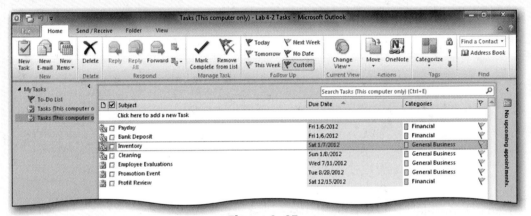

Figure 4–95

Perform the following tasks:

1. Create a Tasks folder named Lab 4-2 Tasks.

2. Create the regular tasks in the Lab 4-2 Tasks folder using the information listed in Table 4–4.

Table 4–4 Tiarpin Music Tasks					
Task	**Task Body**	**Due Date**	**Status**	**Priority**	**Reminder**
Employee Evaluations	Conduct annual reviews	7/11/2012		High	7/5/2012
Promotion Event	Fall outdoor festival	8/28/2012	In Progress	High	
Profit Review	First year profit review	12/15/2012		High	12/1/2012

3. Create the recurring tasks in the Lab 4-2 Tasks folder using the information listed in Table 4–5.

Table 4–5 Tiarpin Music Recurring Tasks			
Task	**Due Date**	**Task Body**	**Recurrence**
Bank Deposit	1/6/2012	CRC Union Bank	Weekly, Monday, Wednesday, Friday
Payday	1/6/2012	Paychecks distributed	Weekly, Friday
Inventory	1/7/2012	Weekly delivery	Weekly, Saturday
Cleaning	1/8/2012	Cleaning by CleanBusinessInc	Weekly, Sunday

4. Categorize the Bank Deposit, Payday, and Profit Review tasks as Financial by creating a new color category.

5. Categorize the remaining tasks as General Business by creating a new color category.

6. Print the tasks in Table Style, and then submit the task list in the format specified by your instructor.

In the Lab

Lab 3: Creating Tasks and Notes

Note: To complete this assignment, you will be required to use the Data Files for Students. See the inside back cover of this book for instructions on downloading the Data Files for Students, or contact your instructor for information about accessing the required files.

Problem: Start Outlook. You are to create a task list for Garmien Catering using the information in Table 4–6. The task list you create is shown in Figure 4–96. You have six events coming up in the next month and want to create the tasks along with the reminders for them. You also want to create notes to remind you about how to prepare for each event.

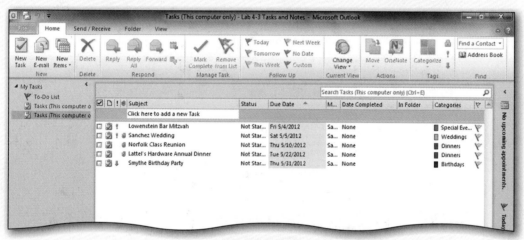

Figure 4–96

Part 1 Perform the following tasks:

1. Create a Tasks folder named Lab 4-3 Tasks, and then create the tasks shown in Table 4–6. Do not create the categories at this time.

Table 4–6 Garmien Catering Tasks

Employee	Due Date	Reminder	Priority	Category
Sanchez Wedding	May 5, 2012	May 1, 2012	High	Weddings
Lowenstein Bar Mitzvah	May 4, 2012	April 29, 2012	High	Special Events
Lattel's Hardware Annual Dinner	May 22, 2012	May 20, 2012	Normal	Dinners
Smythe Birthday Party	May 31, 2012	May 20, 2012	Low	Birthdays
Norfolk Class Reunion	May 10, 2012	May 5, 2012	Normal	Dinners

2. Create the color categories needed for the tasks: Weddings, Special Events, Dinners, and Birthdays. Use the colors of your choice.

3. Categorize the tasks according to the categories shown in Table 4–6.

Continued >

In the Lab *continued*

4. Edit the Sanchez Wedding task. Add the Dinner Options document from the data files as an attachment to the task.

5. Edit the Lattel's Hardware Annual Dinner task. Add the Annual Dinner Schedule document from the data files as an attachment to the task.

6. Edit the Norfolk Class Reunion task. The clients want a menu similar to the one used for the Sanchez Wedding task. Add the Sanchez Wedding task as an attachment to this task.

7. Print the tasks, and then submit the tasks in the format specified by your instructor.

Part 2 Perform the following tasks:

Create a Notes folder named Lab 4-3 Notes, and then create notes using the information in the following list. The resulting notes are displayed in Figure 4–97.

- Check setup space for Sanchez Wedding
- E-mail Lattel's Hardware contact about final schedule
- Confirm Smythe cake colors and decorations
- Get final approval for food list from Lowenstein

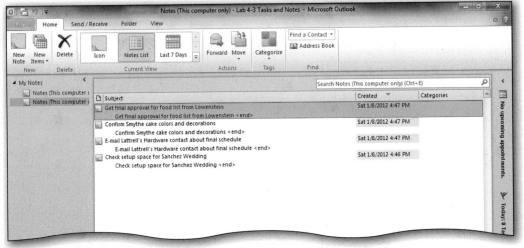

Figure 4–97

2. Print the notes list, and then submit it in the format specified by your instructor.

Cases and Places

Apply your creative thinking and problem solving skills to design and implement a solution.

1: Create Study Group Tasks

Academic

You are in charge of your study group, which consists of students who are taking Computer Science 101 (CIS 101) and Computing and Engineering Technology 122 (CET 122) classes. You are charged with creating tasks for the major tests in each class. Using Table 4–7, create the tasks as shown. Categorize the tasks based upon the Class column. Use the class and test name for the task name. Enter the chapters covered in the task body. Print the final list of tasks, and then submit it in the format specified by your instructor.

Table 4–7 Study Group Tasks			
Class	**Test**	**Due Date**	**Chapters Covered**
CIS 101	Test 1	9/19/2012	1–4
CIS 101	Test 2	11/7/2012	5–8
CIS 101	Test 3	12/12/2012	6–12
CET 122	Exam 1	9/14/2012	1–5
CET 122	Exam 2	10/25/2012	6–10
CET 122	Final Exam	12/20/2012	All

2: Create a Team List

Professional

After attending an executive retreat conference, you now have several bits of information that you would like to create as notes in Outlook, so that later on you can use the ideas from the conference with the rest of your managers and staff. You have created a list of items you want to use as your notes, which is shown in Table 4–8. You indicate which notes will be used for managers and which notes will be used for staff members in the Audience column. Create the notes and categorize them appropriately. Print the notes list and submit it in the format specified by your instructor.

Table 4–8 Retreat Notes	
Note	**Audience**
Encourage employee feedback	Managers
Treat customers as you would like to be treated	Staff
Create environment of shared quality assurance	Managers
Track trends in customer purchasing	Managers
Maintain a positive attitude at all times	Managers, Staff
Follow approved procedures and guidelines	Staff

3: Create a Birthday List

Personal

You typically have problems remembering your friends' birthdays, and want to add them to Outlook to keep better track. Use Table 4–9 to add these birthdays as tasks to your To-Do list. Create them as recurring tasks that begin today but recur indefinitely. Have each task recur yearly on the day of the birthday. Print the task list and submit it in the format specified by your instructor.

Table 4–9 Birthday List		
Name	**Birthday**	**Category**
Bobby	August 25	Friend
Mom	May 3	Family
Max	Feb 19	Family
Dad	June 5	Family
Carla	April 1	Friend

5 | Customizing Outlook

Objectives

You will have mastered the material in this chapter when you can:

- Add a new e-mail account
- Configure junk e-mail options
- Set the default message format
- Create an e-mail signature
- Customize personal stationery
- Adjust calendar settings

- Customize search options
- Create a Quick Step
- Manage Quick Steps
- Create rules
- Configure AutoArchive settings
- Add a news feed

5 | Customizing Outlook

Introduction

Outlook provides many options for customizing your experience when working with e-mail messages, calendars, and other items. From creating custom e-mail signatures to adjusting how the work week is displayed in your calendar, you can make Outlook fit your requirements so that you can use it more efficiently. For example, a rule is a command that tells Outlook how to process an e-mail message. Using rules, you quickly can categorize or flag your e-mail messages as they arrive so that you can identify at a glance which ones you first want to address. You can change the fonts and colors that are used by default as well. Outlook's customization options can help you become more productive.

Project — Adding a New E-Mail Account and Customizing Options

People often have more than one e-mail account. In fact, some people have more than they can remember. Outlook allows you to manage multiple e-mail accounts. That way you can read your e-mail messages from the accounts without the need for several e-mail programs.

   The project in this chapter follows general guidelines and uses Outlook to add a new e-mail account and customize Outlook options, as shown in Figure 5–1.

Overview

   As you read this chapter, you will learn how to customize Outlook as shown in Figure 5–1 by performing these general tasks:

- Add a new e-mail account.
- Customize signatures and stationery.
- Change calendar options.
- Create Quick Steps.
- Manage rules.
- Add and use a news feed.

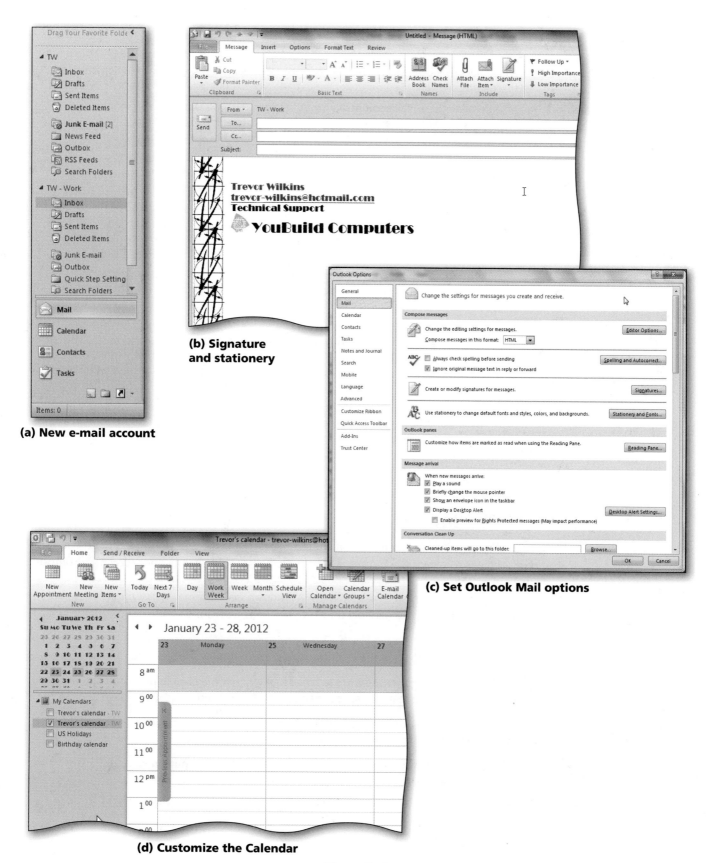

(a) New e-mail account

(b) Signature and stationery

(c) Set Outlook Mail options

(d) Customize the Calendar

Figure 5–1

<table>
<tr><td>Plan
Ahead</td><td>

General Project Guidelines

When customizing Outlook, the actions you perform and decisions you make will affect the appearance, characteristics, and performance of Outlook. As you customize options, such as those shown in Figure 5–1 on the previous page, you should follow these general guidelines:

1. **Determine the e-mail accounts you want to manage with Outlook.** You should include in Outlook the e-mail accounts that you intend to use frequently. If you have an account you rarely use, you may want to consider canceling it. Too many e-mail accounts can lead to confusion over where to find the information you need.

2. **Determine which options you want to customize.** Among the options you can customize are the default e-mail message format, spelling options, personalized signatures, and calendar settings.

3. **Decide what set of actions you want to use as Quick Steps.** A Quick Step is a set of tasks that are automated so that you can perform them with one click. You should identify repetitive tasks you perform and then decide if they should be added as a Quick Step.

4. **Plan rules to use with your e-mail messages.** Rules allow Outlook to process e-mail messages automatically. Determine how you would like your e-mail messages to be processed.

5. **Determine what news feeds you would like to use.** A news feed provides Web site content that is updated frequently. You typically subscribe to a news feed to stay current on topics that interest you. You can find news feeds about practically any topic. Only add the news feeds that you would like to read frequently, instead of those you might never view again.

When necessary, more specific details concerning the above guidelines are presented at appropriate points in the chapter. The chapter also will identify the actions performed and decisions made regarding these guidelines during the customization shown in Figure 5–1.

</td></tr>
</table>

To Start Outlook

If you are using a computer to step through the project in this chapter and you want your screens to match the figures in this book, you should change your screen's resolution to 1024 × 768.

The following steps, which assume Windows 7 is running, start Outlook based on a typical installation. You may need to ask your instructor how to start Outlook for your computer.

1 Click the Start button on the Windows 7 taskbar to display the Start menu.

2 Type `Microsoft Outlook` as the search text in the 'Search programs and files' text box and watch the search results appear on the Start menu.

3 Click Microsoft Outlook 2010 in the search results on the Start menu to start Outlook with your Inbox as the default Mail folder.

4 If the Outlook window is not maximized, click the Maximize button next to the Close button on its title bar to maximize the window.

5 Click the File tab to display the Backstage view Inbox TW – Microsoft Outlook window (Figure 5–2).

Q&A Why does my title bar not match the title bar in Figure 5–2?

If you did not import the data file for this chapter, your title bar will be different. The title bar always displays the name of the Outlook data file.

Figure 5–2

BTW

Q&As
For a complete list of the Q&As found in many of the step-by-step sequences in this book, visit the Outlook 2010 Q&A Web page (scsite.com/out2010/qa).

BTW

BTWs
For a complete list of the BTWs found in the margins of this book, visit the Outlook 2010 BTW Web page (scsite.com/out2010/btw).

Adding New E-Mail Accounts

As you learned in Chapter 1, when setting up an e-mail account, you need to know basic information such as the e-mail address and password. You also need to know the name to use with the e-mail account, as well as how you would like Outlook to display the account. For example, in Figure 5–2, the mailbox is displayed as Inbox – TW. You could use any name you like for the mailbox.

When you first set up Outlook, the Auto Account Setup feature ran and helped you to set up the first e-mail account to be managed by Outlook. When adding an account, you use the Account Settings dialog box. Part of the process includes using the Auto Account Setup feature, which makes it easy to configure the new e-mail account.

Determine the e-mail accounts you want to manage with Outlook.
For the e-mail account you plan to add, make sure you know the account properties and settings before you start to add the account. Gather the following information: type of account, such as e-mail, text messaging, or fax mail; your name, e-mail address, and password; server information, including account type and the addresses of incoming and outgoing mail servers. You typically receive the server information from your e-mail service provider.

Plan Ahead

Depending on your instructor's preferences and your e-mail services, you can perform the steps in this chapter by adding a new e-mail account to Outlook or by opening an Outlook data file provided with the book. Before you can add a new e-mail account in Outlook, you must have an account set up with an e-mail service provider that is different from any other account already set up in Outlook. For example, you might have a Hotmail or Windows Live account that provides e-mail service. If you have not configured this account in Outlook, you can complete the steps in this chapter to do so.

To add a new account, you use the Add Account option from the Backstage view, which lets you add an account using the Add New Account dialog box. If you want to add an account and change advanced settings, you should use the Account Settings dialog box.

In some cases, you may be required to add an extra component. For example, for Hotmail accounts, you might need to install an Outlook connector program. You then would restart Outlook, which would guide you through the steps to add the account.

BTW

Multiple E-Mail Accounts
If you have multiple e-mail accounts configured in Outlook, you can decide which e-mail account to use each time you compose and send a new e-mail message. To select the account from which to send the e-mail message, click the From button in the Untitled - Message window, and then click the desired e-mail account.

To Add a New E-Mail Account

You recently started working for YouBuild Computers as a technical assistant for projects that involve creating Web sites for the company's new Web hosting department. You have a new e-mail account and need to add it to Outlook so that you can manage both personal and work e-mail accounts. Similar to your personal e-mail account, you want the new account to appear as "TW – Work" in Outlook. Because you want to reference your new account by a specific name, which is an advanced setting, you need to use the Account Settings dialog box.

The following steps add a new e-mail account and set the name to TW – Work using the Account Settings dialog box. If you are performing these steps on your computer, enter the name, e-mail address, and password for an e-mail account you own but have not yet added to Outlook.

1
- If necessary, display the Backstage view.

- Click the Account Settings button to display the Account Settings command (Figure 5–3).

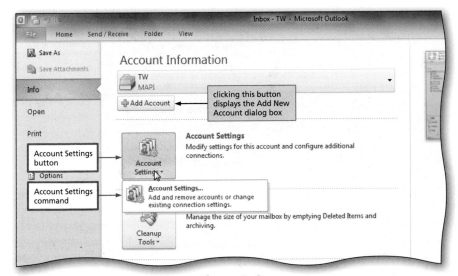

Figure 5–3

2
- Click Account Settings to display the Account Settings dialog box (Figure 5–4).

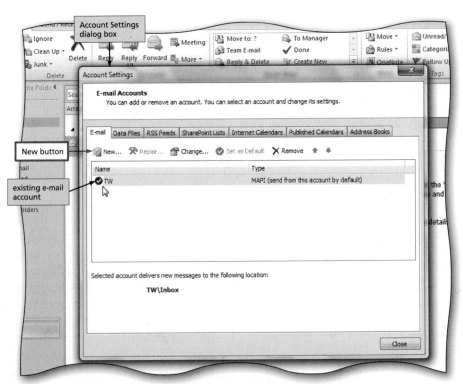

Figure 5–4

• Click the New button (Account Settings dialog box) to display the Add New Account dialog box (Figure 5–5).

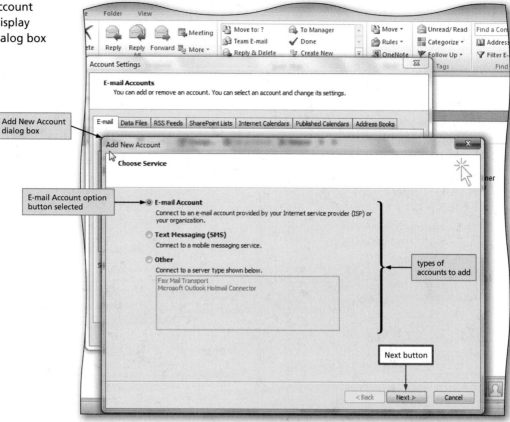

Figure 5–5

• Click the Next button (Add New Account dialog box) to continue to the next step in adding a new account (Figure 5–6).

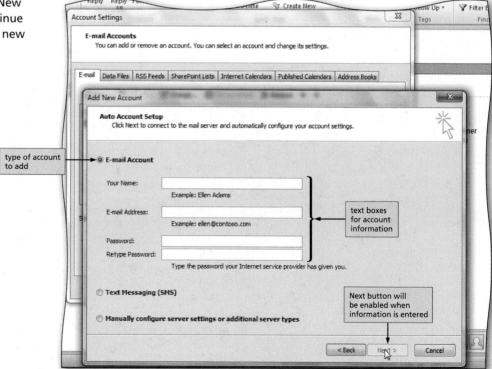

Figure 5–6

5

- Type your name in the Your Name text box to enter a name for the account.

- Type your e-mail address in the E-mail Address text box to enter an e-mail address for the account.

- Type the password for the account in the Password and Retype Password text boxes to enter in the account password (Figure 5–7).

Q&A

What should I enter for the password?

Enter the appropriate password for the e-mail address you just entered.

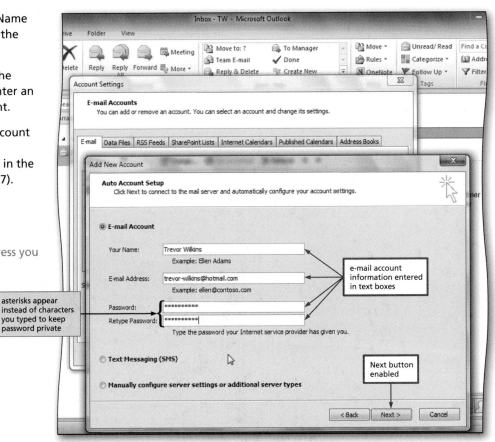

Figure 5–7

6

- Click the Next button (Add New Account dialog box) to let Outlook configure the account (Figure 5–8).

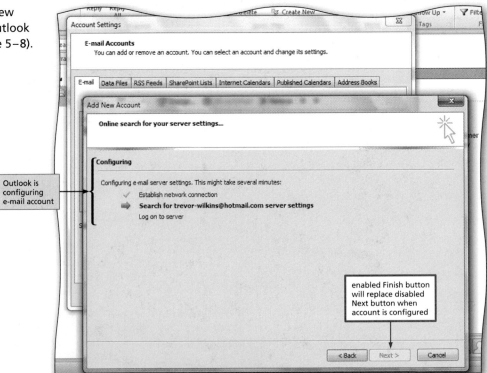

Figure 5–8

7

- After the account is configured, click the Finish button (Add New Account dialog box) to return to the Account Settings dialog box (Figure 5–9).

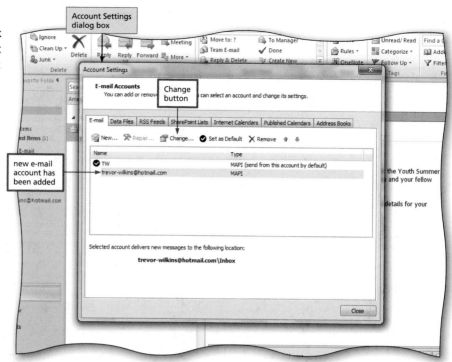

Figure 5–9

8

- If necessary, click the new e-mail account (in this case, the trevor-wilkins@hotmail.com account) to select it.

- Click the Change button (Account Settings dialog box) to display the Windows Live Hotmail Settings dialog box (Figure 5–10).

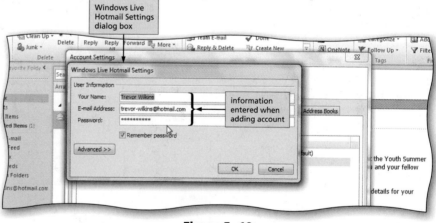

Figure 5–10

9

- Click the Advanced button (Windows Live Hotmail Settings dialog box) to display advanced options (Figure 5–11).

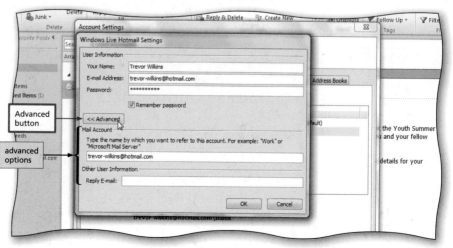

Figure 5–11

• Type **TW - Work** in the Mail Account text box to change the name by which the account is referred (Figure 5–12).

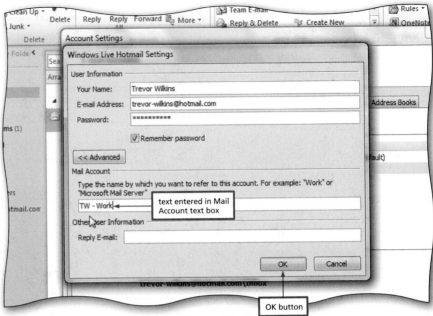

Figure 5–12

• Click the OK button (Windows Live Hotmail Settings dialog box) to close the Windows Live Hotmail Settings dialog box.

• Click the Close button (Account Settings dialog box) to close the Account Settings dialog box (Figure 5–13).

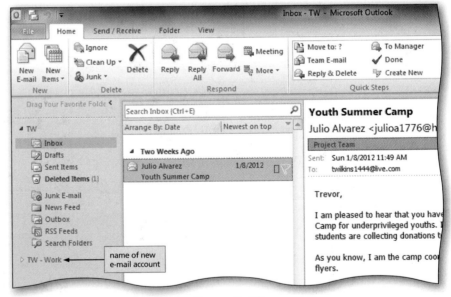

Figure 5–13

Other Ways

1. Click File, click Add Account

To Open an Outlook Data File

If you choose not to add an e-mail account, you need to open the TW – Work Outlook data file from the Data Files provided with the book. Note that using the TW – Work data file might not let you perform all of the steps in this chapter. If you find you cannot perform a series of steps, switch to an Outlook e-mail account to complete the steps. If you do not have access to an Outlook e-mail account, read but do not perform the steps. The following steps open the TW – Work Outlook data file.

1 Click File to display the Backstage view.

2 Click Open in the Backstage view to display the Open commands.

③ Click Open Outlook Data File to display the Open Outlook Data File dialog box.

④ Navigate to the location of the file to be opened (in this case, the USB flash drive), and then double-click the folder that contains the data files for this chapter to open it.

⑤ Click TW – Work to select the file to be opened.

⑥ Click the OK button (Open Outlook Data File dialog box) to open the TW – Work mailbox in your Outlook window.

Working with Junk E-Mail Options

As you learned in Chapter 1, junk e-mail is bulk e-mail, spam, or other unwanted e-mail messages. Outlook uses a junk e-mail filter to control the amount of junk mail you receive. The junk e-mail filter evaluates incoming messages and sends to the Junk E-mail folder those messages that meet the criteria for junk e-mail. You can use the Junk button in the Delete group of the Home tab to override the default criteria when viewing e-mail messages by deciding to block the sender, never block the sender, never block the sender's domain, or never block a group or mailing list.

Using the Junk E-mail Options dialog box, you can change even more settings (Figure 5–14). Table 5–1 describes the options you can adjust using the Junk E-mail Options dialog box.

BTW
Junk E-Mail
It usually is a good idea to check your Junk E-mail folder regularly to make sure no items are labeled as junk inadvertently. If, after clicking the Junk E-mail folder, you find an e-mail message that is not junk, select the e-mail message, click the Junk button (Home tab | Delete group), click Not Junk, and then click the OK button.

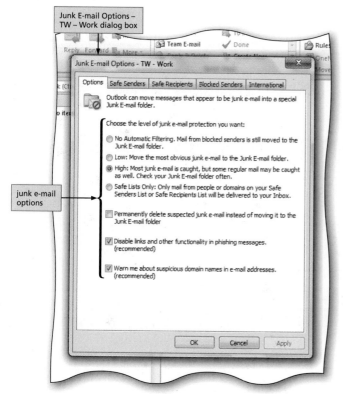

Figure 5–14

Table 5–1 Junk E-Mail Options	
Tab	**Description**
Options	Allows you to choose the level of protection (No Automatic Filtering, Low, High, Safe Lists Only), as well as set whether junk e-mail is deleted, links are disabled in phishing messages, and warnings are provided for suspicious domain names.
Safe Senders	Permits the specification of safe e-mail addresses and domains. E-mail messages from the listed e-mail addresses and domains will not be treated as junk e-mail.
Safe Recipients	Specifies that e-mail messages sent to e-mail addresses or domains in the safe recipient list will not be treated as junk e-mail.
Blocked Senders	Allows you to manage your list of blocked e-mail addresses and domains.
International	Manages which domains and encodings you would like to block based on languages used.

To Configure Junk E-Mail Options

You need to configure junk e-mail options for your work e-mail account. You want to add Microsoft.com to the Safe Sender list because you often receive e-mail messages from Microsoft. The following steps configure the junk e-mail options for the TW – Work account.

1

• Click the TW – Work account in the Navigation Pane to select the TW – Work mailbox (Figure 5–15).

Q&A Why did I have to select the TW – Work account?

To change junk e-mail options for an account, the account first should be selected. If the TW mailbox had been selected, you would have changed junk e-mail settings for that account and not the work account. If you created a new account with a name other than TW – Work, click that account instead.

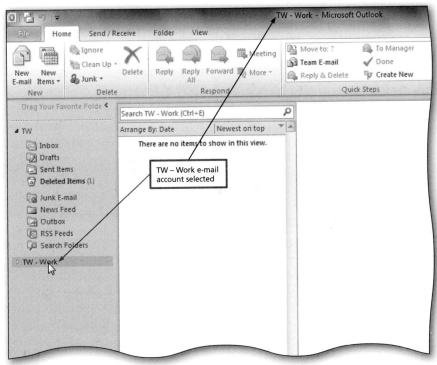

Figure 5–15

2

• Click the Junk button (Home tab | Delete group) to display junk e-mail options (Figure 5–16).

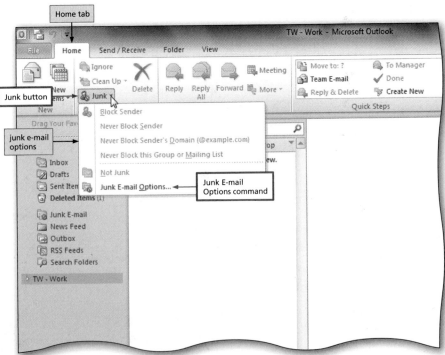

Figure 5–16

3

- Click Junk E-mail Options to display the Junk E-mail Options dialog box (Figure 5–17).

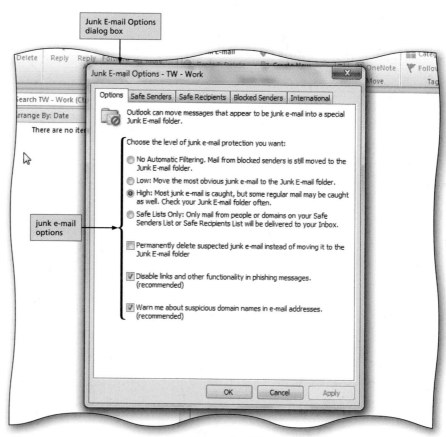

Figure 5–17

4

- Click the Safe Senders tab (Junk E-mail Options dialog box) to display the Safe Senders options (Figure 5–18).

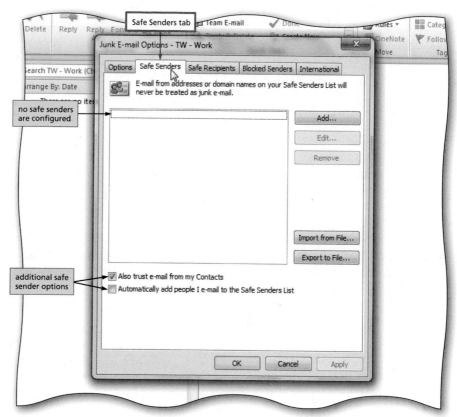

Figure 5–18

5

- Click the Add button (Junk E-mail Options dialog box) to display the 'Add address or domain' dialog box (Figure 5–19).

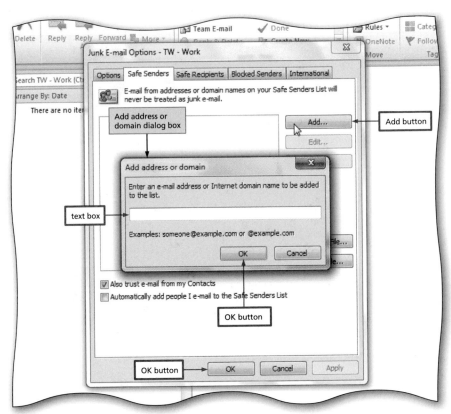

Figure 5–19

6

- Type **@Microsoft.com** in the text box to enter a domain name to add.

Q&A

Do I have to type the @ symbol?

While Outlook recommends that you type the @ symbol to indicate a domain name, you could have left out the symbol. In that case, you would leave it up to Outlook to determine if it is a domain name or e-mail address. Most of the time, Outlook will interpret it correctly; however, to be certain, type the @ symbol.

- Click the OK button ('Add address or domain' dialog box) to add the domain to the Safe Senders List (Figure 5–20).

7

- Click the OK button (Junk E-mail Options dialog box) to close the Junk E-mail Options dialog box.

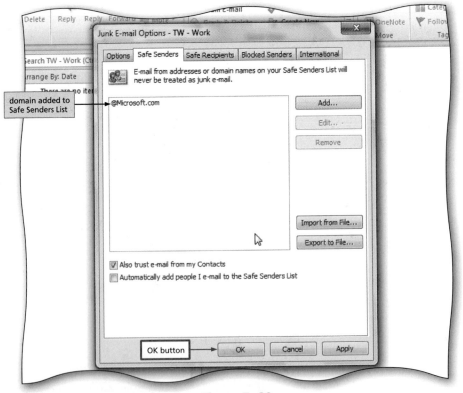

Figure 5–20

Customizing Outlook Options

Most of the customizing options for Outlook can be accessed using the Outlook Options dialog box. The Outlook Options dialog box allows you to change mail, calendar, tasks, notes and journal, search, mobile, language, and advanced settings. You also can customize the Ribbon and Quick Access toolbar as well as manage Add-Ins and work with the Trust Center.

Determine which options you want to customize.   **Plan**
Outlook users often customize their default e-mail message format and spelling options.   **Ahead**
Two other useful and popular options to change are creating one or more e-mail message
signatures and specifying calendar settings:

- **Determine the information to include in your signature.** Some people include only their full name and e-mail address in a signature. At work, you also could include your job title, phone number, office location, and company name. Plan the information for your signature before you add it to your first e-mail message. Select the formats that match your company or personal design, and have any fonts and images available before creating the signature.

- **Determine the calendar settings you need.** Decide on what formatting you would like to use in your calendar. Make sure you have decided on your work week as well. For example, Trevor works Mondays, Wednesdays, Fridays, and Saturdays, and only wants the calendar to display those days.

To Display Outlook Options

To customize Outlook, you use the Outlook Options dialog box. The following step displays the Outlook Options dialog box.

1

- Display the Backstage view.

- Click Options in the Backstage view to display the Outlook Options dialog box (Figure 5–21).

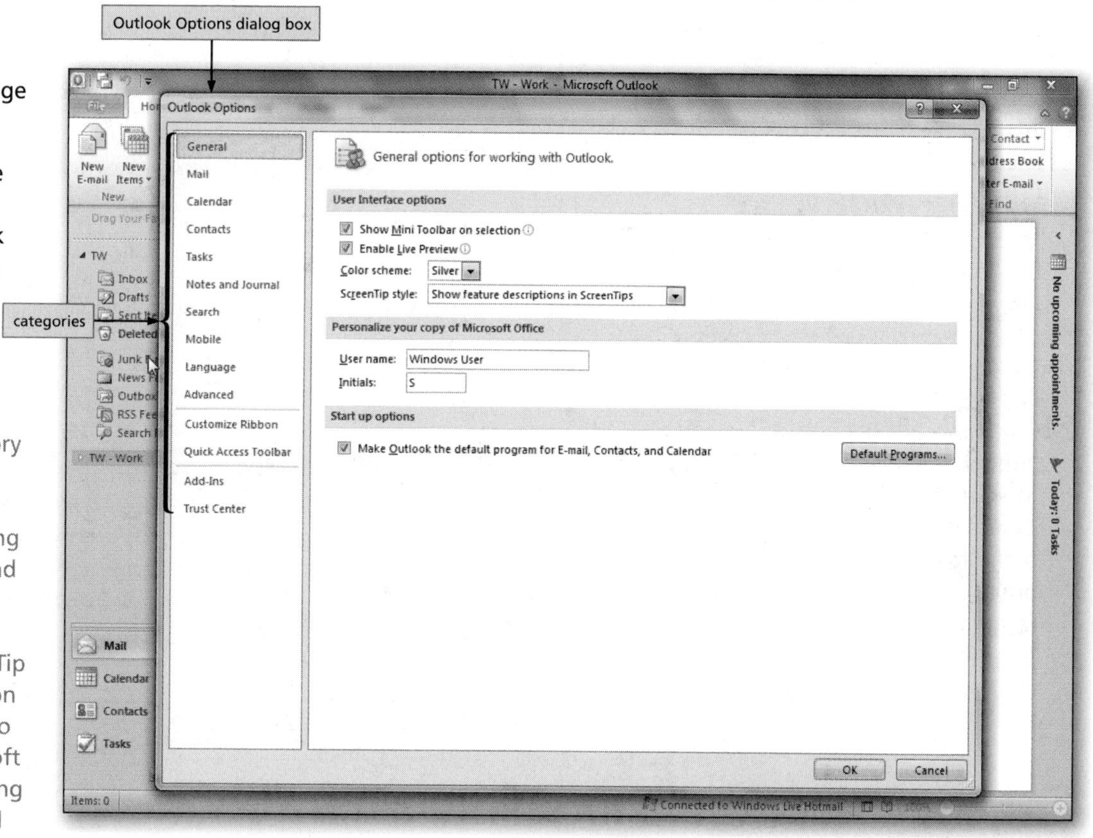

Q&A

What options can I set in the General category?

The General category allows you to customize the user interface by enabling the Mini Toolbar and Live Preview, and changing the Color scheme and ScreenTip style. Personalization options allow you to personalize Microsoft Outlook by specifying your user name and initials, and Start up options allow you to specify whether Outlook should be the default program for e-mail, contacts, and calendar.

Figure 5–21

To Set the Default Message Format

E-mail messages can be formatted as HTML, plain text, or rich text. With plain text, you can include text with no formatting. Rich text provides more formatting options, and HTML provides the most formatting options including various elements that commonly are found on Web pages.

You want to make sure that your e-mail messages use the HTML format by default because this message format allows the most flexibility when composing e-mail messages. The following steps set the default message format to HTML.

1

- Click Mail in the Category list to display Mail options (Figure 5–22).

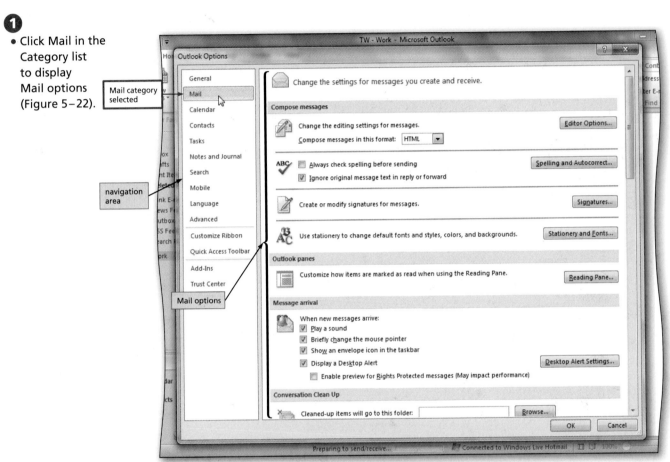

Figure 5–22

2

- Click the 'Compose messages in this format' box arrow to display a list of formatting options (Figure 5–23).

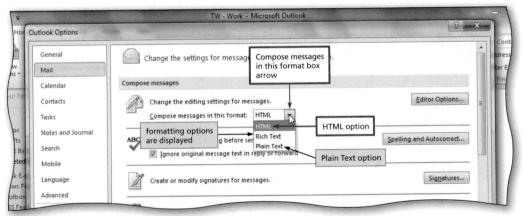

Figure 5–23

3

- Click HTML to set the default message format as HTML (Figure 5–24).

Q&A What if HTML already was selected?

Depending upon who set up Outlook, the default message format already might be HTML. In that case, you can skip Step 3.

Q&A What if I want to choose a different format?

When you display the available message formats, choose the type you want to use. For example, if you want all new e-mail messages to be in plain text format, click the Plain Text option (shown in Figure 5–23).

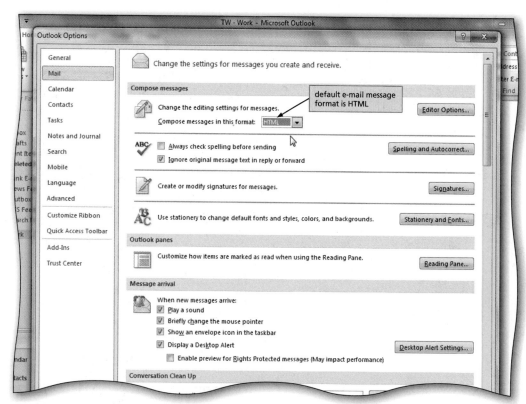

Figure 5–24

To Configure Spell Checking Options

You want the e-mail messages you send to co-workers to be free of spelling and grammar mistakes. To make this task easier, you decide to make sure that spelling and grammar are checked before you send an e-mail message. The following steps configure Outlook to check spelling and grammar before sending an e-mail message.

1

- Click the 'Always check spelling before sending' check box to select the option (Figure 5–25).

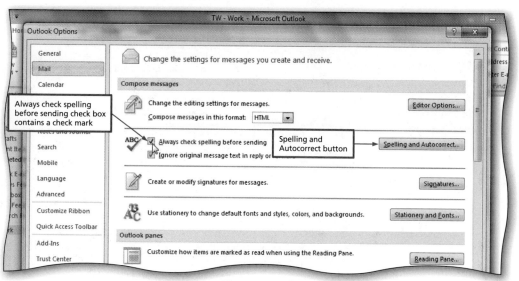

Figure 5–25

● Click the Spelling and Autocorrect button (Outlook Options dialog box) to display the Editor Options dialog box (Figure 5–26).

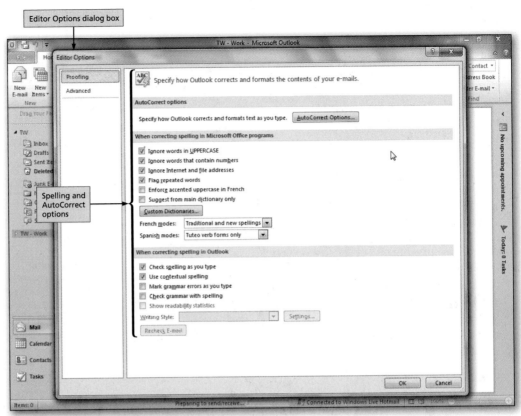

Figure 5–26

● Click the 'Check grammar with spelling' check box to select it (Figure 5–27).

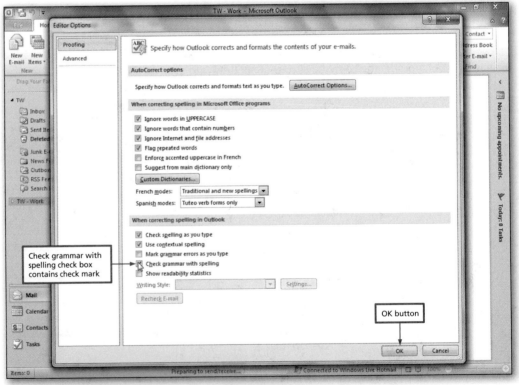

Figure 5–27

4

- Click the OK button (Editor Options dialog box) to close the Editor Options dialog box (Figure 5–28).

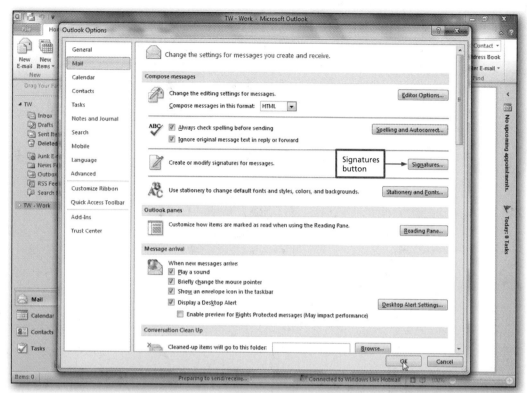

Figure 5–28

Creating Signatures and Stationery

You can configure Outlook to add signatures to your e-mail messages automatically. A signature is similar to a closing set of lines in a formal letter. It can include your full name, job title, e-mail address, phone number, and company information. You even can include business cards in your signature.

If you have more than one e-mail account, you will need to select the account for which you want to create the signature. You can create the signature while you are creating an e-mail message or you can use the Outlook Options dialog box. If you create the signature while writing an e-mail message, you will have to apply the signature to the e-mail message, as it will not be applied automatically. If you create it using the Outlook Options dialog box, it will be added automatically.

In addition to adding signatures to your e-mail messages, you can customize the stationery, which determines the appearance of your e-mail messages, including background, fonts, and colors. You can pick fonts to use in the e-mail message text, or you can select a theme or stationery design and apply that to your e-mail messages.

BTW

The Ribbon and Screen Resolution
Outlook may change how the groups and buttons within the groups appear on the Ribbon, depending on the computer's screen resolution. Thus, your Ribbon may look different from the ones in this book if you are using a screen resolution other than 1024 × 768.

To Create an E-Mail Signature

You decide to create a signature to use when composing e-mail messages using the TW – Work account. The following steps create a signature called Work.

1

- Click the Signatures button (Outlook Options dialog box) to display the Signatures and Stationery dialog box (Figure 5–29).

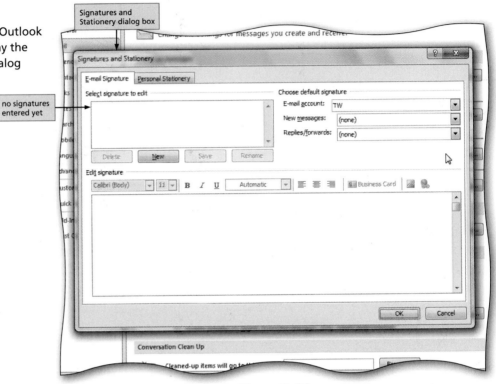

Figure 5–29

2

- Click the New button (Signatures and Stationery dialog box) to display the New Signature dialog box (Figure 5–30).

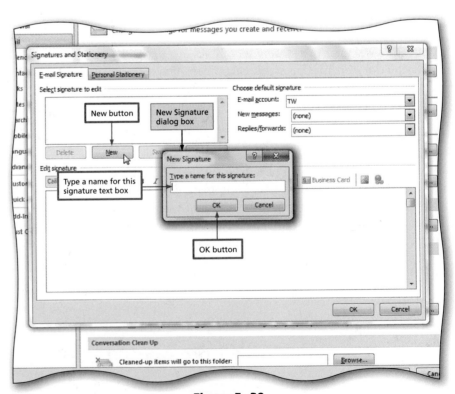

Figure 5–30

- Type **Work** in the 'Type a name for this signature' text box to enter a name for the signature.

- Click OK to create the signature (Figure 5–31).

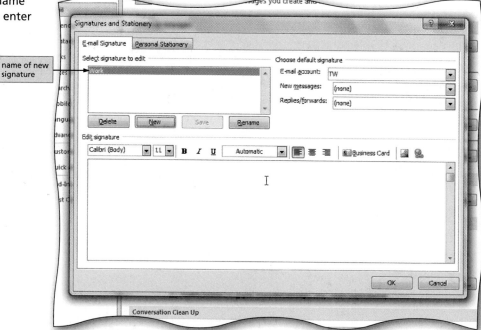

Figure 5–31

To Format an E-Mail Signature

You want to include your name, e-mail address, job title, and the company information as part of the signature. You also want to format the signature so that it is attractive but maintains a professional appearance. The following steps format and add the text for the signature.

1

- Click the Font box arrow to display a list of fonts (Figure 5–32).

Figure 5–32

- If necessary, scroll down until Broadway is visible.

- Click Broadway to select the font.

- Click the Font Size box arrow to display a list of font sizes (Figure 5–33).

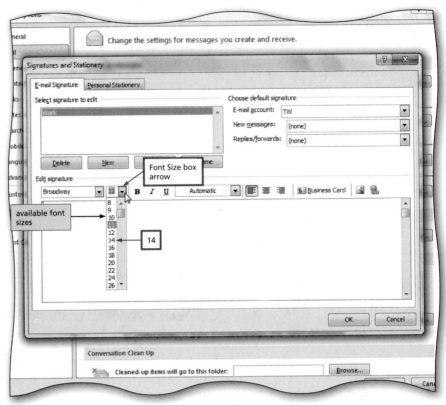

Figure 5–33

- Click 14 to change the font size.

- Click the Font Color box arrow to display a list of colors (Figure 5–34).

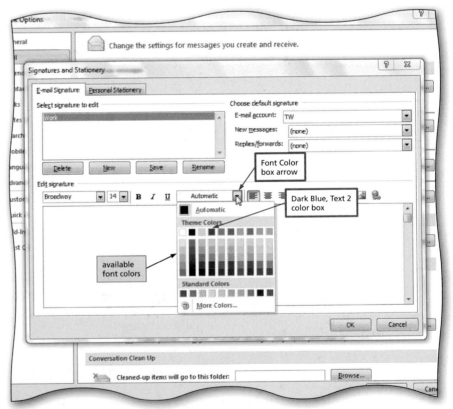

Figure 5–34

4

- Click the Dark Blue, Text 2 color box (column 4, row 1) to change the font color.

- Type `Trevor Wilkins` in the signature body to enter the first line of the signature.

- Click the Font Color box arrow to display a list of colors.

- Click Automatic to change the font color to automatic (Figure 5–35).

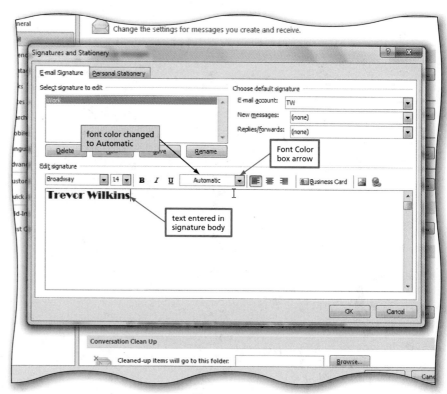

Figure 5–35

5

- Press the ENTER key and then type `trevor-wilkins@hotmail.com` in the signature body to enter the second line of the signature.

- Press the ENTER key and then type `Technical Assistant` in the signature body to enter the third line of the signature.

- Click the Font Size box arrow to display a list of font sizes.

- Click 22 to change the font size.

- Press the ENTER key and type `YouBuild Computers` in the signature body to enter the fourth line of the signature (Figure 5–36).

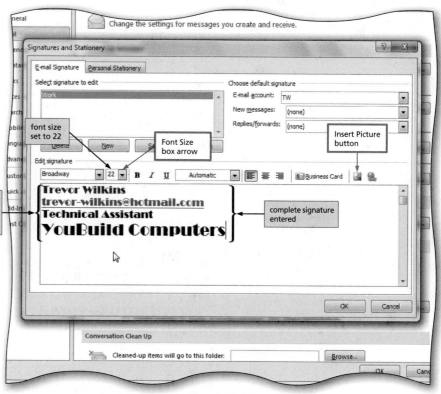

Figure 5–36

To Add an Image to an E-Mail Signature

You can add an image such as a photo or drawing to your signature. You have a copy of the YouBuild Computers company logo and want to include it in your signature. The following steps add the logo picture to the work signature and save the changes.

- Move the insertion point to the beginning of the fourth line.

- Click the Insert Picture button (Signatures and Stationery dialog box) to display the Insert Picture dialog box.

- Navigate to the USB flash drive where you have stored the Data Files for this chapter.

- Click the logo picture file to select it for insertion (Figure 5–37).

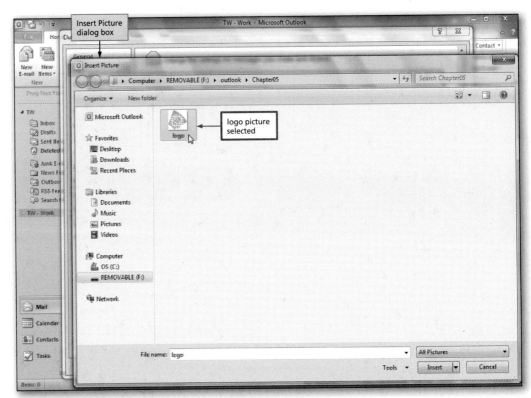

Figure 5–37

- Click the Insert button (Insert Picture dialog box) to insert the picture into the signature (Figure 5–38).

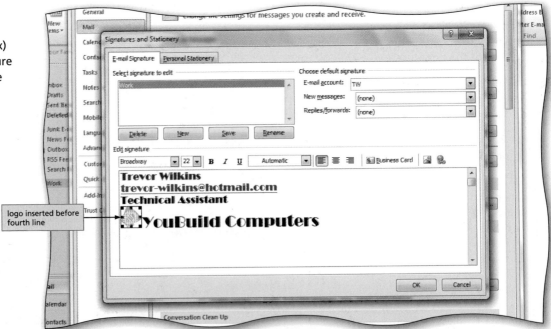

Figure 5–38

3

- Click the Save button (Signatures and Stationery dialog box) to save the changes to the signature (Figure 5–39).

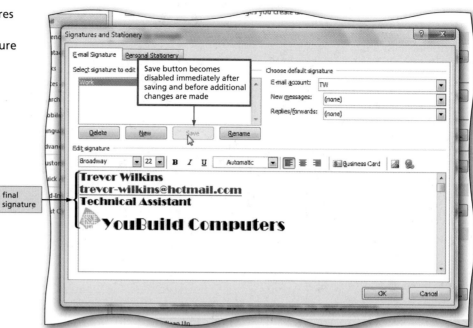

Figure 5–39

To Configure Signature Options

After creating a signature, you need to assign it to an e-mail account. You can assign it to as many accounts as you want. When working with an account, you can set two default signatures: one for new messages and one for replies and forwards.

Because you created your signature for your work account, you want to make it the default for new messages in the TW – Work e-mail account. The following steps set the default signature for new messages from the TW – Work account to the Work signature.

1

- Click the E-mail account box arrow to display a list of accounts.

- Click TW – Work to select the TW – Work account (Figure 5–40).

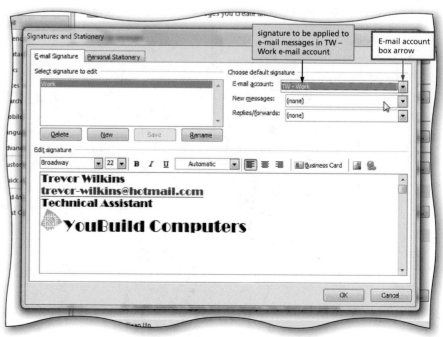

Figure 5–40

- Click the New messages box arrow to display a list of signatures.
- Click Work to make it the default signature for new messages (Figure 5–41).

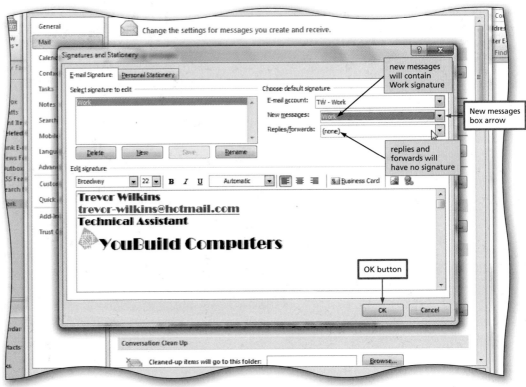

Figure 5–41

- Click the OK button (Signatures and Stationery dialog box) to save the changes to the signature settings, close the Signatures and Stationery dialog box, and return to the Outlook Options dialog box (Figure 5–42).

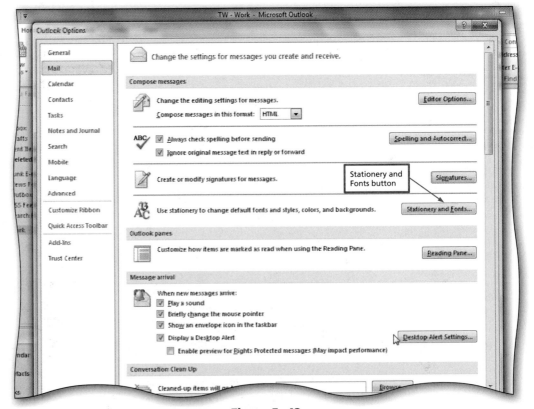

Figure 5–42

To Customize Stationery

You decide to use the Tech Tools stationery for all your work e-mail messages. The following steps change the e-mail message stationery to Tech Tools.

1
• Click the Stationery and Fonts button (Outlook Options dialog box) to display the Signatures and Stationery dialog box (Figure 5–43).

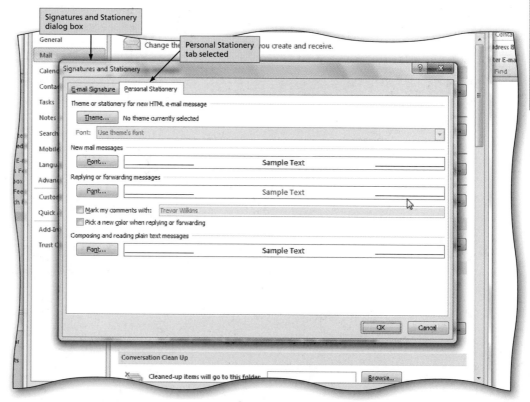

Figure 5–43

2
• Click the Theme button (Signatures and Stationery dialog box) to display the Theme or Stationery dialog box (Figure 5–44).

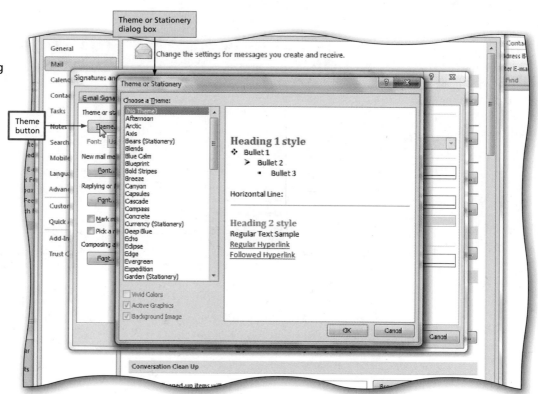

Figure 5–44

- Scroll in the Choose a Theme area until Tech Tools (Stationery) is visible.

- Click Tech Tools (Stationery) to select it as the stationery (Figure 5–45).

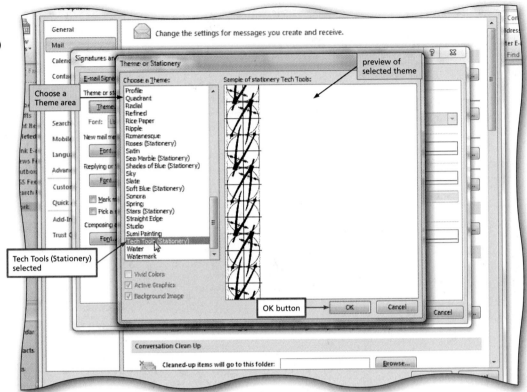

Figure 5–45

④

- Click the OK button (Theme or Stationery dialog box) to apply the theme to the stationery (Figure 5–46).

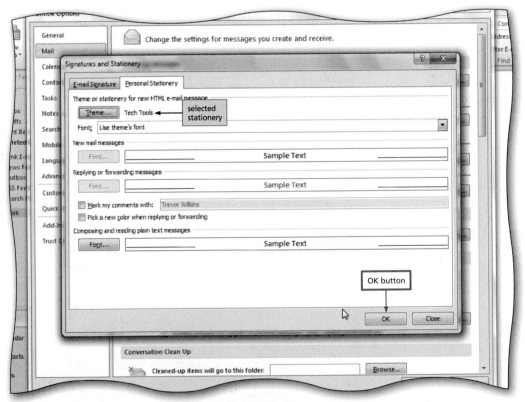

Figure 5–46

5

- Click the OK button (Signatures and Stationery dialog box) to save the theme settings and return to the Outlook Options dialog box (Figure 5–47).

6

- Click the OK button (Outlook Options dialog box) to close the Outlook Options dialog box.

Figure 5–47

To Preview Message Changes

You want to preview the changes you made to your e-mail signature and stationery and see how they look in an e-mail message. The following steps display a new e-mail message without sending it.

1 Click the New E-mail button (Home tab | New group) to create a new e-mail message (Figure 5–48).

2 Close the e-mail message without sending it.

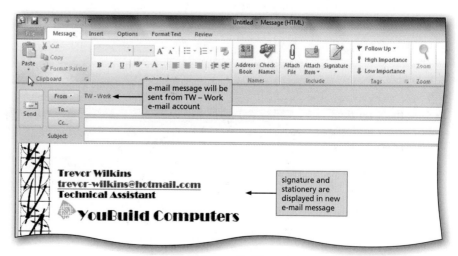

Figure 5–48

Customizing the Calendar

You can customize the Calendar to better suit your needs. For example, you can select the days of your work week and set the displayed time range to reflect the start and end times of your workday. You also can change the default reminder time from 15 minutes to any other interval, such as 5 minutes or a half-hour. Other Calendar options you can customize include the calendar font and current time zone.

To Change the Work Time on the Calendar

You want to customize the work time on the Calendar so that it reflects your work schedule. You normally work from 9:00 AM to 5:30 PM on Mondays, Wednesdays, Fridays, and Saturdays. The following steps change the Calendar settings to match the work schedule and make Monday the first day of the week.

- Open the Backstage view.

- Click Options in the Backstage view to display the Outlook Options dialog box.

- Click Calendar in the Category list in the Outlook Options dialog box to display Calendar options (Figure 5–49).

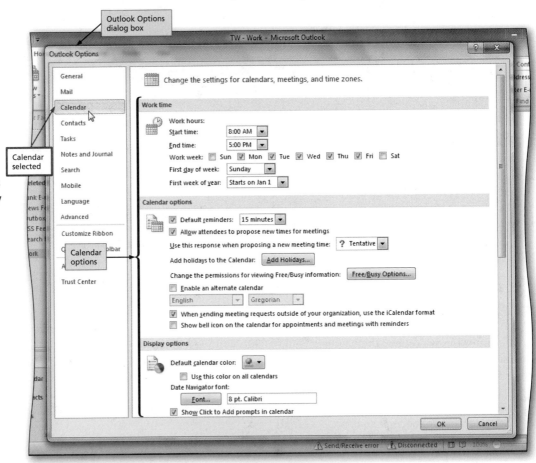

Figure 5–49

2

- Click the Start time box arrow to display a list of start times.

- Select 9:00 AM to change the start time.

- Click the End time box arrow to display a list of end times.

- Select 5:30 PM to change the end time (Figure 5–50).

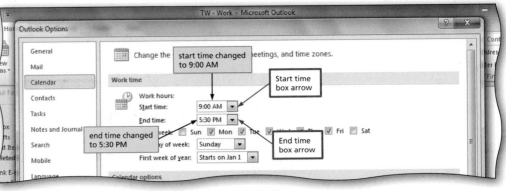

Figure 5–50

3

- Click the Tue check box to deselect it.

- Click the Thu check box to deselect it.

- Click the Sat check box to select it (Figure 5–51).

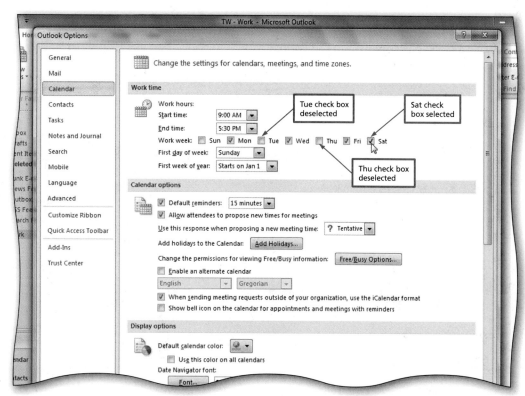

Figure 5–51

4

- Click the 'First day of week' box arrow to display a list of days.

- Click Monday to change the first day of the week to Monday (Figure 5–52).

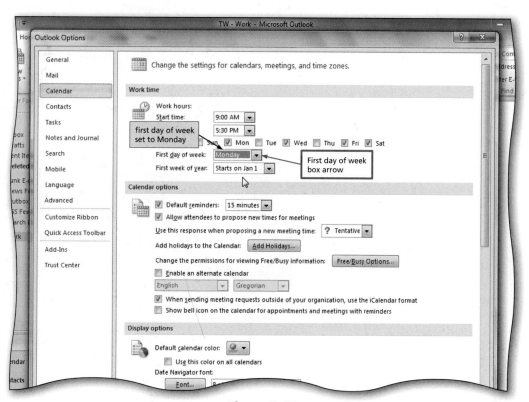

Figure 5–52

To Modify Calendar Options

To further customize the Outlook calendar, you want to increase the time for reminders to 30 minutes. You also have a colleague who lives in the United Kingdom and would like to add her holidays to your calendar so that you know when her office is closed.

The following steps change the time for reminders to 30 minutes and add the holidays from the United Kingdom to the calendar.

- Click the Default reminders box arrow to display a list of times.

- Click 30 minutes to select 30 minutes as the default time for reminders (Figure 5–53).

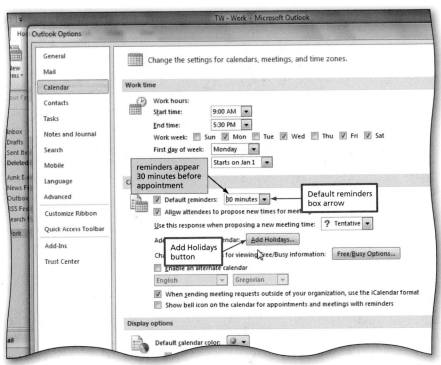

Figure 5–53

- Click the Add Holidays button (Outlook Options dialog box) to display the Add Holidays to Calendar dialog box (Figure 5–54).

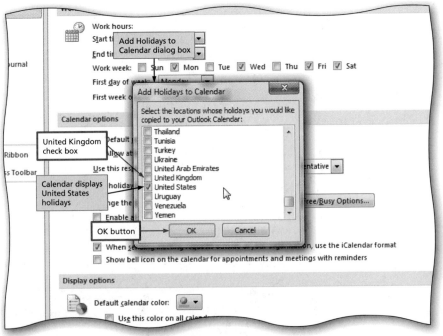

Figure 5–54

- Click the United Kingdom check box to select it.

- Click the OK button (Add Holidays to Calendar dialog box) to import the United Kingdom holidays and display a confirmation message (Figure 5–55).

- Click the OK button (Microsoft Outlook dialog box) to return to the Outlook Options dialog box.

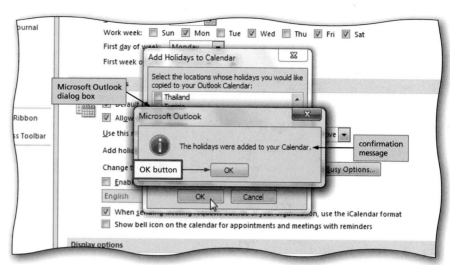

Figure 5–55

To Change Calendar Display Options

After changing the holidays that are displayed on your calendar, you decide to change some display options of your calendar as well. You want to change the calendar font to Broadway to match the signature font, and change the default calendar color to Teal.

The following steps change the calendar display options.

1

- Click the 'Default calendar color' button to display a list of colors (Figure 5–56).

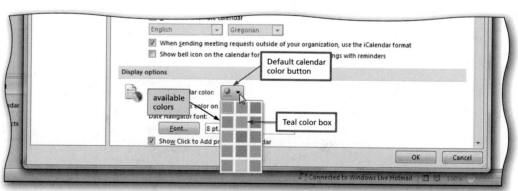

Figure 5–56

2

- Click Teal (column 2, row 2) to change the color to Teal (Figure 5–57).

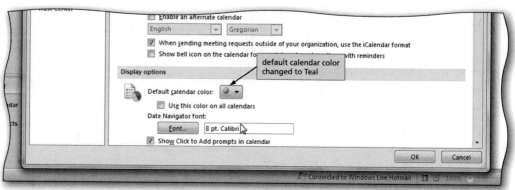

Figure 5–57

● Click the Font button (Outlook Options dialog box) to display the Font dialog box (Figure 5–58).

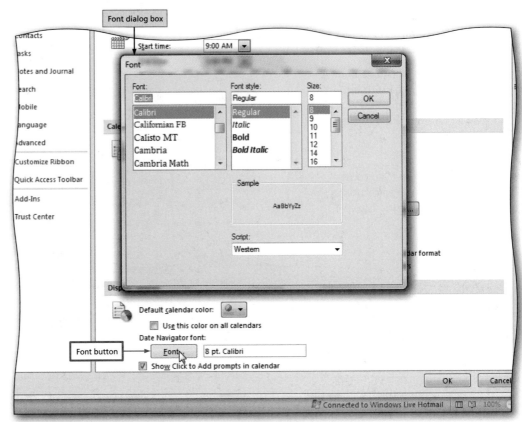

Figure 5–58

④

● Scroll in the Font scroll box until Broadway is visible.

● Click Broadway to select it (Figure 5–59).

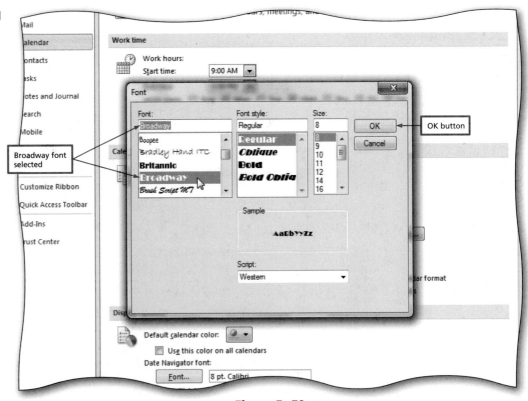

Figure 5–59

5
- Click the OK button (Font dialog box) to return to the Outlook Options dialog box (Figure 5–60).

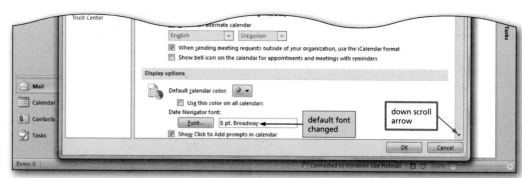

Figure 5–60

To Change the Time Zone Setting

You will be working in a different time zone for a few months while you are in Chicago consulting with a company to create their Web site. You want to learn how to change the time zone of your calendar, so that you can set it to Central Time while you are in Chicago.

The following steps change the time zone to Central Time.

1
- Scroll down until the Time zones settings are visible in the Outlook Options dialog box (Figure 5–61).

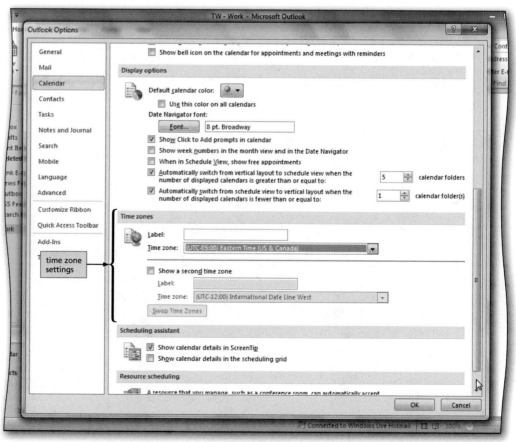

Figure 5–61

- Click the Time zone box arrow to display a list of time zones (Figure 5–62).

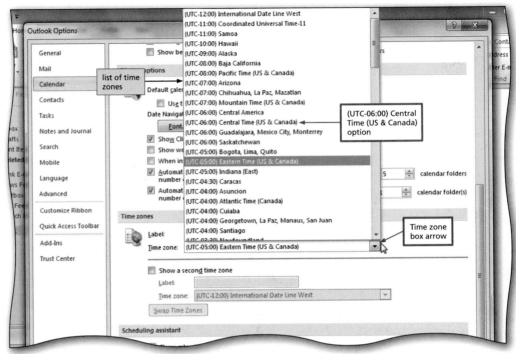

Figure 5–62

- If necessary, click (UTC-06:00) Central Time (US & Canada) to select the time zone (Figure 5–63).

- Click the OK button (Outlook Options dialog box) to close the Outlook Options dialog box.

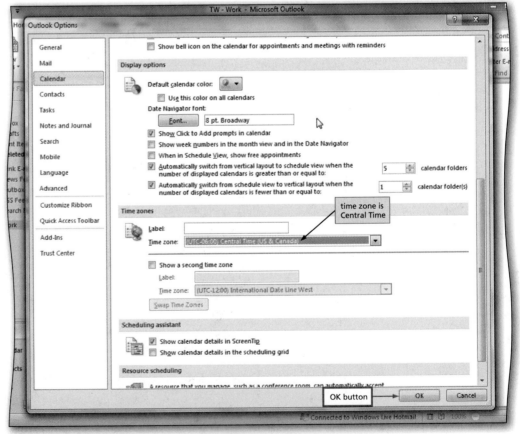

Figure 5–63

To Preview Calendar Changes

You now need to preview the changes you made to see how they look in the calendar. The following steps display the TW – Work calendar.

1 Click the Calendar button in the Navigation Pane to display the Calendar.

2 Show only Trevor's calendar for the TW – Work account.

3 If necessary, click the Work Week button (Home tab | Arrange group) to see the calendar work week (Figure 5–64).

4 Click the Mail button in the Navigation Pane to return to the mailbox.

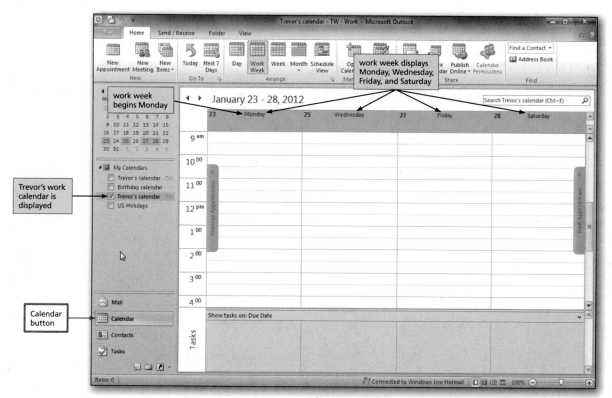

Figure 5–64

Break Point: If you wish to take a break, this is a good place to do so. To resume at a later time, start Outlook and continue following the steps from this location forward.

BTW

Advanced Options
In addition to the various Outlook options presented in this chapter, Outlook allows users to view and change advanced options. To access the advanced options, open the Outlook Options dialog box and then click Advanced in the Category list.

Setting Other Outlook Options

Other Outlook options you can set include customizing Instant Search settings and the Ribbon. When you search Outlook items, such as to find e-mail messages that contain a certain word in the Subject line, Outlook searches the current folder by default. For example, if you are working with sent items, Outlook searches only in the Sent Items folder. However, if you are often searching for items that can be in any one of your folders, you can customize Outlook to search all folders instead. Outlook also highlights in yellow search terms in the search results and improves the search speed by limiting the number of results shown. You can change these default settings by selecting a different highlight color and not limiting the search results.

If you commonly perform certain actions, you can add a button for that action to a tab on the Ribbon. Outlook allows you to customize any tab by adding buttons to it. Outlook also allows you to create your own tabs on the Ribbon.

To Customize Instant Search Options

The following steps change the instant search options to include all folders, highlight search terms in light blue, and display all results.

1

- If necessary, click File to open the Backstage view, and then click Options to display the Outlook Options dialog box.

- Click Search in the Navigation area to display the Search settings (Figure 5–65).

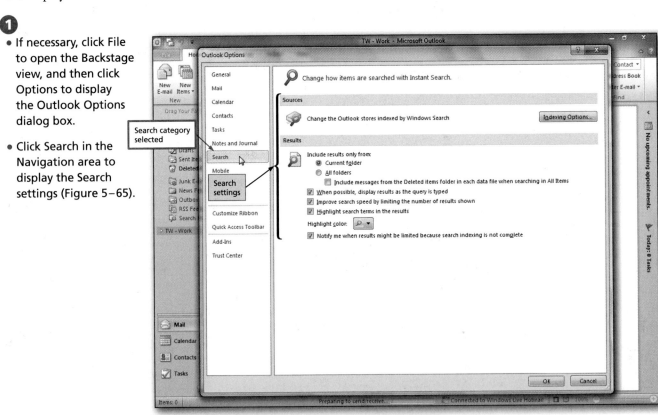

Figure 5–65

• Click the All folders
option button to
configure Outlook to
search in all folders,
not only the current
folder (Figure 5–66).

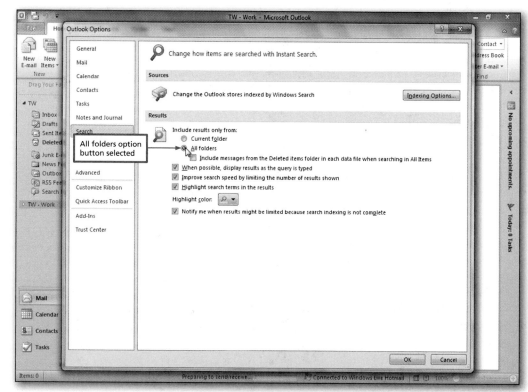

Figure 5–66

• Click the 'Improve
search speed by
limiting the number
of results shown'
check box to remove
the check mark
(Figure 5–67).

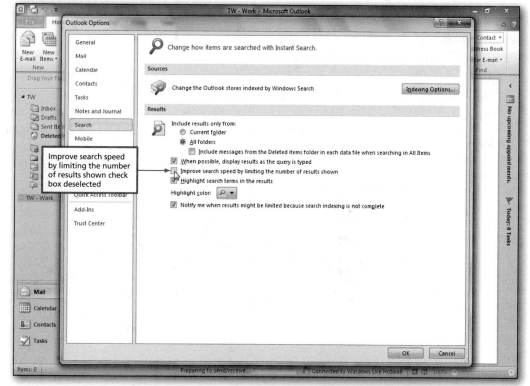

Figure 5–67

- Click the Highlight color button arrow to display a list of colors.

- Click Light Blue (column 3, last row) to select it and change the highlight color to light blue (Figure 5–68).

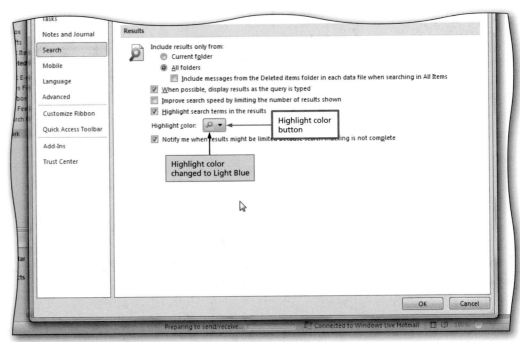

Figure 5–68

To Customize the Outlook Ribbon

You often print Outlook information, and want to add the Print button to the Home tab on the Ribbon. You need to add a group to the Home tab before you can add the command. You decide to add a Printing group to the Home tab and then add the Print command. The following steps add the Print button to a Printing group on the Home tab.

- Click Customize Ribbon in the Navigation area to display the Customize Ribbon options (Figure 5–69).

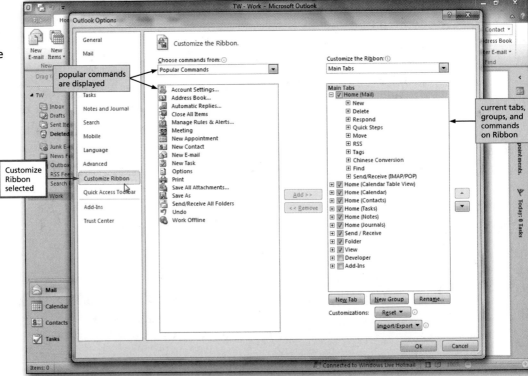

Figure 5–69

2

- Click the New Group button (Outlook Options dialog box) to add a new group to the Home tab (Figure 5–70).

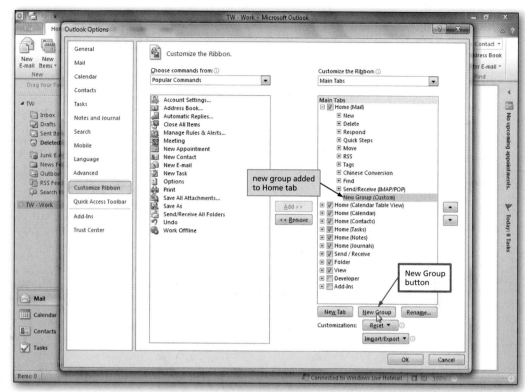

Figure 5–70

3

- Click the Rename button (Outlook Options dialog box) to display the Rename dialog box (Figure 5–71).

Q&A

What can I do with the icons in the Rename dialog box?

When you rename a custom group, you can select an icon to represent that group. The icon appears if the Ribbon is resized so much that the group name cannot be displayed.

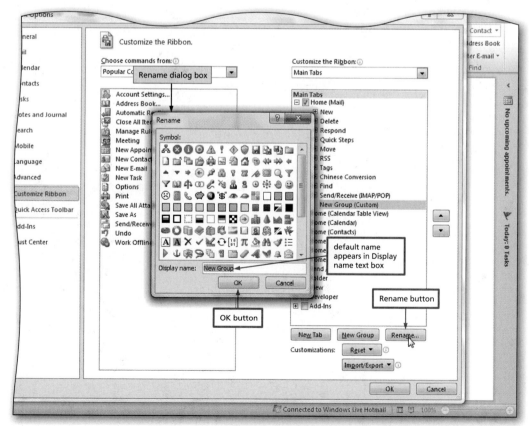

Figure 5–71

4

- Type **Printing** in the Display name text box to enter a name for the group.

- Click the OK button (Rename dialog box) to rename the group (Figure 5–72).

 Why does it say (Custom) next to the name of the new group?

The Custom designation indicates that this is a custom group, and not a default group on the Microsoft Outlook Ribbon. This additional text is not displayed next to the group name on the Ribbon.

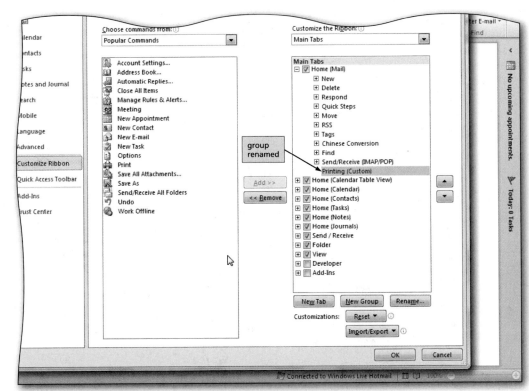

Figure 5–72

5

- Click Print in the Popular Commands list to select it (Figure 5–73).

Figure 5–73

6

- Click the Add button (Outlook Options dialog box) to add the Print command to the Printing (Custom) group on the Home tab (Figure 5–74).

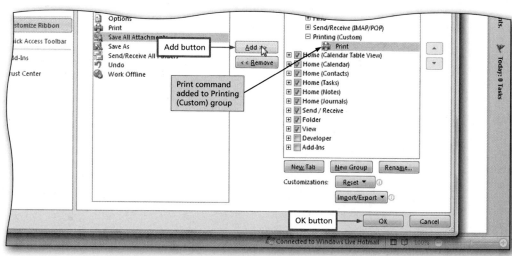

Figure 5–74

7

- Click the OK button (Outlook Options dialog box) to save the changes to the Ribbon and close the Outlook Options dialog box (Figure 5–75).

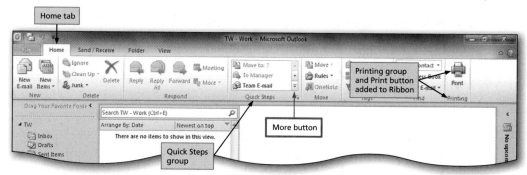

Figure 5–75

Creating Quick Steps

Outlook 2010 introduces a new feature called Quick Steps. A **Quick Step** applies multiple actions at once to an e-mail message. Quick Steps are designed to help you quickly manage your mailbox by automating common tasks. For example, if you commonly read your e-mail messages and move them to a certain location, you could create a Quick Step to perform that action. Table 5–2 lists the Quick Steps included by default in Outlook.

Table 5–2 Quick Steps	
Quick step	**Description**
Move to	Selected message is moved to a folder you have specified
To Manager	Messages are automatically forwarded to your manager
Team E-mail	Messages are forwarded to members of your team
Done	Message is moved to a folder, marked as complete and read
Reply & Delete	Creates a reply to a message, and deletes the original
Create New	Allows you to create your own Quick Step

The first time you use a default Quick Step, Outlook prompts you to configure the Quick Step according to your preferences. You also can use the Create New option to create your own Quick Steps.

Plan
Ahead

Decide what set of actions you want to use as Quick Steps.
You should only create Quick Steps for tasks you are going to perform repeatedly. To take advantage of the timesaving feature of Quick Steps, the tasks you choose to automate should involve more than one step, such as filing messages in a particular folder. Pay attention to tasks you perform frequently, and then determine whether you would save time by using or creating a Quick Step.

To Create a Folder

You want to create a Quick Step for copying selected work e-mail messages to a folder named Work. First, you need to create the Work folder. The following steps create the Work folder.

1 Display the Folder tab.

2 Click the New Folder button (Folder Tab | New group) to display the Create New Folder dialog box.

3 Type **Work** in the Name text box to enter a name for the folder.

4 Click the OK button (Create New Folder dialog box) to create the folder.

To Create a New Quick Step

Now you are ready to create the Quick Step. When you select certain work e-mail messages, you do not want to move them from your mailbox, but rather want to create a copy of each message as a backup.

The following steps create a Quick Step called Work Copy that copies selected messages to the Work folder.

- Display the Home tab.

- Click the More button (Home tab | Quick Steps group) to display the Quick Steps gallery (Figure 5–76).

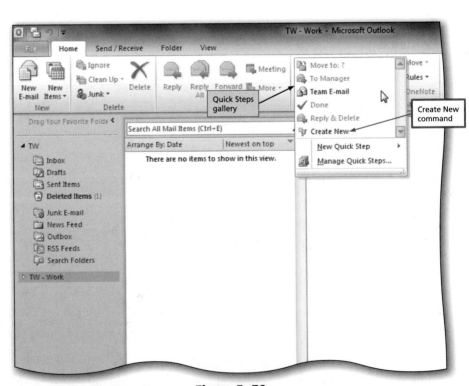

Figure 5–76

2

- Click the Create New command to display the Edit Quick Step dialog box (Figure 5–77).

Figure 5–77

3

- Type **Work Copy** in the Name text box to name the Quick Step.

- Click the Choose an Action box arrow to display a list of actions (Figure 5–78).

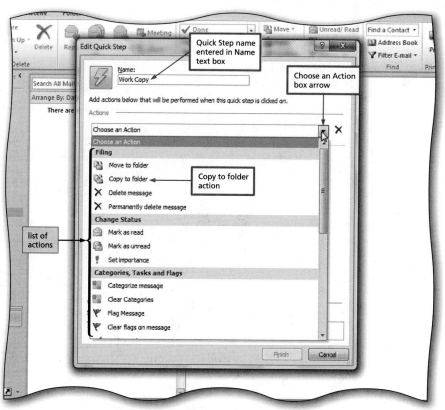

Figure 5–78

4

• Click 'Copy to folder' to select the action (Figure 5–79).

Figure 5–79

5

• Click the Choose folder box arrow to display a list of folders.

• Click Work – TW – Work to choose Work as the folder for the copies (Figure 5–80).

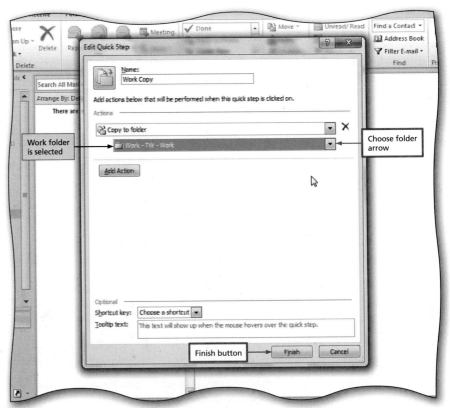

Figure 5–80

6

- Click the Finish button (Edit Quick Step dialog box) to finish creating the Quick Step and close the Edit Quick Step dialog box (Figure 5–81).

Q&A

Instead of creating a new Quick Step from scratch, can I duplicate an existing Quick Step and make some changes?

Yes. To duplicate a Quick Step, click the Manage Quick Steps Dialog Box Launcher (Home tab | Quick Steps group), click the name of the Quick Step to duplicate, click the Duplicate button (Manage Quick Steps dialog box), make the desired changes in the Edit Quick Step dialog box, and then click the Finish button (Edit Quick Step dialog box).

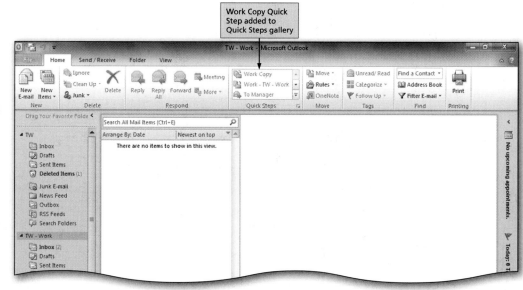

Figure 5–81

To Use a Quick Step

Now that you have created the Quick Step, you can use it. The following steps apply the Work Copy Quick Step.

1

- Click Inbox in the Navigation Pane for the TW – Work account to select the Inbox folder (Figure 5–82).

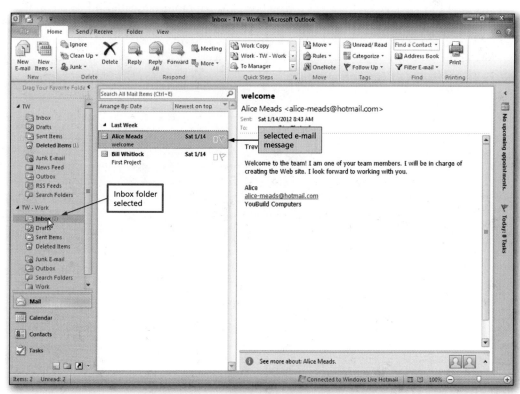

Figure 5–82

2

- Click the Work Copy Quick Step (Home tab | Quick Steps group) to copy the selected e-mail message to the Work folder (Figure 5–83).

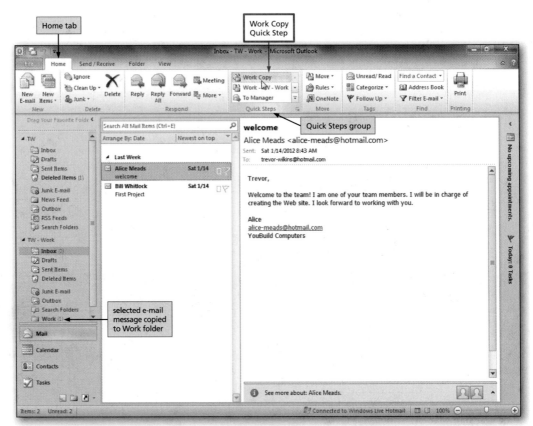

Figure 5–83

To Manage Quick Steps

Using the Manage Quick Steps dialog box, you can modify, create, and delete Quick Steps. You decide that you no longer need the Work Copy Quick Step, so you want to delete it.

The following steps delete the Work Copy Quick Step.

1

- Click the More button (Home tab | Quick Steps group) to display the Quick Steps gallery.

- Click Manage Quick Steps to display the Manage Quick Steps dialog box (Figure 5–84).

Q&A After making changes, can I reset Quick Steps to their default settings?

Yes. Click the Reset to Defaults button (Manage Quick Steps dialog box), and then click the Yes button when the Microsoft Outlook dialog box is displayed.

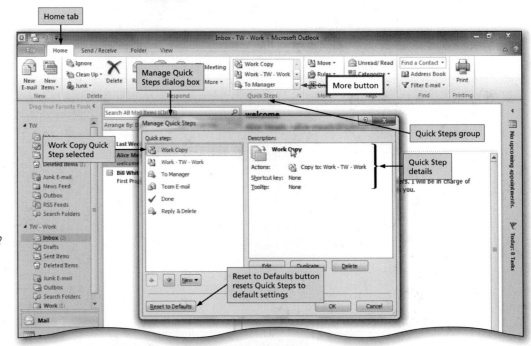

Figure 5–84

- Click the Delete button (Manage Quick Steps dialog box) to delete the selected Quick Step (Figure 5–85).

Figure 5–85

- Click the OK button (Manage Quick Steps dialog box) to close the Manage Quick Steps dialog box (Figure 5–86).

Figure 5–86

Break Point: If you wish to take a break, this is a good place to do so. To resume at a later time, start Outlook and continue following the steps from this location forward.

Working with Rules

To further automate the processing of e-mail messages in Outlook, you can create rules. A **rule** is a set of instructions that tells Outlook how to handle e-mail messages that are in your mailbox. You can create rules that apply to received e-mail messages and rules that apply to sent e-mail messages. You could specify that e-mail messages from a particular user be categorized automatically or placed in a specified folder, for example. Rules can be created from a template or from scratch based upon conditions you specify. Rules apply to an e-mail account, not a single folder or file. If you are working with a data file instead of an e-mail account, you cannot create rules.

<table>
<tr><td>Plan
Ahead</td><td>**Plan rules to use with your e-mail messages.**
Consider using rules to help you manage e-mail messages and keep organized and up to date. If you cannot respond to e-mail messages right away, for example, you could create a rule to send automatic replies. Or if you wanted to flag all e-mail messages from your boss for follow-up, you could create a rule for that. Try to determine what rules you would like to have Outlook run automatically, and which ones you want to run manually.</td></tr>
</table>

To simplify the process of creating rules, Outlook provides a Rules Wizard, which presents a list of conditions for selecting an e-mail message and then lists actions to take with messages that meet the conditions. If necessary, you also can specify exceptions to the rule. For example, you can send certain messages to a specified folder unless they are sent with high importance.

To Create a New Rule

You would like to create a rule to flag all e-mail messages from your boss, Bill Whitlock, for follow-up. This way, you can easily remember to follow up with him on important tasks.

The following steps create a rule that automatically flags e-mail messages from Bill Whitlock. If you are using the TW – Work data file, you cannot create a rule for the e-mail messages in the file. To practice creating a rule, switch to an Outlook e-mail account and use a message from someone other than Bill Whitlock to complete the following steps. Otherwise, read but do not perform the following steps.

- Click the Bill Whitlock e-mail message to select it (Figure 5–87).

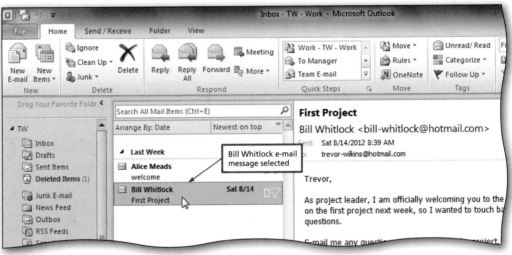

Figure 5–87

❷
- Click the Rules button (Home tab | Move group) to display a list of rule options (Figure 5–88).

Figure 5–88

3

- Click the Create Rule command to display the Create Rule dialog box (Figure 5–89).

Q&A

What should I do if trevor-wilkins@hotmail.com appears in the Sent to text box instead of "me only" as shown in Figure 5–89?

If you opened the TW – Work data file instead of creating an e-mail account at the beginning of this chapter, the trevor-wilkins@hotmail.com e-mail address appears instead of "me only." That means you cannot create a rule for the TW – Work account.

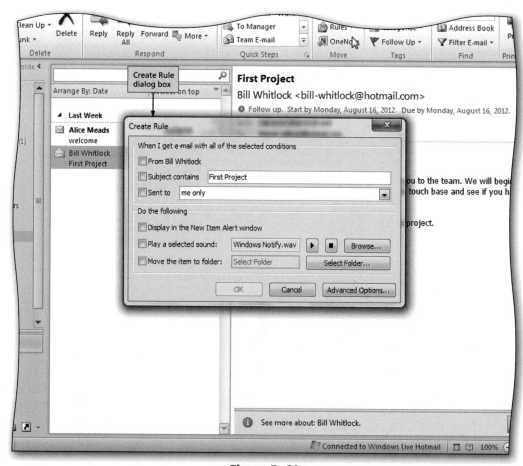

Figure 5–89

4

- Click the From Bill Whitlock check box to select it (Figure 5–90).

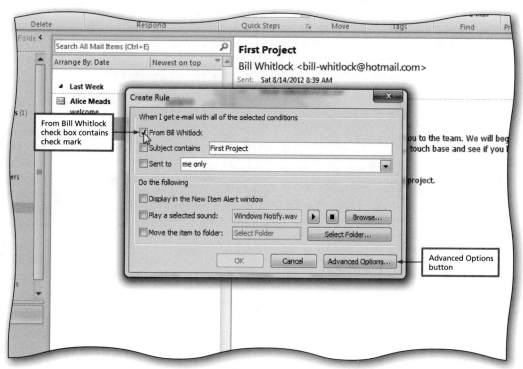

Figure 5–90

5

- Click the Advanced Options button (Create Rule dialog box) to display the Rules Wizard dialog box (Figure 5–91).

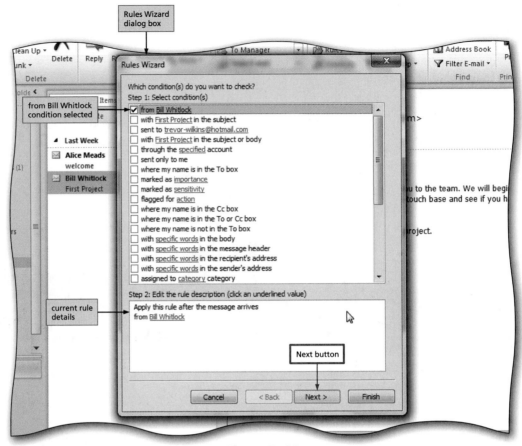

Figure 5–91

6

- Click the Next button (Rules Wizard dialog box) to continue to the next step, where you specify one or more actions to take with a selected message (Figure 5–92).

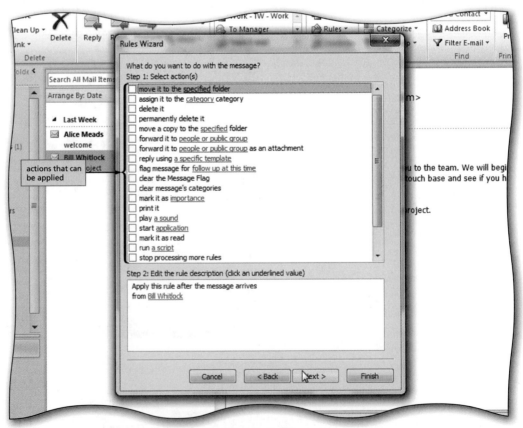

Figure 5–92

• Click the 'flag message for follow up at this time' check box to select it (Figure 5–93).

Q&A

What is the effect of selecting the 'flag message for follow up at this time' check box?

Messages that meet the conditions you specified, in this case, messages from Bill Whitlock, will appear in the message list with a flag icon to indicate the need to be followed up.

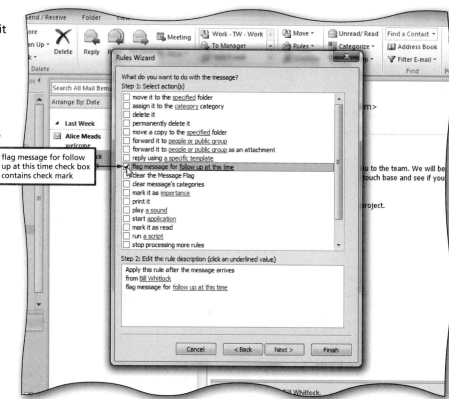

Figure 5–93

• Click the 'follow up at this time' link in the Step 2 area to display the Flag Message dialog box (Figure 5–94).

Q&A

For what can I use the Flag Message dialog box?

You can flag a message for follow up (the default) or for other options, including For Your Information, No Response Necessary, and Reply. You also can specify when to follow up: Today (the default), Tomorrow, This Week, Next Week, No Date, or Complete.

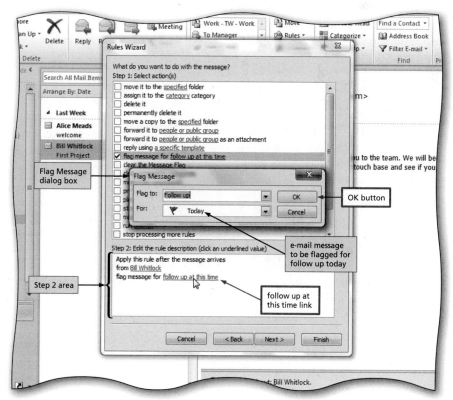

Figure 5–94

9

- Click the OK button (Flag Message dialog box) to accept the default settings and return to the Rules Wizard dialog box (Figure 5–95).

10

- Click the Finish button (Rules Wizard dialog box) to save the Rule.

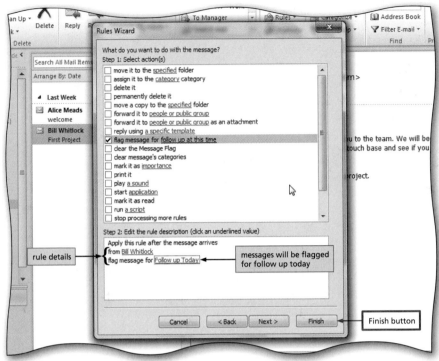

Figure 5–95

Other Ways

1. Click File, click Info, click Rules and Alerts

To Run Rules

Rules that you create run for all incoming e-mail messages received after creating the rule. If you want to apply rules to e-mail messages that you already have received, you use the Rules and Alerts dialog box. The following steps run the newly created rule.

1

- Click the Rules button (Home tab | Move group) to display a list of rule options.

- Click the Manage Rules & Alerts command to display the Rules and Alerts dialog box (Figure 5–96).

Q&A

After I create a rule, can I modify it?

Yes. To modify an existing rule, select the rule you want to modify, click the Change Rule button, and then click the Edit Rule Settings command. Next, make the desired changes in the Rules Wizard. Click the Finish button after making all necessary changes.

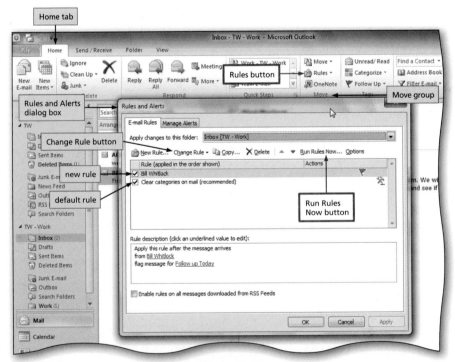

Figure 5–96

2

- Click the Run Rules Now button (Rules and Alerts dialog box) to display the Run Rules Now dialog box.

- Click the Bill Whitlock check box to select it and specify the rule that will run.

- Click the Run Now button (Run Rules Now dialog box) to run the rule (Figure 5–97).

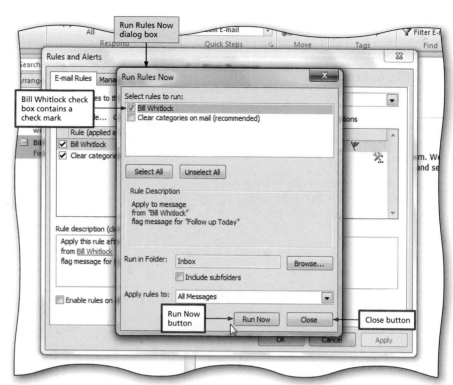

Figure 5–97

3

- Click the Close button (Run Rules Now dialog box) to close the Run Rules Now dialog box.

- Click the OK button (Rules and Alerts dialog box) to close the Rules and Alerts dialog box (Figure 5–98).

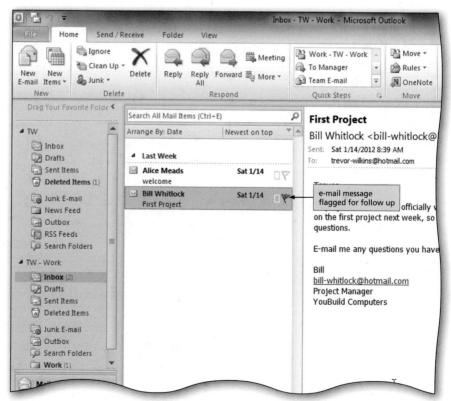

Figure 5–98

To Delete a Rule

Once you no longer need a rule, you should delete it. After further consideration, you decide that you do not need to flag all e-mail messages from your boss; therefore, you decide to delete the rule.

The following steps delete the Bill Whitlock rule.

- Click the Rules button (Home tab | Move group) to display a list of rule options.

- Click the Manage Rules and Alerts command to display the Rules and Alerts dialog box (Figure 5–99).

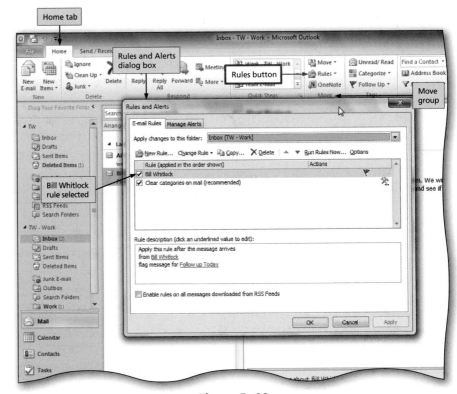

Figure 5–99

- Click the Delete button (Rules and Alerts dialog box) to display the Microsoft Outlook dialog box (Figure 5–100).

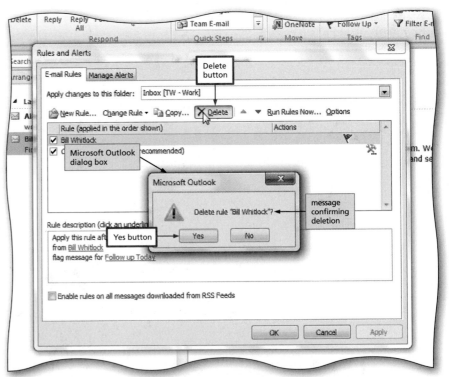

Figure 5–100

- Click the Yes button (Microsoft Outlook dialog box) to delete the Bill Whitlock rule (Figure 5–101).

- Click the OK button (Rules and Alerts dialog box) to close the Rules and Alerts dialog box.

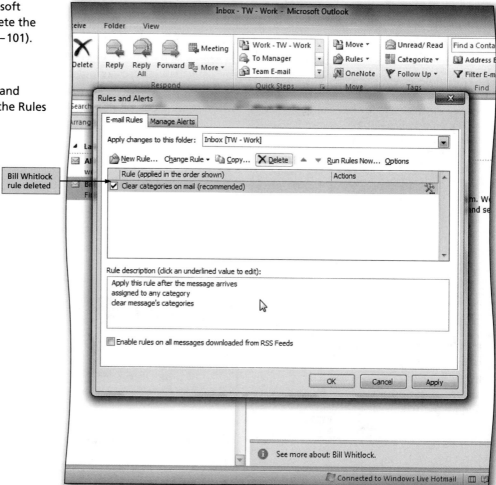

Figure 5–101

To Set Up Automatic Replies

Outlook provides a quick way to set up automatic replies for when you may be out of the office; however, your e-mail account must support automatic replies. If you wanted to set up automatic replies, you would use the following steps.

1. Display the Backstage view.
2. Click Info in the Backstage view to display account information.
3. Click Automatic Replies to display the Automatic Replies dialog box.
4. Click 'Send automatic replies' to turn on automatic replies.
5. Change the Start time to select the day and time for the automatic replies to start.
6. Change the End time to select the day and time for the automatic replies to stop.
7. Select Inside My Organization and enter an e-mail message for e-mail messages to be sent inside your organization.
8. Select Outside My Organization and enter an e-mail message for e-mail messages to be sent outside your organization.
9. Click OK to save the rule for automatic replies.

BTW

Cleanup Tools
In addition to archiving
e-mail messages, Outlook
provides cleanup tools to
help control the size of
your mailbox. To access
the various cleanup tools,
display the Backstage
view, click the Info tab, if
necessary, click the Cleanup
Tools button, and then click
the desired cleanup tool
you want to access.

Configuring AutoArchive

AutoArchive allows you to set up automatic archiving within Outlook so that older
Outlook items are moved to a separate Outlook data file, where you can access them by
opening the file in Outlook. People often forget to back up or archive their messages.
In the case of computer or e-mail failures, important messages could be lost if they are not
backed up or archived. Archiving also allows you to keep your Inbox at a manageable size.
It can be difficult to manage an Inbox that has several hundred messages.

To Set AutoArchive Settings

You decide that you should back up the e-mail messages in your e-mail account. By default, when turned on,
Outlook will archive messages every 14 days. The following steps turn on AutoArchive.

1

- Display the Outlook
  Options dialog box.

- Click Advanced
  in the Category
  list to display
  advanced options
  (Figure 5–102).

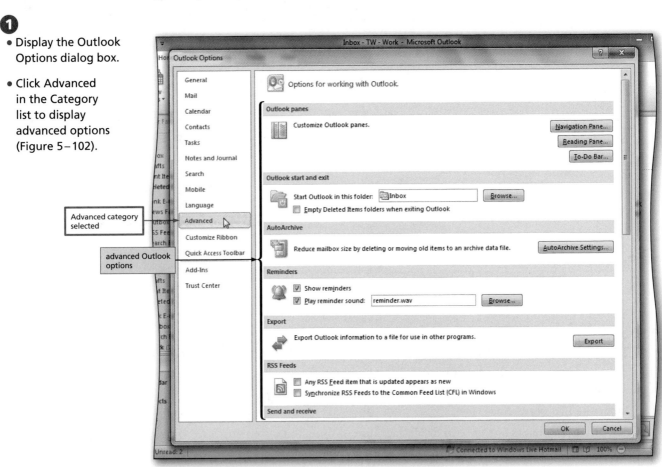

Figure 5–102

- Click the AutoArchive Settings button (Outlook Options dialog box) to display the AutoArchive dialog box (Figure 5–103).

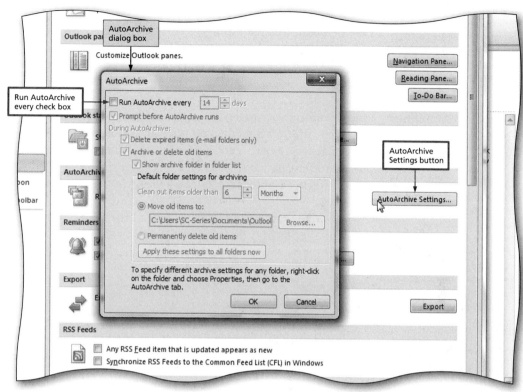

Figure 5–103

- Click the Run AutoArchive every check box to select it and enable AutoArchive (Figure 5–104).

- Click the OK button (AutoArchive dialog box) to close the AutoArchive dialog box.

- Click the OK button (Outlook Options dialog box) to close the Outlook Options dialog box.

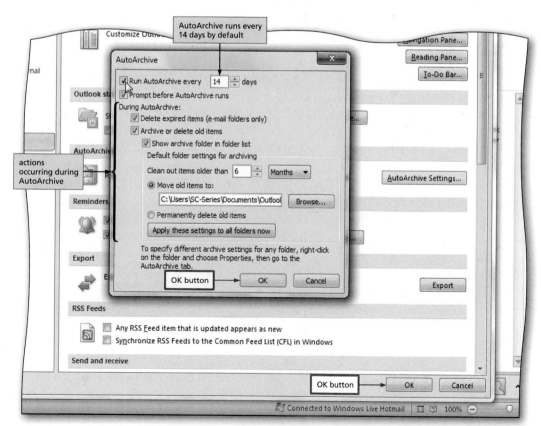

Figure 5–104

BTW

Certification
The Microsoft Office Specialist program provides an opportunity for you to obtain a valuable industry credential — proof that you have the Outlook 2010 skills required by employers. For more information, visit the Outlook 2010 Certification Web page (scsite.com/out2010/cert).

BTW

Quick Reference
For a table that lists how to complete the tasks covered in this book using the mouse, Ribbon, shortcut menu, and keyboard, see the Quick Reference Summary at the back of this book, or visit the Outlook 2010 Quick Reference Web page (scsite.com/out2010/qr).

Working with News Feeds

One of the newer technologies on the Internet is RSS, which stands for Really Simple Syndication. RSS allows Web page authors to easily distribute, or syndicate, Web content. RSS feeds typically are found on news Web sites, discussion boards, blogs, and other Web sites that frequently update their content. For example, the CNN Web site contains two RSS feeds that allow people to view top stories and recent stories in one convenient location. If you frequently visit Web sites that offer RSS feeds, you quickly can review the feed content of all the Web sites in a simple list in your browser by subscribing to their RSS feeds, without having to first navigate to each individual site. If you subscribe to an RSS feed using Internet Explorer, you can access the feed in the Internet Explorer Favorites Center.

If you want to use Outlook to read the feed, you can add the RSS feed using the Account Settings dialog box. Outlook will then let you manage and work with your RSS feed. Some accounts will automatically let you access the feeds from your Web browser if they are using a common feeds folder; however, not all accounts allow for this.

To Subscribe to an RSS Feed

You subscribe to some RSS feeds in your Web browser. You want to use Outlook to view a feed called Life Rocks 2.0 from http://www.nirmaltv.com/feed/. To keep it separate from work, you decide to add it to your personal e-mail account.

The following steps subscribe to the http://www.nirmaltv.com/feed/ RSS feed and display the messages.

1
- Right-click the RSS Feeds folder in the TW mailbox in the Navigation pane to display a shortcut menu (Figure 5–105).

Q&A

What should I do if an RSS Feeds folder does not appear in the TW mailbox?

Right-click the RSS Feeds folder in a different mailbox on your computer.

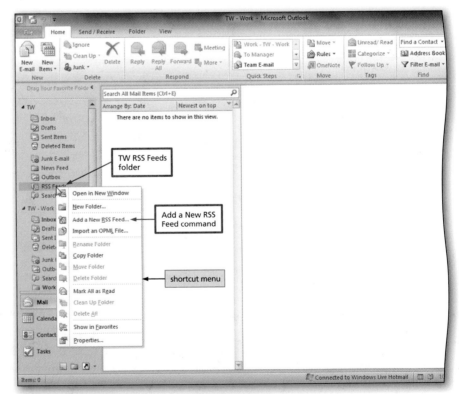

Figure 5–105

2
- Click the Add a New RSS Feed command to display the New RSS Feed dialog box (Figure 5–106).

Figure 5–106

3
- Type `http://www.nirmaltv.com/feed/` in the text box to enter the address of an RSS feed (Figure 5–107).

Figure 5–107

4
- Click the Add button (New RSS Feed dialog box) to add the RSS feed to the RSS Feeds folder.

- Click the Yes button (Microsoft Outlook dialog box) to confirm you want to add the RSS feed (Figure 5–108).

Experiment
- Click the different messages to see what has been posted in the RSS Feeds folder.

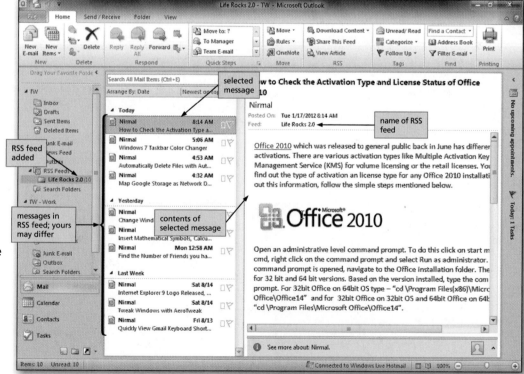

Figure 5–108

To Delete an RSS Feed

When you no longer need to use an RSS feed, you should delete it so that you do not have unwanted messages in your account. The steps on the next page delete the Life Rocks 2.0 RSS feed at http://www.nirmaltv.com/feed/.

1

- Right-click the Life Rocks 2.0 folder in the Navigation Pane to display a shortcut menu (Figure 5–109).

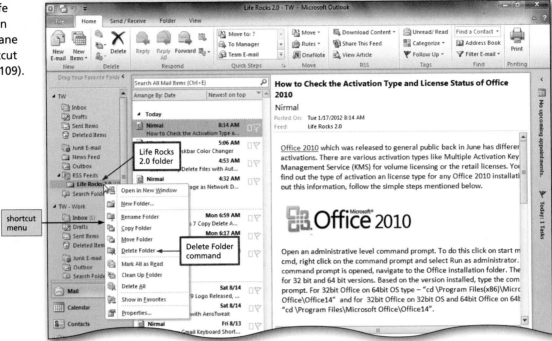

Figure 5–109

2

- Click the Delete Folder command to display the Microsoft Outlook dialog box (Figure 5–110).

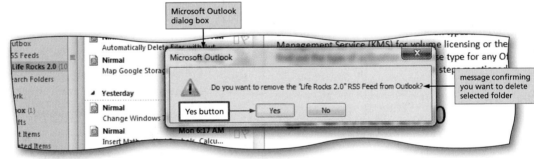

Figure 5–110

3

- Click the Yes button (Microsoft Outlook dialog box) to delete the RSS Feed (Figure 5–111).

Figure 5–111

To Remove an E-Mail Account

When you no longer need an e-mail account, you easily can remove it from Outlook. The following steps remove the TW – Work account.

- Right-click the TW – Work account name in the Navigation Pane to display a shortcut menu (Figure 5–112).

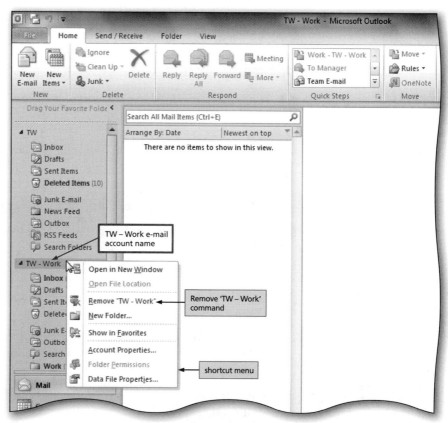

Figure 5–112

- Click the Remove "TW – Work" command to remove the e-mail account from Outlook (Figure 5–113).

Q&A

What should I do if the Remove "TW – Work" command does not appear on the shortcut menu?

If you opened the data file, then Close "TW – Work" appears instead of Remove "TW – Work." In that case, click the Close "TW – Work" command.

- Click the Yes button (Microsoft Outlook dialog box) to remove the TW – Work account.

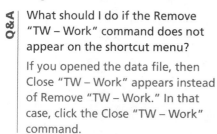

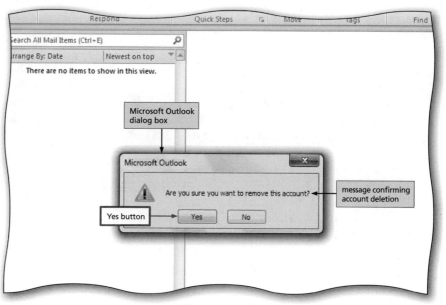

Figure 5–113

To Reset the Time Zone Setting

You should change the time zone back to your original time zone before quitting Outlook. The following steps change the time zone.

1 If necessary, click the File tab to open the Backstage view, and then click Options to display the Outlook Options dialog box.

2 Click Calendar, and then scroll down until the Time Zone settings are visible in the Outlook Options dialog box.

3 Click the Time zone box arrow to display a list of time zones.

4 Click your time zone to select the time zone.

To Quit Outlook

The project is complete. Thus, the following step quits Outlook.

1 Click the Close button on the right side of the title bar to quit Outlook.

Chapter Summary

In this chapter, you have learned how to add an e-mail account, customize Outlook options, create rules, manage Quick Steps, add Rules, and add RSS Feeds. The items listed below include all the new Outlook skills you have learned in this chapter.

1. Add a New E-Mail Account (OUT 238)
2. Configure Junk E-Mail Options (OUT 244)
3. Display Outlook Options (OUT 247)
4. Set the Default Message Format (OUT 248)
5. Configure Spell Checking Options (OUT 249)
6. Create an E-Mail Signature (OUT 252)
7. Format an E-Mail Signature (OUT 253)
8. Add an Image to an E-Mail Signature (OUT 256)
9. Configure Signature Options (OUT 257)
10. Customize Stationery (OUT 259)
11. Change the Work Time on the Calendar (OUT 262)
12. Modify Calendar Options (OUT 264)
13. Change Calendar Display Options (OUT 265)
14. Change the Time Zone Setting (OUT 267)
15. Customize Instant Search Options (OUT 270)
16. Customize the Outlook Ribbon (OUT 272)
17. Create a New Quick Step (OUT 276)
18. Use a Quick Step (OUT 279)
19. Manage Quick Steps (OUT 280)
20. Create a New Rule (OUT 282)
21. Run Rules (OUT 286)
22. Delete a Rule (OUT 288)
23. Set AutoArchive Settings (OUT 290)
24. Subscribe to an RSS Feed (OUT 292)
25. Delete an RSS Feed (OUT 293)
26. Remove an E-Mail Account (OUT 295)

 If you have a SAM 2010 user profile, your instructor may have assigned an autogradable version of this assignment. If so, log into the SAM 2010 Web site at www.cengage.com/sam2010 to download the instruction and start files.

Learn It Online

Test your knowledge of chapter content and key terms.

Instructions: To complete the Learn It Online exercises, start your browser, click the Address bar, and then enter the Web address **scsite.com/out2010/learn**. When the Outlook 2010 Learn It Online page is displayed, click the link for the exercise you want to complete and then read the instructions.

Chapter Reinforcement TF, MC, and SA
A series of true/false, multiple choice, and short answer questions that test your knowledge of the chapter content.

Flash Cards
An interactive learning environment where you identify chapter key terms associated with displayed definitions.

Practice Test
A series of multiple choice questions that test your knowledge of chapter content and key terms.

Who Wants To Be a Computer Genius?
An interactive game that challenges your knowledge of chapter content in the style of a television quiz show.

Wheel of Terms
An interactive game that challenges your knowledge of chapter key terms in the style of the television show *Wheel of Fortune*.

Crossword Puzzle Challenge
A crossword puzzle that challenges your knowledge of key terms presented in the chapter.

Apply Your Knowledge

Reinforce the skills and apply the concepts you learned in this chapter.

Creating a Signature
Instructions: Start Outlook. You will be using the Signatures and Stationery dialog box (Figure 5–114) to create a signature to use when you e-mail members of your debate team.

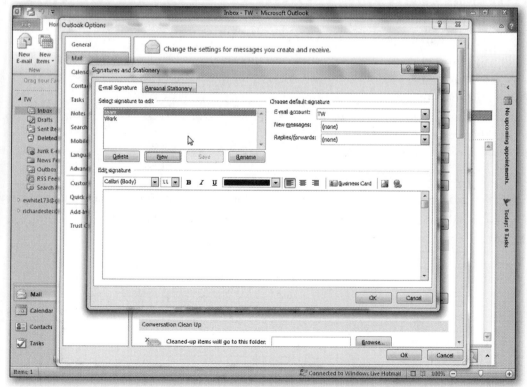

Figure 5–114

Continued >

Apply Your Knowledge *continued*

Perform the following tasks:
1. Display the Outlook Options dialog box. Click Mail and then click the Signatures button to display the Signatures and Stationery dialog box.
2. Click the New button to create a signature. Type `team` as the name of the signature.
3. Change the font to Algerian and the font size to 18.
4. On three lines, enter the following information: your name, your e-mail address, and the text `Debate Team News`.
5. Set the signature to apply to new messages.
6. Click the Personal Stationery tab and click the Theme button.
7. Select the Studio theme as your stationery.
8. Accept the changes in the dialog boxes and then create a new e-mail message addressed to your instructor to display your new signature and stationery.
9. Submit the e-mail message in the format specified by your instructor.

Extend Your Knowledge

Extend the skills you learned in this chapter and experiment with new skills. You may need to use Help to complete the assignment.

Creating and Adding an E-Mail Account
Instructions: You are going to create a Windows Live e-mail account. You will need to read and use the instructions provided by Windows Live to create the account (Figure 5 – 115). You will then add the e-mail account to Outlook and send an e-mail to your instructor.

Perform the following tasks:
1. Open your Web browser and navigate to www.live.com. Click the Sign Up button (or other appropriate button) to create a new account.
2. Follow the instructions to create an e-mail account using your last name as part of the Windows Live ID. If you already have a Windows Live account, create another one for this exercise. Make sure to follow all instructions.
3. Log on to your new e-mail account in the Web browser and, if necessary, follow the instructions to verify your account.
4. Log off of the account and close your Web browser.
5. Start Outlook and open the Account Settings dialog box.
6. Click New to display the Add New Account dialog box and add your e-mail account to Outlook.
7. Use the new Windows Live account to create an e-mail message addressed to your instructor. Submit the e-mail message in the format specified by your instructor.

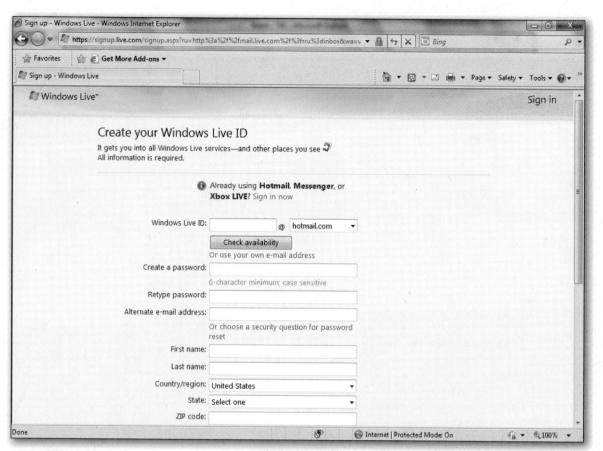

Figure 5–115

Make It Right

Analyze tasks and correct all errors and/or improve the design.

Copying and Modifying a Signature

Note: To complete this assignment, you will be required to use the Data Files for Students. See the inside back cover of this book for instructions on downloading the Data Files for Students, or contact your instructor for information about accessing the required files.

Instructions: Start Outlook. Import the Make It Right 5-1 folder from the Data Files for Students folder into Outlook.

Your boss has sent you an e-mail message using a signature that he suggests you customize for your own use. He also asks you to change the stationery for your messages.

Perform the following tasks:

1. Display the Make It Right 5–1 message in the Outlook Mail window. Open the e-mail message from Richard Estes (Figure 5–116 on the next page).
2. Create a new signature and name it MakeItRight using the Signatures and Stationery dialog box.
3. Change the font to Biondi (or any other font) and the font size to 14. Enter the text from the Richard Estes e-mail as the new signature. Change the name to your name.
4. Using the Personal Stationery tab, change the theme to Level.
5. Save all your changes, and then submit an e-mail message with your signature in the format specified by your instructor.

Continued >

Make It Right *continued*

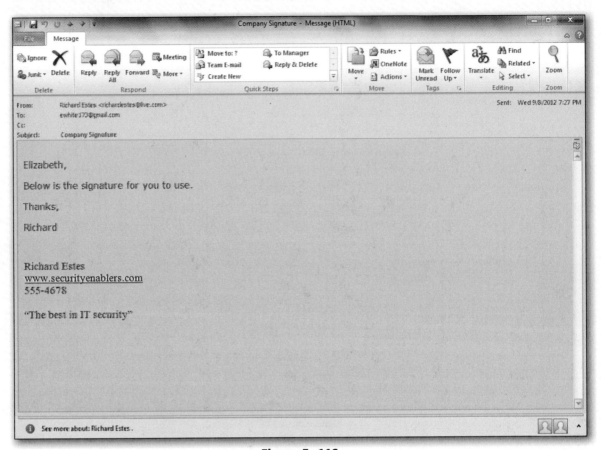

Figure 5–116

In the Lab

Design, create, modify, and/or use signatures and rules using the guidelines, concepts, and skills presented in this chapter. Labs are listed in order of increasing difficulty.

Lab 1: Creating Custom Signatures

Problem: You communicate with the professors for your biology and physics classes via e-mail. They ask all of their students to clearly identify themselves in their e-mail messages. To do so, you will create e-mail signatures for the messages you send to your biology and physics professors. You will use the Signatures and Stationery dialog box to create the signatures (Figure 5–117).

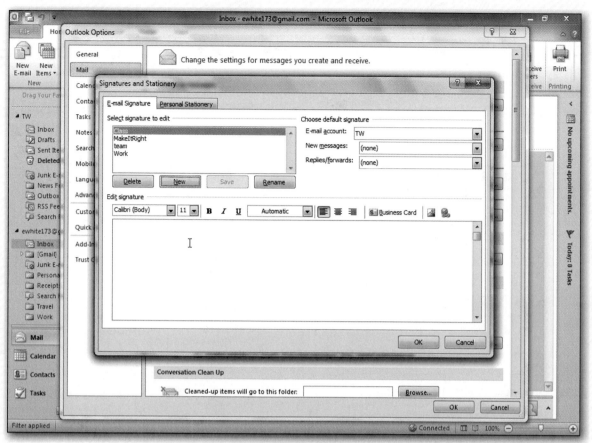

Figure 5–117

Perform the following tasks:

1. Display the Outlook Options dialog box. Click Mail and then click the Signatures button to display the Signatures and Stationery dialog box.

2. Click the New button to create a signature. Type **Biology** as the name of the signature.

3. Change the font to Century and the font size to 16.

4. On three lines, enter the following information: your name, **BIO 202**, and **Professor Sanchez's MW Class**.

5. Using the Biology signature, submit an e-mail message in the format specified by your instructor.

6. Display the Outlook Options dialog box. Click Mail and then click the Signatures button to display the Signatures and Stationery dialog box.

7. Click the New button to create a signature. Type **Physics** as the name of the signature.

8. Change the font to Century, the font size to 18, and the font color to green.

9. On three lines, enter the following information: your name, **PHY 112**, and **Dr. Wood's T Class**.

10. Using the Physics signature, submit an e-mail message in the format specified by your instructor.

In the Lab

Lab 2: Adding an RSS Feed

Problem: You are in charge of ordering new computer parts for your IT department. You regularly use a computer parts Web site (Figure 5–118) that has an RSS feed. You want to add that feed to your Outlook e-mail account.

Figure 5–118

Perform the following tasks:

1. In Outlook, right-click the RSS Feeds folder (or the feeds folder for your e-mail account) and then display the New RSS Feed dialog box.

2. Enter `http://www.newegg.com/Product/RSS.aspx?Submit=RSSDailyDeals` as the address to add.

3. Add the feed to Outlook.

4. Open the first RSS message.

5. Print the message and then submit it in the format specified by your instructor.

In the Lab

Lab 3: Configuring Junk E-Mail

Problem: You occasionally find e-mail you want to read in the Junk E-mail folder for your Outlook e-mail account. You also receive spam from a certain e-mail address. You want to use the Junk E-mail Options dialog box (Figure 5–119) to make sure you receive e-mail messages from some senders, while blocking e-mail from another sender.

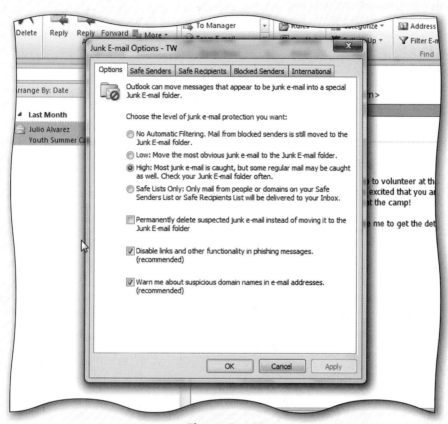

Figure 5–119

Perform the following tasks:

1. In Outlook, display the Junk E-mail Options dialog box.

2. Click the Safe Senders tab.

3. Add www.microsoft.com to the Safe Senders list. Write down what is displayed in the Safe Senders list.

4. Click the Safe Recipients tab. Add ewhite173@gmail.com to the Safe Recipients list. Write down what is displayed in the Safe Recipients list.

5. Click the Blocked Senders tab. Add @crazyedigames.com to the Blocked Senders list. Write down what is displayed in the Blocked Senders list.

6. Submit what you have recorded in the format specified by your instructor.

Cases and Places

Apply your creative thinking and problem solving skills to design and implement a solution.

1: Create Rules

Academic

For three of the classes you are currently taking, create mail folders for each class. Create rules to move messages related to the classes to the appropriate class mail folder. Write a rule for one class that flags messages for follow-up within five days. Write down the rules and then submit your work in the format specified by your instructor.

2: Subscribe to Feeds

Professional

Research and find four RSS feeds for professional development such as http://www.convergemag.com/rss/ or http://www.connectusers.com/feeds/news.rss (both for careers in education). Subscribe to the feeds in Outlook and review some of the messages. Print a message from each feed, write a paragraph summarizing what you feel the sites offer, and submit it in the format specified by your instructor.

3: Create QuickSteps

Personal

Create some Quick Steps to help you in working with your e-mail messages. Create a Family mail folder and an Archive mail folder. Create a Quick Step that stores e-mail messages sent by a family member in the Family folder. Create another Quick Step that flags e-mail messages containing the words *family reunion* for follow-up within a month. Configure the already existing Move to: ? Quick Step to move e-mail messages to the Archive mail folder. Write down the steps you performed to create each Quick Step. Submit your steps in the format specified by your instructor.

NOTES

NOTES

NOTES

NOTES

Appendix A

Project Planning Guidelines

Using Project Planning Guidelines

The process of communicating specific information to others is a learned, rational skill. Computers and software, especially Microsoft Office 2010, can help you develop ideas and present detailed information to a particular audience.

Using Microsoft Office 2010, you can create projects such as Word documents, PowerPoint presentations, Excel spreadsheets, and Access databases. Productivity software such as Microsoft Office 2010 minimizes much of the laborious work of drafting and revising projects. Some communicators handwrite ideas in notebooks, others compose directly on the computer, and others have developed unique strategies that work for their own particular thinking and writing styles.

No matter what method you use to plan a project, follow specific guidelines to arrive at a final product that presents information correctly and effectively (Figure A–1). Use some aspects of these guidelines every time you undertake a project, and others as needed in specific instances. For example, in determining content for a project, you may decide that a chart communicates trends more effectively than a paragraph of text. If so, you would create this graphical element and insert it in an Excel spreadsheet, a Word document, or a PowerPoint slide.

Determine the Project's Purpose

Begin by clearly defining why you are undertaking this assignment. For example, you may want to track monetary donations collected for your club's fund-raising drive. Alternatively, you may be urging students to vote for a particular candidate in the next election. Once you clearly understand the purpose of your task, begin to draft ideas of how best to communicate this information.

Analyze Your Audience

Learn about the people who will read, analyze, or view your work. Where are they employed? What are their educational backgrounds? What are their expectations? What questions do they have?

PROJECT PLANNING GUIDELINES

1. DETERMINE THE PROJECT'S PURPOSE
Why are you undertaking the project?

2. ANALYZE YOUR AUDIENCE
Who are the people who will use your work?

3. GATHER POSSIBLE CONTENT
What information exists, and in what forms?

4. DETERMINE WHAT CONTENT TO PRESENT TO YOUR AUDIENCE
What information will best communicate the project's purpose to your audience?

Figure A–1

Design experts suggest drawing a mental picture of these people or finding photos of people who fit this profile so that you can develop a project with the audience in mind.

By knowing your audience members, you can tailor a project to meet their interests and needs. You will not present them with information they already possess, and you will not omit the information they need to know.

Example: Your assignment is to raise the profile of your college's nursing program in the community. How much do they know about your college and the nursing curriculum? What are the admission requirements? How many of the applicants admitted complete the program? What percent pass the state board exams?

Gather Possible Content

Rarely are you in a position to develop all the material for a project. Typically, you would begin by gathering existing information that may reside in spreadsheets or databases. Web sites, pamphlets, magazine and newspaper articles, and books could provide insights of how others have approached your topic. Personal interviews often provide perspectives not available by any other means. Consider video and audio clips as potential sources for material that might complement or support the factual data you uncover.

Determine What Content to Present to Your Audience

Experienced designers recommend writing three or four major ideas you want an audience member to remember after reading or viewing your project. It also is helpful to envision your project's endpoint, the key fact you wish to emphasize. All project elements should lead to this ending point.

As you make content decisions, you also need to think about other factors. Presentation of the project content is an important consideration. For example, will your brochure be printed on thick, colored paper or posted on the Web? Will your PowerPoint presentation be viewed in a classroom with excellent lighting and a bright projector, or will it be viewed on a notebook computer monitor? Determine relevant time factors, such as the length of time to develop the project, how long readers will spend reviewing your project, or the amount of time allocated for your speaking engagement. Your project will need to accommodate all of these constraints.

Decide whether a graph, photo, or artistic element can express or emphasize a particular concept. The right hemisphere of the brain processes images by attaching an emotion to them, so audience members are more apt to recall these graphics long term rather than just reading text.

As you select content, be mindful of the order in which you plan to present information. Readers and audience members generally remember the first and last pieces of information they see and hear, so you should place the most important information at the top or bottom of the page.

Summary

When creating a project, it is beneficial to follow some basic guidelines from the outset. By taking some time at the beginning of the process to determine the project's purpose, analyze the audience, gather possible content, and determine what content to present to the audience, you can produce a project that is informative, relevant, and effective.

Appendix B

Publishing Office 2010 Web Pages Online

With Office 2010 programs, you use the Save As command in the Backstage view to save a Web page to a Web site, network location, or FTP site. **File Transfer Protocol (FTP)** is an Internet standard that allows computers to exchange files with other computers on the Internet.

You should contact your network system administrator or technical support staff at your Internet access provider to determine if their Web server supports Web folders, FTP, or both, and to obtain necessary permissions to access the Web server.

Using an Office Program to Publish Office 2010 Web Pages

When publishing online, someone first must assign the necessary permissions for you to publish the Web page. If you are granted access to publish online, you must obtain the Web address of the Web server, a user name, and possibly a password that allows you to connect to the Web server. The steps in this appendix assume that you have access to an online location to which you can publish a Web page.

To Connect to an Online Location

To publish a Web page online, you first must connect to the online location. To connect to an online location using Windows 7, you would perform the following steps.

1. Click the Start button on the Windows 7 taskbar to display the Start menu.

2. Click Computer in the right pane of the Start menu to open the Computer window.

3. Click the 'Map network drive' button on the toolbar to display the Map Network Drive dialog box. (If the 'Map network drive' button is not visible on the toolbar, click the 'Display additional commands' button on the toolbar and then click 'Map network drive' in the list to display the Map Network Drive dialog box.)

4. Click the 'Connect to a Web site that you can use to store your documents and pictures' link (Map Network Drive dialog box) to start the Add Network Location wizard.

5. Click the Next button (Add Network Location dialog box).

6. Click 'Choose a custom network location' and then click the Next button.

7. Type the Internet or network address specified by your network or system administrator in the text box and then click the Next button.

8. Click 'Log on anonymously' to deselect the check box, type your user name in the User name text box, and then click the Next button.

9. If necessary, enter the name you want to assign to this online location and then click the Next button.

10. Click to deselect the Open this network location when I click Finish check box, and then click the Finish button.

11. Click the Cancel button to close the Map Network Drive dialog box.

12. Close the Computer window.

TO SAVE A WEB PAGE TO AN ONLINE LOCATION

The online location now can be accessed easily from Windows programs, including Microsoft Office programs. After creating a Microsoft Office file you wish to save as a Web page, you must save the file to the online location to which you connected in the previous steps. To save a Microsoft Word document as a Web page, for example, and publish it to the online location, you would perform the following steps.

1. Click File on the Ribbon to display the Backstage view and then click Save As in the Backstage view to display the Save As dialog box.

2. Type the Web page file name in the File name text box (Save As dialog box). Do not press the ENTER key because you do not want to close the dialog box at this time.

3. Click the 'Save as type' box arrow and then click Web Page to select the Web Page format.

4. If necessary, scroll to display the name of the online location in the navigation pane.

5. Double-click the online location name in the navigation pane to select that location as the new save location and display its contents in the right pane.

6. If a dialog box appears prompting you for a user name and password, type the user name and password in the respective text boxes and then click the Log On button.

7. Click the Save button (Save As dialog box).

The Web page now has been published online. To view the Web page using a Web browser, contact your network or system administrator for the Web address you should use to connect to the Web page.

Appendix C

Microsoft Office 2010 Specialist and Expert Certifications

What Are Microsoft Office Specialist and Expert Certifications?

Microsoft Corporation has developed a set of standardized, performance-based examinations that you can take to demonstrate your overall expertise of Microsoft Office 2010 programs, including Microsoft Word 2010, Microsoft PowerPoint 2010, Microsoft Excel 2010, Microsoft Access 2010, and Microsoft Outlook 2010. When you successfully complete an examination for one of these Office programs, you will have earned the designation as a specialist or as an expert in that particular Office program.

These examinations collectively are called the Microsoft Office 2010 Specialist and Microsoft Office 2010 Expert certification exams. The information in Table C–1 identifies each of these examinations.

Table C–1 Microsoft Office Specialist and Expert Certifications

Certification Exam	Description	Requirement	Credential Earned
Microsoft Word 2010 Specialist	Indicates you have proficiency in using at least 80 percent of the features and capabilities of Word 2010	Successfully complete Exam 77-881	Microsoft Office Specialist: Microsoft Word 2010
Microsoft Word 2010 Expert	Indicates you have proficiency in using Word 2010 at the feature and functionality levels, together with advanced features of Word 2010	Successfully complete Exam 77-887	Microsoft Office Specialist: Microsoft Word 2010 Expert
Microsoft PowerPoint 2010 Specialist	Indicates you have proficiency in using PowerPoint 2010 by creating complex slide shows using sophisticated data presented in visual formats	Successfully complete Exam 77-883	Microsoft Office Specialist: Microsoft PowerPoint 2010
Microsoft Excel 2010 Specialist	Indicates you have proficiency in using at least 80 percent of the features and capabilities of Excel 2010	Successfully complete Exam 77-882	Microsoft Office Specialist: Microsoft Excel 2010

Table C–1 Microsoft Office Specialist and Expert Certifications *(continued)*

Certification Exam	Description	Requirement	Credential Earned
Microsoft Excel 2010 Expert	Indicates you have proficiency in using Excel 2010 at the feature and functionality levels, together with advanced features of Excel 2010	Successfully complete Exam 77-888	Microsoft Office Specialist: Microsoft Excel 2010 Expert
Microsoft Access 2010	Indicates you have proficiency in using Access 2010 by creating, modifying, and extending functionality of basic database objects	Successfully complete Exam 77-885	Microsoft Office Specialist: Microsoft Access 2010
Microsoft Outlook 2010	Indicates you have proficiency in using Outlook 2010 by formatting message content, creating contact records and appointments, scheduling meetings, and sharing schedules	Successfully complete Exam 77-884	Microsoft Office Specialist: Microsoft Outlook 2010

You will notice in Table C–1 that Word and Excel have an Expert certification. The other programs do not.

Microsoft provides one other level of Office certification: 2010 Microsoft Office Master certification. To be certified as a 2010 Microsoft Office Master, you must successfully complete the following exams:

- 77-887: Word 2010 Expert
- 77-888: Excel 2010 Expert
- 77-883: PowerPoint 2010

and either

- 77-885: Access 2010

or

- 77-884: Outlook 2010

Why Should You Be Certified?

Microsoft Office 2010 certification provides a number of benefits for both you and your potential employer. The benefits for you include the following:

- You can differentiate yourself in the employment marketplace from those who are not Microsoft Office Specialist or Expert certified.
- You have proved your skills and expertise when using Microsoft Office 2010.
- You will be able to perform at a higher skill level in your job.
- You will be working at a higher professional level than those who are not certified.
- You will broaden your employment opportunities and advance your career more rapidly.

For employers, Microsoft Office 2010 certification offers the following advantages:

- When hiring or promoting employees, employers have immediate verification of employees' skills.
- Companies can maximize their productivity and efficiency by employing Microsoft Office 2010 certified individuals.

Taking the Microsoft Office 2010 Certification Exams

The Certiport Company administers the Microsoft Office 2010 Specialist and Expert certification exams. You can contact Certiport at 888-999-9830 x138 or at the Web address, http://www.certiport.com. On the Web site, click the Microsoft Office 2010 Specialist link. Be sure to explore the links on these Certiport pages to obtain a thorough understanding of the Microsoft Office 2010 certification exams.

To take an exam, you must register and pay a fee. The fee varies depending on the test and the testing center. Each exam requires that you complete specified tasks using the program on which you are being tested, that is, tasks you would perform while at work. Remember — these are performance-based exams, so you will be using the software, not answering questions about the software.

You can find testing centers by following the links on the Certiport Web site and then clicking Find a Testing Center.

How Do I Prepare for the Microsoft Office 2010 Specialist Exam?

The Shelly Cashman Series offers Microsoft-approved textbooks for the certification exams listed in Table C–1 on pages APP 5 and APP 6. These textbooks can be found by visiting the Web site, www.cengagebrain.com and then entering the search topic, Shelly. Using any of the approved textbooks will prepare you to take and pass the indicated Microsoft Office 2010 Specialist or Expert exam. For a list of skill sets specific to this book, see Table C–2 on pages APP 8 through APP 11. The use of all appropriate Shelly Cashman Series Office 2010 textbooks will prepare you for the 2010 Microsoft Office Master certification.

For further information from Microsoft regarding Microsoft Office 2010 certification, please visit http://www.microsoft.com/learning/en/us/certification/mos.aspx and http://office.microsoft.com/en-us/word-help/should-you-become-a-microsoft-office-specialist-HA001211101.aspx.

Table C–2 Outlook 2010 Certification Objectives	
Skill Set	**Page Number**
Managing the Outlook Environment	
Apply and manipulate Outlook program options	
Set General options	OUT 247
Set Mail options	OUT 248–251
Set Calendar options	OUT 84 OUT 262–268
Set Tasks options	OUT 181 OUT 185
Set Notes and Journal options	OUT 219
Set Advanced options	OUT 270 OUT 290–291
Set Language options	APP 8
Manipulate item tags	
Categorize items	OUT 186–190
Set flags	OUT 198–199
Set sensitivity level	APP 9, APP 11
Mark items as read or unread	OUT 15
View message properties	OUT 14
Arrange the Content pane	
Show or hide fields in a list view	APP 10
Change the Reading view	OUT 13
Use the Reminders Window	APP 11
Use the People pane	APP 11
Apply search and filter tools	
Use built-in Search folders	OUT 139–140
Print an Outlook item	
Print attachments	OUT 33
Print calendars	OUT 103
Print multiple messages	OUT 17
Print multiple contact records	OUT 156
Print tasks	OUT 217
Print multiple notes	OUT 220
Creating and Formatting Item Content	
Create and send e-mail messages	
Specify a message theme	OUT 259–261
Specify message content format	
Plain text	OUT 22
Rich text	OUT 21
HTML format	OUT 21 OUT 248–249
Show or hide the From and Bcc fields	OUT 22
Set a reminder for message recipients	APP 12
Specify the sending account	OUT 237
Specify the Sent items folder	APP 12

Table C–2 Outlook 2010 Certification Objectives *(continued)*

Skill Set	Page Number
Configure message delivery options	APP 13
Configure voting options	APP 14
Configure tracking options	OUT 285–286
Send a message to a contact group	OUT 144 OUT 146
Create and manage Quick Steps	
Perform Quick Steps	OUT 279–280
Create Quick Steps	OUT 276–279
Edit Quick Steps	OUT 279
Delete Quick Steps	OUT 281
Duplicate Quick Steps	OUT 279
Reset Quick Steps to default settings	OUT 280
Create item content	
Insert graphical elements	OUT 256
Insert a hyperlink	OUT 21
Format item content	
Use formatting tools	OUT 253–255
Apply styles	APP 14
Create styles	APP 15
Create themes	APP 16
Use Paste Special	APP 17
Format graphical elements	APP 17
Attach content to e-mail messages	
Attach an Outlook item	OUT 205–206
Attach external files	OUT 30–32
Managing E-mail Messages	
Clean up the mailbox	
View mailbox size	APP 18
Save message attachments	OUT 34–35
Save a message in an external format	OUT 28
Ignore a conversation	APP 18
Use clean-up tools	OUT 290
Create and manage rules	
Create rules	OUT 282–286
Modify rules	OUT 286
Delete rules	OUT 288–289
Manage junk mail	
Allow a specific message (not junk)	OUT 244–246
Filter junk mail	
Never Block Sender	OUT 243
Never Block Sender's Domain	OUT 243
Never Block this Group or Mailing List	OUT 243
Block Sender	OUT 243

Table C–2 Outlook 2010 Certification Objectives *(continued)*

Skill Set	Page Number
Manage automatic message content	
Manage signatures	OUT 257–258
Specify the font	
New HTML messages	OUT 259–261
Plain-text messages	OUT 249
Specify options for replies	OUT 17
Specify options for forwards	OUT 17
Set a default theme for all HTML	
Messages	OUT 259–261
Stationery	OUT 259–261
Fonts	OUT 259–261
Managing Contacts	
Create and manipulate contacts	
Modify a default business card	APP 19
Forward a contact	OUT 127
Update a contact in the address book	OUT 130–131
Create and manipulate contact groups	
Create a contact group	OUT 144–146
Manage contact group membership	OUT 149–151
Show notes about a contact group	OUT 131
Forward a contact group	OUT 149
Delete a contact group	OUT 151
Send a meeting to a contact group	OUT 133
Managing Calendar Objects	
Create and manipulate appointments and events	
Set appointment options	OUT 67–69
Print appointment details	OUT 100–101
Forward an appointment	OUT 98
Schedule a meeting with a message sender	OUT 98
Create and manipulate meeting requests	
Set response options	OUT 97
Update a meeting request	OUT 98
Cancel a meeting or invitation	OUT 96
Propose a new time for a meeting	OUT 98
Manipulate the Calendar pane	
Arrange the calendar view	OUT 61
Change the calendar color	OUT 56 OUT 71
Display or hide calendars	OUT 56
Create a calendar group	APP 17

Table C–2 Outlook 2010 Certification Objectives *(continued)*

Skill Set	Page Number
Working with Tasks, Notes, and Journal Entries	
Create and manipulate tasks	
Create a task	OUT 173–175
Manage task details	OUT 176–181
	OUT 182
Send a status report	OUT 209–211
Mark a task as complete	OUT 211–212
Move or copy a task to another folder	OUT 202
Assign a task to another Outlook user	OUT 206–207
Accept or decline a task assignment	OUT 202
Update an assigned task	OUT 202–203
Use Current view	OUT 102
	OUT 137
	OUT 216
Create and manipulate notes	
Create a note	OUT 218–220
Change the current view	OUT 220
Categorize notes	OUT 220
Create and manipulate Journal entries	
Automatically record Outlook items	APP 22
Automatically record files	APP 23
Edit a Journal entry	APP 23

Outlook Certification

The chapters in this book have covered most of the topics necessary for the Outlook certification; however, you need to know about a few more to be ready for the certification exam.

Working with Outlook Program Options

When working with Outlook, you can configure several options to customize your experience. The Outlook Options dialog box can be used for setting these options.

To Set Language Options

You can use the Outlook Options dialog box to set the Office Language Preferences. Usually, Outlook configures the language settings to match your operating system; however, if you want to change that, you can adjust the Language options.

The following steps set the Language options.

1

- Click File on the Ribbon to display the Backstage view.

- Click Options in the Backstage view to display the Outlook Options dialog box.

- Click Language to display the Language options (Figure C–1).

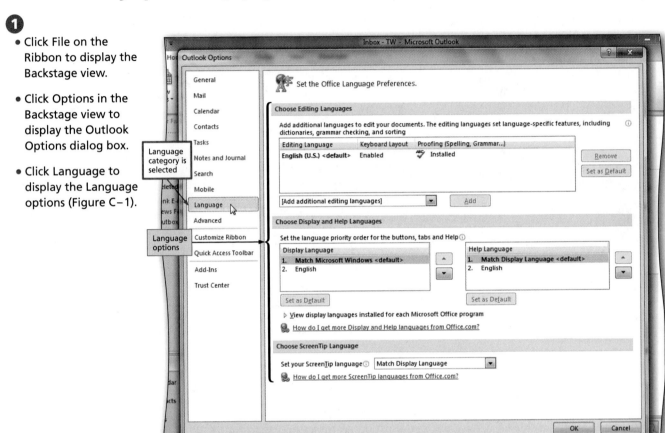

Figure C–1

What types of features do the Language options determine?

They specify the editing and display languages, such as the languages used in the dictionaries, grammar checking, and sorting.

2

- Modify the settings in each area to set the Language options.

- Click the OK button to close the Outlook Options dialog box and save the changes.

To Set the Sensitivity Level for All New Messages

You can set the sensitivity level for all messages by using the Outlook Options dialog box. Sensitivity levels are Normal, Personal, Private, and Confidential. Changing the setting in the Outlook Options dialog box changes the default sensitivity level of all messages created afterwards.

The following steps set the Sensitivity level.

1

- Click File on the Ribbon to display the Backstage view.

- Click Options in the Backstage view to display the Outlook Options dialog box.

- Click Mail to display the Mail options.

- Drag the scroll bar to display the Send messages area (Figure C–2).

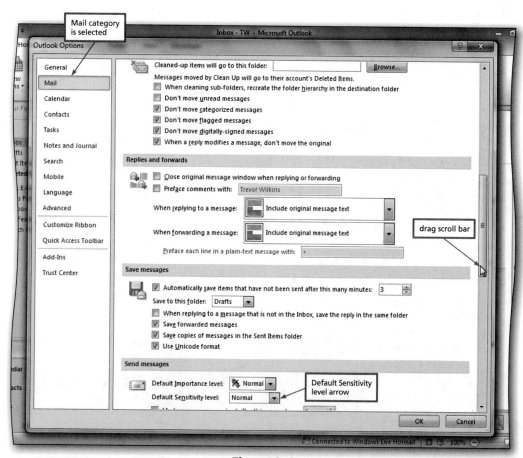

Figure C–2

2

- Click the Default Sensitivity level arrow to display a list of sensitivity levels.

- Click Normal, Personal, Private, or Confidential to set the default sensitivity level for all new messages.

- Click OK to close the Outlook Options dialog box and save the changes.

Working with the Content Pane

When working with the Content pane, you should be able to perform the tasks included in this section for the certification exam.

To Show or Hide Fields in List View

When organizing the Content pane, you can adjust the fields displayed in List view by showing or hiding the fields. You can adjust which fields are displayed using the Show Columns dialog box.

To show or hide a field in List view, perform the following steps.

1

- Click View on the Ribbon to display the View tab.

- Click the Add Columns button (View tab | Arrangement group) to display the Show Columns dialog box (Figure C–3).

2

- Click a column name in the Available columns box that you want to show, and then click the Add button (Show Columns dialog box) to display the column.

- Click a column name in the 'Show these columns in this order' box, and then click the Remove button (Show Columns dialog box) to hide the column.

- Click the OK button (Show Columns dialog box) to close the dialog box and display or hide the columns you selected.

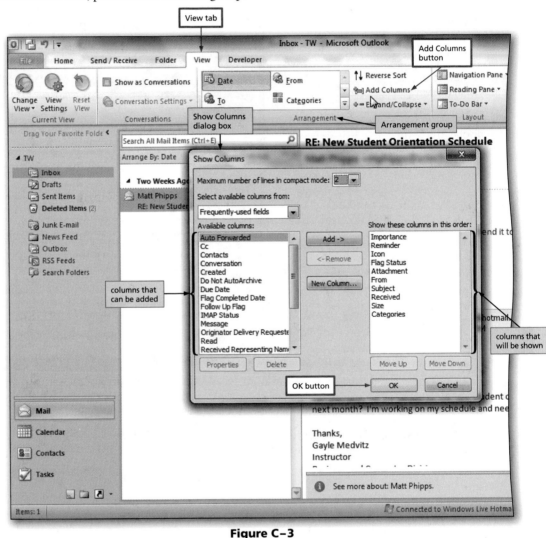

Figure C–3

To Open the Reminders Window

If you have set up reminders for tasks or other items, you can use the Reminders window to view reminders. You can then dismiss the ones you no longer need. For those that require more time, you can choose more time to complete the task and set a snooze interval so that Outlook reminds you about the item again. If you choose to open the Reminders window, you would use the following steps.

1. Click View on the Ribbon to display the View tab.
2. Click the Reminders Window button (View tab | Window group) to open the open the Reminders window.
3. After reviewing the reminders, click the Close button to close the Reminders window.

To Use the People Pane

When you are reviewing a message in Outlook, you can use the People pane to view more information about the contacts associated with the message, such as the senders and receivers of the message. If the message has more than one contact, you can select the contact in the People pane to display individual information, such as e-mails, meetings, and other data that relate to that contact as stored in Outlook.

The People pane is minimized by default; therefore, it needs to be expanded before you can use it. If you choose to use the People pane, you would use the following steps.

1. Select a message in the Message list.
2. If necessary, click the Expand button to expand the People pane.
3. Click a contact icon to see related data for the Contact.
4. After reviewing the data in the People pane, click the Collapse button to collapse the People pane.

Creating and Sending E-Mail Messages

In addition to what you have learned in the chapters, you should also be able to perform the following tasks when working with e-mail messages.

To Change a Sensitivity Level

When composing a message, you can change the sensitivity level. If you choose to change the sensitivity level for a single message, you would use the following steps.

1. While composing a message, click Options on the Ribbon to display the Options tab.
2. Click the More Options Dialog Box Launcher (Options tab | More Options group) to display the Properties dialog box.
3. Click the Sensitivity button to display a list of options.
4. Click a sensitivity option to change the sensitivity level of the message.
5. Click the Close button (Properties dialog box) to apply the changes.

TO SET A REMINDER FOR MESSAGE RECIPIENTS

When composing a message, you can set reminders for message recipients. If you choose to set a reminder for message recipients, you would use the following steps.

1. While composing a message, click the Follow Up button (Message tab | Tags group) to display a menu of follow-up options.

2. Click Custom to display the Custom dialog box.

3. Click the Flag for Recipients check box to select it.

4. Click the OK button (Custom dialog box) to apply the changes.

To Specify the Sent Items Folder

When organizing your messages, you can select which folder to use for storing sent items. To specify the Sent Items folder, a message window must be open; that is, you should be composing an e-mail message. The following steps specify the Sent Items folder.

- Open a new or existing e-mail message.

- Click Options on the Ribbon to display the Options tab.

- Click the Save Sent Item To button (Options tab | More Options group) to display a list of options.

- Click Other Folder to display the Select Folder dialog box (Figure C–4).

- Select a folder or create a new folder to change the Sent Items folder.

- Click the OK button (Select Folder dialog box) to apply the changes.

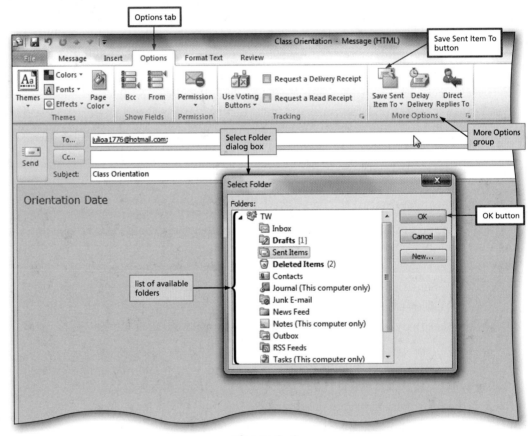

Figure C–4

To Configure Message Delivery Options

When composing a message, you can adjust the delivery options using the Properties dialog box. For example, you can change where replies are sent, delivery dates, expiration dates, saving options, contact information, and categories.

The following steps configure message delivery options.

1

- While composing a message, click Options on the Ribbon to display the Options tab.

- Click the More Options Dialog Box Launcher (Options tab | More Options group) to display the Properties dialog box (Figure C–5).

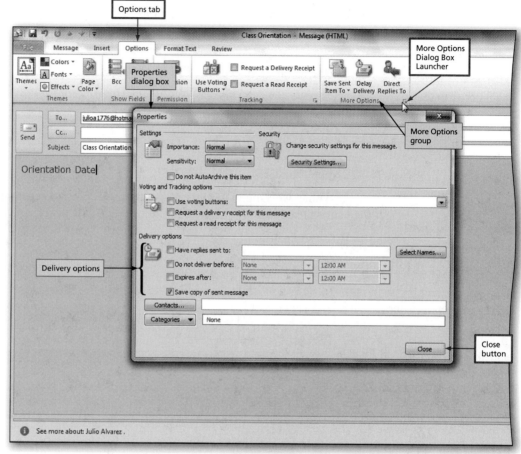

Figure C–5

2

- Select delivery options in the Delivery options area.

- Click the Close button to close the Properties dialog box.

TO CONFIGURE VOTING OPTIONS

When composing a message, you can configure voting options by using the Properties dialog box. For example, you can choose to use voting buttons as well as request delivery and read receipts.

If you choose to configure voting options, you would use the following steps.

1. While composing a message, click Options on the Ribbon to display the Options tab.
2. Click the Use Voting Buttons button (Options tab | Tracking group) to display a list of options.
3. Click Custom to display the Properties dialog box.
4. Select voting options in the Voting and Tracking options area.
5. Click the Close button to close the Properties dialog box.

Using Formatting Tools

When working with message content, you can use several formatting tools to enhance the appearance of the content.

To Apply a Style

While composing a message, you can format text using one of the styles provided in the Styles gallery. The following steps change the style of selected text.

- In an open message, select text that you want to format.

- Click Format Text on the Ribbon to display the Format Text tab.

- Click the More button (Format Text tab | Styles group) to display the Styles gallery (Figure C–6).

- Click a style to change the style of the selected text.

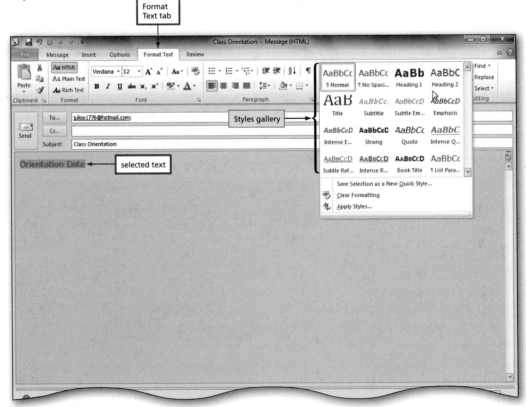

Figure C–6

To Create a Style

You can create custom styles using the Create New Style from Formatting dialog box. First, you format text in your message, and then you use the dialog box to save your style with a name. You can select the custom style from the Styles gallery the next time you decide to use it. The following steps create a new style.

1

- Format and then select text in a message to use the formatting when creating the style.

- Click Format Text on the Ribbon to display the Format Text tab.

- Click the Styles Dialog Box Launcher (Format Text tab | Styles group) to display the Styles dialog box (Figure C–7).

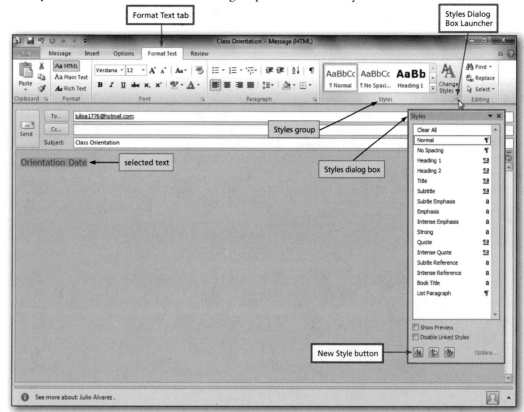

Figure C–7

2

- Click the New Style button (Styles dialog box) to display the Create New Style from Formatting dialog box.

- Type a name in the Name text box to name the new style.

- Click the OK button (Create New Style from Formatting dialog box) to save the style.

To Create a Theme

Besides creating styles, you also can create a theme. When you create a theme, all the formatting of the message is included in the new theme. You then can apply your theme by selecting it from the Themes gallery. The following steps create a new theme.

①

- After formatting a message, click Options on the Ribbon to display the Options tab.

- Click the Themes button (Options tab | Themes group) to display the Themes gallery (Figure C–8).

②

- Click Save Current Theme to display the Save Current Theme dialog box.

- Type a name in the File name text box to name the new theme.

- Click the Save button (Save Current Theme dialog box) to save the new theme.

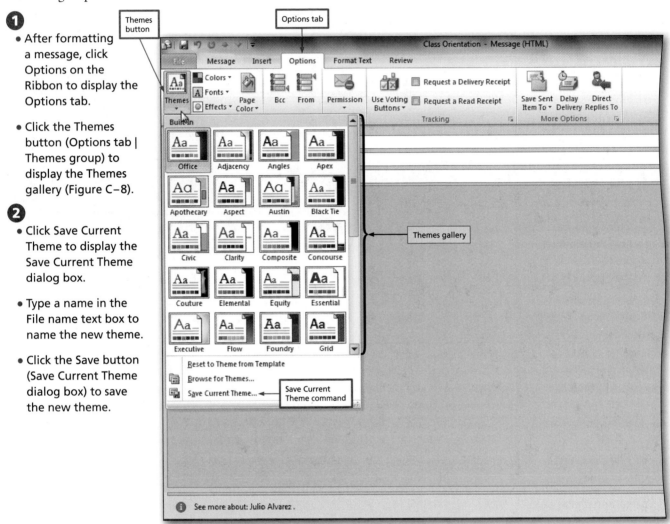

Figure C–8

To Use Paste Special

When pasting content into a message, you can choose different paste options using the Paste Special dialog box. For example, you can paste a paragraph as unformatted text so that no formats are copied from the original source of the text.

The following steps use the Paste Special dialog box.

- After copying content to the Clipboard, open a new or existing message.

- Click the Paste button arrow (Message tab | Clipboard group) to display a list of paste options.

- Click Paste Special to display the Paste Special dialog box (Figure C–9).

2

- Select a paste option in the As box.

- Click the OK button (Paste Special dialog box) to paste the content from the Clipboard using the selected paste option.

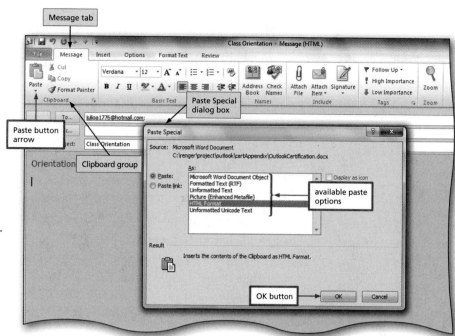

Figure C–9

To Format a Graphical Element

When working with inserted images, clip art, and other graphical elements, you can use the Format tab to change the appearance of the graphical elements. The Format tab is a contextual tab that appears when a graphical element is selected. The available options depend on the selected element.

The following steps format a graphical element.

- Select a graphical element in a message.

- Click Format on the Ribbon to display the Format tab for the element (Figure C–10).

Q&A

What types of formatting can I apply to a graphic?

Using a tool on the Format tab, you can adjust the graphic's color, brightness, or contrast, apply a Picture style, or resize the graphic, for example.

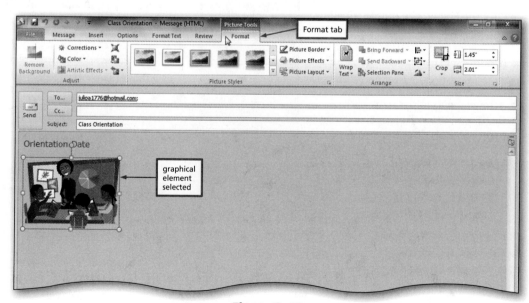

Figure C–10

2

- Click a formatting tool to use it to format the graphical element.

Working with the Mailbox

In addition to the mailbox tasks covered in the chapters, you can choose to ignore conversations among messages when you no longer want to track the conversation. A **conversation** is a complete chain of e-mail messages that share the same subject. When a conversation is ignored, Outlook places the selected message and all future messages in the Deleted Items folder. You also can view your mailbox size to determine whether to delete or archive items to save storage space.

TO IGNORE A CONVERSATION

If you choose to ignore a conversation, you would use the following steps.

1. Click a message in the mailbox to select a message.
2. Click the Ignore button (Home tab | Delete group) to display the Ignore Conversation dialog box.
3. Click the Ignore Conversation button (Ignore Conversation dialog box) to ignore the conversation.

To View Mailbox Size

The following steps view the mailbox size.

- Select the mailbox.

- Click Folder on the Ribbon to display the Folder tab.

- Click the Folder Properties button (Folder tab | Properties group) to display the Properties dialog box for the mailbox.

- Click the Folder Size button (mailbox Properties dialog box) to display the Folder Size dialog box (Figure C–11).

- After viewing folder sizes, click the Close button (Folder Size dialog box) to close the dialog box.

- Click the OK button (Properties dialog box) to close the mailbox Properties dialog box.

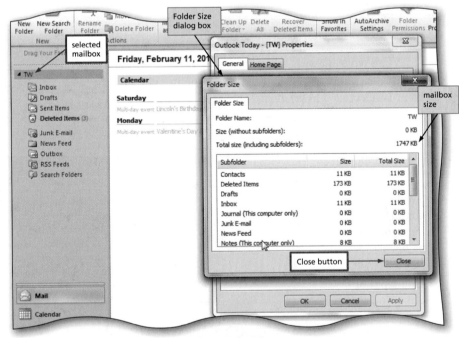

Figure C–11

Working with the Default Business Card

When working with your contacts, you may decide to change the appearance of the default business card. Changing the default business card involves customizing a business card for a blank contact and then using the Developer tab to publish the custom contact formats. After publishing, you then change the properties of the contact folder to use the newly published format. All contacts added will use the customized format.

To Modify a Default Business Card

The following steps modify the default business card format.

1

- Click the Contacts button in the Navigation pane to display the Contacts window.

- Click the New Contact button (Home tab | New group) to display the Untitled – Contact window.

- Double-click the default business card to display the Edit Business Card dialog box (Figure C–12).

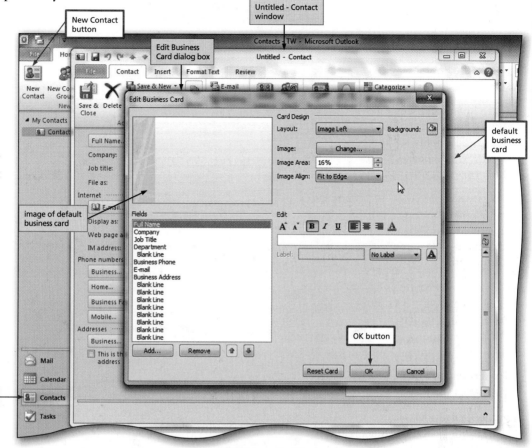

Figure C–12

2

- Use the options in the Edit Business Card dialog box to change the business card fields and design options.

- Click the OK button (Edit Business Card dialog box) to save the changes.

- If the Developer tab is not displayed on the Ribbon, click the File tab to display the Backstage view, and then click the Options button.

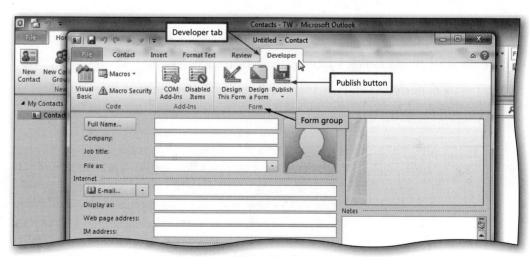

Figure C–13

- Click Customize Ribbon, and then click the Developer check box in the Customize the Ribbon area.

- Click the OK button to add the Developer tab to the Ribbon.

- Click Developer on the Ribbon to display the Developer tab (Figure C–13).

3

- Click the Publish button (Developer tab | Form group) to display a list of options.

- Click Publish Form to display the Publish Form As dialog box.

- Enter a name in the Display name text box to provide a name to display when selecting the form, or business card.

- Enter a name in the Form name text box to provide a file name for the form.

- Click the Publish button (Publish Form As dialog box) to publish the form.

- Close the Untitled – Contact window without saving changes.

- In the Navigation pane, right-click the contact folder to display a shortcut menu.

- Click Properties to display the Contacts Properties dialog box (Figure C–14).

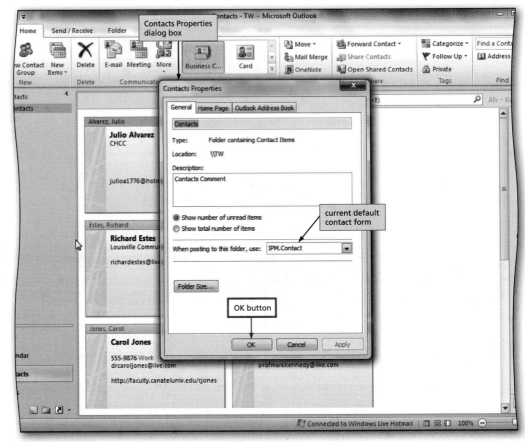

Figure C–14

4

- Click the 'When posting to this folder, use' arrow to display list of forms and business cards.

- Click the name of your form to select it as the default business card.

- Click the OK button (Contacts Properties dialog box) to change the properties of the Contacts folder.

Working with Calendar Groups

Within Outlook, you can create multiple calendars. If you are using an Exchange server for your e-mail, you can arrange calendars in groups for easier access to specific calendars. For example, if you belong to two clubs, you might create a calendar for each club. You then can create a calendar group called Clubs and arrange the two calendars into the Clubs group. If you are using an Exchange server, you may also have access to shared calendars of your colleagues. (The sharing feature is only available on an Exchange server.) If you have shared calendars, you can create a calendar group for those serving on the same committee or project and arrange the calendars in the group for quick access to everyone's schedule.

To Create a Calendar Group

The following steps create a calendar group.

1. Click the Calendar button in the Navigation pane to display the Calendar window.
2. Click the Calendar Groups button (Home tab | Manage Calendars group).
3. Select the appropriate group option to create a group.
4. Enter a name for the group and click the OK button to create the group.

Working with Journal Entries

In Outlook, you may want to keep track of actions that you have performed in relation to specific contacts. You can have Outlook automatically record these actions as Journal entries. A Journal entry can track items such as e-mail messages, meetings, and Microsoft Office files.

To View Journal Entries

To view the Journal, you need to add the Journal button to the Navigation pane. The following step adds the Journal button to the Navigation pane and displays the Journal entries.

1

- Click the Configure buttons arrow in the Navigation pane to display a menu.

- Point to Add or Remove Buttons to display a menu of buttons to display on the Navigation pane.

- Click Journal to add the Journal button to the Navigation pane.

- Click the Journal button to view Journal entries (Figure C–15).

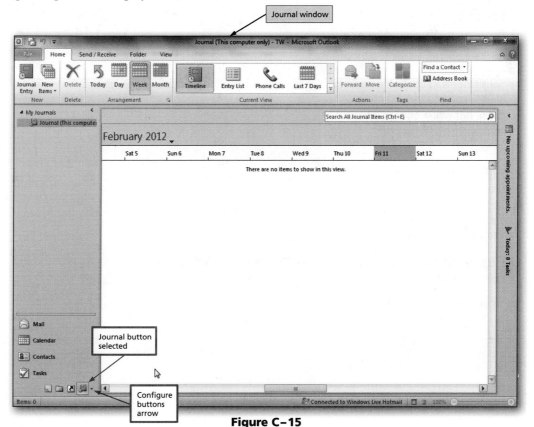

Figure C–15

To Automatically Record Outlook Items

You can change the Journal options so that Outlook automatically records items for particular contacts. The following steps turn on automatic recording for Outlook items.

- Click File on the Ribbon to display the Backstage view.

- Click the Options button in the Backstage view to display the Outlook Options dialog box.

- Click Notes and Journal to display the Notes and Journal options.

- Click the Journal Options button (Outlook Options dialog box) to display the Journal Options dialog box (Figure C–16).

- Select items in the 'Automatically record these items' list box to identify items to be recorded.

- Select contacts in the 'For these contacts' list box to identify contacts associated with the items to be recorded.

- Click the OK button (Journal Options dialog box) to start automatically recording journal entries.

- Close the Outlook Options dialog box.

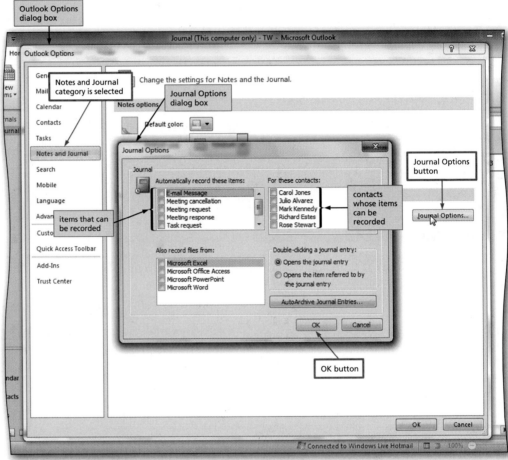

Figure C–16

To Automatically Record Files

You also can automatically record files in your Journal. If you choose to automatically record files, you would use the following steps.

1. Click File on the Ribbon to display the Backstage view.
2. Click the Options button in the Backstage view to display the Outlook Options dialog box.
3. Click Notes and Journal to display the Notes and Journal options.
4. Click the Journal Options button (Outlook Options dialog box) to display the Journal Options dialog box.
5. Select files in the 'Also record files from' list box to identify files to be recorded.
6. Click the OK button (Journal Options dialog box) to start automatically recording journal entries.
7. Close the Outlook Options dialog box.

To Edit a Journal Entry

After a Journal entry has been created, you can edit it. The following steps edit a Journal entry.

1

- Click the Journal button in the Navigation pane to view the Journal.

- Double-click an entry to display the Journal Entry window (Figure C–17).

2

- Edit the journal entry as necessary.

- Click the Save & Close button (Journal Entry tab | Actions group) to save the changes and close the Journal Entry window.

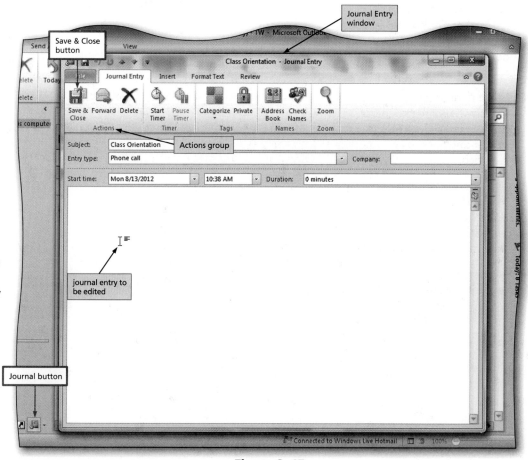

Figure C–17

Index

Quick Reference Summary

Microsoft Outlook 2010 Quick Reference Summary					
Task	**Page Number**	**Mouse**	**Ribbon**	**Shortcut Menu**	**Keyboard Shortcut**
Add Attachment to Contact	OUT 131		Attach File button (Insert tab | Include group), select file, click Insert		
Add E-Mail Account	OUT 238		Account Settings button (File tab | Info tab) *or* Add Account button (File tab | Info tab)		
Add Holidays to Calendar	OUT 264	Add Holidays button (Outlook Options dialog box)			
Add Image to E-Mail Signature	OUT 256	Insert Picture button (Signatures and Stationery dialog box)			
Add Name to Contact Group	OUT 149		Add Members button (Contact Group tab | Members group)		
Add RSS Feed	OUT 292			Right-click RSS Feeds folder, click Add a New RSS Feed	
Appointment, Change Date for	OUT 80	Double-click appointment, change date *or* Drag appointment to different date in Date Navigator			CTRL+O, change date
Appointment, Change Time for	OUT 79	Double-click appointment, change time *or* Drag appointment to different time slot in appointment area			CTRL+O, change time
Appointment, Create	OUT 62, OUT 64	Drag to select time slots, type appointment title	New Appointment button (Home tab | New group)		CTRL+SHIFT+A
Appointment, Delete	OUT 82		Delete button (Calendar Tools Appointment Series tab *or* Calendar Tools Appointment tab | Actions group)	Delete	DELETE
Appointment, Save	OUT 69	Close button, Yes to save changes	Save & Close button (Appointment tab | Actions group)		

Microsoft Outlook 2010 Quick Reference Summary *(continued)*

Task	Page Number	Mouse	Ribbon	Shortcut Menu	Keyboard Shortcut
Appointment, Set Recurrence Options for	OUT 72		Recurrence button (Appointment tab | Options group)		
Appointment, Set Reminder for	OUT 68		Reminder box arrow (Appointment tab | Options group)		
Appointment, Set Status for	OUT 67		Show As box arrow (Appointment tab | Options group)		
Assign Task	OUT 206		Assign Task button (Task tab | Manage Task group)		
Assign Theme to Stationery	OUT 259	Mail category, Stationery and Fonts button (Outlook Options dialog box), Theme button (Signatures and Stationery dialog box)			
Attach File to E-mail Message	OUT 30	Drag file to message area	Attach File button (Message tab | Include group *or* Insert tab | Include group)	Copy, right-click message area, click Paste	
Attach Outlook Item to Task	OUT 205		Outlook Item button (Insert tab | Include group)		
Attachment to Contact, Change	OUT 134	Double-click contact, click attachment, click Attach File button (Insert tab | Include group), select file, click Insert	Attach File button (Insert tab | Include group), select file, click Insert		
Attachment to Contact, Remove	OUT 135	Double-click contact, click attachment, press DELETE			DELETE
Attachment, Add to Contact	OUT 131		Attach File button (Insert tab | Include group), select file, click Insert		
Attachment, Add to Task	OUT 203		Attach File button (Insert tab | Include group)		
Attachment, Preview	OUT 33	Click message header, click attachment			
Attachment, Save	OUT 35		Save As button (Attachment Tools Attachments tab | Actions group), Save button (Save Attachment dialog box)	Save As	
AutoArchive Settings, Configure	OUT 290	Advanced category, AutoArchive Settings button (Outlook Options dialog box)			
Business Card, Modify Default	APP 19	Contacts button in Navigation pane, New Contact button (Home tab | New group), double-click default business card			
Calendar Group, Create	APP 21	Calendar button in Navigation pane, Calendar Groups button (Home tab | Manage Calendars group)			

Microsoft Outlook 2010 Quick Reference Summary *(continued)*

Task	Page Number	Mouse	Ribbon	Shortcut Menu	Keyboard Shortcut
Calendar Options, Set	OUT 262	Calendar category (Outlook Options dialog box)			
Calendar, Accept Meeting Request	OUT 96		Accept button (Meeting tab | Respond group)		CTRL+ALT+R
Calendar, Change Default Color	OUT 265	Calendar category, Default calendar color button (Outlook Options dialog box)			
Calendar, Change Time Zone for	OUT 267	Calendar category, Time zone box arrow (Outlook Options dialog box)			
Calendar, Delete Personal Calendar	OUT 108		Delete Calendar button (Folder tab | Actions group)	Delete Calendar	
Calendar, Display Day View	OUT 62		Day button (Home tab | Arrange group)		CTRL+ALT+1
Calendar, Display Different Month in	OUT 80	Click left or right scroll arrow			PAGE UP or PAGE DOWN
Calendar, Display List View	OUT 102		Change View button (View tab | Current View group), click List		
Calendar, Display Month View	OUT 60		Month button (Home tab | Arrange group)		CTRL+ALT+4
Calendar, Display Personal Folder	OUT 56	Click folder check box			
Calendar, Display Schedule View	OUT 60		Schedule View button (Home tab | Arrange group)		CTRL+ALT+5
Calendar, Display Week View	OUT 59		Week button (Home tab | Arrange group)		CTRL+ALT+3
Calendar, Display Work Week View	OUT 58		Work Week button (Home tab | Arrange group)		CTRL+ALT+2
Calendar, Export Subfolder	OUT 104		Import button (File tab | Open tab), Export to a file (Import and Export Wizard)		
Calendar, Go to Specific Date	OUT 57	Click date in Date Navigator	Go To Dialog Box Launcher (Home tab | Go To group)		CTRL+G
Calendar, Import Subfolder	OUT 108		File | Open tab | Import | Import from another program or file (Import and Export Wizard)		
Calendar, Print Table Style	OUT 103		Change View button (View tab | Current View group), click List, Print button (File tab | Print tab | Table Style)		CTRL+P
Calendar, Print Weekly Calendar Style	OUT 100		Change View button (View tab | Current View group), click Calendar, Print button (File tab | Print tab | Weekly Calendar Style)		CTRL+P
Calendar, Recurrence Options, Set for Appointment/Event/ Meeting	OUT 72		Recurrence button (Appointment tab | Options group)		

Microsoft Outlook 2010 Quick Reference Summary *(continued)*

Task	Page Number	Mouse	Ribbon	Shortcut Menu	Keyboard Shortcut
Calendar, Reminder, Set for Appointment/Event/Meeting	OUT 68		Reminder box arrow (Appointment tab | Options group)		
Calendar, Remove Default Calendar from Appointment Area	OUT 56	Click Calendar check box in My Calendars Pane (to remove check mark)			
Cancel Meeting	OUT 98		Cancel Meeting button (Calendar Tools Meeting tab | Actions group)		
Categorize E-Mail Message	OUT 197		Categorize button (Home tab | Tags group)	Right-click e-mail message's category column, click category	
Categorize Multiple Tasks	OUT 190		Select tasks, click Categorize button (Home tab | Tags group)	Select tasks, right-click one task's category column, click All Categories	
Categorize Task	OUT 189		Click task, click Categorize button (Home tab | Tags group)	Right-click task's category column, click All Categories	
Category, Create	OUT 186		Categorize button (Home tab | Tags group)		
Category, Delete	OUT 213	Delete button (Color Categories dialog box)			
Category, Rename	OUT 193		Categorize button (Home tab | Tags group), click All Categories, click category, click Rename	Right-click task's category column, click All Categories, select category, click Rename button	
Change Attachment to Contact	OUT 134	Double-click contact, click attachment, click Attach File button (Insert tab | Include group), select file, click Insert	Attach File button (Insert tab | Include group), select file, click Insert		
Change Meeting Time	OUT 98	Double-click meeting, change time *or* Drag meeting to new time			
Change Notes View	OUT 220		Notes List (Home tab | Current View group)		
Change Task View	OUT 216		Change View button (Home tab | Current View group)		
Change Work Time on Calendar	OUT 262	Calendar category (Outlook Options dialog box)			
Configure Junk E-Mail Options	OUT 244		Junk button (Home tab | Delete group)		

Microsoft Outlook 2010 Quick Reference Summary *(continued)*

Task	Page Number	Mouse	Ribbon	Shortcut Menu	Keyboard Shortcut
Contact Group, Create from E-Mail Message	OUT 146		New Items button (Home tab | New group), click More Items, click Contact Group, enter name, click Add Members button (Contact Group tab | Members group), click Members text box, enter e-mail address		
Contact Group, Create from Existing Contacts	OUT 144		New Contact Group button (Home tab | New group), enter name, click Add Members button (Contact Group tab | Members group)		
Contact List, Preview	OUT 152		File tab | Print tab		
Contact List, Print	OUT 156		Print button (File tab | Print tab)		
Contact List, Print Only Selected Items	OUT 154		Print Options button (File tab | Print tab), Only selected items option button, Print		
Contact List, Select Style	OUT 153		File tab | Print tab		
Contact View, Change	OUT 137		More button (Home tab | Current View group), click view		
Contact, Create	OUT 126		New Contact button (Home tab | New group)		CTRL+SHIFT+C
Contact, Create from E-Mail Message	OUT 127			Right-click e-mail address in e-mail message, click Add to Outlook Contacts	
Contact, Create from Existing Contact	OUT 129		New Items button (Home tab | New group), click Contact from the Same Company		
Contact, Edit	OUT 130	Double-click contact			
Contact, Find by Searching for E-Mail Address	OUT 139	Click Search All Contact Items text box, type search text			CTRL+E
Contact, Find from Any Outlook Folder	OUT 142	Click folder in Navigation Pane, type search text in Find a Contact search box (Home tab | Find group)			
Contacts, Sort	OUT 138		Reverse Sort button (View tab | Arrangement group)		
Conversation, Ignore	APP 18		Select message, Ignore button (Home tab | Delete group), Ignore Conversation button (Ignore Conversation dialog box)		
Create Appointment	OUT 62, OUT 64	Drag to select time slots, type appointment title	New Appointment button (Home tab | New group)		CTRL+N
Create Category	OUT 186		Categorize button (Home tab | Tags group)		
Create Contact	OUT 126		New Contact button (Home tab | New group)		CTRL+SHIFT+C

Microsoft Outlook 2010 Quick Reference Summary *(continued)*

Task	Page Number	Mouse	Ribbon	Shortcut Menu	Keyboard Shortcut
Create Contact from E-Mail Message	OUT 127			Right-click e-mail message, click Add to Outlook Contacts	
Create Contact from Existing Contact	OUT 129		New Items button (Home tab | New group), click Contact from the Same Company		
Create Contact Group from E-Mail Message	OUT 146		Copy e-mail address, click New Items button (Home tab | New group), click More Items, click Contact Group, enter name, click Add Members button (Contact Group tab | Members group), click Members text box, paste e-mail address		
Create Contact Group from Existing Contacts	OUT 144		New Contact Group button (Home tab | New group), enter name, click Add Members button (Contact Group tab | Members group)		
Create E-Mail Signature	OUT 252		Options button (File tab), Mail category, Signatures button		
Create Event	OUT 84		New Appointment button (Home tab | New group), click All day event		
Create Folder in Inbox	OUT 36		New Folder button (Folder tab | New group)	New Folder	
Create Meeting	OUT 93		New Meeting button (Home tab | New group)		
Create New E-mail Message	OUT 9		New E-mail button (Home tab | New group)		CTRL+N
Create Note	OUT 218		New Note (Home tab | New group)		CTRL+N
Create Personal Folder	OUT 54		New Calendar button (Folder tab | New group)		CTRL+SHIFT+E
Create Quick Step	Ch 5		More button (Home tab | Quick Steps group), click Create New		
Create Recurring Task	OUT 183		New Task button (Home tab | New group), Recurrence button (Task tab | Recurrence group)		
Create Rule	OUT 282		Rules button (Home tab | Move group)		
Create Task	OUT 173		New Task button (Home tab | New group)		
Create Task with Due Date	OUT 176		New Task button (Home tab | New group), click Due date box arrow		
Create Task with Priority	OUT 179		New Task button (Home tab | New group), click Priority box arrow		

Microsoft Outlook 2010 Quick Reference Summary *(continued)*

Task	Page Number	Mouse	Ribbon	Shortcut Menu	Keyboard Shortcut
Create Task with Reminder	OUT 180		New Task button (Home tab | New group), click Reminder check box, click Reminder date box arrow		
Create Task with Status	OUT 177		New Task button (Home tab | New group), click Status box arrow		
Current View, Change for Contacts	OUT 137		More button (Home tab | Current View group), click view		
Custom Date, Flag E-Mail Message with	OUT 199		Follow Up button (Home tab | Tags group), click Custom	Right-click e-mail's flag column, click Custom	
Customize Ribbon	OUT 272	Customize Ribbon category (Outlook Options dialog box)			
Customize Stationery	OUT 259	Mail category, Stationery and Fonts button (Outlook Options dialog box)			
Date, Go to	OUT 57	Click date in Date Navigator	Go To Dialog Box Launcher (Home tab | Go To group)		CTRL+G
Day View, Display in Calendar	OUT 56		Day button (View tab | Arrangement group)		CTRL+ALT+1
Default Calendar, Remove from Appointment Area	OUT 56	Click Calendar check box in My Calendars pane (to remove check mark)			
Default Color, Change for Calendar	OUT 265	Calendar category, Default calendar color button (Outlook Options dialog box)			
Default Message Format, Set	OUT 248		Options button (File tab), Mail category, Compose messages in this format box arrow		
Delete Appointment	OUT 82		Delete button (Calendar Tools Appointment Series tab *or* Calendar Tools Appointment tab | Actions group)	Delete	DELETE
Delete Category	OUT 213	Delete button (Color Categories dialog box)			
Delete E-mail Message	OUT 22	Drag to Deleted Items folder	Delete button (Home tab | Delete group)		DELETE or CTRL+D
Delete Event	OUT 87		Delete button (Calendar Tools Appointment tab | Actions group)		DELETE
Delete Note	OUT 221		Delete button (Home tab | Delete group)		
Delete Personal Calendar	OUT 108		Delete Calendar button (Folder tab | Actions group)	Delete Calendar	DELETE
Delete RSS Feed	OUT 294			Right-click RSS feed, click Delete Folder	

Microsoft Outlook 2010 Quick Reference Summary *(continued)*

Task	Page Number	Mouse	Ribbon	Shortcut Menu	Keyboard Shortcut
Delete Rule	OUT 288		Rules button (Home tab | Move group), click Manage Rules and Alerts, click Delete button (Rules and Alerts dialog box)		
Delete Task	OUT 212		Remove from List button (Home tab | Manage Task group) *or* Display task, click Delete button (Home tab | Delete group)	Right-click task, click Delete	DELETE
Deleted Items Folder, Move E-mail Message to	OUT 22	Drag to Deleted Items folder	Delete button (Home tab | Delete group)		DELETE or CTRL+D
Display Calendar in List View	OUT 102		Change View button (View tab | Current View group), click List		
Display Outlook Options	OUT 247		Options button (File tab)		
Due Date, Create Task with	OUT 176		New Task button (Home tab | New group), click Due date box arrow		
Edit Contact	OUT 130	Double-click contact			
E-Mail Account, Add	OUT 238		Account Settings button (File tab | Info tab) *or* Add Account button (File tab | Info tab)		
E-Mail Account, Remove	OUT 295			Right-click account, click Remove *account*	
E-Mail Message, Attach File to	OUT 30		Attach File button (Message tab | Include group *or* Insert tab | Include group)		
E-Mail Message, Categorize	OUT 197		Categorize button (Home tab | Tags group)	Right-click e-mail message's category column, click category	
E-Mail Message, Categorize Using Quick Click	OUT 198	Click category column for e-mail message			
E-Mail Message, Change Format to Plain Text	OUT 21		Plain Text button (Format Text tab | Format group)		
E-Mail Message, Check Spelling	OUT 24		Spelling & Grammar button (Review tab | Proofing group)		F7
E-Mail Message, Close	OUT 15	Click the Close button	Close button (File tab)		
E-Mail Message, Compose New	OUT 8		New E-mail button (Home tab | New group		CTRL+N
E-Mail Message, Delete	OUT 22		Delete button (Home tab | Delete group)	Delete	DELETE
E-Mail Message, Flag for Follow-Up	OUT 198		Follow Up button (Home tab | Tags group)	Right-click e-mail's flag column, click option	
E-Mail Message, Flag with Custom Date	OUT 199		Follow Up button (Home tab | Tags group), click Custom	Right-click e-mail's flag column, click Custom	
E-Mail Message, Forward	OUT 19		Forward button (Home tab | Respond group)		CTRL+F

Microsoft Outlook 2010 Quick Reference Summary *(continued)*

Task	Page Number	Mouse	Ribbon	Shortcut Menu	Keyboard Shortcut
E-Mail Message, Mark as Read	OUT 15		Unread/Read button (Home tab | Tags group)	Mark as Read	CTRL+Q
E-Mail Message, Mark as Unread	OUT 15		Unread/Read button (Home tab | Tags group)	Mark as Unread	CTRL+U
E-Mail Message, Open	OUT 14	Double-click message header			CTRL+O
E-Mail Message, Print	OUT 15		Print button (File tab | Print tab)	Quick Print	CTRL+P
E-Mail Message, Read	OUT 14	Select message in message list and read in Reading Pane			
E-Mail Message, Reply	OUT 17		Reply button (Home tab | Respond group)		CTRL+R
E-Mail Message, Reply All	OUT 17		Reply All button (Home tab | Respond group)		CTRL+SHIFT+R
E-Mail Message, Save Response in Drafts Folder	OUT 27		Save button (Quick Access Toolbar)		CTRL+S
E-Mail Message, Send	OUT 11	Send button in message header			ALT+S or CTRL+ENTER
E-Mail Message, Set High Importance for	OUT 32		High Importance button (Message tab | Tags group)		
E-Mail Signature, Create	OUT 252		Options button (File tab), Mail category, Signatures button		
E-Mail Signature, Format	OUT 253	Mail category, Formatting options (Signatures and Stationery dialog box)			
Event, Create	OUT 84		New Appointment button (Home tab | New group), click All day event check box	New All Day Event	CTRL+SHIFT+A
Event, Delete	OUT 87		Delete button (Calendar Tools Appointment tab | Actions group)		DELETE
Event, Save	OUT 86		Save & Close button (Event tab | Actions group)		
Event, Set Recurrence Options for	OUT 88		Recurrence button (Event tab | Options group)		
Export Calendar Subfolder	OUT 104		Import button (File tab | Open tab), Export to a file (Import and Export Wizard)		
Fields, Show or Hide in List View	APP 10		Add Columns button (View tab | Arrangement group), column name, Add button (Show Columns dialog box)		
File Attached to Contact, Remove	OUT 135	Double-click contact, click attachment, press DELETE			DELETE
File, Attach to Contact	OUT 131		Attach File button (Insert tab | Include group), select file, click Insert		

Microsoft Outlook 2010 Quick Reference Summary *(continued)*

Task	Page Number	Mouse	Ribbon	Shortcut Menu	Keyboard Shortcut
File, Attach to E-mail Message	OUT 30		Attach File button (Message tab | Include group)		
File, Attach to Task	OUT 203		Attach File button (Insert tab | Include group)		
Files, Record Automatically	APP 23		Options button (File tab), Notes and Journal, Journal Options button (Outlook Options dialog box)		
Find Contact by Searching for E-Mail Address	OUT 139	Click Search All Contact Items text box, type search text			CTRL+E
Find Contact from Any Outlook Folder	OUT 142	Click folder in Navigation Pane, type search text in Find a Contact search box (Home tab | Find group)			
Flag E-Mail Message for Follow-Up	OUT 198		Follow Up button (Home tab | Tags group)	Right-click e-mail's flag column, click option	
Flag E-Mail Message with Custom Date	OUT 199		Follow Up button (Home tab | Tags group), click Custom	Right-click e-mail's flag column, click Custom	
Folder, Create in Inbox	OUT 36		New Folder button (Folder tab | New group)	New Folder	CTRL+SHIFT+E
Folder, Create Personal Calendar	OUT 54		New Calendar button (Folder tab | New group)		
Folder, Move E-mail Message to	OUT 37	Drag e-mail message to folder	Move button (Home tab | Move group)	Move, click folder name	
Format E-Mail Signature	OUT 253	Mail category, Formatting options (Signatures and Stationery dialog box)			
Forward E-mail Message	OUT 19		Forward button (Home tab | Respond group)	Forward	CTRL+F
Forward Task	OUT 208		Forward button (Task tab | Actions group)		CTRL+F
Go to Date	OUT 57		Go To Dialog Box Launcher (Home tab | Go To group)		CTRL+G
Graphical Element, Format	APP 17		Select graphic, formatting tool (Format tab)		
High Importance, Set for E-mail Message	OUT 32		High Importance button (Message tab | Tags group)		
Holidays, Add to Calendar	OUT 264	Add Holidays button (Outlook Options dialog box)			
Image, Add to E-Mail Signature	OUT 256	Insert Picture button (Signatures and Stationery dialog box)			
Import Personal Subfolder	OUT 108		Import button (File tab | Open tab), Import from another program or file (Import and Export Wizard)		

Microsoft Outlook 2010 Quick Reference Summary *(continued)*

Task	Page Number	Mouse	Ribbon	Shortcut Menu	Keyboard Shortcut
Importance, Set to High for E-mail Message	OUT 32		High Importance button (Message tab | Tags group)		
Invite People to Meeting	OUT 94		New Meeting button (Home tab | New group), type e-mail address and subject, click Send		
Item, Attach to Task	OUT 205		Outlook Item button (Insert tab | Include group)		
Journal Entries, View	APP 21	Configure buttons arrow in Navigation pane, Add or Remove Buttons, Journal			
Journal Entry, Edit	APP 23	Journal button in Navigation pane, double-click journal entry			
Junk E-Mail Options, Configure	OUT 244		Junk button (Home tab | Delete group)		
Language Options, Set	APP 8		Options button (File tab), Language (Outlook Options dialog box)		
List View, Display for Calendar	OUT 102		Change View button (View tab | Current View group), click List		
Mailbox Size, View	APP 18		Folder Properties button (Folder tab | Properties group), Folder Size button (mailbox Properties dialog box)		
Manage Quick Steps	OUT 280		More button (Home tab | Quick Steps group), click Manage Quick Steps		
Mark Task as Complete	OUT 211		Mark Complete button (Home tab | Manage Task group)	Right-click task, click Mark Complete	
Meeting Cancellation Notice, Send	OUT 98	Send Cancellation button in message header	Cancel Meeting button (Calendar Tools Meeting tab | Actions group), Send Cancellation button		
Meeting Time, Change	OUT 98	Double-click meeting, change time *or* Drag meeting to new time			
Meeting Time, Propose New	OUT 98		Propose New Time button (Calendar Tools Meeting Occurrence tab | Respond group)		
Meeting, Cancel	OUT 98		Cancel Meeting button (Calendar Tools Meeting tab | Actions group)		
Meeting, Create	OUT 94		New Meeting button (Home tab | New group)		CTRL+SHIFT+Q
Meeting, Invite People to	OUT 94		New Meeting button (Home tab | New group), type e-mail address and subject, click Send		
Member, Add to Contact Group	OUT 149		Add Members button (Contact Group tab | Members group)		
Message Delivery Options, Set	APP 13		More Options Dialog Box Launcher (Options tab | More Options group), select delivery options (Properties dialog box)		

Microsoft Outlook 2010 Quick Reference Summary *(continued)*

Task	Page Number	Mouse	Ribbon	Shortcut Menu	Keyboard Shortcut
Message Format, Change to Plain Text	OUT 21		Plain Text button (Format Text tab | Format group)		
Message Format, Set Default	OUT 248		Options button (File tab), Mail category, Compose messages in this format box arrow		
Message List, Arrange by Date	OUT 8	Click Arrange by: Date column heading		Date	
Message List, Show in Groups	OUT 8		Show In Groups button (View tab | Arrangement group | More button)	Show in Groups	
Month View, Display in Calendar	OUT 60		Month button (Home tab | Arrange group)		CTRL+ALT+4
Move E-mail Message to Folder	OUT 37	Drag e-mail message to folder	Move button (Home tab | Move group)	Move, click folder name	
Multiple Tasks, Categorize	OUT 190		Select tasks, click Categorize button (Home tab | Tags group)	Select tasks, right-click one task's category column, click All Categories	
Name, Add to Contact Group	OUT 149		Add Members button (Contact Group tab | Members group)		
Name, Remove from Contact Group	OUT 150		Remove Member button (Contact Group tab | Members group)		
Note, Create	OUT 218		New Note (Home tab | New group)		CTRL+N
Note, Delete	OUT 221		Delete button (Home tab | Delete group)		
Notes View, Change	OUT 220		Notes List (Home tab | Current View group)		
Open E-mail Message	OUT 14	Double-click message header			CTRL+O
Options for Junk E-Mail, Configure	OUT 244		Junk button (Home tab | Delete group)		
Options for Spell Checking, Set	OUT 249		Options button (File tab), Mail category, Always check spelling before sending check box		
Outlook Data File, Open	OUT 7		Open Outlook Data File button (File tab | Open tab), select file, Open button		
Outlook Item, Attach to Task	OUT 205		Outlook Item button (Insert tab | Include group)		
Outlook Items, Automatically Record	APP 22		Options button (File tab), Notes and Journal, Journal Options button (Outlook Options dialog box)		
Outlook Options, Display	OUT 247		File tab	Options button		
Paste Special, Use	APP 17		Paste button arrow (Message tab | Clipboard group), Paste Special, select option (Paste Special dialog box)		

Microsoft Outlook 2010 Quick Reference Summary *(continued)*

Task	Page Number	Mouse	Ribbon	Shortcut Menu	Keyboard Shortcut
People Pane, Use	APP 11	Message in message list, contact icon			
Personal Calendar, Delete	OUT 108		Delete Calendar button (Folder tab | Actions group)	Delete Calendar	DELETE
Personal Folder, Create	OUT 54		New Calendar button (Folder tab | New group)		CTRL+SHIFT+E
Personal Folder, Display	OUT 56	Click check box in My Calendars pane			
Personal Subfolder, Import	OUT 108		Import button (File tab | Open tab), Export to a file (Import and Export Wizard)		
Plain Text, Change Message Format to	OUT 21		Plain Text button (Format Text tab | Format group)		
Preview Attachment	OUT 33	Click message header, click attachment			
Preview Contact List	OUT 152		File tab | Print tab		
Print Calendar in Table Style (List View)	OUT 103		Table style (File tab | Print tab)		CTRL+P
Print Calendar in Weekly Style	OUT 100		Weekly Calendar style (File tab | Print tab)		CTRL+P
Print Contact List	OUT 156		Print button (File tab | Print tab)		
Print E-mail Message	OUT 15		Print button (File tab | Print tab)	Quick Print	CTRL+P
Print Only Selected Items in Contact List	OUT 155		Print Options (File tab | Print tab), Only selected items option button, Print		
Print Tasks	OUT 217		Print button (File tab | Print tab)		
Priority, Create Task with	OUT 179		New Task button (Home tab | New group), click Priority box arrow		
Propose Meeting Time	OUT 98		Propose New Time button (Calendar Tools Meeting Occurrence tab | Respond group)		
Quick Click, Set	OUT 195		Categorize button (Home tab | Tags group), click Set Quick Click	Right-click task's category column, click Set Quick Click	
Quick Click, Use to Categorize E-Mail Message	OUT 198	Click category column for e-mail message			
Quick Step, Create	OUT 276		More button (Home tab | Quick Steps group), click Create New		
Quick Step, Use	OUT 279		Quick Step button (Home tab | Quick Steps group)		
Quick Steps, Manage	OUT 280		More button (Home tab | Quick Steps group), click Manage Quick Steps		
Quit Outlook	OUT 38, OUT 109	Click Close button	Exit button (File tab)		

Microsoft Outlook 2010 Quick Reference Summary *(continued)*

Task	Page Number	Mouse	Ribbon	Shortcut Menu	Keyboard Shortcut
Read E-mail Message	OUT 14	Message header in message list			
Recurrence Options, Set for Appointment	OUT 72		Recurrence button (Appointment tab | Options group)		
Recurrence Options, Set for Event	OUT 88		Recurrence button (Event tab | Options group)		
Recurring Task, Create	OUT 183		New Task button (Home tab | New group), Recurrence button (Task tab | Recurrence group)		
Refine Search	OUT 141		Search All Contact Items text box, click More button (Search Tools Search tab | Refine group), click property		CTRL+E
Reminder, Create Task with	OUT 180		New Task button (Home tab | New group), click Reminder check box, click Reminder date box arrow		
Reminder, Set for Appointment	OUT 68		Reminder box arrow (Appointment tab | Options group)		
Reminder, Set for Message Recipients	APP 12		Follow Up button (Message tab | Tags group), Custom, Flag for Recipients (Custom dialog box)		
Reminders Window, Display	APP 11		Reminders Window button (View tab | Window group)		
Remove Attachment to Contact	OUT 135	Double-click contact, click attachment, press DELETE			DELETE
Remove E-Mail Account	OUT 295			Right-click account, click Remove *account*	
Remove Name from Contact Group	OUT 150		Remove Member button (Contact Group tab | Members group)		
Remove Task	OUT 212		Remove from List button (Home tab | Manage Task group) *or* Delete button (Home tab | Delete group)	Right-click task, click Delete	DELETE
Rename Category	OUT 193		Categorize button (Home tab | Tags group), click All Categories, click category, click Rename button	Right-click task's category column, click All Categories, select category, click Rename button	
Reply to E-mail Message	OUT 17		Reply button (Home tab | Respond group)	Reply	CTRL+R
Ribbon, Customize	OUT 272	Customize Ribbon category (Outlook Options dialog box)			
RSS Feed, Delete	OUT 294			Right-click RSS feed, click Delete Folder	

Microsoft Outlook 2010 Quick Reference Summary *(continued)*

Task	Page Number	Mouse	Ribbon	Shortcut Menu	Keyboard Shortcut
RSS Feed, Subscribe to	OUT 292			Right-click RSS Feeds folder, click Add a New RSS Feed	
Rule, Create	OUT 282		Rules button (Home tab | Move group)		
Rule, Delete	OUT 288		Rules button (Home tab | Move group), click Manage Rules and Alerts, click Delete button (Rules and Alerts dialog box)		
Rule, Run	OUT 286		Rules button (Home tab | Move group), click Manage Rules and Alerts, click Run Rules Now button (Rules and Alerts dialog box)		
Run Rule	OUT 286		Rules button (Home tab | Move group), click Manage Rules and Alerts, click Run Rules Now button (Rules and Alerts dialog box)		
Save Appointment	OUT 69		Save & Close button (Appointment tab | Actions group)		
Save Attachment	OUT 33		Save As button (Attachment Tools Attachments tab | Actions group), Save button (Save Attachment dialog box)		
Save E-Mail Message in Drafts Folder	OUT 27	Save button on Quick Access Toolbar	Save option (File tab | Save tab)		
Save Event	OUT 86		Save & Close button (Event tab | Actions group)		
Schedule View, Display in Calendar	OUT 60		Schedule View button (Home tab | Arrange group)		CTRL+ALT+5
Search Options, Set	OUT 270	Search category (Outlook Options dialog box)			
Search, Refine	OUT 141		Search All Contact Items text box, click More button (Search Tools Search tab | Refine group), click property		CTRL+E
Select Style for Contact List	OUT 152		File tab | Print tab		
Send E-mail Message	OUT 8	Send button (message window)			ALT+S
Send Meeting Cancellation Notice	OUT 99	Send Cancellation button in message header	Cancel Meeting button (Calendar Tools Meeting tab | Actions group), Send Cancellation button		
Send Status Report	OUT 209		Send Status Report button (Task tab | Manage Task group)		
Sensitivity Level, Set for New Messages	APP 9		Options button (File tab), Mail (Options dialog box), Default Sensitivity level list box		

Microsoft Outlook 2010 Quick Reference Summary *(continued)*

Task	Page Number	Mouse	Ribbon	Shortcut Menu	Keyboard Shortcut
Sensitivity Level, Set for Single Message	APP 11		More Options Dialog Box Launcher (Options tab | More Options group), Sensitivity button (Properties dialog box)		
Sent Items Folder, Specify	APP 12		Save Sent Item To button (Options tab | More Options group), Other Folder, select folder (Select Folder dialog box)		
Set Calendar Options	OUT 264	Calendar category (Outlook Options dialog box)			
Set Default Message Format	OUT 248		Options button (File tab), Mail category, Compose messages in this format box arrow		
Set Junk E-Mail Options	OUT 244		Junk button (Home tab | Delete group)		
Set Quick Click	OUT 195		Categorize button (Home tab | Tags group), click Set Quick Click	Right-click task's category column, click Set Quick Click	
Set Search Options	OUT 270	Search category (Outlook Options dialog box)			
Set Signature Options	OUT 257	Select settings (Signatures and Stationery dialog box)			
Set Spell Checking Options	OUT 249		Options button (File tab), Mail category, Always check spelling before sending check box		
Signature Options, Set	OUT 257	Select settings (Signatures and Stationery dialog box)			
Signature, Create for E-Mail	OUT 252		Options button (File tab), Mail category, Signatures button		
Sort Contacts	OUT 138		Reverse Sort button (View tab | Arrangement group)		
Spell Checking Options, Set	OUT 249		Options button (File tab), Mail category, Always check spelling before sending check box		
Spelling, Check as You Type	OUT 24		Spelling & Grammar button (Review tab | Proofing group)	Right-click error, click correct word	F7
Stationery, Assign Theme to	OUT 259	Mail category, Stationery and Fonts button (Outlook Options dialog box), Theme button (Signatures and Stationery dialog box)			
Stationery, Customize	OUT 259	Mail category, Stationery and Fonts button (Outlook Options dialog box)			
Status Report, Send	OUT 209		Send Status Report button (Task tab | Manage Task group)		
Status, Create Task with	OUT 177		New Task button (Home tab | New group), click Status box arrow		

Microsoft Outlook 2010 Quick Reference Summary *(continued)*

Task	Page Number	Mouse	Ribbon	Shortcut Menu	Keyboard Shortcut
Status, Set for Appointment	OUT 67		Show As box arrow (Appointment tab | Options group)		
Style, Apply	APP 14		Select text, More button (Format Text tab | Styles group), select style		
Style, Create	APP 15		Select formatted text, Styles Dialog Box Launcher (Format Text tab | Styles group), New Style button (Styles dialog box), enter name (Create New Style from Formatting dialog box)		
Subscribe to RSS Feed	OUT 292			Right-click RSS Feeds folder, click Add a New RSS Feed	
Table Style (List View), Print Calendar in	OUT 103		Table style (File tab | Print tab)		CTRL+P
Task View, Change	OUT 216		Change View button (Home tab | Current View group)		
Task, Assign	OUT 206		Assign Task button (Task tab | Manage Task group)		
Task, Attach File to	OUT 203		Attach File button (Insert tab | Include group)		
Task, Categorize	OUT 189		Click task, click Categorize button (Home tab | Tags group)	Right-click task's category column, click All Categories	
Task, Create	OUT 173		New Task button (Home tab | New group)		
Task, Create with Due Date	OUT 176		New Task button (Home tab | New group), click Due date box arrow		
Task, Create with Priority	OUT 179		New Task button (Home tab | New group), click Priority box arrow		
Task, Create with Recurrence	OUT 183		New Task button (Home tab | New group), Recurrence button (Task tab | Recurrence group)		
Task, Create with Reminder	OUT 180		New Task button (Home tab | New group), click Reminder check box, click Reminder date box arrow		
Task, Create with Status	OUT 177		New Task button (Home tab | New group), click Status box arrow		
Task, Forward	OUT 208		Forward button (Task tab | Actions group)		CTRL+F
Task, Mark Complete	OUT 211		Mark Complete button (Home tab | Manage Task group)	Right-click task, click Mark Complete	

Microsoft Outlook 2010 Quick Reference Summary (continued)

Task	Page Number	Mouse	Ribbon	Shortcut Menu	Keyboard Shortcut
Task, Remove	OUT 212		Remove from List button (Home tab | Manage Task group) or Delete button (Home tab | Delete group)	Right-click task, click Delete	DELETE
Task, Send Status Report for	OUT 209		Send Status Report button (Task tab | Manage Task group)		
Task, Update	OUT 202	Double-click task			
Tasks, Print	OUT 217		Print button (File tab | Print tab)		
Theme, Assign to Stationery	OUT 259	Mail category, Stationery and Fonts button (Outlook Options dialog box), Theme button (Signatures and Stationery dialog box)			
Theme, Create	APP 16		Themes button (Options tab | Themes group), Save Current Theme, enter name (Save Current Theme dialog box)		
Time Zone, Change in Calendar	OUT 267	Calendar category, Time zone box arrow (Outlook Options dialog box)			
Undo	OUT 9	Undo button on Quick Access Toolbar			CTRL+Z
Update Changed Meeting	OUT 95	Change meeting time, click Send Update button			
Update Task	OUT 202	Double-click task			
Voting Options, Set	APP 14		Use Voting Buttons button (Options tab | Tracking group), Custom, set voting options (Properties dialog box)		
Week View, Display in Calendar	OUT 59		Week button (Home tab | Arrange group)		CTRL+ALT+3
Weekly Style, Print Calendar in	OUT 100		Weekly Calendar style (File tab | Print tab)		CTRL+P
Work Time, Change on Calendar	OUT 262	Calendar category (Outlook Options dialog box)			
Work Week View, Display in Calendar	OUT 58		Work Week button (Home tab | Arrange group)		CTRL+ALT+2